LIVING IN THE ENDLESS CITY

The Urban Age Project by the London School of Economics and Deutsche Bank's Alfred Herrhausen Society

Edited by Ricky Burdett and Deyan Sudjic

LIVING

ENDLES

IN THE

SS CITY

INTRODUCTION

Foreword	Wolfgang Nowak	6
Living in the Urban Age	Ricky Burdett and Philipp Rode	8
The Architecture of the Endless City	Deyan Sudjic	44
The Economies of Cities	Saskia Sassen	56

CITIES

MUMBAI		68
Managed Chaos	Deyan Sudjic	86
Democracy and Self-Interest	K. C. Sivaramakrishnan	90
A Matter of People	Darryl D'Monte	94
Looking for the Bird of Gold	Suketu Mehta	102
The Static and the Kinetic	Rahul Mehrotra	108
The Long View	Charles Correa	116
Beyond the Maximum	Geetam Tiwari	122
SÃO PAULO		128
The Urban Giant	Deyan Sudjic	146
Filling the Political Vacuum	Jeroen Klink	150
The Cultures of the Metropolis	Gareth A. Jones	156
Looking for a Shared Identity	José de Souza Martins	162
Worlds Set Apart	Teresa Caldeira	168
The Mirage and Its Limits	Raul Juste Lores	176
Living on the Edge	Fernando de Mello Franco	182
ISTANBUL		188
The City Too Big to Fail	Deyan Sudjic	206
Bridging Histories	İlhan Tekeli	210
The Hinge City	Richard Sennett	218
It's Istanbul (not Globalization)	Hashim Sarkis	224
The Violence of Change	Asu Aksoy	232
The Contours of Concrete	Ömer Kanıpak	240
Measuring Success	Çağlar Keyder	246

DATA

Vital Statistics: Nine Cities Compared 252

Understanding the Numbers Justin McGuirk 292

Understanding What People Think Tony Travers 308

REFLECTIONS

Boundaries and Borders Richard Sennett 324

No Frills and Bare Life Alejandro Zaera Polo 332

City Solutions to Global Problems Nicholas Stern, Dimitri Zenghelis and Philipp Rode 342

Democracy and Governance Gerald E. Frug 350

The Urban Earthquake Anthony Williams 356

Uneven Landscapes Sophie Body-Gendrot 360

From Utopia to Youtopia Alejandro Aravena 368

Surviving in an Urban Age David Satterthwaite 374

Getting to Work Fabio Casiroli 380

Facing the Metro Challenge Bruce Katz 388

On the Ground Adam Kaasa with Marcos Rosa and Priya Shankar 396

INDEX

Notes 414

Credits 416

Contributors 419

Urban Age Conference Participants 421

Index 428

Editors' Acknowledgments 431

FOREWORD

Wolfgang Nowak

Cities are political programmes made visible. They are mirrors of society and systems of governance of the country in which they are located. Successful cities demonstrate the viability of social systems. In cities, all of the world's problems and conflicts are crowded together in a confined space. In growing metropolises the first, second and third worlds come into direct contact with each other. Cities have to deal with religious and cultural confrontations, terrorism, economic crises, pandemics, and, of course, migration issues. Centuries ago, cities believed they could protect themselves against problems with walls. Today people try to protect themselves against unresolved problems through gated communities within cities.

We are experiencing a crisis of responsibility between citizens and government – and not only in Western cities and states. Citizens experience their own powerlessness walking through their city every day, and they interpret it as powerlessness on the part of the government. In particular, young people are often radically disoriented by the experience and become vulnerable to any kind of ideological discipline. Occasional 'attacks' through a ruthless enforcement of special interests, e.g. by prestige buildings, only reinforce doubts about the government and its ability to serve the common good. The kind of conflicts that occur in cities can only be resolved, however, by mediating between different value perceptions. Learning and mediating and the willingness to see through other people's eyes are core competencies for the successful governance of a city. Nowadays legitimacy results not only from elections; it develops when a mayor achieves a significant contribution as an impartial entity to improving the situation of citizens, and takes a stand against the repeated threat of growing cities disintegrating into unbridled individual interests.

The growth of cities is currently unstoppable. The constitutions of European cities were designed to address problems of the twentieth century. They are hardly appropriate to today's challenges. Some cities have become urban regions which are limited in their development by 'historic' national and city borders. In many countries, it is national rather than municipal government that holds the strings to planning decisions. In effect, these cities are governed from outside. But nations will increasingly depend on cities and their economic success. New forms of governance for cities are required. To a certain extent, we find ourselves in a hiatus: the old form is no longer effective and the new form is not clearly visible yet. A new generation of mayors proves on a daily basis that they can not only endure political conflicts, but also resolve them. Some have even stepped up to become heads of state. They have managed to mobilize the expertise of all citizens for better solutions. Cities put high demands on their leaders. They must succeed in not only managing a confusion of issues, problems and contradictions, but in linking them into a common will in an ongoing process. Once this has been achieved, a city becomes a visible, political programme of change, one that replaces the old ideologies of the twentieth century.

Since 2005, the London School of Economics and Deutsche Bank's Alfred Herrhausen Society – together with mayors, city planners, state governments, architects, scientists, community groups and committed local people – have studied growing, and in some cases shrinking, cities of the twenty-first century. *The Endless City*, published in 2007, described the outcome of the first two years of collaboration. This book, *Living in the Endless City*, covers the following three. Given the fact that the twenty-first century is the 'urban age', the work was extended to cities in India, Latin America and the Mediterranean. The result was an international 'think-and-do tank', linking people across continents and political systems, ready to learn from and with each to find better solutions for cities of the future.

In recognition of the value of this work, Deutsche Bank decided to fund a new research centre at the London School of Economics in 2010, which is now in full operation under the banner of LSE Cities. The objective of LSE Cities is to consolidate and build upon accumulated knowledge and serve as the centre of the evolving network of urbanists at a global level.

None of this would have been possible without the personal endorsement of Deutsche Bank's CEO, Dr Josef Ackermann, whose commitment to the project has been outstanding. We wish to thank him and the Alfred Herrhausen Board for their continued support of this joint initiative.

During the Urban Age Conference in Mexico City in 2006, the conference participants visited a large informal neighbourhood whose residents suffered from lack of basic infrastructure and resources. In the middle of this misery we were surprised to find a building that had a transformative effect on the young people from the area. Organized as a local citizens' initiative, this small arts centre was an island of hope in a hopeless environment. We responded by setting up the Deutsche Bank Urban Age award, a US$100,000 prize, which is given annually to projects, which demonstrate responsible partnering and that improve the social and physical environment of a city. Since 2007 the prize has been awarded in Mumbai, São Paulo, Istanbul and Mexico City, to projects that have reacted to intolerable conditions. They reacted positively, by working together on projects, without violence or extreme crime, either of which would have negated their existence as engaged citizens of their own city. They motivated themselves and others to break away from enforced passivity to find better solutions for human coexistence. The award gives a voice to those in the city who have no lobby. They are ambassadors of new ideas.

This volume describes our collective work between 2007 and 2010, including the conferences, the research and surveys, and the local awards. All parties in the Urban Age project are united by a common goal: to find a grammar for the success of cities. Scepticism is clearly justified given the major problems faced, especially by the cities in Asia, Africa and Latin America. And yet, I am confident that we will make it; as the former Brazilian President Lula once put it, with utopia in our hearts, but both feet firmly anchored in the real world.

Wolfgang Nowak is Director of Deutsche Bank's Alfred Herrhausen Society

LIVING IN THE URBAN AGE

Ricky Burdett and Philipp Rode

Why Cities? Why Now?

This book investigates the links between the physical and the social in cities.
It is not an academic exercise, but one that stems from a sense of urgency that
something needs to be done to address the dynamics of urban change described by
the statistics on the front cover. With half of the seven billion people on earth living in
cities, a substantial proportion of global GDP will be invested in energy and resources
to accommodate a mass of new city dwellers over the next decades.[1] The form of
this new wave of urban construction and the shape of our cities will have profound
impacts on the ecological balance of the planet and the human conditions of people
growing up and growing old in cities. That is why cities, and their design, matter.

It is not the first time that city form and social development attract global
attention. Social reformers in Europe and North America in the late-nineteenth and
early-twentieth centuries were preoccupied by similar concerns. In the aftermath of
the Industrial Revolution cities were swamped by new migrants in search of jobs and
opportunities. But, at a considerably slower pace and smaller scale than the current
wave of global urbanization. London grew from 1 million to become the world's first
megacity of 10 million. It took over a hundred years to get there. Lagos, Delhi and
Dhaka, are today growing at the rate of over 300,000 people per year. Mumbai is set
to overtake Tokyo and Mexico City as the world's largest city in the next few decades
with over 35 million people. The order of magnitude is radically different.

Last time round, planners reacted to overcrowding and congestion with a heavy
hand. Entire communities in traditional city cores were ripped apart to create clean
and healthy new urban environments to house the urban poor. Road widening
schemes and large-scale blocks replaced the fine grain of city streets. Suburbanization
led to the separation of city functions, fuelling urban sprawl before we became aware
of the consequences on climate change and social alienation. Are we are about to
repeat the same mistakes, but at a grander and more dramatic scale?

The cities being built and transformed today will have far greater consequences,
both locally and globally. The way they are changing is not encouraging. The
investigations of the Urban Age project, which forms the basis of this publication,
find that cities are becoming more spatially fragmented, more socially divisive
and more environmentally destructive. The objective, of course, is quite different.
Governments, public agencies and the private sector are driving this change to
improve living conditions of existing and new city dwellers, responding to a real

2%

of the earth's surface is occupied by cities

53%

of the world's population lives in cities

market demand resulting from global economic growth and restructuring.

In Chinese cities like Shanghai, for example, strong growth has seen the new middle class triple the amount of space they occupy in the space of a few decades, moving from pre-industrial housing conditions to apartments with running water, reliable electricity and modern domestic facilities. Formally planned or illegally constructed neighbourhoods are emerging on the peripheries of older cities while new dormitory towns – gated communities or mass housing schemes – are appearing on the edges of Istanbul, São Paulo or Mumbai, as illustrated in the essays that follow. The problem is that the bulk of what is being built today, which could stay with us for hundreds of years, may have even more negative impacts on the urban communities they are designed to serve than the ones built by the well-intentioned social reformers of the last centuries.

A few examples serve to illustrate this point. In Istanbul, the government is building 3 million housing units in 20 years. All around the millennial city, rows of bland, 20-storey tower blocks surrounded by tarmac are emerging, reminiscent of the most alienating social housing projects built across Europe and the United States in the mid-twentieth century. Some of these have since been demolished because of their social dysfunctionality, yet the same ubiquitous typology continues to be erected around the world. Despite a recent slowdown, São Paulo continues its march towards endless sprawl fuelled by a planning ideology that finds four-hour commuting patterns acceptable in a city that accepts about one thousand new cars on its streets every day. Many other metropolitan areas of the fast-growing economies would have similar stories to tell. Mumbai's cynical attempts to redevelop Dharavi, India's largest slum located on valuable land near the centre, with large commercial blocks replacing the fine urban grain of one of the city's most sustainable communities, raises the spectre of 1960s 'slum clearance' programmes that devastated the social life and urban structure of so many European and American cities. While the inevitable forces that drive improvement and growth must be embraced, it is time to ask ourselves whether we have got the planning formula right.

On balance, the answer from this publication is probably 'no'. The impact of this emerging urban landscape on people and the environment, with very few exceptions, is likely to be negative. Before considering the findings and reflections of the Urban Age experts on the forces and contradictions that are shaping this new wave of urban change, it may be helpful to give an overview of the global impact of cities at economic, environmental and social level.

The Global Urban Context

With a population share of just above 50 per cent, but occupying less than 2 per cent of the earth's surface, urban areas concentrate 80 per cent of economic output, between 60 and 80 per cent of global energy consumption, and approximately 75 per cent of CO_2 emissions.[2] Seventy-five per cent of the world's population is expected to be concentrated in cities by 2050 – a large proportion in megacities of several million people each and massively urbanized regions stretching across countries and continents. As the maps on pages 26 to 43 reveal, these patterns of human and urban development are not equally distributed across the surface of the globe. Cities in developing countries continue to grow due to high birth rates and by attracting migrants, while rural settlements are transformed into urban regions. At the same time, some cities of largely urbanized developed countries have had to adapt to profound economic restructuring with shrinking populations.

LIVING WITHIN OUR MEANS

While high levels of urbanization have gone hand-in-hand with increased energy consumption (measured by the 'ecological footprint'), some countries have been able to maintain relatively high standards of social well-being (measured by the United Nation's composite Human Development Index) without indulging in unacceptable levels of over-consumption that challenge the earth's capacity to sustain balanced and equitable growth. This graph, developed by LSE Cities, is part of the 'Green Cities' chapter of *The Green Economy*, a study commissioned by the United Nations Environment Programme (Geneva, 2011).

Urbanization level in 2005

- >90%
- 80-90%
- 70-80%
- 60-70%
- 50-60%
- 40-50%
- 30-40%
- 20-30%
- <20%

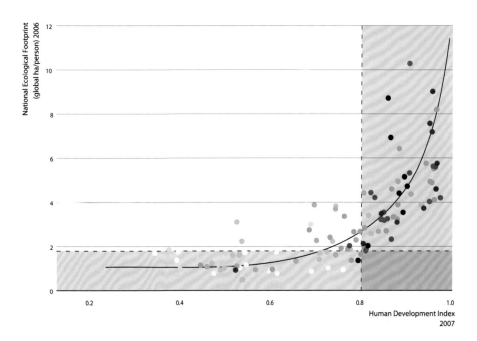

While urbanization has helped to reduce absolute poverty, the number of people classified as urban poor is on the rise. Between 1993 and 2002, 50 million poor were added to urban areas while the number of rural poor declined by 150 million.[3] Urban growth puts pressure on the local environment that disproportionately affects disadvantaged people who live in precarious structures in more vulnerable locations such as riverbanks and drainage systems, all of which are exposed to flooding, mudslides and other hazards linked to climate change. Regular flooding in São Paulo, Istanbul and Mumbai – not to mention New Orleans or Jakarta – indicate the immediacy of the problem and its costs on human lives.

Cities of different wealth levels impact the environment differently. As their economies become more prosperous, with wider and deeper patterns of consumption and production, their environmental footprint is increasingly felt at a global level. In terms of carbon emissions, energy, electricity and water consumption, dwelling and transport patterns, there is a very marked difference between cities in developed and developing countries. Whereas cities in Europe, the US and Brazil, for example, have a lower environmental impact than their respective countries, cities in India and China have a much larger impact owing to their significantly higher income levels compared with their national averages.

But why are so many cities continuing to grow? From an economic perspective, cities bring people and goods closer together, help overcome information gaps, and enable idea flows.[4] National development of countries has always been linked to the growth of its cities, as witnessed by the fact that manufacturing and services have increased their share of global GDP to 97 per cent, and most of these activities are located in urban areas.[5]

Mirroring their economic performance, as cities grow in size, they leave a strong imprint on the planet. The World Bank has estimated that while urban populations in the developed world have grown only about 5 per cent, their built-up area has increased by 30 per cent between 1990 and 2000. For developing world cities, the growth of populations was 20 per cent against a 50 per cent increase in urbanized

33%

of city dwellers live in slums

land. Annually, the amount of built-up land per person has increased by 2.3 per cent in cities in industrialized nations and 1.7 per cent in developing world cities.[6] These statistics are living evidence that the 'endless city' is not simply a metaphor, but a description of a real physical phenomenon which applies just as much to Los Angeles and Phoenix in the United States, as it does to Mexico City or São Paulo.

As argued above, much of this expansion has occurred with the growth of peripheral development triggered by suburban lifestyles and a combination of land speculation, weak planning control and greater population mobility. The rapid expansion of car use has gone hand in hand with horizontal expansion. Increasing motorization continues to create an infrastructure legacy that matches those of the cheap oil period of the 1950s and 1960s, bringing with it a landscape of urban motorways, flyovers and tunnels that has a negative impact on the quality of the urban environment, causing physical severance and acoustic and air pollution. Even though fuel is no longer cheap, this has not stopped Mexico City spending most of its transport budget on the Segundo Piso, a double-decker flyover in the middle of the city, or Mumbai investing millions of dollars in the much disputed Bandra-Worli Sea Link across one of its stunning bays. Meanwhile Boston has invested over US$5 billion on the Big Dig, demolishing the 1960s elevated motorway that scarred the centre for decades. Many others have followed suit.

Despite an ongoing debate on the links between physical structure and energy use in cities, there is growing evidence that urban environments with higher-density residential and commercial buildings, a well distributed mix of uses and public transport reduce the energy footprint. Research has shown that the so-called 'compact city' model has lower per-capita carbon emissions as long as good public transport is provided at the metropolitan and regional level.[7] Despite this evidence and important efforts like the C40 movement, the majority of cities globally are following the less sustainable model of urban growth. It is left to a handful of urban pioneers, like Copenhagen, Seattle, Singapore or Bogotá, to implement radical, but highly successful policies that have dramatically reduced their energy footprint, reduced commuting times and improved quality of life.

But, what do these numbers and statistics mean for both those who inhabit and those who build the city? How can the 'old' model of urbanity that has supported human existence for centuries serve us to comprehend the emerging form of 'cityness' that the new century of massive global urbanization is delivering? What is the complex relationship between urban form and city life; and how can we intervene at governance level, as policymakers, urban designers and planners to bring about positive change? These are some of the questions that have been addressed by the Urban Age project to which we now turn.

Experiencing the Urban Age Project
A sequel to *The Endless City*, this book adds to the global debate on the future of cities with new research on Mumbai, São Paulo and Istanbul, yet builds on the accumulated knowledge and experiences of six other cities – New York, Shanghai, London, Mexico City, Johannesburg and Berlin.[8] It is a distillation of more than five years of collaborative work that has brought together several hundred people who perhaps, before the Urban Age project, did not see themselves as 'urbanists' per se. Traffic engineers, mayors, criminologists, architects, sociologists, planners … perhaps, but not urbanists.

Yet, over time, as each one of us was confronted with a different spatial reality, the need to understand our distinct viewpoints *in relation to the urban* came sharply into focus. The more we observed the complex processes of social and economic change, the more we became aware – as Saskia Sassen puts it – that the materiality of the city itself allows it to survive, while nation-states, companies, kingdoms and enterprises come and go. Paradoxically, though, it became clear that that very materiality (its 'architecture') is subject to continuous, at times violent, modification that accounts for the resilience of some cities and the failure of others to adapt to economic change and deal with the consequences of transition. Confronting urban realities across the world has confirmed that city dwellers can do better than those who live in rural areas. Like the poorest Mumbaikars, we have found that many see their city as a 'bird of gold', a place of fortune, where you can change your destiny and fly.[9] As the figures above show, city dwellers get jobs; they produce and earn more. They can have better access to education and health. They can more easily become part of a networked, global society. But, at the same time, they consume and pollute more. They are exposed to extreme floods, violence, disease and wars. Many live without rights to land, shelter or votes, entrapped in a vicious cycle of social and spatial exclusion. It is these fragmented topographies that bring the informal and the formal close together, rendering them interdependent within the contemporary urban landscape.

The essays in this book reveal that it has become difficult for many of the Urban Age experts to talk about their own discipline without reference to the spatial dynamics of urban change. As Wolfgang Nowak has described in the Foreword, this process started in 2005, when the first Urban Age conference took place in New York, followed in quick succession by five other conferences over the following two years. The second phase continued in three hotspots of global metropolitan growth. The first took place in November 2007 in Mumbai, India's economic powerhouse where 44 newcomers per hour are swelling the 'Maximum City'.[10] The second occurred in December 2008, at the height of the global recession, in São Paulo, Brazil's most populous and dynamic city growing at the rate of 11 people per hour. The final conference of the series was held in November 2009 in Istanbul, with claims to being Europe's largest city (even though a third of its residents live on the Asian side) where 12 new residents per hour contribute to its success as one of the most resilient urban economies in the world.[11] Not only do these cities represent world regions that are growing rapidly today, but their metropolitan areas expanded exponentially during the twentieth century: Mumbai by 1,978 per cent, São Paulo by 7,916 per cent and Istanbul by 'only' 1,305 per cent since 1900, even though it has quadrupled since 1980. By contrast, London only grew by 16 per cent over the same period.[12]

Each conference was attended by 300 to 400 people, with presentations given by up to 80 local and international experts covering subjects as diverse as urban governance, security and crime, transport and mobility, housing and public space as well as the impact of cities on the environment and sustainability. The Urban Age team carried out studies on wider regional trends, working with local municipalities and institutions as part of year-long research projects that generated the material and ideas discussed at the conferences and included in this book.[13]

The Mumbai conference became the focus of debate on urbanization of Indian cities – including Bangalore, Kolkata and Delhi – and at a time of significant restructuring of urban governance in the world's largest and most cumbersome democracy. In São Paulo, we explored how South American cities – including Buenos Aires, Lima, Bogotá and Rio de Janeiro – were responding to different economic

75%

of the world's CO_2 emissions are produced by cities

and social pressures, especially in relation to inequality and security. In Istanbul, we focused on how the profound social, cultural and economic change in a city with a 'deep history', inhabited for over 2000 years, is affecting its spatial and political landscape.

A Road Map for the Reader

The book is divided into three sections: 'Cities' contains visual essays and analytic texts which mirror the content of Urban Age conferences held in the three core cities from 2007 to 2009; 'Data' is a compendium of vital statistics of all nine Urban Age cities, accompanied by a critical narrative and the results of opinion polls carried out among local residents; 'Reflections' collects the thoughts of scholars and practitioners who have followed our project, offering their perspectives on the lessons learnt for the twenty-first-century city.

Following this introductory text, the first two essays frame the critical thematic axes of the book: built form and the urban economy. Tackling the relationship between architecture and cities head-on, Deyan Sudjic offers a critique of the limits of the current discourse within the design professions when it comes to addressing the pragmatics and the poetics of 'Living in the Endless City'. Reviewing recent projects in the three Urban Age case studies, he argues that architecture has remained on the edge of the conversation about cities, and makes a rallying call to architects to get off the fence and address what cities might become. Taking a different view, Saskia Sassen tackles the complex economies of global cities, arguing that their resilience and survival are interdependent on indeterminate infrastructure and built form. Using examples from Istanbul, Mumbai and São Paulo, she describes how backward, often informal, sectors serve advanced sectors and their high-income employees, concluding that urban manufacturing plays a critical role in extending the deep histories of global cities in current times and that the specialized differences of cities have specific spatial requirements in order to allow their complex economies to grow and survive.

In the essays that investigate Mumbai in the context of other Indian cities, the authors offer different insights on governance, civic engagement, exclusion, urban culture and mobility. A common theme runs through the texts, that despite the immense poverty of its residents and inadequacy of its infrastructure, Mumbai has lessons to offer other cities around the world. The sheer density of human occupation, which Suketu Mehta describes as 'an assault on one's senses', cuts through all the essays, as does the notion of resilience and ingenuity of its residents. Mehta connects the vibrant social economy of slums like Dharavi to the realities of Lisbon and Istanbul, arguing that the tabula rasa approach to slum redevelopment is totally out of step with the needs of a more inclusive urban society, especially one that is so lacking in resources.

Equally critical of the ambitious top-down vision for Mumbai as a 'Global City', Darryl D'Monte argues that there are many cities in Mumbai, constituted by different social and cultural identities that run the risk of being stamped out by the current coalition of state bureaucrats and vested interests. Building on this theme, Rahul Mehrotra gives a new reading of how Mumbai functions for its diverse constituencies through its 'kinetic' dimension; a city of festivals, events, in perpetual motion, continually renewing itself. Geetam Tiwari agrees that a high population density has implicit benefits in terms of energy consumption, and while she applauds the fact that over 50 per cent of Mumbai's population commute to work by foot or by bicycle, she bemoans the failure of the state to build a public transport policy based on this uniquely efficient urban structure and the lifestyles of Indian cities.

Arguing that Mumbai is as politically fragmented as it is spatially, K. C. Sivaramakrishnan explains the power dynamics and struggles between central nation, state and local communities in the light of a much-vaunted government initiative (the 74th Constitutional Amendment) to devolve power downwards, which, he argues, is resulting in a significant loss of accountability. It is left to the architect of the failed attempt to decongest old Bombay with a new centre at Navi Mumbai, Charles Correa, to reflect wryly that current plans for Mumbai are more hallucinations than visions, and that the establishment should look again at the city's own DNA. Rather than build a city for cars for people who cannot afford them, he proposes a single, networked and balanced system based on public transport to cope with the inevitable crisis Mumbai will face with the 'monstrous' prospect of becoming the largest city in the world where today over 6 million people live in slums.

The strength of the culture of social entrepreneurship and civic engagement stands out as a dominant theme emerging from the essays on São Paulo and other South American cities. Buenos Aires, Lima, Rio and Bogotá have responded to extreme political and economic developments from the 1970s onwards – dictatorships, revolutions, economic miracles and disasters – with a mixture of Latin hopelessness and pragmatism that reflects little faith in governments and their institutions. Jeroen Klink addresses the institutional vacuum that has shaped urban development of this highly urbanized continent, where lack of investment and political will has, to his mind, fuelled a vicious cycle of poverty, environmental degradation and socio-spatial exclusion that has failed to make the most of the potential offered by South American cities and nations.

Despite being a classic 'second city', São Paulo occupies a class of its own. With over 30,000 dollar millionaires, one of the largest and powerful cities of the BRIC nations whose economies keep driving global growth, São Paulo – as Fernando de Mello Franco argues – has fully exploited (to the point of exhaustion) its unique geographic location on a high plateau with rivers flowing inland to the rest of the continent, fuelling its strong export economy. Raul Juste Lores extends the narrative by describing the city as an octopus stretching out in all directions, way beyond its political state and municipal boundaries, invading its precious water reservoirs and giving in to the pressures of land speculation that has seen the emergence of shopping malls, gated communities and business centres around the sprawling edges of this sprawling city.

Recalling Georg Simmel's preoccupations with how people would cope with the overstimulation of the metropolis, Gareth Jones suggests that the capacity for everyday life to hold on to the quality of contingency and connection is the mechanism through which excluded social groups – young people, gangs, ethnic minorities – are able to hang together in places where there is low public confidence in public institutions: politicians, planners or the police. His view that contemporary social life is marked on the urban landscape of Mexico City, Buenos Aires and Lima is further developed by Teresa Caldeira in her account of how social difference is spatialized in São Paulo through a process of exclusion that keeps people apart. Challenging the voyeuristic model of the rich/poor divide in neighbourhoods where extreme wealth sits cheek by jowl with impoverished *favelas*, she describes how the edges of the city have become increasingly segregated, with poorer people pushed out to areas without infrastructure and with high levels of crime, while the affluent

growth in the number of urban poor between 1993 and 2002

remain in guarded enclaves either in the centre, or move even further out to car-dependent 'secure' developments.

Echoing Teresa Caldeira's identification of the different modalities of social cohesion defined through religion, graffiti, language, gangs or crime, José de Souza Martins focuses on São Paulo's 'transitive' multicultural immigrant communities that populate the city's strong neighbourhoods – Italian, Jewish, Spanish, Arab, German, Russian, and Ukrainian as well as *Nordestinos* (from northeast Brazil) and the more protected Japanese and Korean communities. He describes the city as being peculiar and multicultural. Not because it accepts the cultural diversity of those who arrive in it without conflict, but mainly because it ensures each example of diversity is allowed to be what it has always been, while the fact of their daily coexistence is embraced and leads to new forms and innovations.

The essays on Istanbul and its geopolitical hinterland revolve around the impact of globalization on city form and social equity, especially in a context of such physical specificity. Provocatively, Richard Sennett synthesizes this debate into a question. Does Istanbul in the future want to look more like modern Frankfurt or Renaissance Venice as it faces the challenges of global capitalism? Deyan Sudjic takes this visual analogy further by describing Istanbul as a city as beautiful as Venice or San Francisco, but 'once you are away from the water [it becomes] as brutal and ugly as any metropolis undergoing the trauma of warp-speed urbanization.'[14]

Sennett's reference to a pre-modern Venice provides an interpretative framework for post-modern Istanbul. The first 'hinge city' of the Mediterranean, Venice imported spices from India, slaves from North Africa and cloth from Asia, and then sent finished goods to Europe and the East. This notion of city as workshop, with building and places that allow for the making of things to maintain its 'hinge' status, resonates with Saskia Sassen's identification of the primacy of urban manufacturing, even in the most global of global cities. When the environment becomes homogenized and informality is neutralized from the public spaces of the city, the 'hinge begins to rust' and the city becomes dysfunctional as a social mechanism.

Hashim Sarkis develops this argument further, using spatial models based on Mediterranean historiography to analyze Istanbul's ambivalent relationship within its wider context. This complements Ömer Kanıpak's visual narrative of how the city is shaped by nature and its dynamic topography. He decodes Istanbul's millennial DNA by explaining how water and steep escarpments are omnipresent, creating a uniform, accessible landscape for the residents, irrespective of their social or economic class. Observing recent urban developments in Arab cities of the wider Mediterranean area like Beirut, Cairo and Aleppo, Sarkis concludes that Istanbul has managed to maintain, albeit in a manicured way, a unifying geography over historic epochs and to display synchronicity among its historic layers.

Instead, Asu Aksoy and İlhan Tekeli offer a trenchant criticism of the impact of the 'new round' of globalization on the city's spatial and social infrastructure. While Aksoy invokes the notion of 'worldliness' as a positive cocktail of openness, liberalism, pragmatism, democratic culture and global 'embeddedness', she shares Tekeli's concern at the combined risks of an aggressive real estate market and the gargantuan building programme of the government's own housing agency TOKI. Soft targets have been identified by the municipality; the historic Tarlabaşı district, with its abandoned Greek Orthodox churches and dilapidated nineteenth-century houses now occupied by Kurdish populations living side by side with local Gypsy populations and illegal African immigrants, is slated for a clean up. The bulldozer-led, forced relocation of Roma families from the Sulukule district has already occurred, giving way to a new development of neo-Ottomanesque houses for the city's new middle classes. Such heavy-handedness sits awkwardly within a culture that for decades has learnt how to make do, where the informality which gave rise to the *gecekondu* (illegal houses 'built at night' by immigrants) has spread to work (street hawkers), transport (*dolmuş*, shared taxis) and even music and construction. Perhaps this is why Tekeli is not over-critical of the 'hybrid form' of development control that Istanbul has now mastered – half planned, half unplanned – to service its hybrid political economy.

Unintentionally, this half-conclusion provides a way in for Çağlar Keyder to address the tricky question of how to measure success. He makes the point that the history of Istanbul's spatial expansion was not straightforward – in the sense that the accommodation of population growth required ad hoc arrangements regarding land ownership – and that the commodification of land has become a necessity to realize the shared liberal and globalizing agenda which for the first decade of the twenty-first century has united the national leaders in Ankara with Istanbul's city fathers.

The 'Data' section includes information on all nine Urban Age cities, laid out in diagrams drawn to the same scale to invite comparison. Assembled from different sources, the data have been checked and revised to ensure, wherever possible, consistency and accuracy. Each set of diagrams illustrates measures that capture various aspects of population distribution, density, age, inequality and employment as well as administrative boundaries, public transport and modal splits. Where relevant and available, information has been provided at the municipal, metropolitan and regional scales. Particular attention is given to patterns of residential densities found across the nine cities, with detailed maps and diagrams illustrating the urban form of the peak density areas in all cities.

In his extended essay, Justin McGuirk provides an interpretative commentary on the data, which probes and questions their meaning. The aim is to sketch an impression (that is, all 'facts' can do) about what the data really tell us, a guide to finding interpretations and readings in the wall of numbers. Moving from the impersonal and quantitative to the subjective and qualitative, Tony Travers provides a parallel interpretative narrative of the results of three opinion polls commissioned by the Urban Age among the residents of Mumbai, São Paulo and Istanbul. Travers' text makes reference to a similar study carried out in London, allowing a four-city comparison to be made regarding what people's opinions are on each city's government and other issues including security, crime, education, public transport and the environment.

Polling of this kind is important for mayors and local governments in testing what people do and do not like about their neighbourhoods and cities. Personal safety emerges as a key issue in major metropolitan areas and the polling makes clear that in São Paulo and Istanbul there is a significant issue here. Health care and other public services are seen as poor in some developing cities, while the 'range of shops' can be an important reason for residents liking where they live. Perhaps, the unexpected overall conclusion from these soundings is that there is no overwhelming feeling within the four cities that life is bad.

The final section contains a number of personal reflections by individuals who have been closely associated with the Urban Age project from the outset, as well as some relative newcomers. Architects, mayors, sociologists and transport planners offer their views on the trends observed in the Urban Age cities, providing a cross-section of opinions on the interactions between physical and social aspects of cities.

Richard Sennett immediately addresses the contradictions of these interactions by focusing on the fundamental difference between 'borders' and 'boundaries' and their socializing or alienating potential on urban residents, noting that the impermeable boundary is replacing the porous border in the new spaces of the contemporary city. Alejandro Zaera-Polo reflects on how a 'no frills' culture, spurred on by cheap money from the 1990s onwards, has given rise to a new form of homogenized building types that satisfies the need of global capital. Nicholas Stern, Dimitri Zenghelis and Philipp Rode explore how cities can play a significant role in mitigating the negative effects of climate change by developing a new model of green cities that reduces energy consumption and pollution. By comparing the governance structures of three Urban Age cities, Gerald Frug explains how national, state and municipal interests are often in conflict and rarely succeed in providing a democratic voice for the city's contested electorate. Anthony Williams extends this political theme with a parable of how difficult it is for a city leader to steer a clear course between the opposing needs of different urban constituencies, while Sophie Body-Gendrot reflects on how violence, inequality and disorder have been spatialized in all the Urban Age cities.

Moving to a smaller scale, Alejandro Aravena addresses the need to find a flexible and affordable solution to the core building block of city form – the house – presenting the radical and innovative Elemental housing prototype as a viable response to the imprecise demands of the informal economy. David Satterthwaite turns to another core issue – survival – for the poorest city dwellers who are most at risk due to environmental hazards, poor governance and political exploitation. Fabio Casiroli extends our understanding of exclusion by explaining how the different patterns of mobility affect the residents of Istanbul, São Paulo and Mumbai in profoundly different ways, while Bruce Katz defines the problematic economic status of metropolitan areas in the US, offering scenarios for improvement through investment in urban jobs, innovation and export-orientated economy based on green technologies. Finally Adam Kaasa, with Marcos Rosa and Priya Shankar, brings us back to the ground by framing the Deutsche Bank Urban Age Awards – which have accompanied the Urban Age project since 2007 – with an understanding of the role of marginal groups in reclaiming the spaces of their own cities.

Concluding and Looking Forward

These multiple narratives provide a cross-section of the social and spatial dynamics of Mumbai, São Paulo and Istanbul, offering general insights on the state of cities at the beginning of the twenty-first century. The disparate and, at times, bracing accounts of how cities can brutalize both citizens and the environment remind us of the challenges and threats faced by the next generation of urban leaders who are tasked with steering their cities through what will be complex and difficult times.

But, the narratives also suggest that cities are uniquely placed to harness their human and environmental potential, guiding urban growth towards greater social and environmental equity. This will be the main task for mayors, governors and city leaders of the emerging Mumbais, São Paulos and Istanbuls.

Faced with similar threats and challenges more than a century ago, the city fathers of Barcelona, Paris, Chicago or Amsterdam had the vision to build new 'pieces of city' to accommodate the surge of new urban dwellers. A hundred and fifty years later, the streets, avenues, parks, homes and civic institutions conceived by Ildefonso Cerdà, Baron Haussmann, Daniel H. Burnham or Hendrik Petrus Berlage – the first urbanists of the Modern Era – have demonstrated long-term sustainability, adapting to cycles of economic and social change with buildings and spaces that are both robust and resilient. The spatial DNA of the city fabric and its social institutions have worked together to accommodate and support diverse communities, providing them with a sense of place and identity. In these cities, the physical and the social have been successfully interlinked.

The next generation of urban leaders has an opportunity to make a difference, building on the spatial and social DNA of their cities, rather than import generic models that cater to the homogenizing forces of globalization. The recent histories of Barcelona or Bogotá, among others, suggest a way forward. By introducing radical measures that work with the spatial and social fabric of the city, successive mayors have turned their cities round, making the most of their urban and human assets. Rediscovering the fragile thread that links physical order to human behaviour will be the main task of this Urban Age, a world where 75 per cent of us will be living in cities.

WHERE PEOPLE CONCENTRATE

The uneven distribution of people across the globe is revealed by the intensity of colour that marks where the highest population densities will live in 2015. Continuously inhabited Metropolitan Regions are already concentrated in the Indian subcontinent and the Pacific Rim with a 12th of the world's population in the River Ganges plain and a similar proportion in the Yangtze Basin and the North China plain. Clusters of high population density appear in the cities and urban regions of Europe and the United States, and the coastal regions of Africa and the Americas. Urban areas over 25,000 people begin to show up as brighter dots on the map (in contrast to

the sparsely populated or uninhabited areas
in black), highlighting the fact that cities and
Metropolitan Regions make up only 2 per cent
of the world's surface, yet are lived in by 53 per
cent of its inhabitants.

People/km²

0
1 – 5
5 – 25
25 – 250
250 – 1,000
1,000 and over

London
Berlin
Istanbul
Shanghai
Mumbai
Johannesburg

THE HUMAN FOOTPRINT

Scientists estimate that human activities have had a direct impact on 83 per cent of the world's land surface. Only large areas of desert, tundra, tropical forest and icecaps are untouched by permanent roads, buildings, infrastructure or agriculture. While human activity appears to have fully saturated the surface area of Europe, the Indian subcontinent, Eastern China and Central America, North America displays an asymmetric distribution from East to West, while coastal regions of South America and large sub-areas of sub-Sahara Africa are well covered. Urban settlements are distributed across the network of the accumulated human footprint across space and time.

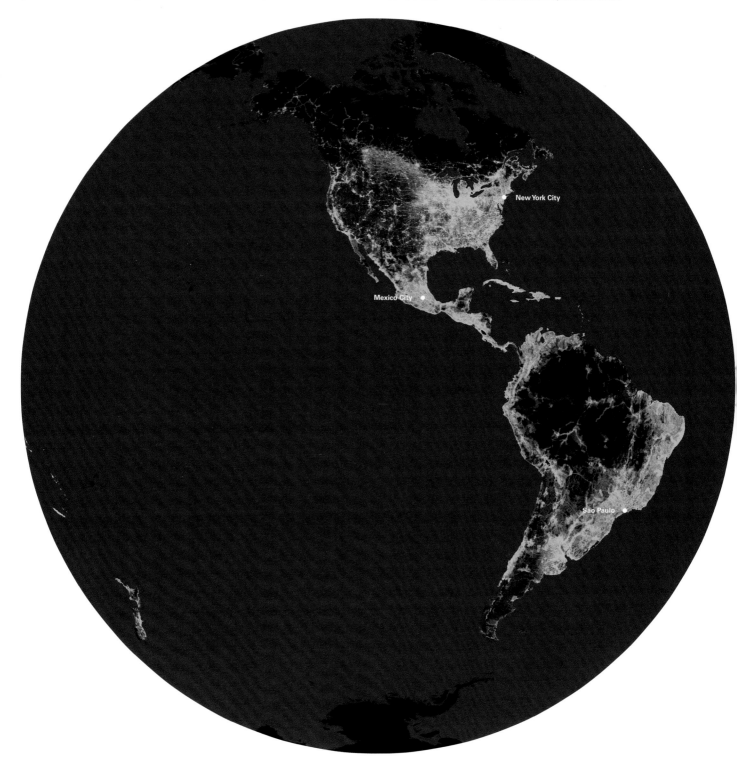

Least influenced

Most influenced

London

Berlin

Istanbul

Shanghai

Mumbai

Johannesburg

CONNECTING BY AIR

Cities are the meeting points of global flows of capital, goods and people. Despite the negative impact on the environment, air travel between cities and metropolitan regions has increased at an exponential rate, fuelled by cheaper flights and market competition. Airports have become essential to the global positioning – or repositioning – of existing or emerging centres of finance, tourism and trade. The intensity of the lines illustrated in this map, which charts routes between nine Urban Age cities, reveals the relative concentration of communications between these engines of the world economy. The busy New York-London route tops the chart with

54 direct daily trips, followed by London-Berlin (22 flights), New York-Mexico City and London-Istanbul (12 flights each) and London-Johannesburg (10 flights). Surprisingly perhaps, it is short, intra-regional routes that have the most intense schedules with 240 daily flights from São Paulo to Rio de Janeiro, 196 from Washington to New York and 101 from London to Amsterdam.

Number of annual flights per route

1 – 500
500 – 1,500
1,500 – 3,000
3,000 – 6,000
6,000 – 10,000
10,000 – 20,000
20,000 – 45,000

London

Berlin

Istanbul

Shanghai

Mumbai

Johannesburg

CONNECTING BY SEA

Despite the increase in air traffic, commercial shipping remains of global significance in distributing goods and connecting major hubs along the coastal regions of four continents. Reflecting their historic geographical location as natural harbours at the crossing point of major international routes, many port-cities have continued to grow and play an important role in the global economy of the twenty-first century. The map reflects the level of commercial activity across the world's oceans and shows the size of port activity measured in terms of annual container traffic (TEU – Twenty Foot Equivalent Unit). While the top five ports are located in Asia – Singapore, Shanghai,

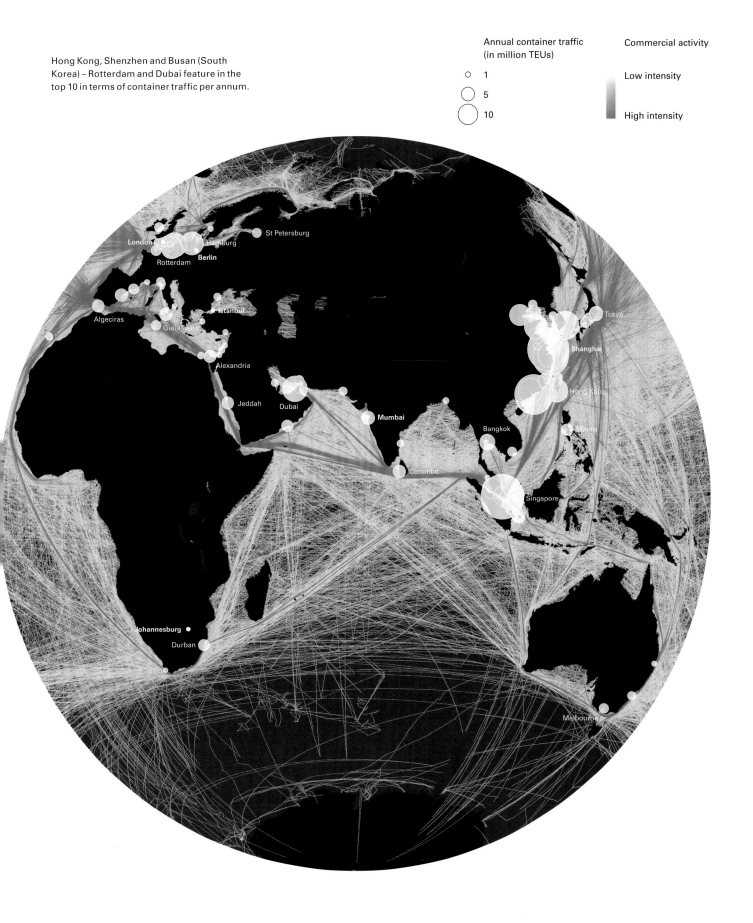

Hong Kong, Shenzhen and Busan (South
Korea) – Rotterdam and Dubai feature in the
top 10 in terms of container traffic per annum.

Annual container traffic
(in million TEUs)

○ 1

◯ 5

◯ 10

Commercial activity

Low intensity

High intensity

St Petersburg

London Hamburg
Rotterdam **Berlin**

Algeciras

Gioia Tauro

Istanbul

Alexandria

Jeddah

Dubai

Mumbai

Colombo

Bangkok

Tokyo

Shanghai

Hong Kong

Manila

Singapore

Johannesburg ○

Durban

Melbourne

WHERE CITIES ARE GROWING

There are dramatic regional differences in the pace and scale of urbanization. The map charts the size and growth of a selection of world cities with more than 750,000 people from 1950 (dark green circle) to 1990 (light green circle) and indicates the projected growth to 2025 (white circle) based on UN predictions. While many European and North American cities (such as London, New York and Paris) had reached their peak by 1950, Japanese and Latin American cities (most notably Tokyo, Mexico City and São Paulo) grew most in the following four decades. But, over the next 20 years, the biggest and fastest growing city regions will be in Africa (Kinshasa and Lagos)

Vancouver

Chicago

New York City

Los Angeles

Havana

Mexico City

Bogotá

Lima

São Paulo

Rio de Janeiro

Buenos Aires

and Asia, with some of the most intense levels of urbanization in India and China (especially in Dhaka, Delhi, Karachi and Mumbai).

Population (in millions)

○ 1
○ 5
○ 10

Year

● 1950
● 1990
2025

London
Paris
Berlin
Moscow
Madrid
Istanbul
Cairo
Tehran
Delhi
Karachi
Beijing
Tokyo
Shanghai
Hong Kong
Khartoum
Mumbai
Dhaka
Manila
Bangkok
Madras
Lagos
Singapore
Kinshasa
Jakarta
Dar es Salaam
Johannesburg
Sydney

HOW FAST CITIES ARE CHANGING

Kinshasa, Dhaka or Delhi will each grow at the rate of one new inhabitant every 75 seconds by 2025. At the same time cities such as Berlin, St. Petersburg, Havana and Seoul are likely to see their populations shrink, reflecting differential patterns of economic and population growth. The most rapidly growing cities are located in areas where population densities are already high, reflecting the accelerating rural-to-urban migration and natural birth rates in developing regions. The provision of urban infrastructure in these rapidly growing cities will have a significant impact on environmental sustainability and quality of life of urban residents.

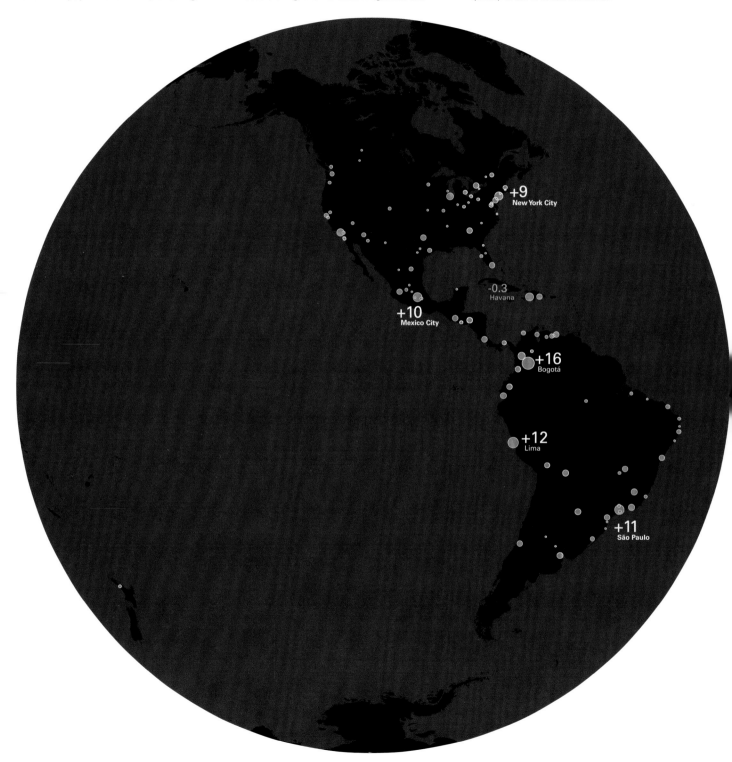

+9 New York City

-0.3 Havana

+10 Mexico City

+16 Bogotá

+12 Lima

+11 São Paulo

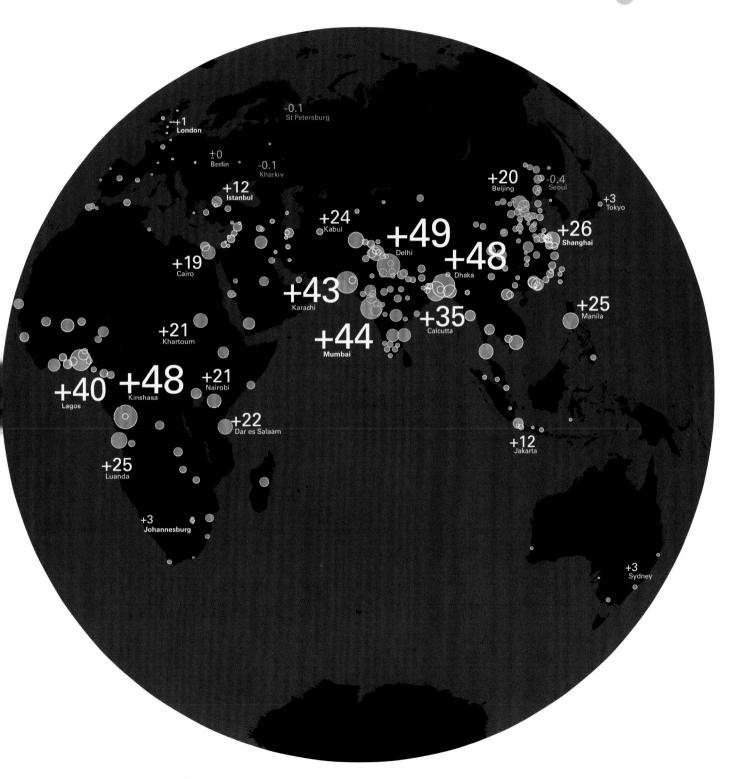

Persons per hour

+10
+30
+50

-0.1
St Petersburg

+1
London

±0
Berlin

-0.1
Kharkiv

+12
Istanbul

+24
Kabul

+20
Beijing

-0.4
Seoul

+3
Tokyo

+49
Delhi

+26
Shanghai

+48
Dhaka

+19
Cairo

+43
Karachi

+35
Calcutta

+25
Manila

+44
Mumbai

+21
Khartoum

+21
Nairobi

+48
Kinshasa

+40
Lagos

+22
Dar es Salaam

+12
Jakarta

+25
Luanda

+3
Johannesburg

+3
Sydney

WHERE URBAN ECONOMIES ARE GOING

Tracking the change in the rate of Gross Value Added (the domestic output of metropolitan regions) for 150 world cities between 1993 and 2010 reveals the geo-political shift that has occurred at a global level over the last decades. Both Eastern Europe and the Asian 'tiger economies' have demonstrated strong economic growth that mirrors a commensurate increase in population and regional migration patterns. While many metropolitan regions were hit hard by the 2007–2009 global recession, a cluster of Asian and Latin American cities have demonstrated resilience in their performance based on innovation, investment in urban manufacturing and export-oriented economies.

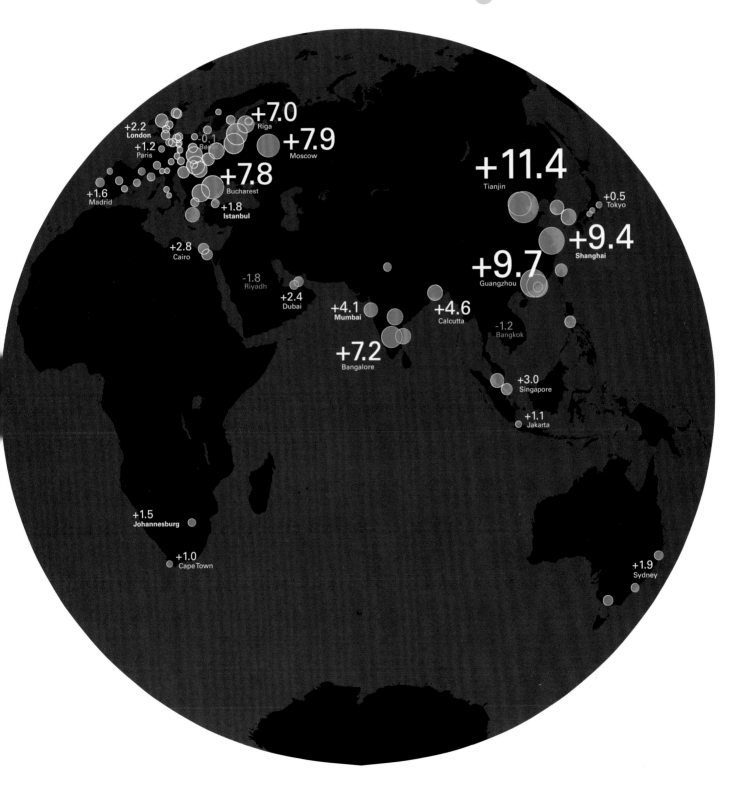

Average annual growth rate in Gross Value Added

+1.00
+5.00
+10.00

+2.2
London

+1.2
Paris

+7.0
Riga

-0.1
Berlin

+7.9
Moscow

+11.4
Tianjin

+0.5
Tokyo

+1.6
Madrid

+7.8
Bucharest

+1.8
Istanbul

+9.4
Shanghai

+2.8
Cairo

-1.8
Riyadh

+9.7
Guangzhou

+2.4
Dubai

+4.1
Mumbai

+4.6
Calcutta

-1.2
Bangkok

+7.2
Bangalore

+3.0
Singapore

+1.1
Jakarta

+1.5
Johannesburg

+1.0
Cape Town

+1.9
Sydney

THE HUMAN POTENTIAL OF CITIES

The quality of life and expectations of city dwellers vary significantly according to which part of the world they inhabit. The distribution of the Human Development Index (HDI) – a composite measure developed by the United Nations to track educational attainment, life expectancy and economic development – suggests that the global South is catching up with the North. While many cities of the global North reach comfortable HDI levels (anything above 0.8 is considered high), Latin American cities are showing a significant improvement, followed closely by urban areas in India and China, while African cities are still trailing behind. In all these regions a fair number of the

largest cities outperform their national averages, reflecting the potential of cities to provide benefits to their residents through better urban and social infrastructure such as schools, health centres and improved sanitation.

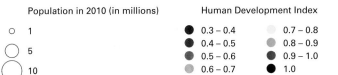

Population in 2010 (in millions)

○ 1

○ 5

○ 10

Human Development Index

● 0.3 – 0.4
● 0.4 – 0.5
● 0.5 – 0.6
○ 0.6 – 0.7
○ 0.7 – 0.8
● 0.8 – 0.9
● 0.9 – 1.0
● 1.0

HOTSPOTS OF RISK

Like wealth and social well-being, environmental risk is unequally distributed across the globe, with large sub-regions of Africa, Asia, the Middle East and Latin America disproportionately exposed to earthquakes, volcanoes, floods, landslides and drought. In urban areas where there is a greater concentration of human beings, the problems are exacerbated, especially in cities located near rivers, waterways and oceans, or in close proximity to fertile plains – all of which are under threat of flooding or sea-level rise brought about by global warming. When compared to the map indicating 'Where people concentrate' (pages 26-27), it becomes clear

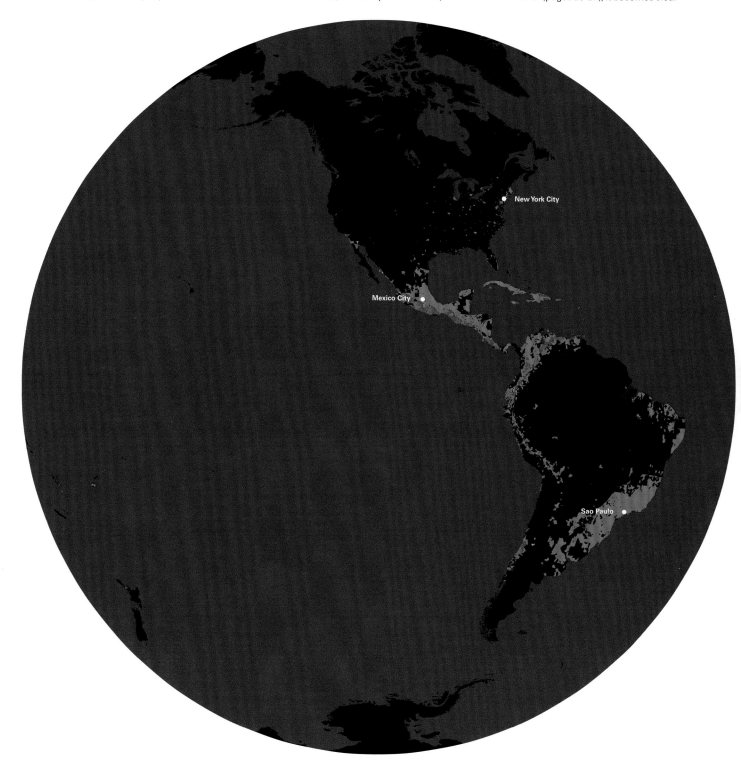

that areas which are attracting climate change
refugees fleeing to cities in search of protection,
are prone to high mortality rates.

High mortality risk from type of hazard

All of the risks described below
Drought, earthquakes and volcanoes
Flood, landslides, earthquakes and volcanoes
Drought, flood and landslides
Earthquakes and volcanoes
Flood and landslides
Drought

THE ARCHITECTURE OF THE ENDLESS CITY

Deyan Sudjic

NEW ARCHITECTURAL PARADIGMS

With some of the highest densities in the world, and extremes of wealth and poverty that coexist in close proximity, Mumbai has produced one of the world's more unexpected new building types, the high-rise palace. Perkins+Will are the architects responsible for oil billionaire Mukesh Ambani's Antilia project, a 24-storey-high tower in the city, which is both a sprawling home and a base for his business.

Architecture may sit on the edge of the conversation about cities, but it has a way of providing the language in which it is conducted. Architecture can suggest what is, in my view, essentially a fallacy: that a city is a kind of work of art, that it is to be understood as beautiful – or it can find a way to embrace the disorder and chaos of a living city, and through that, try to find the means of understanding and predicting their behaviour. Architecture is ready to embrace both utopian and dystopian ideas about the nature of the city. Buckminster Fuller's vision of a giant dome covering most of Manhattan to protect it from pollution could be understood as both a gesture of despair and of hope.

As a point of view, architecture can be breathtakingly ambitious, offering utopian visions of what cities can be, amounting to a kind of magical realism. It is fascinating to find a new generation returning to some of the Modernist dreams of the 1960s, and finding in them signs of hope for a less trivial role for architecture than the one which it is often reduced to, a kind of cosmetic branding. As a slice of what a city might be like, Alison and Peter Smithson's Robin Hood Gardens in London's East End was social housing as conceived by the architectural elite, a dream of streets in the sky, of the sense of community that comes from density. Forty years later, the local authority is determined to demolish it in the belief that it blights the lives of its inhabitants, while activists campaign for its protection as a historic landmark. There are similar cases across Europe and North America. If Minoru Yamasaki's American Institute of Architects award winning Pruitt-Igoe complex in St Louis had not been dynamited as uninhabitable in the 1970s, it would undoubtedly be the subject of a preservation campaign today.

It is an ambition which is sometimes out of step with popular and political perceptions. But when it is not trying to change the world with a single dramatic idea, architecture is also about small tangible things. At the smallest, and the most tangible level, it is the contribution to life in Mumbai's slums made by the activists who found the resources to design and construct communal latrines that have started to make life for Dharavi's inhabitants safer – providing an alternative to the risky practice of defecating on railway tracks; more hygienic, but above all more civilized.

At the opposite extreme in scale and ambition, are the masterplans of Zaha Hadid, working on the shape of a new Istanbul, or Jacques Herzog and Pierre de

A FOCUS ON DETAIL

Alejandro Aravena belongs to an architectural tradition that engages in the social aspects of the profession. His work on the Elemental project has taken a clear-eyed view of the issues that are involved in allowing the poor to live in decent conditions within the exploding cities of the global South. His approach is based on land tenure, density and affordability, rather than technocratic or formal solutions, without losing his commitment to design values.

Meuron's design for a new cultural centre for São Paulo on the site of the city's former bus station, torn down 30 years after it was built in an attempt to recreate a revitalized downtown for the city. These are big projects that suggest that it is possible to push an entire city in a new direction simply through the exercise of will – and a certain amount of investment.

The Urban Age project is driven by a particular vision of the city as a social and physical artefact, that for all its inequalities, dangers and squalor has a great deal to offer. It does not take a dispassionate view, though I believe it does maintain a scrupulous use of research data. Engagement is not necessarily a handicap to gaining insight into the essential nature of the city.

Throughout human history cities have been a focus of economic opportunity. They have offered some measure of security, at least when set off against the risks posed by marauders, brigands and landlords in the countryside. They have been places in which humans have been able to make the most of their creative possibilities. As a unit of organization they have been less problematic than the nation-state. Of course cities have seen pogroms and racial strife, but since the birth of the nation-state they have been a cosmopolitan alternative, offering tolerance and freedom. Even though its density has in fact suggested a way of minimizing man's ecological footprint, the city is associated with pollution, dirt and disease. The city has been the most effective vehicle ever devised for lifting huge numbers of people out of the countless generations of poverty that have overshadowed many forms of rural life.

And yet, the city has also had a persistently bad press. From the medieval attempts to limit London's growth to within the city walls, to the ruralist anarchism portrayed in William Morris's *News from Nowhere*, and a London which has been abandoned, and in which Parliament Square is a dung heap, marked by the fluttering of worthless banknotes. There has been a continuing sense of moral panic about the city. In art and literature, the city has often been presented in the most negative of terms. And once the *bien pensant* were able to take to the air at the start

THE BIG PICTURE

Zaha Hadid's take on shaping the redevelopment of a slice of what was an industrial area on Istanbul's waterfront is bold in its spatial approach, and reflects the grand manner of city making, recalling Haussmann's Paris and Cerdà's Barcelona in its sweep. Her clients have had to address complex land-ownership issues. If they succeed, they will have created a new business centre for the city.

of the twentieth century, and to see how cities looked from the clouds, spreading apparently endlessly and aimlessly, they quickly began to present what they saw as a sickness despoiling the once beautiful face of the earth.

Of course at ground level, from the perspective of daily life, the picture is somewhat different. From inside the Urban Age perspective it is easy to miss this negative interpretation of the city. We may question, or regret the evolution of the city. In the year that I was born, Bombay, as it was still called, had less than 3 million people. São Paulo was about the same size. And Istanbul had less than 2 million. In the course of my still middle-aged life, it has grown to 15 million: a translation that is daunting, to say the least. At heart though, we see cities as essentially offering possibilities. But in Prague in 2010, at Václav Havel's forum on the future of the city, Ricky Burdett and I were challenged in our far from uncritical, but fundamentally positive view of the nature of the city, and the growth of mankind's urban population, by a battery of architects and thinkers who viewed the mushrooming of the cities of Asia, Africa and Latin America with nothing but dismay. For them the appropriate response is not to be found in the palliatives of

The Society for the Promotion of Area Resource Centres is a recently established initiative by Mumbai's slum dwellers to bring a measure of dignity to life in settlements such as Dharavi by providing better sanitation. Rahul Mehrotra's architectural practice has designed a number of communal lavatories for SPARC. Using bamboo, steel and solar collectors, these four-storey structures have become significant local centres.

more efficient public transport systems, or more equitable social housing for more people. For some of them, the world has too many people, engaged in using up the world's finite resources at a rate that will rapidly destroy it. Their only solution is some form of more or less benign Malthusian inspired population control. In their view, to discuss the forms that cities might take, and the provision of infrastructure that might make them work better, is somehow little more than ornamental.

When seen against the scale of the problem of a world that might in the not too distant future reach 10 billion people, it is difficult to argue with any credibility, or even more importantly, perhaps with much chance of success, that the future of the world depends on the poor having fewer children in order to maintain the comfort of the rich. This is not a universal outcome. According to George Monbiot, for example, it is not population that is the key challenge: there are plenty of signs that it has already passed its maximum rate of increase. The problem is the way in which cities make use of the resources that they have at their disposal. Almost as pessimistic are those who may not be driven primarily by ecological arguments, but who still suggest that the endless agglomerations of settlement that we see taking shape across the world do not constitute cities in any meaningful sense.

At one level, these are aesthetic positions. Endless cities look ugly from the air. And even on the ground, they fail to live up to Renaissance Florence. To most of the specialists, the academics, the engineers, the lawyers, this is an essentially frivolous viewpoint. And perhaps it is. And yet this is precisely the way in which the vast majority of the citizens of these cities understand them. How do buildings look and feel within the city, how do they come together to define their public spaces? What can architects, physical and master planners and landscape architects do to make cities work better?

To perhaps the two key figures defining this debate in the architectural world, Rem Koolhaas and Leon Krier, who come at the issue from what might appear to be opposite ends of the architectural spectrum, but in fact have common roots in the Architectural Association school in London of the 1970s, the answer used to be

CULTURAL COMPLEX, LUZ

São Paulo is using Herzog & de Meuron's project to build an open cultural complex for the city's dance theatre and other cultural institutions as a major piece of urban renewal. Due to be completed by 2016, it will occupy the site of a sprawling bus station built in the 1960s that became associated with street crime.

nothing. The urban settlements that have arisen so quickly to accommodate both the absolute growth in the world's population, and the shift from the country to the city, cannot be understood as cities as the world once saw them.

Krier and Koolhaas knew each other when they taught at the AA and Zaha Hadid was a student there at the time. They came away with strikingly divergent views of the nature of the contemporary city, but just as political extremes have a way of backing into a common position, so Krier and Koolhaas's apparently radically divergent analyses have odd echoes of each other. Krier began his journey into architecture as an admirer of Le Corbusier, and later claimed to have been traumatized by the actual experience of Marseilles and the Ville Radieuse. It set him on a path that eventually returned him to an exploration of the nature of the traditional city, and to the declaration that it was the duty of any real architect not to build at all. In Krier's view, to do so was to take part in the crime of the destruction of mankind's greatest creation, the European city. 'A responsible architect cannot possibly build today ... Building can only mean a greater or smaller degree of collaboration in a civilized society's process of self-destruction.' 'I can only make Architecture,' he said in the 1970s, 'because I do not build. I do not build because I am an Architect.'

Koolhaas took an equally jaundiced view of the possibilities offered by architecture, but he found the edge cities and junk space of airports and malls offering more promising material for inquiry than the Tuscan squares and Parisian arcades that Krier explored. Koolhaas was fascinated by the impact of the speed of urban transformation and the way that it was creating such previously unknown phenomena as the development of the Gulf States, and Lagos, and China, where traditional concepts of architecture are an irrelevance. But his final conclusion was not so different from Krier's: architects who focused on building were in some way missing the point. There have been some significant shifts in both their positions since then. Krier met the Prince of Wales, and Koolhaas began working in China.

Krier claims to celebrate what he calls the humility of the traditional city, a

RECONFIGURING THE CITY

Emre Arolat's architectural practice has flourished as Istanbul has set about rebuilding itself, to become the focus for the emerging post-Soviet nations around it. He has designed the Santral cultural complex for Istanbul's Bilgi University, on the site of a redundant power station.

world of what he calls 'robust, handsome, but unpretentious streets', enhanced by the occasional, judiciously placed monument in Classical style. He believes that it is not difficult to go on building places with the qualities of the centre of Oxford, Prague or Ljubljana. It is a measure of the extent of his skill as a polemicist, and perhaps also the hunger for his view of the city, that he has made his position the architectural policy of the next King of England, as well as of the current Mayor of Rome. Krier has disciples everywhere from Florida to Romania. He is the father of what his American followers call New Urbanism, of which the Prince of Wales's development project at Poundbury, in Dorset, is the prime British example.

Krier believes that it is possible to reject the transformations of the past 50 years, and heal the damage that has been done, by following his prescriptions.

'You get more architecture out of low buildings that have high ceilings than you do from high buildings with low ceilings,' he has suggested. And he offers firm guidelines on how to achieve the right balance of public and private space in a city. 'More than 70 per cent public is too much, less than 25 per cent is too little'.

Krier claims that he has won the argument on city planning. All that is left is to banish plate-glass skyscrapers, and the exhibitionism of the current crop of architectural stars. 'Modernism represents the negation of all that makes architecture useful: no roofs, no load bearing walls, no columns, no arches, no vertical windows, no streets, no squares, no privacy, no grandeur, no decoration, no craftsmen, no history, no tradition. In fact neo-modernists have had to admit that there is no true substitute for the traditional fabric of streets and squares.'

Koolhaas also believes that the contemporary city is not a city in the way that it used to be understood, but his remedy to this insight, is not to seek to ameliorate what he sees, but to accept that it is the world's attitudes that need to change. Koolhaas's nostalgic lament is for a moment when the architectural imagination had the power to transform a city. In the way that Cerdà created a new Barcelona, Haussmann rebuilt Paris, and Olmsted designed Central Park. It is a role that has escaped the contemporary generation of architects. It is a position that not all architects accept. The masterplan is a continuing preoccupation of designers. Quite what a masterplan might be is still under discussion. It can be a density diagram, a set of circulation routes, a sculptural vision, or a narrative, a concept in words and pictures of what city life might be like.

The masterplan in the context of the Urban Age is an attempt to crystallize some sense of coherence to the anything but coherent transformation of exploding cities. Such projects in São Paulo, or Mumbai, or Istanbul, are rarely comfortable academic exercises. They are driven by violent change, and instability. And yet the very pace of change, and the openness of their elites to experiment, that has allowed these cities to offer the architectural avant-garde an opportunity to look at new directions.

Zaha Hadid's experiments for the redevelopment of the Istanbul waterfront, a city with which she has a strong personal connection, will take many years to realize. The Kartal Pendik masterplan is huge, at 500 hectares (nearly 2 square miles), it is planned to have 6 million square metres (over 60 million square feet) of space and could one day accommodate 100,000 people. Hadid's masterplan catches the eye with its glittering images, but it is not to be understood as essentially an architectural proposal. It is a script for a segment of a city that would be designed by many people. Hadid's work in Istanbul can be understood as city-shaping in the grand manner.

Given the massive change that Istanbul has gone through in the last two decades, Hadid's design – the result of an initiative of a group of private landowners, led by Bülent Eczacıbaşı working with the city authorities, has already been five years in the making, and has yet to start on site – is equally ambitious. The city has doubled in population in two decades, but despite the construction of such retail centres as the Kanyon complex – also built by Eczacıbaşı – it is still a city whose functioning is constrained by its monocentric structure. Kartal, on the Asian side of the city divided by the Bosporus stitched together by twin suspension bridges, attempts to give the city a second hub, providing an alternative to the Levent business district. A complex set of interlocking sites, some former industrial areas, looking over the sea of Marmara, others stone quarries at the side of the E5

PUTTING ON A BRAVE FACE

*Poundbury is the Prince of Wales'
development in Dorset that attempts to create
a sense of community by replicating traditional
urban forms. The masterplan is based on
Leon Krier's view of urbanism. He sees the ills
of twenty-first-century life as rooted in the
architectural forms that cities have taken on,
rather than the social or economic issues that
have provoked them.*

motorway, Hadid's plan takes advantage of useful existing transport connections to
include provision for a high-rise zone that will serve as a central business district,
luxury housing, cultural facilities, with a waterfront defined by a marina and hotel
cluster. Hadid has created what she calls a 'soft grid', a device that follows in the
steps taken by cities since the Roman period and before, all the way through to
Haussmann's Paris, New York, by way of Edinburgh's new town, to define urban
development. The idea of a grid, and the legal and financial controls that serve to
guarantee its long-term survival, is what can convince a developer to build a house
in an isolated setting, secure that it will one day be flanked by other buildings of
predictable scale and function to form a unified whole.

Hadid describes her grid as a calligraphic script that can be used to define both
integrated streets, but also free-standing structures. A set of lateral routes through
the area will serve to link it with the neighbourhood on either side, linking to the
primary longitudinal routes that connect the seafront with its hinterland. Hadid's
work in Istanbul shows what can happen when an innovative architect gets the
chance to plan old cities in new ways.

Istanbul is also a city that has been quick to learn from cities that de-
industrialized before it. The site of the Ottoman Empire's first electric power station,
SantralIstanbul, is an example of culture-led urban renewal. A mix of theatres,
galleries and libraries in a complex of recycled nineteenth-century buildings and
new developments, serves to create a new sense of the value of the city's recent past.

Alejandro Aravena's Elemental project, based in Chile, approaches the biggest

EVERY ACHIEVEMENT REQUIRES A SACRIFICE

GOING WITH THE FLOW

OMA's impact on architectural thinking has been crucial, even if they have taken a sceptical position on the ability of architecture to play the part it once had in cultural life. They have preferred to operate at the level of the city, rather than of the individual building, as exemplified in this competition strategy for Hong Kong's West Kowloon Cultural District.

challenge facing cities undergoing explosive growth: the issue of housing the poor, through design at the most detailed level. Elemental is a collaboration between Aravena in his university base, and the Chilean Oil Company that helps fund it, and seeks to allow the poor to remain in city centres, to give them a stake in their communities. In one of those cyclical shifts, three decades after the architectural profession for the most part retreated from its interest in social housing, Aravena's work is part of a worldwide refocus of architects on the problem of building housing to densities and designs that their occupants can afford. Elemental's strategy is to use the limited funds available to build minimal formal provision, 35 m² per occupant, in the expectation that the residents will expand the home themselves when resources allow. It is an attempt to inject the security of tenure, and building standards of the formal sector to the self-sufficiency of the *barrios* and the *favelas*. In the manner of such initiatives, it is an idea that has spread rapidly, with the Elemental projects not confined to Chile, but now appearing in Mexico, and the United States, with more to come.

At the other extreme, the transformation of exploding metropolises is seeing the appearance of freakish new building forms, represented at their most extreme in Mumbai, where the combination of massive densities with an explosion of affluence is symbolized by the 24-storey high, 150-metre tall Antilia project for the oil billionaire Mukesh Ambani. Described as the world's largest house, the 24-storey-high tower, designed by Ralph Johnson of Chicago based Perkins + Will architects, seems to symbolize the collision between rich and poor. It is the product of extreme

conditions, creating what is a new typology, but also one with curious echoes of the towers of San Gimignano. And it shows both the visibility and the impotence of contemporary architecture in the new city.

I began by suggesting that architecture has been on the edge of the conversation about the city. The issue here is perhaps the essential duality of architecture, which is both the most pragmatic of arts, in its obligation to provide shelter, but also the most speculative in its pursuit of ideas and emotions.

At the start of the Urban Age conferences, Rem Koolhaas and Peter Eisenman, not helped by my chairmanship, conducted a difficult debate between themselves. Their audience expected pragmatism, and got only the kind of speculation it understood as frivolous. So Koolhaas and Eisenman retreated into a private professional language that served only to suggest the seeming irrelevance of architecture.

But architecture's speculative aspects can in fact have much to say about its pragmatic obligations that is important. It has been at the centre of speculations about what cities might be, and it has been seeking to find a critical way of addressing what they might become. What it has to do now is to frame those speculations in a way that will let them be heard beyond the edge of the conversation.

THE ECONOMIES OF CITIES

Saskia Sassen

MULTIPLE WORLDS IN THE CITY

Manufacturing jobs appear to have deserted Western cities, but the picture is actually more complex than it seems. In developed cities, the global North and South can coexist. Migrants represent both ends of the scale: some work in the low-wage economy, while others have the skills to work in finance.

Within a given period of time – centuries or millennia – enterprises, kingdoms and nation-states are born and die in their thousands. With rare exceptions, cities go on. At best, they change names. The materiality of the city itself allows it to survive. Once there, it stays. In contrast, the more abstract framing of kingdoms and nation-states, and even enterprises, means they can disappear with few traces. A city destroyed is the source for its re-building. Of the three Urban Age cities under review here, Istanbul and Mumbai are dramatic instances of this endurance across millennia and across diverse forms of political organization. But São Paulo also has a history of centuries feeding into its current configuration.

These deep histories of cities are easily overlooked in contemporary analyses of the advanced knowledge economy. Such an economy is assumed to be new, to come from a type of intelligence that is contemporary, with today's 'creative classes' the key actors. The notion is that cities need such classes in order to be advanced economies. From this perspective, the history of a city is at best of little use, and at worst an obstacle to entering the advanced knowledge economy. The prescription is to bring the new economy down from up high *into* one's city.

I find this a partial prescription at best. It may hold for cities that lack much of an economic history. But cities' deep histories matter in today's major global cities. It seems extreme to dismiss the long and enormously complex economic histories of Istanbul and Mumbai as part of their rise as global cities in today's modernity. A first argument I want to develop is that these deep histories of today's global cities have become, if anything, more important in current times. They feed the complex economies of these cities. There is a dynamic relation between such histories and the particular strengths and specialized differences of global cities. In contrast, the Keynesian city of the mid-twentieth century did not much need that deep history.

There is a parallel obscuring of a second articulation that is a key part of the present economy in today's global cities. It is between the advanced economic sectors and backward-looking sectors, which are assumed not to belong in an advanced urban economy and thus considered an anachronism. A second argument I want to develop here is that many of these so-called backward sectors are actually servicing the advanced economic sectors and their high-income employees. Parts of the traditional small enterprise sector and of the informal economy service particular components of the advanced sectors in a city. In some specific sectors, their articulation with the advanced economy is an inversion of the historic relationship

between manufacturing and services. One instance is what we refer to as 'urban manufacturing'; it services the design industries, thereby inverting the historic relation between manufacturing and services.

The visual orders and topographies of global cities do not help our effort to recover these articulations. On the one hand, the increasingly homogenized landscapes and built environments of the glamour zone tend to obscure the fact that specific urban histories feed particular specialized advantages, and hence a connection to the past. The past is easily petrified into beautiful ruins and as a tourist destination. Cities' state-of-the-art glamour zones also speak the language of disconnection. But when we recover these articulations, some of the trends evident in each of the cities of the Urban Age project become more understandable, whether through the specialized differences present everywhere across these cities, or through the juxtaposition of urban glamour zones and poverty zones. In its most extreme format, each global city has a global slum, either next to it or in its centre.[1]

The Management of Empires

Though a partial element of the story, we need to recover the relationship of today's advanced economic sectors with older material economies and the organizational capabilities they implied. Trading, the management of empires, manufacturing, mining, agriculture, these and others mobilized diverse capabilities. At various historic transitions some of these capabilities jumped organizing logics: they could be used, albeit in a different way, in a subsequent new economic order that succeeded the one from which they originated. One instance of such a jump are Chicago's famous 'pork bellies', which became the input for financial futures. A second instance is the shift of particular manufacturing sectors towards servicing service industries, rather than being serviced by the latter, as was the case originally.

The idea that such a relationship exists between present and past economies has been lost in much academic research and general commentary about the knowledge economy. The latter is seen as new and non-material, whence it is easy to assume that its existence is predicated on the *overcoming* of the older material economies of a place, a city, a region. The contemporary understanding of the knowledge economy is that it is about abstract knowledge and the talent of the so-called 'creative classes' and 'symbolic knowledge workers'.[2] I find we have overvalued this class of workers, and that one consequence is a devaluing of material economies, notably manufacturing, and of workers who deal with materials. Such a devaluing of manual work holds, even when this work is part of new and state-of-the-art economic sectors.

Two links are lost in analyses that conceive of the knowledge economy as a sort of opposite, radically different economy from the older material economies. The first, briefly described above, is with the knowledge embedded in older material economies of craft workers and skilled manual work. They are evicted from the standard account about the knowledge economy. This eviction often also affects knowledge workers directly involved in material economies, such as computer engineers who provide the hardware.

The other link that is lost is with the city. Particular types of material economies, including those I refer to as urban manufacturing, are a critical component of multiple knowledge sectors today. These kinds of urban material economies matter enormously for cities and vice versa. Urban manufacturing, both formal and informal, thrives in cities and could, if properly recognized, contribute to creating a more distributed type of economy – producing more mid-level jobs and firms with mid-level rather than hyper profits. This urban production is mostly highly specialized, but in ways that the 'knowledge economy' analysis simply overlooks. Unlike mass manufacturing, it needs to be in cities or urban areas because it is networked, based on multiple supplier and contractor links, and needs direct contact with customers. Moreover, it varies enormously between cities, thereby reflecting the particularity of a city's economic history. For instance, when major producers of fibre optics, LEEDs, and other glass components of advanced economic sectors sought to expand their volumes, one of the sites that became a destination was Toledo, Ohio. This old industrial city was more favourable for the establishment of factories compared with high-tech cities such as Austin.[3] Why? Because it has an old history as a major centre for the manufacturing of traditional industrial glass products, and a knowledgeable manufacturing workforce that could be trusted with the new types of glass production.

In cities with extreme inequalities, where the advanced economy captures a disproportionate share of income and profits, more and more components of urban manufacturing shift to slum areas. This is also evident in São Paulo, Mumbai and Istanbul. All three have long histories of manufacturing, and all three have seen the emergence of a new type of urban manufacturing that services the leading sectors – from design industries to the cultural sector. Whether in cities or in slums, urban manufacturing often goes unrecognized by economic development experts and planners, or is misunderstood as an obstacle to an advanced urban economy. The spaces and visual orders of urban manufacturing do not fit the image of the advanced economy, and thus are easily misunderstood as merely backward leftovers.

We have come to understand the fact that our current political economy needs and generates a growing number of global cities across the world. Together these cities form a multi-sited, state-of-the-art infrastructure for global actors – economic and cultural, professionals and immigrants. But we also have a far less noticed rise of global slums in major cities in the global South.[4] Most slums are not global, just like most cities are not. But some slums are becoming actors with global projection, no matter the multiple immobilities of their inhabitants. Dharavi in Mumbai is perhaps the best known of these slums. It is also one of the most developed ones, with its many informal enterprises catering to some of the major economic sectors in the city. São Paulo has several major slums, some quite internationalized, with migrant workers and small entrepreneurs from Peru and other neighbouring countries.

To put it in extreme terms, we might ask what the rise of global cities and global slums tell us about cities in our global modernity.

Economic History and Its Consequences

Recognizing the link between older material economies and current components of the knowledge economy helps us to understand why these components can vary sharply across cities, and why these specialized differences keep getting reproduced. Each of the three cities of Istanbul, Mumbai and São Paulo has particular, specialized differences beyond the more routinized activities that are evident in all cities. Recognizing these differences also allows us to see that interdependence rather than competition is far more likely among many of the large global cities in the world.

What is usually understood as coming out of the heads of talented professionals turns out to have profound links with the economic histories of cities. By this I mean those histories, inevitably mostly material, that forged a city's modern economy. However, this holds for cities with somewhat complex and diverse economies; it does

1724 French Blue
0051 Aqua
1726 Turquoise
1711 Emerald
0796 Mint
2031 Evergreen
1312 Slate
1089 Gold
2325 Orchid
2002 Berry
1608 Cranberry
0009 Red
1674 Raspberry
0193 Purple
2026 Lapis

OLD SOLUTIONS FOR NEW CITIES

American Apparel is described by its founder, Dov Charney, as a company that uses a vertically integrated business model to minimize the use of subcontractors and offshore labour. Knitting, dyeing, sewing, distribution and design all happen in their Los Angeles factories. It is a model that directly responds to the analysis of manufacturing in developed cities. Fascinatingly, Charney's father was an architect, who worked for Moshe Safdie on Habitat 67, and studied urban design at Harvard.

not hold for towns that emerged around one single industry or firm, such as a mine or steel mill whose death has often meant the death of the town itself.

The argument I am making here is twofold. On the one hand, I suggest that major components of today's knowledge economy started with the knowledge embedded in the material practices of older economies, which eventually fed more abstract forms of knowledge. On the other, I argue that insofar as these older material economies of cities were diverse, each city wound up with a specific type of specialized knowledge economy. Cities that lack a complex economic history can eventually buy into the knowledge economies; thus the strategy adopted by some cities to attract 'creative classes' will work for more routinized knowledge economies, which can be standardized and easily sold.

Ultimately, however, that highly diversified entity we refer to as 'the knowledge economy' could not simply emerge from the heads of the creative classes, no matter how brilliant they might be. Cities are complex systems and enablers of creative activities. Why would these original economic histories of making not extend into our present? This approach also helps us to recognize how our major cities have each partly made their own economic history.

Recognizing that the deep economic history of a place feeds its specialized knowledge economy carries various political implications. One consequence is that it returns value to earlier material economic practices; the craft workers and the mental work embedded in those practices. Another is that cities actually compete with each other far less than is typically argued in mainstream discussions. Firms have different preferences; not all global cities will do. Thus when Boeing, the aircraft manufacturer,

LEAPFROGGING TECHNOLOGY

The technology of the mobile phone connects migrants working in the affluent world with their roots. At the same time, it demonstrates how what were once less developed economies can leapfrog the West. From an absence of fixed line telephones, Africa and Asia have moved directly to using mobile phones as a simple substitute for the cash transfers of the banking system.

decided to enter the global knowledge economy, that is to say, sell its manufacturing expertise on the global market, it did not even consider New York City as a location for its new headquarters. It chose Chicago, today a major knowledge economy hub, in good part based on its heavy industrial past. The upshot is that a city's leadership can make a far tougher bargain with large corporations aiming at setting up offices, and make far fewer concessions than has been typical over the last twenty years. Urban governments should also work much harder at collaborating with other cities – for instance, with the other cities that share offices of a given firm. This need for collaboration among cities will be critical as we begin to confront our major environmental challenges. Effective greening of our economies will require active participation of all actors in and across cities, and much exchange of best practices and just plain communication about what works.

How much the specificity of a city and an urban region matters can vary considerably, depending on multiple factors, including the city's positioning in local and global markets. The Urban Age newspapers have examined the particularities of each of the Urban Age cities in great detail. This specificity matters more than is usually assumed, and in ways that are not generally recognized. The policy implication of my argument is that there is too great a focus on competition and not enough on specialized differences among cities – and the resulting possibility of greater bargaining power vis-à-vis global firms, and of coalitions among cities worldwide confronting those same corporations.

Urban Manufacturing: A Historic Inversion

A very different way in which the deep economic history of a place shapes its present specialized advantages is through urban manufacturing. There are two aspects often overlooked in discussions about urban economies – whether small or large, global or local. One of these aspects is the fact that there are actually multiple articulations between 'backward' and advanced sectors in these cities, no matter how different the urban spaces within which they take place. The second, a critical instance of the first, is that a particular type of manufacturing is very much part of today's urban service economies, including the most advanced ones. When we started our research about this in the 1990s, we chose to call it 'urban manufacturing'.

Urban manufacturing is geared to design sectors of all sorts (from jewellery to furniture design, from architecture to interior decoration), cultural industries (theatres and opera houses need sets and costumes, museums and galleries need display settings for their collections), building trades (customized woodwork and metalwork), and to other sectors that are very much part of advanced service-based economies (the staging in luxury shops and restaurants, displays in corporate headquarters, and so forth).[5]

Urban manufacturing has several characteristics: firstly, it needs an urban location because it is deeply networked and operates in contracting and subcontracting chains; secondly, it is often fairly customized and hence needs to be in close proximity to its customers and to a diverse pool of first-rate craft workers; thirdly, it inverts the historic relation between services and manufacturing (historically services developed to serve the needs of manufacturers) in that it serves service industries.

A very advanced and rapidly growing type of urban manufacturing is emerging out of the diversity of projects to green our economies. It is a mix of more standard manufacturing and the features of urban manufacturing I described above. For much of the 1980s and 1990s, most policy analysts and government economic development agencies in a city such as New York, for instance, did not recognize the existence of a specifically urban manufacturing sector. Policy was oriented towards retaining the large, standardized factories, as these were far more visible and known, and had more sizeable workforces. But these were precisely the ones for which it made no sense to stay in the city: they did not need the urban economy with its multiple supplier and contracting chains and diverse craft talent pools. Finally, these were the decades in which government policy makers easily fell under the spell of powerful corporate services and finance, with their rapidly increasing numbers of very high-income employees and extremely high profits. Eventually, the cultural sector and tourism joined the list of glamorous and desirable sectors. What was not clear was the extent to which urban manufacturing was growing partly as a result of the growth of these advanced service sectors, including cultural industries. For this reason, perhaps, urban governments generally did not support the sector, even though it was often extremely vulnerable given the sharp rise in the costs of manufacturing in cities dominated by high-profit making corporate services. Indeed in the case of New York City we see that the more dynamic the advanced corporate services and the cultural sector, the more dynamic the urban manufacturing sector; and in addition, the more difficult it became for the latter to meet its basic needs (space, reasonable energy costs, technical and banking support, and so on).

Chicago has one of the most developed initiatives to support urban manufacturing, including establishing educational institutions with an emphasis on the diverse crafts involved. An intense initiative to use the manufacturing knowledge base of Chicago is for example the Chicago Manufacturing Renaissance Council's work on a new type of education of manufacturing workers that combines elements of the knowledge economy with fabrication skills. Its aim is to use advanced knowledge to manufacture the new types of products that the greening of our economy will require. Thus its Wind Turbine Supply Chain Project seeks to link local manufacturing companies to the emerging wind turbine sector, a cutting-edge sector that requires complex machined inputs. This is the type of advanced manufacturing that Europe (wind power) and Japan (hydrogen car batteries) have excelled at. It is interesting to note that of the nearly 16,000 factories employing 660,000 workers in Illinois, three quarters are in the Chicago metropolitan area.[6] This is urban manufacturing at a grand scale.

Just as urban manufacturing is intimately connected with – not opposed to – an advanced urban economy, so also is much of the economic informalization that has appeared in major global cities in North America, Western Europe, Latin America and to a lesser extent, Japan. This in turn helps to explain a mostly overlooked development: the proliferation of an informal economy of creative professional work in cities worldwide, consisting of, among others, artists, architects, designers, and software developers.

One way of capturing these somewhat invisible dynamics is to think of the urban economy as traversed by multiple specialized circuits. Thus an analysis of the diverse circuits that connect a given sector to various urban activities shows us that even finance, when disaggregated into such circuits, is linked to urban manufacturing suppliers, often through the design and building trades element, including the installation of advanced security devices throughout corporate office buildings.

Many smaller cities nowadays have the skilled workers and the potential for a small-scale urban manufacturing sector via the growth of an advanced service economy. This is due to the earlier mentioned trend towards the urbanization of economic activities, so that even a mining or manufacturing-based regional economy feeds the growth of specialized corporate services in cities: firms in all economic sectors nowadays are buying more insurance, legal and accounting services. The specialized services needed by more routinized economic sectors (heavy manufacturing, mining, industrial agriculture, transportation) are also more routinized, and hence can be produced in smaller and more provincial cities – they do not need a global city. The presence of a growing advanced services sector, along with the resultant growth of a high-income workforce with a strong preference for urban living, generates the conditions for a demand for urban manufacturing. Such urban living today entails a bundle of demands: for elegant restaurants and shops, for museums and cultural events, for customized furniture and metalwork, and for the rehabilitation of older buildings to new high-end uses. This potential is easily killed due to little or no recognition and support from policy makers, and even from analysts and researchers.

The privileging of advanced services easily misses the opportunity to articulate the multiple components of urban economies more strongly and effectively. One can reach a multiplier effect whereby the whole is more than the sum of its parts – that is, the network effect that lies at the heart of urban manufacturing. It is not only finance and high-tech sectors that are networked. What is more, in this networked urban manufacturing, there is a collective action dilemma that can work to the advantage of the city: a single firm cannot move out without losing the network effect. Thus, individual firms that need particular types of networks are more likely to stay in the town. A town that puts in the effort and resources necessary to develop urban manufacturing is likely to be in a win-win situation if there is a demand for these products, which means that it needs some type of dynamic service economy. This would then be a very different angle from which to look at the service economy: ensuring a dynamic advanced services sector is a condition for having a dynamic urban manufacturing sector, but only if the latter is supported in sustaining the added costs of operating in a city with a vigorous service economy.

The visual convergence and homogenizing of the state-of-the-art built environment of today's global cities easily tricks us into assuming that their economies are also becoming similar. But this is only partly so. Similar looking landscapes may contain very different types of economic operations and very different moments of a firm's multi-sited processes. Overlooking these differences leads to a number of spurious conclusions and possibly policies, which can all cause damage to the overall social and political health of a city. If all urban economies are similar in today's global age, then cities are indeed in desperate competition with each other. At its most extreme, this could on the one hand mean that being competitive requires going all out for hyper-luxury to draw rich and powerful firms and people, and on the other, a race to the bottom for the rest of a city's people and firms. We have indeed seen elements of this over the last two decades, with the leadership of cities engaging in a brutal and brutalizing competition to attract companies, the creative classes, luxury tourism, grand museums, and ensuring the availability of working classes that are reliable and low-wage.

I have sought to argue here that a more careful examination suggests that there is far less competition among cities than hits the urban eye. Standardization is a key feature of our global age, but we need to situate it and its consequences more precisely. We cannot assume that standardization in our complex global modernity is the same as it was in the Keynesian epoch of mass manufacturing and mass construction of suburban housing.

Part of the confusion and the difficulty in capturing the importance of the specialized differences of cities in the current period is due to the globalizing of production standards for the built environment. Thus the state-of-the-art office district, luxury consumption space and high-income neighbourhood all need to meet certain requirements. However, while the office buildings may share the same standards and thereby have multiple standardized visual markers, this does not mean that the work that gets done inside is necessarily the same. To recognize these economic differences across similar state-of-the-art office buildings, we need to use a lens that can capture high levels of economic specialization. In contrast, the office buildings of the mid-twentieth century spoke the language of office work – 'we are about office work' – and they were in fact about office work, with mostly clerical and supervisory jobs. Today's office buildings in global cities are about highly specialized professional and managerial work; most office jobs are elsewhere – in the suburbs, in small towns, in offshore clerical 'factories'. I argue that this kind of built environment is more akin to an infrastructure: necessary but indeterminate. That means that if the state-of-the-art built environment that produces a homogenized urban visual order is actually an indeterminate infrastructure, it can accommodate enormous economic differences. Under these conditions, convergence and homogenization of the built environment becomes an envelope, a standard applied to potentially very different economic contents. The question of competition is partly demoted from its dominant position in explanations and in policies. Instead, more attention needs to go to the other side of the story – the particular specialized sectors that might inhabit that homogenized landscape. By recoding these homogenized landscapes – the hyperspace of global business – as an infrastructure, the emphasis on what inhabits the infrastructure is shifted to how it gets used.

These analytic disassemblings should help in moving us towards a more in-depth explanation of urban spatial organization. Here I focused particularly on two aspects that I consider critical.

One is the weight of the economic histories of major cities. To take the most extreme and unexpected case, the knowledge economy, I argued that some of its important components come from these deep economic histories of a place. For instance, when one thinks of a city like Istanbul, with a history of three millennia, it is almost inconceivable to think that its rich and complex past does not matter today in multiple newly mediated ways. One particular mediation is the capacity to extract the knowledge component from older material economic practices. Once extracted it can be commodified and sold, a key capacity of our global modernity. The premium we place on such (extracted) knowledge components and on their global mobility, ironically re-values the old economic history of a place.

The other is the articulation of the advanced urban economy with spaces we do not see as connected, as part of our global modernity. And this is a second irony. The survival of economies of these other spaces – having to know how to fix, how to make, how to connect – is exactly what makes them useful to the new urban economy. One component of this is that the making of an expanded state-of-the-art built environment over the last two decades has brought with it a growing demand for craft workers who know how to work with metal, wood, stone, plaster, silk and paints.

Both of these aspects open up a whole new urban terrain, which I see as part of our global modernity. At the heart of the most dynamic sectors in global cities we can find an assemblage of enormously diverse spaces and actors. The visual order of global cities renders these articulations invisible.

CIT

MUN

Beyond the high-rise city, religious festivals regularly transform Mumbai's waterfront.

Temples, mosques, synagogues and churches make this India's most cosmopolitan city.

Density comes at a price: every day brings another death on the railway.

The rich live well here, and the poor are never far away.

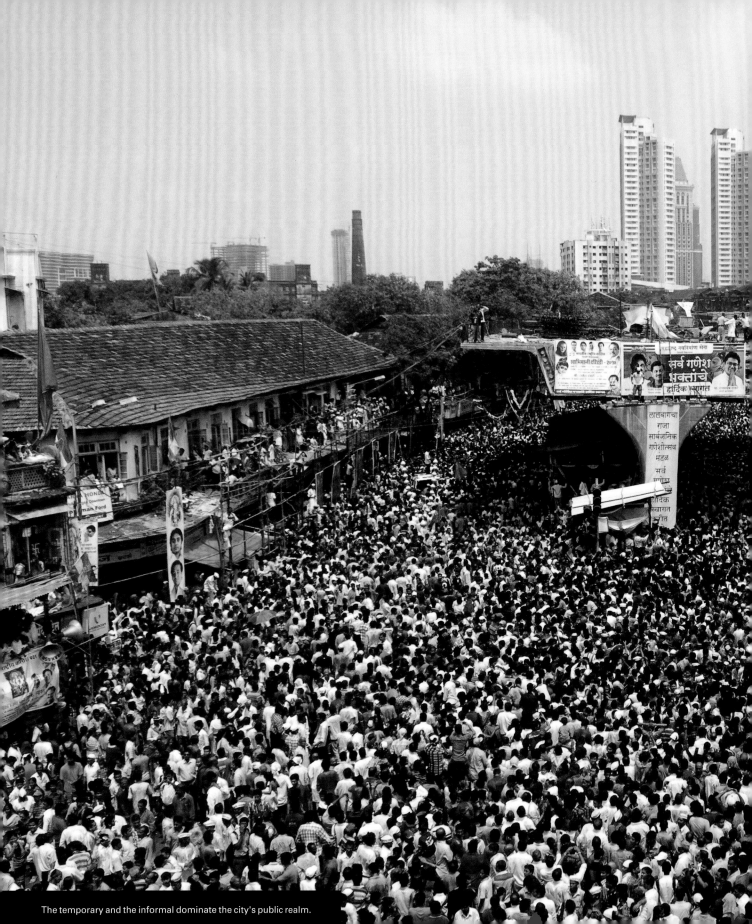

The temporary and the informal dominate the city's public realm.

Formal housing offers little more space than the slums.

In a crisis, the city prides itself on its cohesion.

When the classrooms flooded, schools took to the street.

MANAGED CHAOS

Deyan Sudjic

If the Urban Age is an investigation that marks the transformation of the world
from a predominantly rural to a predominantly urban one, this transition has
not yet fully occurred in India. In time it will happen there too. The country today still
has a rural majority, even as the world as a whole has shifted in the other direction.
But, like China, India has a profound interest in maintaining its rural hinterland.
Both countries are vast, and their populations account for a third of humanity.
They have both, in their own ways, started to emerge from underdevelopment and
have been forced to question with more or less enthusiasm some of the fundamentals
of the political creeds on which their societies are based. Indian democracy and
its legal system are always spoken of as the country's two key advantages in its
increasingly overt competition with China. But these can be seen as handicaps as
well as advantages.

China does not want to see its cities overwhelmed, and forbids free internal
movement. India's constitution guarantees it, even if the Gandhian ideology on which
Indian independence was founded displayed a profound antipathy towards the idea
of the city. Instead India was to be rooted in the self-sufficiency of village life. It was
an antipathy that easily merged with the English horror at the industrial city. The
attitudes that India's Oxbridge-educated elite picked up about cities, at first hand in
some cases from Ruskin and Morris, could be represented as alien creations that left
incomers reduced to squalor.

Many of India's big cities indeed have colonial roots: Calcutta, or Kolkata as it is
now called, also has European foundations. Nationalist unrest drove the British to
move their Imperial capital out of Calcutta and Bengal to a new site on the edges of
the ancient city of Delhi in a simultaneous search for a more peaceful setting and a
symbolic claim to rooting itself in Indian tradition. And it was post-colonial partition
that saw the tragic population exchanges that crowded Delhi and Mumbai with
refugees from Pakistan.

India now has a hierarchy of cities spread across the country, with Mumbai,
Delhi, and Bangalore the most dynamic, and experiencing the most rapid growth,
while Kolkata struggles to find a wider role. But even in Mumbai, the heart of India's
financial sector, 65 per cent of employment is in the informal sector, as opposed to 83
per cent in the country as a whole.

Throughout the long years of India's command and control economy, its cities
appeared as frozen in time, like the elderly Ambassador cars built on production

55%

of Mumbai's population lives in slums

65%

of Mumbai's workforce is employed in the informal sector

lines and shipped from Britain. Liberalization has ushered in an Indian middle class, attracting back the non-resident Indians, the educated diaspora, who have made their money in Silicon Valley and the Gulf, creating a potential economic superpower. Establishing fast food outlets and shopping malls – with attempts to introduce supermarkets resisted in some states by violent protests – India has begun to explore liberal market approaches to city infrastructure. And with these first results now visible, it is questioning their effectiveness.

The new India is impatient with the things that don't work in its cities: the traffic jams, the shortcomings of infrastructure, the bureaucracy. It wants to see big changes and has invested in huge projects like Delhi's new metro system.

Like China, India is finding new ways of doing things that involve profound political shifts. Even Kolkata, with its long and proud tradition as the centre of Indian Marxism and literary intellectuals, has begun to experiment with market forces. But while China is able to ignore or suppress dissent, when Bengal's farmers protested against the Special Economic Zones declared to support the industrialists wanting factories to build a 1-Lakh Rupees (US$2,243 or €1,646) people's car, the state government had to change its mind.

Bangalore and Delhi have also struggled with attempts at liberalizing their approaches to planning work effectively. Alone among Indian cities, Kolkata has made real steps towards a genuine locally centred civic government, rather than remaining entirely in the hands of a state with a vast rural hinterland. But India's administrative complexities and its overlapping systems of state, city and federal power, mean for example that Mumbai's city government found it impossible to introduce the plan of vaccinations for all newcomers. It planned to set up reception centres at their point of entry: the railway stations in the city. But it could not do it: the city was simply unable to come to a legally binding agreement with India's nationally-owned railway administration about the level of rent to be paid for the use of railway land. It is a nicety that is hard to conceive of in the context of China's ruthless subjugation of all other interests to state power. When it comes to something like vaccination in stations, what the party wants, the party ensures that it gets.

For all its recurring episodes of inter-communal violence, Mumbai is a city with the ethnic and religious diversity of a true world city. Its roots go back to the successive waves of European colonization of India. The Portuguese handed over the cluster of islands and fishing villages that constituted Bombay to the British crown in the eighteenth century. The 20,000 inhabitants of that time have swollen to an estimated 19 million in the region today, as a port became successively a mill town, a railway hub, a financial centre, and a world centre for the cinema industry. Its architectural expression ranges from the hallucinogenic translation of high-Victorian gothic from England to the subcontinent of the Chhatrapati terminal, designed by F. W. Stevens, with the swagger of St Pancras, to the Gate of India, to, in more recent times, the lyrical restraint of Charles Correa's careful synthesis of Modernism with India's climate and social conditions. But these are the sharp focus landmarks in the daunting world of Mumbai's slums and hostels geared towards single male migrants and the huge red-light areas that cater for them.

In Bangalore, rapid success has brought with it the problems of affluence. Endless commutes in India's Silicon Valley are encouraging its big IT employers to think about mixing housing with industry to achieve a more decentralized city that could help them run their businesses more efficiently. But the experience of privatized new towns here, as in Delhi, has not been encouraging. Privatized house building, based on a mirage of southern California that is so attractive to India's affluent classes, has too often stopped at the apartment complex gate, and offered no pavement, and no transport links that can allow surrounding settlements the access that they need to provide service jobs.

In Mumbai, a city in which water and power are erratic, in which the suburban railway network is so overcrowded that commuters who fall off the trains are killed every day, the private sector has been asked to create alternative forms of settlements that can provide solutions. All this is occurring in a highly centralized political context where, even though the councillors of Mumbai's Municipal Corporation are locally elected, the state still holds ultimate control.

Other liberal attempts to deal with Mumbai's chronic overcrowding, its constrained site and continuing attraction to rural migrants have also been questioned, including the issue of the city's 300,000 street vendors, of whom just a few thousand are licensed. Yet of the 12 million residents of Greater Mumbai, almost 6.5 million live in slums. Mumbai's slums are of two kinds: the authorized, for which the municipal authority has a responsibility to provide basic services, and the unauthorized, which are subject to demolition, and for which there is no duty for the city to provide power or water. There are impossible densities, 82,000 people per km^2 (213,118 per square mile) in Dharavi, the largest of the city's slums. Authorized slums are outnumbered by the 60 per cent that are illegal. Some of the illegals rely on unauthorised standpipes, and a few have no water at all.

Mumbai is the city that inspired Suketu Mehta's *Maximum City*. It is a city unlike any other. One that offers more lessons to the world, even as it vigorously looks for ways to put India's newfound economic power to work to find its own solutions to the challenges threatening to overwhelm it.

DEMOCRACY AND SELF-INTEREST

K. C. Sivaramakrishnan

HIERARCHIES OF DEMOCRACY

Indian democracy is conducted on three levels: union, state and city. It is a system that has, until now, been too ready to privilege the states' interests as a trade-off for the central government in New Delhi, at the expense of the nation's cities.

An apt saying attributed to Tip O'Neill, former Chairman of the United States Congress, is, 'All politics is local'. Many countries aspire to the title of being a good democracy. A true test will have to show if democracy is alive and kicking, not just at the national or local level, but across the country. If this yardstick is applied, India has some distance to go. The much-touted 74th constitutional amendment and democratic decentralization have had an uneven course so far. The exercise to amend the constitution to provide a constitutional status and mandate for local bodies was initiated by the late prime minister, Rajiv Gandhi, but the initial focus was on the *panchayats,* the system of five locally elected elders who oversee local matters. Later, it was felt that the enlarged structure of representation should be provided for urban local bodies as well, but Rajiv Gandhi's amendment bills did not pass muster in parliament. The succeeding government of V. P. Singh attempted to provide composite legislation for both rural and urban local bodies, but that government did not last long enough. Eventually it was left to the Narasimha Rao government and two parliamentary committees to rework the amendments, which became law as the 73rd and the 74th amendments in 1993.

To briefly summarize salient features of the 74th amendment: urban settlements are classified as corporations, municipalities or *nagar panchayats* (a hybrid designed for settlements in transition from rural to urban). All three categories, broadly labelled as *nagarpalikas*, are to be constituted with representatives elected from territorial constituencies called wards. One-third of the seats as well as the chairperson's position are to be reserved for women.

Elections are mandatory and to be conducted by constitutionally created State Election Commissions. Each municipal ward or a group of them should also have ward committees. Additionally, District Planning Committees and Metropolitan Planning Committees are envisaged for dealing with issues common to municipalities and rural areas in a district as well as multiple municipal agglomerations.

The structure envisaged by the 74th amendment is elaborate. For a total of 101 city corporations and 1,430 municipalities and 2,091 *nagarpalikas* in the country, nationwide elections have now been held two to three times. The number of elected representatives for all the urban local bodies is about 70,000. Of the 3,640 chairpersons of these bodies at least one-third are women, while the All India Council of Mayors is currently also headed by a woman. These are all visible signs

of significant changes in the representative structure of the *nagarpalikas*. The question is whether they amount to a functioning or effective democracy. Evidence indicates there are several deficits.

The first may be described as the 'decentralization deficit'. In the Indian constitution, the powers of the state are embedded in three lists: the Union List pertaining to the government of India, the State List and the Concurrent List. Local government falls under the State List. If the domain of a state government is regarded as complete with respect to the items on the State List, then the domain of the local bodies can only be subsidiary or delegated from the State List. Although the 74th amendment identifies as many as 18 functions that are part of the 12th Schedule of the Constitution as pertaining to *nagarpalikas*, by and large the state governments consider the assignment of these functions as not mandatory but discretionary. Debates about this view have taken place within as well as outside the courts. The factual position is that the functional domain of the *nagarpalikas* is largely decided by state governments and therefore highly uneven across the country. Even a service like water supply, which is considered a basic municipal duty, is performed by state governments or para-statal agencies in states such as Uttar Pradesh, Tamil Nadu, Karnataka and Kerala.

To cite another example, urban planning (including town planning) is mentioned as the very first item in the 12th Schedule to the constitution, yet this function is rarely performed by a city corporation or a municipality. Invariably, a development authority set up as para-statal body performs it, and in recent years town planning has become a highly contentious matter taking up significant time in cases at the High Courts and the Supreme Court.

Even where some functions are devolved, government control is pervasive. The state government reserve's administrative deficit is a result of the financial deficit. The sum total of municipal revenues and expenditure is less than 5 per cent of the government's as a whole.

The role of the municipal chairpersons or the mayor is also unclear. While the Municipal or City Council has a tenure of five years under the constitution, the term of the mayor or the chairpersons varies from one state to another. In most of the states, the mayors and the chairpersons are elected by and from the elected councillors. In Tamil Nadu, Uttar Pradesh and Madhya Pradesh they are elected directly by voters, although this does not entitle them to any significant power. In fact, most municipal laws vest the executive powers in an appointed official.

A major casualty of this situation is accountability. Although the structure envisaged by the 74th amendment is elaborate, the provisions with regards to decentralization within a city are vague. At the municipal ward level, the constitution provides for a committee of one or more wards but the composition of such a committee is left to be decided by the state government, except in Kerala, where members of a ward committee are elected by various groups. The criteria for allocation of responsibilities between the city and the ward levels are also not specified. Ward committees, where they exist, have not emerged as effective platforms for local participation. Similarly, in large cities the constitution envisages an intermediate level for groups of wards. Here again, the arrangements are left to the state governments.

In a few states such zonal formations or committees do exist, but they are comprised almost exclusively of municipal councillors. Since the ward committees do not have adequate participation and the zonal committees virtually exclude representatives from the public, lack of proximity between the elected representatives and the people has become yet another issue.

In a globalized world where the limits of national sovereignty are under daily strain, demands of local autonomy raise doubts and fears about state or national integrity. Yet it has long been understood that even the most powerful of the national or state governments is not powerful enough to deal with its cities. Similarly, even the largest city, with all its resources, cannot superimpose itself as a substitute for the state. Power sharing between the centre and the state has been a difficult process in India. The 74th amendment has introduced a new dimension of power sharing between the states and the local governments.

Finally, one should also take note of the readiness of the people to participate in matters of city management or development. Many Indian cities are blessed with numerous community-level and non-government organizations, although there is a significant hiatus between them and the elected representatives. Structures can indeed facilitate or restrict participatory processes. And that is an issue crucial in addressing the deficits in a democracy.

A MATTER OF PEOPLE

Darryl D'Monte

THE LIFE AND DEATH OF GREAT INDIAN CITIES

Mumbai's history, as a city that grew to service a colonial administration within the constraints of its geography, accounts for its extraordinarily high densities. It is time to understand that 'slum' is as inappropriate a word for its informal communities as it was for Jane Jacobs's Greenwich Village.

Mumbai means different areas to different people and many citizens are only slightly aware that it ranks as a megacity with more than 10 million inhabitants. This is partly because Greater Mumbai, the city peninsula proper, occupies 438 square kilometres (169 square miles), yet is often confused with the Mumbai Metropolitan Region, which is almost 10 times bigger (4,355 square kilometres or 1681.5 square miles) and includes the outlying townships of Kalyan and Thane, which are one million-plus cities in their own right. Even experts compound the confusion by not clarifying which entity they are referring to. For instance, in a paper for a Berlin conference in September 2010, Professor D.P. Singh from the Tata Institute of Social Sciences in Mumbai, stated: 'The population of Mumbai is growing much faster than any other cities [sic] in India'. He was referring to the urban agglomeration. He and his colleagues have provided the demographic data for the Municipal Corporation's Mumbai Human Development Report (HDR) 2009.

Mumbai's HDR cites the international think-tank, City Mayors, which in 2006 ranked Mumbai as the world's largest city, referring to the southern tip of the peninsula as 'probably the world's largest core city and densest'. As a consequence, there is confusion over the population as well as the extent of migration. Many experts conjure up images of a city bursting at the seams, yet a study for the Planning Commission showed more than two decades ago that India's urban growth is in fact not rapid when compared with Africa and Latin America. When compared with its South Asian neighbours like Pakistan, Nepal, Bangladesh and Sri Lanka, India doesn't have a primary city, but a reasonably even spread of cities and towns. Hyderabad and Bangalore are growing faster than the four major metropolises of Mumbai, Delhi, Kolkata and Chennai. In 1988, the National Commission on Urbanisation, headed by architect Charles Correa, reiterated this. In the fairly urban state of Maharashtra, the cities of Pune, Nashik and Nagpur are growing far faster than Mumbai. The International Institute for Environment & Development in London released a report titled 'The Transition to a Predominantly Urban World' in 2007, which listed 11 Indian cities out of the 100 fastest growing (in population) in the world; only Delhi, Hyderabad and Bangalore figured among these.

Political parties and some NGOs have raised the spectre of hordes of migrants pouring into Mumbai, but reality has been different. People do not stream into Mumbai because of its bright lights. They come for jobs, not homes, and they live in far worse conditions than they used to once they get here. The push out of their rural

FLATTENING THE CURVE

While still growing at a strong pace with respect to other world cities, the number of people moving into Mumbai has slowed in recent decades reflecting a period of economic and industrial restructuring.

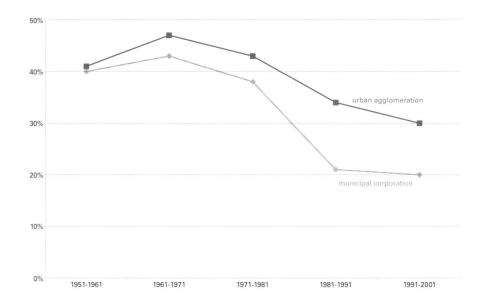

homes is far greater than the pull of the city. No academic institution, not even the Mumbai-based International Institute for Population Sciences (IIPS), has a clear idea of how many enter the city every day. Two decades ago, it was loosely put at 500 families a day, and that figure was close to the total number of migrants. According to the last census in 2001, Greater Mumbai had a population of just under 12 million; thus it has presumably a population of somewhere close to 14.5 to 15 now, Dr R.B. Bhagat of the IIPS told Urban Age. Migration as a proportion of the total population is also declining. In the 1970s, the proportion of migrants was close to 60 per cent, with a natural increase of 40 per cent. The proportions have now been reversed. This is no surprise, considering that formal employment in the city is declining, with the closure of mills, heavy engineering units, chemical factories and even some multinational industries. While no poor migrant would automatically qualify for jobs in manufacturing, they would be employed in casual ancillary services. Now, there is a saturation even of rag and scrap pickers, which are right at the bottom of the employment ladder, as Jaime Lerner told Urban Age in São Paulo.

While the rate of growth may not be dramatic, size does matter. The outlying areas of the Metropolitan Region are expanding faster than the core, especially the 100 square kilometres (38.6 square miles) of the island-city. 'Mumbai's geography is the constant,' underlines Dr Bhagat, 'there has been a demographic and democratic transition.' The southernmost tip, just outside the 'Fort' erected by the East India Company, is still extremely dense. The C Ward there, which is only 1.8 square kilometres (0.69 square miles) large and comprises areas like Bhuleshwar, has 114,000 people per square kilometre (295,337 per square mile), according to the 2001 Census. At one time, these densities were certainly the highest in the world, and may still be. However, as levels of education have increased, families are splitting up, with young couples preferring to live in small flats in the distant northern suburbs, even if it means commuting to work. In a new collection of essays, Correa remarks that the high densities of Indian cities are deceptive, because – unlike in the West and in the Asian Tiger economies – they are not symbolized by high-rise buildings but 'through an extraordinary high occupancy per room'. Something like seven out of every 10 Mumbaikars live in a single room, which includes the 54 per cent who live in slums.

These densities were the result of history, when the 'natives' had to cluster in large numbers in *chawls* or working-class tenements, outside the Fort and more salubrious precincts. These migrants worked in the port and, from the mid-nineteenth century onwards, in the cotton mills. Because the commercial district was located at the south of the island city, as the main district still is, its geography also compelled people to live cheek by jowl with each other. But topography and economics have been tempered by culture: in areas like Girgaum, there are *wadis* or precincts that are predominantly populated by one community. In this area, Hindu Pathare Prabhus, one of the oldest communities, live cheek by jowl with the next *wadi* with Hindus from the trading communities of Gujarat and 'East Indian' (after the company) Catholics (to which minuscule community this writer belongs). This is why historians refer to the many cities in Mumbai, which make it indeed the most cosmopolitan of Indian metropolises, and it explains its tremendous vibrancy and diversity. Mumbaikars tend to relate primarily to their neighbourhood, with communal tension arising only when specific incidents occur after provocation.

While the number of migrants is increasing in absolute numbers, though not in relative ones, they do stir the imagination of so-called 'sons-of-the-soil'. In the worst riots Mumbai has ever faced, over the destruction of a mosque in north India in the early 1990s, there were dire rumours about the large presence of Bangladeshis (shorthand for Muslims) who could easily slip through the porous eastern Indian border and travel incognito to Mumbai. Being the Mumbai editor of *The Times of India* at the time, I sent teams of reporters to uncover these illegal aliens – who were conspicuous by their absence. The terrorist attacks of 2007 haven't caused many ripples because the culprits were from Pakistan, not home grown. However, chauvinist parties, particularly a splinter of the Hindu right-wing Shiv Sena, have in recent years targeted north Indians – specifically cab drivers – for taking away their jobs.

According to the Washington-based Population Institute, Mumbai's urban agglomeration will in 2020 be the world's most populous at 28.5 million, with Tokyo trailing at 27.3 million. Whatever direction Mumbai takes will have a bearing on the future of cities in developing countries. This is partly due to its sheer size, but also its diversity, its specific problems (housing and transport being two of the most pressing) and, not least, the democratic framework in which it functions. There is a sharp contrast with China in general and Shanghai in particular, with which it is frequently compared, with regards to the last issue. Singapore and Hong Kong are also frequently held up as Asian exemplars.

Yet to project Mumbai as a 'world-class city', as the Bombay First think-tank (inspired by its London counterpart, also led by corporate interests) constantly pleads for, is turning a blind eye to its priorities, mainly the overwhelming poverty of its citizens. One must remember that India, despite its near-two-digit GDP growth, is home to the largest number of poor people in the world. In the UN's Human Development Report, released in October 2010, a new Multidimensional Poverty Index, developed with the Oxford Poverty & Human Development Initiative, shows that the eight poorest Indian states have more poor people than the 26 poorest sub-Saharan African countries put together.

And there is no city in India, probably in the world, and certainly no megacity, with as large a proportion of its residents living in slums, officially put at 54 per cent or around 8 million people in Greater Mumbai. Mumbai, incidentally, is the former industrial and current commercial capital of the country. In September 2010, the Municipality reluctantly revealed that 2.5 million people (belonging to nearly 500,000 families, which officially fall under BPL or Below the Poverty Line) lived on less than US$13 (a month per head). It had unearthed this fact in January but kept it under wraps, after surveying the 1.1 million families that claimed support under the BPL category. A similar exercise conducted in the late 1990s revealed only 27,331 such families (an obvious underestimate). As slum activist Simpreet Singh says: 'A steep rise in the number of the poorest of the poor exposes the lack of inclusiveness of the current development model.'

A second problem is the astronomical price of real estate, especially for commercial space, in the two central business districts of Nariman Point and the Bandra-Kurla Complex (BKC) to the north. In one high-rise apartment complex in the reclaimed area of Nariman Point, apartments have exchanged hands for US$2,000 per square foot (US$21,520 per square metre), which must approximate the highest rates in the world. Reports about Nariman Point losing out to its competitors in the north and the real estate boom on 280 hectares (1.08 square miles) of mill land in midtown Mumbai must be understood in conjunction with the fact that in upmarket areas, a single-bedroom flat is virtually impossible to find. Or, for that matter, any open space at all. Indeed, Mumbai has the unique distinction of possessing 0.03 acres (1,306 square feet) of open space for every thousand people, while the norm is 4 acres or 0.016 square kilometres (174,240 square feet). It works out to a single square metre (10.76 square feet) per person, which must be the lowest in the world. The fact that Mumbai hasn't imploded due to the sheer pressure of urban growth is a testament to the innate humanity of its ordinary people.

Dharavi, said to be Asia's largest slum, lies cheek-by-jowl with the Bandra-Kurla Complex. In a draft document on Dharavi, prepared by Sheela Patel, who heads the Society for the Promotion of Area Resource Centers (SPARC) with the Kamala Raheja Vidyanidhi Institute of Architecture and Environmental Studies (the Hindi acronym is KRVIA), writes: 'The metropolis of Mumbai is often called Slumbai or Slumbay with probably the largest number of slum-dwellers in the world. Dharavi – really an informal township within the metropolis – is one of the world's 30 mega-slums and Asia's largest. Spread over 212 hectares (0.82 square miles), it presents a very vibrant mosaic often of thousands of small businesses and hundreds of thousands of residents, of different religions, castes, languages, provinces, and ethnicities, dependent on each other and the city socially, culturally and economically. Its enterprising residents manufacture garments, leather goods, foods and pottery, besides running a flourishing – and unique – recycling business.' One should not, however, romanticize what is essentially dirty, casual work. Dharavi needs *more* planning, but of the humane, inclusive kind.

In 2004, a former New York-based architect, Mukesh Mehta, persuaded the state government to redevelop Dharavi. It was to have five sectors and be thrown open to international bidding. It had attracted nearly 80 real estate giants for the Rs.9,250 crore (US$2.1 billion or €1.5 billion) 0.4 square kilometre (0.154 square mile), new high-rise township, but slum politics fortunately has got in its way. Sundar Burra of SPARC, a former Indian Administrative Service official, is not impressed. 'The developers were to pay a premium to the government and, in return, were to get incentive Floor Space Index (FSI) so that they could build more commercial and other structures to sell in the open market,' he writes. 'A part of the profit was to cross-subsidize the free housing and infrastructure. Given the inflated land prices in the area, developers would have made windfall gains and Government would have earned substantial revenues … Perhaps the most important objection is that the entire plan was conceived without any

CONNECTING TO THE GRID

Because Mumbai's slums are officially regarded as illegal settlements, the municipal government is reluctant to provide them with water and power. The ad-hoc provision of basic services becomes a pawn in power struggles between local politicians eager to buy votes from slum residents.

community participation and is a classic example of top-down planning.'

This negates the rationale of resettlement, because it ignores Dharavi as a work-cum-living space. As one of the most intensive recycling centres in the country, residents in Dharavi use their homes to sort scrap materials and sew, in addition to hundreds of other occupations. With the redevelopment scheme currently proposed, they will likely be unable to afford the monthly charges in the new high-rise redevelopment and will instead sell out to move to another slum colony. The best solution for Dharavi – and, indeed, other slum pockets in the city – is to grant fixed-duration leasehold (not ownership) rights to squatters, which will enable families to build incrementally – for instance, when a son gets married. In return, they should pay the Municipality a monthly rent – at say Rs.300 a family and 1.6 million families (at five a family), this would translate into Rs.48 crore (US$10.8 million or €7.9 billion) a month, which would be sufficient to provide water, lighting and sanitation. This would also generate employment in the slum for a modest range of house-builders.

If the proposed scheme goes through, Dharavi will be privatized and gentrified, complete with a golf course. All this has a bearing on the governance of Mumbai. There have been calls to establish Mumbai as a separate city-state – *à la* Singapore – seceded from the rest of Maharashtra, not to mention India. Although Mumbai accounts for a larger share of the income and corporate taxes paid in the country, this would be dangerous because it militates against the very essence of the democratic

One of Mumbai's many slums, all of which house nearly 60 per cent of the city's population, roughly the same number of people living in London today. These precarious structures are exposed to health and environmental risks, while their inhabitants lack a public voice.

process. Aside from this, the collection of direct taxes is disproportionately high because head offices of companies with nationwide operations are based in the city. The aim should be to bring about a more cohesive integration of Mumbai into Maharashtra – so that, for instance, some Rs.15,000 crore (US$3.4 billion or €2.5 billion) are not spent on road projects in the city but diverted to irrigation and other schemes in Vidarbha and other depressed regions where literally thousands of farmers have been committing suicide due to droughts and consequent debts in recent years.

The call for a CEO for Mumbai should also be treated with caution. Mumbai is not a corporate entity that lends itself to better corporate governance, but a highly variegated and diverse city. As any municipal commissioner will testify, there are pulls and pressures at every move from political parties that are represented in the corporation. The city could certainly be run better, and there is no reason why a hands-on mayor cannot be elected to do the job, as is the case in New York and London. Doing so might also address the allegation that the state government's constituency is in rural areas with ministers treating Mumbai as a cash cow; for although Maharashtra is still a predominantly rural society, like the rest of India, it should be administered in a more comprehensive, rather than exclusionary, way.

In 2007, executives of US companies with a market cap of over US$1 trillion (€734 billion) held a closed-door meeting in New York with their Indian counterparts. The agenda was to discuss how to make Mumbai a major financial centre, yet the dilemma in projecting Mumbai as a world-class city excludes people from this process. In the demonization of slum dwellers, who occupy less than a 10th of the city's area, sought to be disenfranchised by politicians and community leaders, decision makers posit a 'them' versus 'us' dichotomy. However, if the homeless are a majority, they surely deserve to be accorded a priority in planning.

Public transport is an illustrative case in point. In this megacity, more commuters

LEARNING FROM DHARAVI

Despite its deprivation, the world has come
to see Dharavi as a model for sustainable
development; a place in which people can
live and work in close proximity. But it is
under threat from the move to formalize
the settlement, and remains a challenging
environment in which to live.

use public transport than anywhere else in the world. Only 4.7 per cent of commuters
use private motorized transport, while around 90 per cent either walk or use buses
and trains. World Bank studies show that as many as 56.3 per cent of non-'commuters'
walk or cycle to work; an appropriately high number given that more than half the
population lives in slums. This compares to a total of 81 per cent of public transport
users in Tokyo.

The Centre for Science and Environment in New Delhi has shown that a car
requires 23 m^2 (247.5 square feet) to park, including the space needed for entry and
exit. Since Delhi had as many car users (920,723 registered) as in the rest of the three
metropolitan cities put together in 2007, it estimates that the physical space occupied
by cars equals that of the capital's slum dwellers. Since Mumbai's squatters occupy
only 9 per cent of the city's area, it would be interesting to know what proportion is
occupied by cars. More importantly, one wonders which is a bigger nuisance? And
who are vilified in the public discourse?

Mumbai can opt for inclusive growth, where each neighbourhood is self-
contained and a mix of classes and masses. Here, the world's poorest and super rich
(industrialist Ambani has built a US$1 billion (€734 million) skyscraper for his family
of five, said to be the world's most expensive residence) rub shoulders. This proximity
provides security to pedestrians because the roads are never empty; urban violence
and crime *à la* São Paulo are absent. There is symbiosis: the homeless provide maids,
drivers and the like to their more fortunate neighbours.

Alternatively, Mumbai can also go the way of several other megacities by creating
high-rise ghettoized enclaves for the rich, surrounded by a mass of powerless citizens.
Already, Mumbai is emulating the worst design of São Paulo's famous Paraisópolis
multi-storeyed apartment complex, with a swimming pool on each balcony. And the
state has sanctioned a 117-storey posh 'iconic' housing tower. Urban Age conferences
have helped put these crucial urban issues in perspective.

LOOKING FOR THE BIRD OF GOLD

Suketu Mehta

INDIA'S WORLD CITY

Mumbai is the city that, above all others, attracts India's poor, but it is also the place that is the jumping off point for India's migration to Europe and America. It has become the key to understanding the nature of the emerging world city.

On 27 July 2005, Mumbai experienced the highest recorded rainfall in its history – 37 inches (94 cm) in one day. The subsequent flood demonstrated the worst and the best of the city. Hundreds of people drowned, but, unlike the situation after Hurricane Katrina hit New Orleans, there was no widespread breakdown of civic order. Even though the police were absent, the crime rate did not go up and that was because Mumbaikars were busy helping each other. Slum dwellers went to the motorway and took stranded drivers into their homes and made room for one more person in shacks, where the average occupancy is seven adults to a room. Volunteers waded through waist-deep water to bring food to the 150,000 people stranded in train stations. Human chains were formed to get people out of the floodwaters. Most of the government machinery was absent, but nobody expected otherwise. Mumbaikars helped each other, because they had lost faith in the government helping them. On a planet of city dwellers, this is how most human beings are going to live and cope in the twenty-first century.

With an estimated population of around 15 million people within its municipal limits, Mumbai is the biggest, fastest, richest city in India. A city that is an island-state of hope in a very old country, simultaneously experiencing a boom and a civic emergency. Because of the reach of Bollywood movies, Mumbai is also a mass dream for the peoples of India. If you take a walk around Mumbai you'll see that everything – sex, death, trade, religion – is lived out on the pavement. It is a maximum city: maximum in its exigencies, maximum in its heart.

Why do people still live in Mumbai? Every day is an assault on one's senses; from the moment you get up, to the transport you take to go to work, to the offices you work in, to the forms of entertainment you are subjected to. The exhaust fumes are so thick the air boils like a soup. There are too many people touching you, in the trains, in the lifts, when you go home to sleep. You live in a seaside city, but the only time you get anywhere near the sea is for an hour on Sunday evening on a filthy beach. It doesn't stop when you're asleep either, for the night brings the mosquitoes out of the malarial swamps, the thugs of the underworld to your door, and the booming loudspeakers of the parties of the rich and the festivals of the poor. Why would you want to leave your brick house in the village with its two mango trees and its view of small hills in the east to come here?

So that some day your eldest son can buy two rooms in Mira Road, at the northern edges of the city. And the younger one can move beyond that, to New Jersey.

Your discomfort is an investment. Like ant colonies, people here will easily sacrifice their temporary pleasures for the greater progress of the family. One brother will work and support all the others, and he will gain a deep satisfaction from the fact that his nephew is taking an interest in computers and will probably go on to America. Mumbai functions on such invisible networks of assistance. In a Mumbai slum, there is no individual, there is only the organism. There are circles of fealty and duty within the organism, but the smallest circle is the family. There is no circle around the self.

India frustrates description because everything you can say about it is true and false at the same time. Yes, it could soon have the world's largest middle class. But it now has the world's largest underclass. And so, with Mumbai, everything is expanding exponentially: the call centres, the global reach of its film industry, its status as the financial gateway to India, as well as the slums, the numbers of absolutely destitute, the degradation of its infrastructure. The city's planners have their eyes set firmly on Shanghai as a model for Mumbai. The government approved a McKinsey-drafted document titled 'Vision Mumbai', which aims to turn Mumbai into 'a world-class city by 2013'. As the architect Charles Correa noted of the plan, 'There's very little vision. They're more like hallucinations.'

Mumbai needs to dramatically upgrade essential civic services: roads, sewers, transport, health, security. But, as one planner said to me, 'The nicer we make the city, the larger the number of people that will come to live there.' The greatest numbers of migrants to Mumbai now come from the impoverished north Indian states of Uttar Pradesh and Bihar. Mumbai's problems cannot be solved until Bihar's problems are. You have to keep them down on the farm. And that means that agriculture has to become viable again for the small farmer. Abolishing trade-distorting subsidies in the United States and the EU would go a long way towards making, say, Indian cotton competitive with American cotton. Mumbai is at the mercy of national and international factors beyond its control.

Then there are the steps that Indian governments could take. There is no reason Mumbai should be the capital of Maharashtra state. Shifting the state government to Navi Mumbai, across the harbour, as was originally intended, would free up large amounts of space in the congested office district of Nariman Point. Beyond that, there has to be legislation that establishes a strong executive authority for the city, with real decision-making power. The office of the mayor is currently no more than a figurehead; the city is run at the whim of the chief minister, and the state's interests are not necessarily those of the city. There are smart and brave architects and planners who are attempting to work with the state government. But they are trying to reason with people who come from the villages, who do not have a metropolitan sensibility. Mumbai needs a mayor with vision and political power to push through the enormous infrastructural projects that the city so badly needs. The city, which contributes 37 per cent of all the taxes paid in India, gets only a small fraction of it back from the central government in the form of subsidies.

Land should be opened up in the southeastern part of the island, much of which is occupied by a naval and commercial port. Mumbai doesn't need a naval base; it could be relocated further down the coast. Efficient use of the eastern docklands could also alleviate the pressure; the city needs schools, parks, auditoria, public spaces. Instead, it gets luxury housing and shopping centres. The example of the mill areas, in the centre of the city, where 600 acres (0.94 square miles) that were desperately needed for public use have instead been given over to developers, does not bode well for the city.

As with other megacities of the world, what Mumbai needs is not slum demolition but slum rehabilitation. People who live without clear title in our cities are branded, en masse, as 'slum dwellers'. A slum is a matter of definition, and the weight of the word hangs heavy over the poor. What is a slum? You and me don't like it, so we call it a slum. The people in the slums of Mumbai have another word for it; *basti*, which means community. A *basti* abounds in community spaces – in the line to the toilet, in the line at the water tap, in the patches of empty ground, in front of the hundreds of little shops servicing every human need. The construction of the *basti* is crucial to the 'spirit of Mumbai' that saves the city time and again, through floods, riots, and terror attacks.

Each room in the *basti* is exquisitely custom-built, every detail of it, including the walls and the ceilings. Each room is different, and, over the decades, they become suited to the owner's needs. They are endlessly flexible, with partitions and extra storeys according to the number of family members that live there. They are coloured, outside and in, to their owners' taste. Look at a slum colony anywhere in the world: it is multi-coloured. Then look at the public housing that replaces it when it's demolished: it is monochromatic.

We marvel at Lisbon's old city, we pay a premium to live in Trastevere, the Marais or the East Village – all of which were 'slums' a hundred years ago. Young people now want to live where the other half lived. A young Jewish friend of mine in New York was looking for an apartment in New York's Lower East Side. When her grandmother heard about it, she reminded her, 'I spent my life trying to get out of that place'.

The moral of this story is: don't demolish slums, but improve them. Give them private toilets – or make the communal ones nicer. Shore up the roofs, give them clean water and reliable electricity. Most of all, give them tenure, 99-year leases on the land underneath their shacks. The poor already live exactly where they want to live, and have made an architecture and an urban plan that they can live with. They don't need planners. And when they are presented with the big plans that the city has for them, they don't understand them. That is because much of the conversation around planning is deliberately arcane, like a Latin mass. It serves the function of setting up an exclusive class of individuals who are the intermediaries between God and man, between the politicians and developers who have their visions of the city and the ordinary people who have to inhabit them.

There's an epic land grab under way in Mumbai called the SRA (Slum Rehabilitation Authority) scheme, under which, if 70 per cent of the residents of a 'slum' agree to have the colony demolished in exchange for project housing built mostly by private developers, the views of the other 30 per cent don't matter. As it was explained to me on a visit to the Jogeshwari neighbourhood, '70 per cent is 100 per cent'.

The people I knew when I was researching my book in the 1990s, who were active in the riots, in the underworld, in politics, are now in real estate. The builders are distributing money to them with open hands. Documentation needed to establish residency in the slum, and thus consent to its demolition, are things like ration cards, electricity bills, rent receipts. All of them are being forged liberally. The areas reserved for 'green zones' in the slums are now being made into 'gardens', pitiful open patches of paved-land in between the tower blocks, with scraggly brown grass.

The drive is towards verticality. The builders get an FSI ratio of 2.5 for building flats for slum dwellers. Each flat has a maximum of 270 square feet (25 square metres) of 'carpet area'. That's enough for a small living room and a small bedroom, divided by a small kitchen. There are niches for the cupboard areas. Each flat has a private bathroom. The buildings are supposed to have working lifts. All this sounds good. That is, until you speak to people who've moved into the flats. 'Our *sanskruti* (culture) is not there in the flat system,' an elderly man explained ruefully, looking around at series of tower blocks. Cities all over the world are tearing down high-rise public housing while Mumbai is building it, hundreds of thousands of these tower block flats.

Who builds these structures, in Mumbai, São Paulo, Istanbul? Somewhere in the world, in a government planning office, must sit a mad architect. From this lair, he designs all the public housing in the world. Modern slum rehabilitation is the war of the individual against the communal, of anomie against community.

So where can we look for real solutions? The architect Rahul Mehrotra once explained to me that planning in Mumbai is an exercise in futility. The nicer you make the city – adding roads and train tracks, improving housing stock – the greater the number of people that will be attracted to Mumbai from the destitute villages, swamping the roads, trains and houses. So how do we fix its problems?

In 2007, I was on the jury of the Urban Age project in Mumbai, to be given out to the best project in the city that had the potential to significantly affect the lives of its inhabitants, and one that could be successfully replicated in other cities around the world. We considered huge projects funded by the World Bank, by the state government, and by private developers: roads, housing estates, architectural wonders. And in the end, the jury members, who included the former Mayor of Washington, one of the world's leading architects, the country's biggest Bollywood star, and I decided to give thc Urban Age award to a better toilet (see pp. 396–411).

Out of the hundred-odd entries we had received, only one came handwritten in Marathi, the local language. It was a home-grown project from a group of local residents. Hundreds of them shared a public toilet, which was a pretty disgusting place, as you might imagine. Because it was everybody's property, it was nobody's; the municipal sweepers often didn't show up, and it was a site of filth and disease. It was worst for the women, who had nowhere else to go. So the residents came up with a solution: they put a couple of rooms on top of the building housing the toilet, and made it an educational centre. They planted flowers around the toilet. The community centre offered simple English and computer classes, and became a social centre for the neighbourhood. To get to the community centre, you had to pass the toilet, and so people started taking responsibility for the cleanliness of it; nobody wants to study computers on top of a filthy place.

Now the structure was no longer just a toilet, to be resorted to only when your need was urgent. It became a place around which the young people of the area started hanging out, and it started becoming a community centre. In short, the condition of the toilet improved dramatically, as the people who used it made sure to clean up afterwards, because their neighbours and families were all around, and literally on top of them.

So we gave US$100,000 (€73,393) to this group of local residents who had come up with an ingenious as well as indigenous solution that needed very little investment, and could be replicated in areas of informal housing around the world. The best moment, for me, came during the awards ceremony; Angela Merkel, the Chancellor of Germany, personally gave out the award on a stage in Mumbai. The prizewinners came in a bus to the grand hall, dressed in ill-fitting suits that they had rented for the occasion. When Frau Merkel gave them the cheque, they accepted it with grace and shook her hand, but when they encountered the municipal bureaucrat who was in charge of their area, they knelt down as one and touched his feet in reverence. They knew who had the power to make day-to-day change in their lives, and it was not the Chancellor of Germany. Watching this made me admire the local residents all the more, and made me realize: these people are survivors.

One of the most potent forms of storytelling, the one with perhaps the greatest narrative drive, is the story of crime. People living in big cities are fascinated by crime – they read about it in the tabloids, avidly follow sensational trials on television, and vote for politicians who promise to fight crime by any means necessary.

In the roaring 1990s Mumbai thought of itself as a violent, gang-ridden city. Hundreds of people were dying every year in wars between rival gangs, and extrajudicial killings by the police. The city was convinced of its own menace. The newspaper headlines, the movies, suited both the gangsters and the police. The gangsters because it increased their stature in society – after all, they live on fear, fear is their fuel; and the police because the public, afraid of crime, granted them the highest power – the power to take a life without a trial. I got the sense of a city straining to imagine itself more violent than it actually was.

I saw this same phenomenon in Lisbon, in a squatter settlement centrally located in the city called Cavo da Moura. Some 7,000 people live there, mostly migrants from Cape Verde. They serve a function in the city, working as day labourers and domestic servants. They've been living there since the 1960s, without any major problems. But the city's developers have their eyes on this prime piece of land. So they've enlisted the press to their cause. I saw, for example, a lurid magazine cover: 'With the Police in the Barrio'. It had pictures of bodies, the police handcuffing young black men facedown on the ground, and a map of the area, like it was a war zone. The article painted a picture of a crime-and-drug-ridden ghetto, a constant danger to the gentry of Lisbon. Articles like this sensationalize the area, and give the municipal government a pretext for demolishing it, to rid it of immigrant crime.

The story is the same in Istanbul. It is one of the safest cities in Europe, but the fastest growing segment of housing here are the gated communities, both in the city centre and in the suburbs. These communities are a reaction to crime, or the perception of crime. As a result, people pay enormous sums to hire private security guards. If you look at what people in these gated communities actually pay every month in maintenance fees, it would be cheaper to get mugged every month. But they don't mind paying, because the story they are fascinated by is the myth of the monster coming out of the slums.

Wherever we live, we all have a stake in helping the people of mega-cities like Mumbai. The desperation of slum-dwellers in cities like Mumbai directly affects the economic fortunes of people in New York or Los Angeles. It's as important for London to understand Mumbai as it is for Mumbai to understand London, if for no other reason than that the next generation of Londoners is being born in Mumbai.

So why do people still live in Mumbai? 'Mumbai is a bird of gold,' a Muslim man in Jogeshwari, whose brother was shot dead by the police in the riots, and who lives in a shack without running water or a toilet, told me. A golden bird, try to catch it if you can. It flies quick and sly, and you'll have to work hard to catch it, but once it's in your hand, a fabulous fortune will open up for you. This is one reason why anyone would still want to come here, leaving the pleasant trees and open spaces of the village, braving the crime and the bad air and polluted water. It is a place where your caste doesn't matter, where a woman can dine alone at a restaurant without being harassed, and where you can marry the person of your choice. For the young person in an Indian village, the call of Mumbai isn't just about money. It's also about freedom.

THE STATIC AND THE KINETIC

Rahul Mehrotra

SIDE BY SIDE

Many worlds coexist in Mumbai. One is an India of Hindu traditions, where cows are sacred. Another is an India of multinational capitalism. This creates a tension that is crucial to the city's position as a global centre.

Cities in South Asia are characterized by physical and visual contradictions that coalesce in a landscape of incredible pluralism. Historically, particularly during the period of British colonization, the distinct worlds active within these cities – which could be economic, social or cultural – occupied different spaces and operated under different rules. The aim of their separation was to maximize control and minimize conflict between these, often opposing, worlds.[1] However, today these worlds share the same space, but they understand and use it differently.[2] Massive waves of distressed rural migration during the latter half of the 1900s triggered their convergence into a singular, but multifaceted entity. Combined with the inadequate supply of urban land and the lack of the creation of new urban centres, this resulted in extremely high densities in existing cities. With the emergence of a post-industrial, service-based economy, the intertwining of these worlds within the same space is now even greater.[3]

In this post-industrial scenario, cities in India have become critical sites for negotiations between elite and subaltern cultures. The new relationships between social classes in a post-industrial economy are quite different from those that existed in state-controlled economies.[4] The fragmentation of the economy in service and production sectors has spatially resulted in a new, bazaar-like urbanism, which has woven its presence throughout the entire urban landscape.[5] This is an urbanism created by those outside the elite domains of the formal modernity of the state. It is a 'pirate' modernity that has to slip under the laws of the city simply in order to survive, without any conscious attempt at constructing a counterculture.[6] With the retreat of the state in the course of the 1980s and 1990s (in different measures across South Asia), the space of the 'everyday' is where economic and cultural struggles are articulated. These common spaces have been largely excluded from the cultural discourses on globalization, which focus on elite domains of production in the city.[7]

Today, Indian cities are comprised of two components occupying the same physical space. The first is the Static City. Built of more permanent material such as concrete, steel and brick, it forms a two-dimensional entity on conventional city maps and is monumental in its presence. The second is the Kinetic City. Incomprehensible as a two-dimensional entity, this is a city in motion – a three-dimensional construct of incremental development. The Kinetic City is temporary in nature and often built with recycled material: plastic sheets, scrap metal, canvas and waste wood. It constantly modifies and reinvents itself. The Kinetic City's building blocks are

not pieces of architecture, but spaces that hold associative values and that support their residents' lives and livelihoods. Patterns of occupation determine its form and perception. It is an indigenous urbanism that has its particular 'local' logic. It is not necessarily the city of the poor, as most images might suggest; rather it is a temporal articulation and occupation of space, which not only creates a richer sensibility of spatial occupation, but also suggests how spatial limits are expanded to include formally unimagined uses in dense urban conditions.[8]

The Kinetic City presents a compelling vision that potentially allows us to better understand the blurred lines of contemporary urbanism and the changing roles of people and spaces in urban society. The increasing concentrations of global flows – of money and goods – have exacerbated the inequalities and spatial divisions of social classes. In this context, an architecture or urbanism of equality in an increasingly unequal economic world requires looking deeper to find a wide range of places to mark and commemorate the cultures of those excluded from the spaces of wealth and economic boom. These don't necessarily lie in the formal production of architecture, but often challenge it. Here the idea of a city is an elastic urban condition, not a grand vision, but a 'grand adjustment'.

The Kinetic City can be seen as the symbolic image of the emerging urban South Asian condition. The processions, weddings, festivals, hawkers, street vendors and slum dwellers or *katchi abadis*, all create an ever-transforming streetscape – a city in constant motion where the very physical fabric is characterized by continuous change. The Static City, on the other hand, dependent on architecture for its representation, is no longer the single image by which the city is read. Thus architecture is not the 'spectacle' of the city, nor does it even comprise the single dominant image. In contrast, festivals such as Diwali, Dussehra, Navratri, Muharam, Durga Puja, Ganesh Chaturthi and many more, have emerged as the spectacles of the Kinetic City. Their presence in the everyday landscape is pervasive and dominates the popular visual culture of Indian cities. Festivals create a forum through which the fantasies of the subalterns are articulated and even organized into political action.

In Mumbai for example, the popularity and growth of the Ganesh festival has been phenomenal.[8] During the festival, which occurs in August or September, numerous neighbourhoods transform temporarily with lights and decorations. New spaces are created to house the idol of Ganesh for 10 days. During this festival period, family, neighbourhood and city events mark the celebrations. On the last day, a large part of the population carries the idol in long processions ultimately to be immersed in the sea. Each procession carries tableaux, depicting images of both local as well as global concerns, with Lord Ganesh mediating the outcomes. This representation is not based on formal scriptures or predetermined rules; instead human ingenuity breaches the boundaries between the local and the global, the historic and contemporary.[9] They convey the hybrid urgencies of metropolitan India. The neighbourhood processions weave along predetermined routes.[10] Each procession vies against other neighbourhood processions to showcase the intensity of their followings. Set against the backdrop of the Static City, the procession culminates in the immersion of the idol as it is bid farewell amid chants inviting Ganesh to resurrect his presence the following year.

Immersion becomes a metaphor for the spectacle. As the clay idol dissolves in the water of the bay, the spectacle comes to a close. There are no static or permanent mechanisms to encode it. Here the memory of the city is an 'enacted' process – a temporal moment as opposed to buildings that contain the public memory as a static or permanent entity.[11] Within the Kinetic City, meanings are not stable; spaces get consumed, reinterpreted and recycled. The Kinetic City recycles the Static City to create a new spectacle.

This transformative ability of the Kinetic City becomes even more vivid in the events that play out at Mumbai's Town Hall every year on 15 August, India's Independence Day. The Public Works Department (PWD) subverts the meaning and symbolism of the architecture of this Classical building by reconfiguring it for an annual ceremony when the Governor of the State addresses the citizens. To ensure protection from the monsoon rains, the PWD builds a structure, a sort of large porch, which is attached to the building. Built overnight in bamboo and cloth, the decorative trim and other ornamental highlights graft onto this Classical building a local and perhaps traditional sensibility that momentarily transforms the architecture.

The conservationists protest each year decrying this as an abuse of the legislation that protects heritage buildings, but they ignore the fact that this as a reversible action, well within the bounds of even the holiest of preservationists' canons.[12] The intended image of this symbol of colonial power, a celebrated asset of the Static City, is subverted and re-colonized by the Kinetic City. The PWD alters the significance of this building momentarily to expand the margins of the Kinetic City.

This kind of action takes on a critical dimension when it is compared with accepted practices of historical preservation. Debates about the conservation of the Static City have often revolved around the notion of 'cultural significance', which emerged clearly in the conservation debate in the 1980s.[13] Implicit in the common definition of the phrase is the belief that 'significance' is static. It is a definition that is object-centric (devoid of life) with its roots in the debate propagated by the antiquarians of the Renaissance.[14] What is the validity of such a notion where cultural memory is often an enacted process, as in the Kinetic City? Or where meanings are as fluid as the Kinetic City itself and often complicated in post-colonial conditions by the fact that the users and custodians of historic environments in the Static City are from different cultures than those that created them?

What then is our cultural reading for the Kinetic City, which now forms a greater part of our urban reality? If the production or preservation of architecture or urban form has to be informed by our reading of cultural significance in this dynamic context, it will necessarily have to include the notion of 'constructing significance' both in the architectural as well as conservation debates.[15] In fact, an understanding that 'cultural significance' evolves, will truly clarify the role of the architect as an advocate of change (versus a preservationist who opposes change) – one who can engage with both the Kinetic and Static City on equal terms. Under such conditions, a draining of the symbolic import of the architectural landscape leads to a deepening of ties between architecture and contemporary realities and experiences. This understanding allows architecture and urban typologies to be transformed through intervention and placed in the service of contemporary life, realities, and emerging aspirations. Here, the Static City embraces the Kinetic City and is informed and remade by its logic.

The phenomenon of bazaars in the Victorian arcades in the old Fort Area, Mumbai's Historic District, is emblematic of this potential negotiation between the Static and Kinetic City. The original use of the arcades was twofold. First, they provided spatial mediation between building and street. Second, the arcades were a perfect response to Bombay's climate. They served as a zone protecting pedestrians from both the harsh sun and lashing rains. Today, with the informal bazaar occupying

NEW SLUMS FOR OLD

Just as it once was for Manhattan and London, the troubling question for Mumbai is the longevity of the new housing developments that have taken the place of the demolished slums of the recent past.

the arcade, its original intent is challenged. This emergent relationship of the arcade and bazaar not only forces a confrontation of uses and interest groups, but also demands new preservation approaches. For the average Mumbai resident, the hawker provides a wide range of goods at prices considerably lower than those found in local shops. Thus, the bazaars in the arcades are thriving businesses. For the elite and for conservationists, the Victorian core represents the old city centre, complete with monumental icons. In fact, as the city sprawls, dissipating the clarity of its form, these images, places, and icons acquire even greater meaning for preservationists as critical symbols of the city's historic image. Consequently, hawking is deemed illegal by city authorities that are constantly attempting to relocate the bazaars.

The challenge in Mumbai is to cope with the city's transformation, not by exaggerating its dualism, but by attempting to recognize these opposing conditions as being simultaneously valid. The existence of two worlds in the same space implies that we must accommodate and overlap varying uses, perceptions, and physical forms. The arcades in the Fort Area possess a rare capacity for reinterpretation. As an architectural solution, they display an incredible resilience; they can accommodate new uses while keeping the illusion of their architecture intact.

One design solution might be to re-adapt the functioning of the arcades. They could be restructured to allow for easy pedestrian movement and accommodate hawkers at the same time. They could contain the amorphous bazaar encased in the illusion of the disciplined Victorian arcade. With this sort of approach, the key components of the city would have a greater ability to survive, because they could be more adaptable to changing economic and social conditions. There are no total solutions in an urban landscape characterized by both permanence and rapid transformation. At best, the city could constantly evolve and invent solutions for the present through safeguarding the crucial components of our historically important 'urban hardware'. Could 'Bazaars in Victorian Arcades' become an authentic symbol of an emergent reality of temporary adjustment? Clearly the Static and Kinetic Cities go beyond their obvious differences to establish a much richer relationship

INFRASTRUCTURE AND ITS IMPACT

Its railway network has been essential to the growth of Mumbai. It has made possible an economic infrastructure that supports a dense network of enterprises: from the tiffin men who feed office workers, to the textile workers who sew shirts for Europeans.

both spatially and metaphorically than their physical manifestations would suggest. Here affinity and rejection are simultaneously played out – in a state of equilibrium maintained by a seemingly irresolvable tension. The informal economy of the city vividly illustrates the collapsed and intertwined existence of the Static and Kinetic Cities. The *dabbawalas* (literally translated as 'tiffin men') are an example of this relationship between the formal and informal, the static and kinetic. The tiffin delivery service, which relies on the train system for transportation, costs approx Rs.200 (US$4) per month. A *dabbawala* picks up a lunch tiffin from a house anywhere in the city. Then he delivers the tiffin to one's place of work by lunchtime and returns it to the house later in the day. The *dabbawalas* deliver hundreds of thousands of lunch boxes every day. The efficiency of Mumbai's train system, the spine of the linear city, enables this complex informal system to work. *The dabbawalas* have innovatively set up a network that facilitates an informal system to take advantage of a formal infrastructure. The network involves the *dabba* or tiffin being exchanged up to four or five times between its pickup and return to the house in the evening. The average box travels about 30 km (18 miles) each way. It is estimated that around 200,000 boxes are delivered around the city per day, involving approximately 4,500 *dabbawalas*. In economic terms, the annual turnover amounts to roughly 50 million Rupees or about a US$1 million.[16]

Entrepreneurship in the Kinetic City is an autonomous and oral process that demonstrates the ability to fold the formal and informal into a symbiotic relationship. The *dabbawalas,* like several other informal services that range from banking, money transfer, courier, and electronic goods bazaars, leverage community relationships and networks and deftly use the Static City and its infrastructure beyond its intended margins. These networks create a synergy that depends on mutual integration without the obsession of formalized structures. The Kinetic City is where the intersection of need (often reduced to survival) and unexploited potentials of existing infrastructure give rise to new innovative services. The trains in Mumbai are emblematic of a kinetic space, supporting and blurring the formal and the informal, slicing through these worlds while momentarily collapsing them into a singular entity. Here the self-consciousness about modernity and the regulations imposed by the Static City are suspended and redundant. The Kinetic City carries local wisdom into the contemporary world without fear of the modern, while the Static City aspires to erase the local and re-codify it in a written 'macro-moral' order.[17]

The issue of housing most vividly demonstrates the reordering process of the Kinetic City by the Static City. In Mumbai, for example, approximately 60 per cent of the city's population does not have access to formal housing. This population lives on approximately 10 per cent of the city's land in settlements that are locally referred to as slums. It is believed that about 70 per cent of the city's population works in the informal sector. This number has risen with the new liberal economy that curtails bargaining capacity through fragmenting labour in the cities. Despite its informal nature, this population's productivity allows Mumbai to be competitive on a global scale.[18] This subaltern population lives in the interstitial spaces of the cities – road edges, drainage channels (*nalla* spaces), edges of railway lines – and must engage in innovative means of negotiating everyday life. Satellite dishes and a web of electrical wires and cables juxtapose these homes covered by plastic sheets or with walls made of empty drums. These developments represent a kaleidoscope of the past, present and future compressed into an organic fabric of alleys, dead ends and a labyrinth-like mysterious streetscape that constantly modifies and reinvents itself. Like a twitching organism the Kinetic City locates and relocates itself through the city in perpetual motion. Regular demolitions exacerbate the tenuous occupation of land by the inhabitants of these settlements. The demolitions inhibit any investment the occupants might make in their physical living conditions. Flow, instability and indeterminacy are basic to the Kinetic City. Thus the Kinetic City is a fluid and dynamic city that is mobile and temporal (often as a strategy to defeat eviction) and leaves no ruins. It constantly recycles its resources leveraging great effect and presence with very little means.

This only heightens the growing contradictions in the islands of increasing concentration of wealth manifest physically in the gated communities throughout the city and in the edge city suburbs. The popular metaphorical reference to 'making Bombay Shanghai' is emblematic of the one-dimensional imagination that planners and politicians bring to bear on decisions about the city's development.[19] An obvious extension of the Shanghai metaphor is the notion of remaking the city in a singular image and using architecture as the spectacle to represent a global aspiration. The radical transformation of the physical nature of the city is seen as the most immediate method to make the city viable for integration in a global network of cities and economies. New motorways, flyovers, airports, corporate hotels and convention centres (followed by a secondary development of museums, galleries, parks and progressive urban regulations demonstrating further compliance with international urban standards) are all critical elements for the Static City to achieve this perceived integration. Such global implications also raise political questions that challenge the democratic processes of city governance.[20]

Ambiguity regarding the urban form of Mumbai and its dominant image, prompts the question: whose city is it anyway? This question goes beyond the politics of occupation and challenges the processes by which the city is made. The making of the city is perhaps most critical when negotiating between the Static and Kinetic Cities; for it is also an effective point of intervention. Through the city-making process, globalization and its particular transgressions in the urban landscape are realized, but it is also how the Kinetic City can simultaneously resist or participate in globalization as well as reconfigure itself socially, culturally and spatially.

The growing movement of slum associations and networks in Mumbai is a potent illustration of these points of effective intervention. These associations engage with the formal world of the Static City while mediating the inherent contradictions of issues of legality, informality and the mobile and temporal strategies of the Kinetic City. The most successful of these movements is the alliance between an NGO, The Society for the Promotion of Area Resource (SPARC), a CBO, The National Slum Dwellers Federation (NSDF), and the Mahila Milan, an organization of poor women. This alliance is essentially united in its concerns for securing land and access to urban infrastructure. It has successfully negotiated between the formal and informal worlds in the city and across national boundaries with a network of other alliances working with slum dwellers around the world.

Besides representing efforts to reconstitute citizenship in cities, these efforts form what Arjun Appadurai refers to as ' deep democracy'. The depth refers to '…[a] model that produces poor communities able to engage in partnership with more powerful agencies – urban, regional, national and multilateral – that purport to be concerned with poverty and citizenship … vertical collaborations and partnerships with more powerful persons and organizations together form a mutually sustaining cycle of process. This is where depth and laterality become joint circuits along which pro-poor strategies can flow.'[21] It is through this restructuring of the city-making process that the Kinetic and Static Cities can be intertwined beyond the physical and better engage the inhabitants of the city.

The urbanism of Mumbai represents a fascinating intersection where the Kinetic City – a landscape of dystopia, and yet a symbol of optimism – challenges the Static City – encoded in architecture – to reposition and remake the city as a whole.[22] The Kinetic City forces the Static City to re-engage itself in present conditions by dissolving its utopian project to fabricate multiple dialogues with its context. Could this become the basis for a rational discussion about coexistence? Or is Mumbai's emergent urbanism inherently paradoxical, and are the coexistence of the Static and Kinetic Cities and their particular states of utopia and dystopia inevitable? Can the spatial configuration for how this simultaneity occurs actually be formally imagined? The Kinetic City obviously cannot be seen as a design tool, rather as a demand that conceptions of urbanism create and facilitate environments that are versatile and flexible, robust and ambiguous enough to allow this kinetic quality of the city to flourish. Perhaps the Kinetic City might be the tactical approach to take when dealing with the urbanism of the temporary, of high densities and intensities? In spite of these many potential disjunctures, what this reading of the city does celebrate is the dynamic and pluralist processes that make the urban Indian landscape. Within this urbanism, the Static and Kinetic Cities necessarily coexist and blur into an integral entity, even if momentarily, to create the margins for adjustment that their simultaneous existences demand.

THE LONG VIEW

Charles Correa

THE PREHISTORY OF THE CITY

Mumbai was shaped first as a colonial trading harbour, and second by its railways: a junction between the strategic movement of military power, and the commercial demands of business.

In this essay I would like to highlight some crucial lessons Mumbai could provide to help us identify key urban issues around the globe, especially in the developing world.

Public Transport

The development of a public transport system for Bombay was not an afterthought. Right from the start, it was essential to the city's DNA. The island on which the city sits is really an elongated breakwater, protecting the harbour from the open sea. To service the port, located at the southern end of this island, the British constructed two major railway lines. One of them ran north and west, and was used to carry troops up to the Khyber Pass. The other ran north and east, and took British businessmen to the city that was then called Calcutta. Starting at the southern end of the city, both lines travel roughly parallel to each other, along the length of the island, before they reach the mainland where they part ways.

Stations were constructed along these two railways lines, and, around these stations housing was built to provide affordable accommodation for migrants working in the mills that were located northwards from Parel and Lalbagh, and in offices at the southern end of the island. Interchanges between the two railway lines, like Dadar and Bandra, grew more swiftly because they provided even greater access and economic opportunity.

The very successful urban structure of the current city of Mumbai is therefore due not to any prescient planning, but to the two engineers who laid out the original railway tracks. They created corridors of demand that could support a much higher frequency of trains and buses that could run at lower fares. This would be impossible in the evenly distributed sprawl of Delhi or Chandigarh. It is precisely this mobility, and the potential for interaction, available to all its citizens, that lies at the heart of Mumbai's success. Much is made of the energy, the 'get-up-and-go' spirit of this city, especially when compared with Chennai or Kolkata. But do we ever ask ourselves how much of this is due to the greater mobility of the average citizen? After all, cities are characterized by interaction, and about the synergy that it generates. Perhaps the real goal of city planners should not be that of the 'city beautiful', but that of the 'city as network', as synergy.

Mumbai is not alone in this. Other examples of linear cities partly conditioned by their physical context and partly by the intrinsic logic of public transport include Manhattan and Bogotá. And, of course, London, which is arguably the most liveable

URBAN DNA

Mumbai grew along the railway corridors planned by British engineers to connect the port to the Indian subcontinent. As the city grows to become the largest in the world, the infrastructure has become inadequate.

of all the giant metropolises of the world. For while it has a plentiful supply of beautiful parks and terraced houses, London also has an excellent public transport system consisting of interlinked underground lines, trains and buses that take you right across the city (soon to be enhanced by the new GB£16 [US$25.3 / €18.5] billion Crossrail high-speed underground line). How did this happen? Because when it became clear in the nineteenth century that London's growth was exponential, the underground system was extended beyond the immediate residential suburbs, opening up large swathes of land on the fringes of the city to development opportunities. During the 1920s and 1930s, developers followed, creating a mix of residential neighbourhoods near these underground stations. In short, London is a vivid example of how public transport can structure a city's growth – a case of supply generating demand – with extremely positive results.

Today our cities in India (and perhaps elsewhere as well) pay little attention to public transport. They are allowed to develop in a sprawling manner. Or, if planned, they are laid out as a matrix of sectors, unstructured by any corridor of demand. Then, decades later, when we attempt to insert a public transport system, it has to be heavily subsidized. For trying to retrofit public transport after a city has developed, is a very expensive proposition. But what if, as was the case in Mumbai, we integrate public transport with land-use right from the start? It would be cheaper to build and would also structure the city along high-density corridors, making the system more economical to operate. And even if there is some subsidy to the transport system, it is

ENVISIONING A NEW CITY

With a leap of imagination, Mumbai could escape its old geographical constraints and create a functioning metropolis that stretches over the boundaries set by its origins and allow it to function in a new way, bringing together existing settlements.

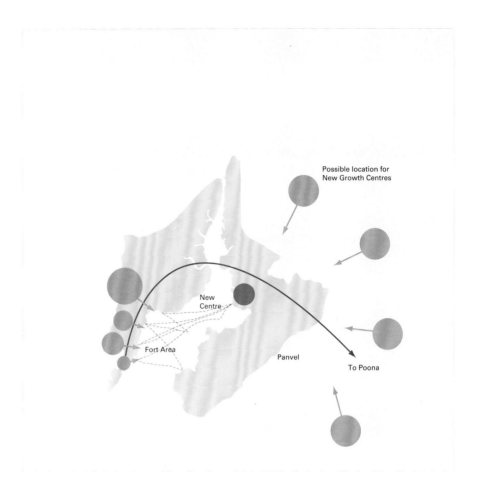

Possible location for New Growth Centres

New Centre

Fort Area

Panvel

To Poona

really an indirect subsidy on housing, since the city's mass transport system opens up more urban land, bringing the price of housing down to affordable levels.

The same system of cross-subsidy operates in North America, except that affordable suburban housing has become possible only at the cost of building a vast network of highways for cars. This is a form of subsidy that some Americans consider problematic, since private car commuting patterns have destroyed the fabric of cities right across the United States. Unfortunately, the danger of this situation is not understood by India's urban elites. Cars are proliferating in our cities, leading to ever-bigger traffic jams. And so the next step is already well under way: the demand for more flyovers and bigger expressways, all of which come with huge price tags that effectively pre-empt the availability of any budget for public transport. It is a tragedy that prevails in almost every one of our cities.

And yet, here's the simple truth: Bombay's railways were built not to lose money but to generate it. The railways of India were all funded by private capital, as were the railways of Europe and North America. Investors like Vanderbilt, Morgan, and Harriman made fortunes by investing in the railways during the nineteenth century. To deal with the scale of urban growth that lies ahead, we must understand the invaluable lesson that Mumbai's DNA teaches us: public transport infrastructure must not be the last to enter the scene. Given the pace of change, there are crucial advantages in making it one of the first.

Governance

Right from the start, Bombay attracted people from all over India: Gujaratis, Parses and Punjabis from the north, Bengalis and Biharis from the east, Tamils and Keralites from the south – and each made huge contributions to the success of the city. The powerful financial institutions of Bombay – the Stock Exchange, the commodities market, and so forth – derived their strength from the energy and enterprise that Gujarat brought to the city. The British made them all welcome, including a community of Baghdadi Jews – one of whom, Victor Sassoon, was responsible for connecting the seven islands with landfill, and thus in effect creating the city as we know it today.

Bombay can therefore be considered India's first, and perhaps the only, cosmopolitan city in recent history. Was this intentional? Three centuries ago, the British started in Madras, which has always been dominated by the local Tamil population, and was never likely to become cosmopolitan. Then they moved to Calcutta, and made it the second city of the Empire. Still, after two centuries of trying, it remains an essentially Bengali city. And yet, during the same time span, European cities like Vienna, Paris, London and Berlin became great cosmopolitan centres. Someone must have noticed the crucial difference that a pluralistic citizenry makes, not only to Bombay's culture but also to its economic vitality – and hence the importance of attracting a diverse population. If this is true, then it is one of the earliest and most effective urban examples of social engineering – and although it may not have been proclaimed in any formal policy document, it might well exist in the India Office in London just as subtle notes in the margins of some files.

Because of narrow parochialism and religious bigotry, our politicians today are rapidly destroying this pluralism. The damage to the city is immeasurable. When political parties shout slogans like 'North Indians go home!', they are actually destroying the city. For a city is a network of people, goods and services. Demolish those networks and you destroy the city – and thus the wealth of the nation. The Indian political establishment, at state as well as federal level, keeps proclaiming that they want Mumbai to become a world financial centre, a world city. And yet the politicians in Mumbai have been allowed to do exactly the opposite. They seem not to understand that the fundamental reason a trading post or a business centre thrives is that the merchants feel secure and protected. It is a principle as old as Samarkand.

The Future

The scale of urban growth that lies ahead is the key issue. This is why the lessons of Mumbai's original DNA are of such crucial importance. Despite the waves of migrants that kept pouring in, the city had no squatters right up to World War II, because of the availability of land provided by the two railway corridors. Squatter colonies started to appear only in the 1950s – an explicit sign that public transport was not opening up new land fast enough and that demand had started to overtake supply.

In 1964 the population of Bombay was 4.5 million, of which only 10 per cent were squatters. By 1980 the population had reached 8 million, of which 50 per cent (4 million) were squatters. Today greater Mumbai has a population of over 17 million, of which the government estimates that 60 per cent (over 10 million!) are squatters. We should have responded by creating new job centres in new locations, connected by new public transport way back in 1964.

This was the prime objective of the masterplan for Navi Mumbai (New Mumbai):

an urban vision that involved re-directing Bombay's growth towards the waterfront around the harbour, and from there inland, towards the hinterland of the state of Maharashtra. At the core of this project was a sequence of new mixed urban centres that fed off new public transport arteries. Navi Mumbai was a strategy to transform the energy of Bombay into a polycentric urban system around the harbour, aimed at allowing it to become, once again, one of the finest of things: a city on water. For there are physical and visual dimensions to economic and social issues, and the decisions they precipitate are what planning is about. But unfortunately these objectives and strategies were never adequately implemented, nor perhaps ever even understood, by the state government.

Public transport is crucial to the urban equation. After all, migrants do not come to cities looking for housing; they come in search of work. So they try to live as close as possible to their workplaces or to some form of transport that will take them there. Thus affordable housing is not an isolated problem. It is the product of an equation that includes at least two other crucial parameters: job location and available transport. In India, very few people have access to cars, which is why public transport is so crucial. It means people can get to their job, their school, their doctor, their friends.

Today's Mumbai is expected to grow into a city of 24 million within a decade. That seems monstrous. Unless we realize that the size of a city can be mitigated by its structure. A single-centred city of 10 million people could be a disaster. But what if the same population was distributed across five interconnected centres of 2 million each? One success story is the Bay Area of San Francisco, which has a total population of over 4 million, and yet San Francisco itself is a city of just about 800,000 inhabitants. The Randstad in Holland is an even better example: here the main cities of Amsterdam, Rotterdam, The Hague and Utrecht, and a range of smaller cities, form a single integrated urban system, well connected by rapid rail, and no one city is out of scale. Nearer to home in India, the many towns and cities of Kerala or Goa, together form a single balanced habitat.

Coda

Over the last few years, there has been much talk of transforming Mumbai into a world city. But by any standards, Bombay was already a world city 60 years ago! The tragedy is that as it has been growing larger and larger, it has actually diminished since then into a monstrous provincial town.

BEYOND THE MAXIMUM

Geetam Tiwari

WALKING TO WORK

The future of Mumbai, and perhaps also of the planet, depends on how the city deals with the car. Despite the launch of the low-cost Nano, India is still a country with very low car ownership that continues to give the taxi a special position.

Urban travel in Indian cities predominantly happens through walking, cycling and public transport, including intermediate public transport (IPT). Despite high growth rates of motorized two-wheelers and cars in the last two decades (at 15 per cent and 10 per cent per annum respectively), car ownership has remained relatively low, at between 3 to 13 per cent of the households, while that of two-wheelers has stalled between 40 to 50 per cent. The latter is the same as the bicycle ownership in cities of different sizes.[1] The variation in modal shares among these three seems to have a relationship between city size and per capita income. Small- and medium-size cities have a lower income than the megacities. Therefore the dependence on cycle rickshaws and bicycles is higher in smaller cities. In some medium-size cities (with populations of 1 to 3 million), private buses have been introduced. Public-sector-run state transport corporations have been responsible for running inter-city routes. Other than the four megacities (Delhi, Mumbai, Kolkata and Chennai), Bangalore and Pune are the exceptions in which municipal corporations have been running significant numbers of buses. Other cities have skeletal bus services provided by the city municipality. Intermediate public transport modes like tempos, cars and cycle rickshaws assume importance as they are necessary to meet travel demands in medium-size cities in India, such as Lucknow, Hubli, Varanasi, Kanpur and Vijayawada. These vehicles have minimal regulations in terms of road-worthiness certifications, which are issued by the transport authorities; their operations have been left to the private operator. Often they have been found to cause serious emission and safety violations. However, there is no policy or project that can improve the operation of para-transit modes. Often the fare policy stipulated by the government is not honoured by the operators, and the road infrastructure also does not include facilities for these modes. As a result, the operators have to violate legal policies to survive.

Of India's 285 million urban residents, nearly 100 million people live in urban slums. Travel patterns of people living in informal housing or slums are very different from residents in formal housing. Generally, cycling and walking account for 50 to 75 per cent of the commuter trips for those in the informal sector. The formal sector is dependent on buses, cars and two-wheelers. This implies that despite high risks and a hostile infrastructure, low-cost modes are used because their users do not have any choice; they are the captive users of these modes. Public transport is the predominant mode of motorized travel in megacities. Buses carry 20 to 65 per cent of the total number of passengers, excluding those who walk.[2] The minimum cost of

public transport use still means that between 20 to 30 per cent of a family income, for the nearly 50 per cent of the city population living in unauthorized settlements, is spent on simply moving around.

Since transport is a state responsibility under the Indian constitution, the country's central government did not have a policy or investment plan for urban transport infrastructure until 2006. City governments attempted to solve transport crises as isolated road improvement projects. Despite investments in road infrastructure and plans for land use and transport development, cities continue to face the problem of congestion, traffic accidents and air and noise pollution, which are all on the increase. Investments in road-widening schemes and grade-separated junctions that primarily benefit personal vehicle users (cars and two-wheelers), have dominated government expenditure. In Delhi, for example, the total funds allocated for the transport sector in 2002–2003 have doubled in 2006–2007. However, 80 per cent of the funds have been allocated for road-widening schemes that benefit primarily the car and motorcycle users. In 2006–2007, 60 per cent of the funds were earmarked for public transport, which primarily meant work on a metro system.[3] Cars are owned by less than 15 per cent of the households in Delhi. Therefore, an investment in car-friendly infrastructure will not benefit a majority of the commuters.

In the name of promoting public transport, demand for rail-based systems (metro, LRT and monorail) has been pursued by several cities. This despite the fact that the rail-based systems are capital intensive, capacity is underutilized and the system requires capital and operating subsidies. The existing metro systems in Kolkata, Chennai and Delhi carry less than 20 per cent of the available capacity. All three systems have been running with operating losses.[4] Nevertheless, the government in Delhi has decided to expand the metro system. Similarly the state governments of Maharashtra, Karnataka and Andhra Pradesh have decided to invest in metro systems.[5] While these systems will only cater for a small proportion of the total number of journeys (less than 5 per cent), they are still being pursued by the city authorities and promoted as investment projects in which the private sector can participate. The Mumbai metro rail project has been approved as the first MRTS project being implemented as a public private partnership (PPP) project.

Traffic and transport improvement proposals prepared by consultants before the Jawaharlal Nehru National Urban Renewal Mission (JNNURM), include proposals for road widening, grade-separated junctions and metro systems. While the road-widening and junction-improvement schemes were implemented in only a few cities, public transport remained in the reports only because the finances required for metro projects are beyond the capacity of state or city governments.

Different Indian cities are either implementing or looking at new public transport systems, be it a metro system, high-capacity buses or a sky bus. The argument given for introducing new technologies is that they will serve the high-density demands that are expected on a few corridors in the city. In the last two decades, comprehensive traffic and transport plans have been drawn up for at least 20 cities. Travel forecasts for the next 30 years have been used to justify the proposals for light rail or metro systems. Indian cities have high-density developments in the form of urban slums. But even a subsidized metro system is too expensive for slum dwellers.

Cities have grown as multi-node centres with mixed land-use patterns. Often formal and informal housing coexist, which in turn results in short journey lengths. This is one of the reasons why the demand for metro systems in Indian cities is low. Metro systems are capital-intensive systems (on average they demand Rs.2,000 to

LOOKING AT THE LONG TERM

Infrastructure investment in Mumbai has been focused on financial returns, rather than on projects that have favoured the development of the city. Its future success depends on bringing these two divergent strands closer together.

3,000 million/km, or US$45 to 67 / €32.6 to 49 million/km). It is not suitable to meet the mobility requirements of the majority of city residents. For the same price a 30- to 50-kilometre bus network can be developed, including the use of modern buses. This would benefit 30 to 50 times more people than a metro system. The cost of a single metro trip is at least Rs.45 (US$1.01 / €0.74) compared with Rs.15 (US$0.34 / €0.25) for a bus trip. Since cars and personal two-wheelers provide a flexible door-to-door service, it is not easy to attract these users to the metro, even if they can afford the cost. Tickets have to be subsidized at least 10 to 15 times more heavily than a bus ticket for the same journey. All rail-based systems depend on buses, three-wheelers and rickshaws as feeder modes to increase their catchment area, and it is only long-distance travellers (with journeys of at least 15 km) are likely to use a feeder mode. Therefore, in order to realize the social benefits of metro systems, city structures have to change completely.

A draft national urban transport policy was introduced in 2004 and adopted in 2006. At the same time the national government introduced the Jawaharlal Nehru National Urban Renewal Mission to upgrade the crumbling infrastructure of urban areas. Under JNNURM, the government of India has identified 63 cities for which it will provide assistance in upgrading their road infrastructure.[6] Detailed guidelines have been provided to ensure that public transport gets priority in these cities. For getting approval for transport projects, the guidelines recommend that the transport infrastructure improvement schemes are in compliance with the National Urban

RIDING OVER POVERTY

Carving a high-level motorway through the midst of a densely packed city to create a toll road may offer better conditions for international bankers and help to make Mumbai a global financial centre, but it alienates most of its citizens.

Transport Policy (NUTP). Since NUTP's focus is on public transport, pedestrians and bicycles, cities are modifying the earlier road expansion projects to Bus Rapid Transit (BRT) and bicycle-inclusive plans. BRT and bicycle-inclusive plans have been approved by the central government for six cities and another four cities are at different stages of preparation. It seems that pedestrian and bicycle facilities are not the focus of these projects. On six-lane arterial roads, two lanes are reserved for public transport buses, but there seems to be a reluctance to provide a quality facilities for pedestrians and cyclists. This is reflected in the priority for space allocation for various modes in a restricted right of way. In order to accommodate two lanes for cars as well as an exclusive lane for buses, pedestrians and cyclists have been given less than desirable space. This is despite the fact that nearly 50 per cent of journeys are made on foot, by bicycle, or by intermediate public transport systems. The main motivation for preparing BRT projects has been to become eligible for the grant aid offered by the central government. It is yet to be seen whether public transport, non-motorized-vehicle and pedestrian-friendly infrastructure is created when these projects are implemented.

Although implementation of BRTs has commenced in Delhi, at times it seems that accommodating the demands of the major stakeholders like the 'Transport Industry' in the Delhi Metro Rail Corporation (DMRC), the public works department, Light Rail Transit and monorail industries in the planning and investment agenda is the primary focus. Providing an efficient and safe means of transport to the majority of the population, and using public money in the most efficient way is not the driving force for implementing BRTs in Delhi. The company that has been established to implement the project, the Delhi Integrated Multi-Modal Transport System (DIMTS), is also preparing plans for light rail transit and monorail. BRTs' road designs have been modified to 'improve' car flow so that after the construction of the BRT lanes, car users do not suffer, even if it means reducing safety and convenience to pedestrians and cyclists.

In view of the recently implemented measures and current investment priorities we should expect an increase in the use of private vehicles (both motorized two-wheelers and cars) by high- and middle-income households in all Indian cities and use of bicycles and walking by low-income urban residents, despite the hostile environment. At present over 20,000 people a year are the victim of fatal traffic accidents and another 400,000 are seriously injured in urban areas. This number is likely to double in the next decade, creating a major public health crisis, and with this increase in the use of two-wheelers and cars, congestion and environment pollution will also continue to deteriorate.

It is clear that the public-transport agenda has failed in Indian cities. With the fascination for capital-intensive rail-based projects, investments in pedestrian, bicycle and road-based public transport infrastructure continues to be neglected. Today public transport users are largely the people who are using these modes not out of choice, but because of financial constraints. With a rise in income the ownership of private vehicles is increasing, people prefer to use private vehicles that can provide them with door-to-door connectivity.

The failure of the public transport agenda also reflects the failure of our democratic process because the present mechanism of planning and decision-making does not allow inclusion of the demands of the majority of the city residents, who are pedestrians, cyclists and public transport users. On the one hand, the policy makers are concerned about the growing levels of congestion and pollution, while on the other, transport policies continue to encourage the use of private vehicles.

SÃO P

Latin America's largest city exploded in the second half of the twentieth century.

Where the unplanned meets the planned in uneasy mutual interdependence.

Traffic and security fears make the rich helicopter commuters.

Landmark architecture by Oscar Niemeyer in the midst of chaos.

The lack of investment in transport infrastructure handicaps the city.

São Paulo's flourishing city-centre street market.

Brazil's economic boom is transforming the nature of housing.

Security remains a preoccupation at every level.

THE URBAN GIANT

Deyan Sudjic

Urban Latin America is one thing. Urban South America is quite another. The former is dominated by Mexico City, by far the largest city of the two entities with Miami as its other putative, though offshore, capital. Perhaps that's why South America is a construct that appeals to Brazil's boosters. Geographical fine-tuning allows the Metropolitan Region of São Paulo with 19 million people to make an unblushing claim to be the unchallenged leader if not of Latin America, then at least of South America, of which it is indisputably the largest city.

Even if São Paulo, for all its economic dynamism, sometimes suspects that it lags behind Mexico City – not just in size, but in its cultural and political clout – it is certainly way ahead of Rio de Janeiro. When Juscelino Kubitchek, Oscar Niemeyer's greatest patron, transferred his government to Brasília, it was a huge political gesture, turning away from the colonial coastal capital to establish a new kind of country with Brasília at its geographical heart. One unintended consequence was that it tilted the balance between the country's two largest cities even further towards São Paulo. Rio still has its remarkable natural setting, but it is a place in which once languid embassies are now hemmed in by angry *favelas*.

But that sense of confidence and self assertion, marked by the building of Brasília, is a reflection of the rather different status that South American cities have when compared with some of the other regions visited by Urban Age. By comparison with Shanghai, with its strongly centralist government, cities in South America display a much more sophisticated level of 'social entrepreneurship' and civic engagement. There, active pressure groups, religious, ethnic and political groups – in the wealthy districts as well as the highly organized *favelas* – are not beholden to central government. South America also has the benefit of civic initiatives that *can* pay off. Brazil has the example of Curitiba and beyond that, the work done by reforming mayors in Bogotá, a city that with 8 million people is far more relevant in terms of scale.

In the last 10 years, Bogotá has built more than 50 new schools, mostly of some architectural distinction, a tangible investment in the quality of life of some of the city's poorest inhabitants. It has done a lot, not just to reduce truancy rates, but also to create a sense of inclusion. The city has initiated a vigorous programme to build new libraries, and an impressive public transport system based on special rapid transit bus lanes, which has succeeded in persuading commuters to leave their cars at home. Bogotá has tackled crime through its visible commitment to social justice,

5.8%

percentage of Brazil's population who live in São Paulo

11.9%

percentage of Brazil's GDP produced by São Paulo

bringing its murder rate down from frightening levels, and raising literacy in its overwhelmingly young population. Bogotá shows its neighbours what can be done, given will, organization and rational priorities.

In the network of South American cities, São Paulo certainly eclipses Buenos Aires, which, despite its nineteenth-century Classical architecture and its European airs has still to regain the equilibrium of its time in the sun in the 1940s when Argentina could have been another Australia. Argentina's farmers were still angry enough with their government's economic policies to ignite the protest fires that left Buenos Aires trapped in a cloud of choking smoke in the winter of 2008, which did nothing to reinforce Buenos Aires' pretensions to be taken seriously as a metropolis.

Yet Brazil's huge size, and population in excess of 180 million, gives it a different urban pattern to that of its South American neighbours Argentina, Peru and Colombia, which each have one overwhelmingly dominant city. One in every three Argentinians and Peruvians live in their capital cities compared with only one in every nine Brazilians who live in São Paulo. Lima's dominance in Peru has virtually destroyed the national system of cities, a trend that was not even halted by the dismantling of Lima's public transport system in the early 1990s following the government's espousal of the most aggressive neo-liberal reforms in South America. Given the city's unique physical setting, constrained by mountains and the sea, and the absence of growth controls, Lima could develop into a 300 kilometres (182 miles) long linear megacity that encroaches on adjacent low-value desert land; an unsustainable scenario in an environment where water supply and transport accessibility are already at their limits.

São Paulo and Mexico City are very different models of what a city can be. Mexico City's roots go far back into the Pre-Colombian past. São Paulo was a tiny colonial outpost until the beginning of the last century. São Paulo is now the largest city in one of the world's most important new economies, representing the B in that uncomfortably named entity, BRIC, of which the other three members are India, China and Russia.

Brazil is the country that is able to build and launch its own satellites. It has the 10th largest market in the world, and an art biennale that has global clout. São Paulo's GDP is in excess of US$10,000 (€7,339) per head, and counts 30,000 dollar millionaires. It has an economy that has powered past that of Mexico, to become bracketed by booming India and Russia, which together have reshaped the geography of the global economy. A very large part of Brazil's economic strength can be ascribed to the extraordinary growth of São Paulo. Barely recognizable as a city a century ago, it has exploded in size from just 240,000 people in the early years of the last century. Despite a recent slowdown in its economic prowess, it has been a job-creating machine, absorbing successive waves of migrants: from Europe and Japan, as well as from Brazil's poor northeast. By many measures, it is an unqualified success.

And yet, it is a country and a city that cannot control crime. In 2007 Brazil found itself unable to trust the safety of its skies after a series of crashes, and it was paralyzed by air traffic restrictions. The clichés about São Paulo come thick and fast. It has more private helicopters registered to its citizens than any other city in the world. Its prison system is in a permanent state of insurgency. Its tribes of street children are brutalized by both crime and the police. It is also the city whose reforming mayor earned himself world-wide publicity when he reclaimed the public realm by banning outdoor advertising, leaving the ghostly traces of billboards stripped of their posters and the charred surfaces revealed by neon signs that have been dismantled. And it is a centre for media that has created the *telenovela*, spreading a very particular kind of Brazilian culture to audiences around the world.

São Paulo is the classic second city, built on an industrial explosion from almost nothing. And it is that industrial base that makes the Brazilian economy different. It has moved far beyond the natural-resource based boom-and-bust cycles of its neighbours. São Paulo could have been a Manchester, a Shanghai or a Chicago. But in the special circumstances of Brazil, where Rio lost the will to work after it ceded its capital-city status to Brasília, São Paulo is a second city that became a first city. Its infrastructure may be in a ramshackle state. Its crime really is an issue. But like Johannesburg, São Paulo has the vitality and drive that keeps it moving. São Paulo is an authentic metropolis with the racial diversity to prove it with a Japanese and an Arab quarter as well as a Balkan district.

In urban and architectural terms, Brazil is still overshadowed by the remarkable generation that began by creating Rio's Great Corbusian monument: the Ministry of Education. It may have lost the remarkable landmark building skills of Oscar Niemeyer who made Brazilian architecture from the 1940s to the 1960s world famous. The remarkable architectural talent of Lino Bo Bardi, who arrived from Italy in São Paulo after World War II has not yet been overtaken by her successors. But in the shape of the Campana brothers São Paulo has developed its visibility as a centre for creative design.

In urban terms the question that faces it is how to address the inequalities, and the fractured nature of its public services. If it does that it could yet find itself becoming a Tokyo, where prosperity and organization overcame an equally random pattern of dizzyingly rapid growth.

FILLING THE POLITICAL VACUUM

Jeroen Klink

THE NEW BRAZIL

Brazil has finally emerged as an economic powerhouse with a growth rate to match India's and China's, but it is still struggling to find a political underpinning to match its success. These are issues that the country is only just beginning to address.

The development trajectory of the Latin American continent in the 1980s has commonly been interpreted as 'the lost decade', specifically in light of the debt crisis and the subsequent cumbersome structural adjustment programmes. The region suffered a second, perhaps less visible setback in the 1990s, from which it has been trying to recover only recently. While many Latin American countries witnessed an intense socio-economic, technological and regulatory adjustment process associated with shifts in national development models, with often dramatic impacts on cities and metropolitan areas, there was a surprising lack of a solid and transparent institutional and regulatory framework that could guide these transformations in Latin American city regions in a sustainable manner. This institutional vacuum was all the more dramatic considering the continent's relatively urbanized profile. Large city regions and metropolitan areas had often been the spatial nodes of authoritarian, Keynesian-style, and nationally driven strategies aimed at import substitution, industrialization and nation building. As such, challenges at the national and the metropolitan and regional scale – including social exclusion, environmental degradation and overall loss of competitiveness – became increasingly interdependent. As argued by several Latin American urban development scholars, the continent's city regions were entering a new stage of internationalization while historical deficits – in terms of access to basic services and land as well as sustainable and predictable sources of finance – had not been addressed satisfactorily yet, to say the least.[1] As a matter of fact, during a large part of the 1990s, the suspicion was that in many Latin American metropolitan areas socio-spatial disparities had actually grown.[2]

Three Examples: Santiago, Buenos Aires and Bogotá

A few examples serve to illustrate the shift in patterns of urbanization across Latin America.[3] Greater Santiago generates about half of Chile's GDP, while approximately two-thirds of the country's population is concentrated in the city regions of Santiago, Valparaíso and Concepción. Although the Chilean development model has generally been recognized for its achievements in terms of growth and poverty reduction, Santiago has increasingly faced rapid sprawl, reduction of environmental quality, socio-spatial segregation and escalating intra-metropolitan disparities. The perception among the population is one of increasing violence. At the same time, Chile lacks specific institutional structures for its metropolitan areas. In Santiago governance is fragmented over three provinces (one being Santiago itself, which is

ANYTHING GOES

Newcomers to São Paulo demonstrate resilience in making the most out of any urban opportunity, creating a viable micro-economy – homes, shops and even sports centres – beneath one of the city's busiest flyovers.

in turn subdivided in 32 municipalities). In practice, senior level government ends up 'crowding out' local bodies that have relatively little say in the organization and management of inter-municipal services.

Along the same lines, even though Greater Buenos Aires does not exist as a formal political and administrative body as such, its Metropolitan Region, loosely defined as the Autonomous City of Buenos Aires with its surrounding 32 cities, concentrates approximately half of the production and a third of the population of Argentina. In the 1990s, the city region experienced a traumatic process of productive restructuring and de-industrialization. The lack of clear structures for metropolitan governance, as reflected in a complex and overlapping set of responsibilities divided between a strong province, the federated city, peripheral local governments and the institutions of the national government, made it all the more difficult to develop effective strategies to deal with the rapidly growing intra-metropolitan disparities and environmental degradation. Not surprisingly, Greater Buenos Aires witnessed a proliferation of suburban gated communities and metropolitan sprawl during this period.[4]

Greater Bogotá, roughly composed of the central city of 7 million inhabitants and 24 surrounding municipalities, all together generate around 30 per cent of the national GDP and contained one-fifth of Colombia's population in 2003. The opening up of the Colombian trading regime reinforced the region's attractiveness and its role as a national economic powerhouse. By 2010, the city region was expected to have grown from 8 million to 9.6 million inhabitants. However, there is no formal arrangement to deal with the challenges being faced by the region, including increasing levels of pollution of the Bogotá River, the inter-municipal transportation of cargo and people, solid waste disposal and land-use planning in environmentally sensitive areas. Nevertheless, the Regional Roundtable of the Bogotá-Cundinamarca region, which was launched at the beginning of 2002 – involving national government, the state government of Cundinamarca, the city of Bogotá, 116 surrounding municipal administrations and three environmental special purpose districts – proved successful. Its aim was to create an informal multi-stakeholder policy network that was to leverage the effectiveness of a highly fragmented metropolitan system.

The Brazilian Context

The scenario played out in Brazil in the 1990s was no exception to this pattern of socio-economic and territorial restructuring. From the mid-1980s onwards, the highly centralized and authoritarian Brazilian model felt the pressure of democratization and decentralization, which accompanied the collapse of the debt-financed macro-economic expansion and the globalization of production. The severe financial and fiscal crisis of the 1990s represented a shift in the macro-economic and regulatory environment, and led to the opening up of the trade regime, deregulation and privatization, without compensating technological and industrial policies from the federal level.[5]

These transformations set the stage for the increasing influence of the so-called centrifugal forces of the international economy on the Brazilian economy, which were directly mediated by spatial strategies at the state and local level. While the 1988 constitution consolidated a decentralized framework, with more resources and responsibilities for local and state governments, the effect in the deregulated and market-friendly configuration of the 1990s was that Brazilian federal relations became increasingly competitive.[6] City regions and metropolitan areas were key arenas in this process of restructuring of global production systems and regulatory regimes. The industrial sector implemented a strategy of 'concentrated de-concentration',[7] locating some of their activities outside the relatively high-cost metropolitan areas like São Paulo, but not moving too far away from the so-called 'polygon' (formed by the states of Minas, Rio, São Paulo, Rio Grande do Sul, Espírito Santo and Paraná), in order not to lose out from the positive innovation and incubation effects of the larger metropolitan areas.[8] This created a scenario of increased competition among city regions and states in the polygon region.

The institutional and political vacuum in which Brazilian metropolitan areas were operating in the 1990s also affected cities that, at least until then, were considered to be model cases of good urban governance and urban planning in the Latin American context. For example, Curitiba has been widely benchmarked as the sustainable and well-planned city, specifically so in light of its perceived capacity to guide city growth through investments in financially accessible and good quality public transportation, which were also linked to land use and urban planning.[9] Recent developments have shown that this picture does not quite match the reality of Greater Curitiba. The intense process of metropolization, which is reflected in an increasingly dense pattern of functional interdependences between the central city and its outskirts, has in a painfully clear manner revealed the main structural deficiencies of what has been labelled as the Curitiba model. In the metropolitan masterplan, elaborated in 1978 and updated recently, a warning had been issued that development should not occur in the eastern zone of the metropolitan area, in which the environmentally sensitive areas and the watersheds that provide approximately 70 per cent of the urban water supply are concentrated. However, this is exactly where urban growth has occurred. Part of this distorted land-use pattern can be attributed to the subsidies, tax incentives and land grants that had been given by the state and local government to attract industries away from the more expensive locations in the state of São Paulo, as part of a more aggressive local economic development policy. The investments made in 1996 by car manufacturers Audi, Renault and Volkswagen in the city of São José dos Pinhais, a city on the outskirts of Greater Curitiba located close to environmentally sensitive areas, should be directly associated with these policies.

Like so many other Brazilian metropolitan areas, Curitiba has little control over its land market, as reflected by the growth of slums and irregular settlements in both the city and its outskirts. In spite of progressive federal legislation (the 'statute of the city'), which increases the leverage of local governments over land markets, at least in theory, it has not provided a real solution to the dilemma, given that it lacks a built-in mechanism for the coordination of municipal masterplans. Thus, in practice, the bulk of Brazilian metropolitan land markets are guided by a patchwork of localized plans that have been elaborated on the basis of different criteria and methodologies, without incorporating a more strategic view on the sustainable development of the metropolitan areas as a whole.

In that sense, Greater Curitiba is no different than other Brazilian metropolitan areas, where the low end of the real estate market is pushed out to risky, flood-prone and environmentally sensitive areas, reinforcing a vicious cycle of poverty, environmental degradation and socio-spatial exclusion. For instance, in Guaratuba, an environmentally sensitive area where the federal government is investing in slum upgrading, informal and unregulated development grew by 70 per cent in the 1990s. At the same time, Curitiba's highly acclaimed integrated public transportation system has not been able to cope with the rapid growth in inter-municipal journeys between the central city and the metropolitan outskirts. Since the late 1990s, congestion and private car ownership have grown exponentially. According to data collected by the municipality of Curitiba, car ownership in the city grew by 78 per cent between 2000 and 2009.[10]

Seven Big Cities

Nevertheless, even in this relatively adverse macro-institutional environment, social and institutional innovation has occurred in Brazil. The case of the so-called ABC region, seven cities located in the southeastern part of Metropolitan São Paulo, which collectively represent one of Brazil's industrial heartlands (sometimes called the Brazilian Detroit), is paradigmatic. Until the 1990s, this city region was host to the bulk of the country's car production and a substantial part of its petrochemical industries. From the 1990s onwards, it faced the negative consequences of economic restructuring, while lacking an effective framework for collaborative governance. Being a highly politicized region that had participated actively in the process of Brazilian democratization, the region reacted by organizing an innovative institutional response, which mobilized both local stakeholders and the state government. This led to the creation of an inter-municipal consortium in 1991, a Regional Chamber for Participatory Strategic Planning coordinated by the state created in 1998, and an Economic Development Agency established in 1999, with active participation from the private sector. Despite the usual complexities that surround multi-stakeholder participatory planning processes, this more flexible system of governance of variable geographies has been instrumental in mobilizing and articulating a series of regional projects in infrastructure (road systems, sewerage), environmental planning (legislation for watershed protected areas) and economic development (avoiding tax wars, information systems, support policies to small- and medium-sized enterprises). Interestingly enough, this institutional arrangement, which was embedded in the specific socio-historical context of the seven cities of the ABC region that have a common identity, gradually emerged alongside the existing – and largely inoperative – model of the 1970s, which had tried to organize all of the 39 cities of the Metropolitan Region of São Paulo. The success of parallel moves from inside the system illustrates the benefits of a more participatory approach among different stakeholders that have resulted in the creation of effective regional and metropolitan institutions.

The Missing Metropolitan Agenda

Alongside this social and institutional learning that happens 'on the ground', it should be acknowledged that governments in Latin America have increasingly become aware of the interdependence between their metropolitan areas and national welfare. The Brazilian government, for example, created a new framework law on inter-municipal consortia, which significantly strengthened the institutional and organizational capacity of these bodies. Likewise, the federal government in Argentina, in close collaboration with the Inter-American Development Bank, has launched an ambitious programme aimed at the institutional, managerial and organizational strengthening of metropolitan areas across the country. Nevertheless, the Brazilian experience clearly shows that there is an absence of a broader national strategy for metropolitan areas, which could both guide and enable a programme of incentives aimed at the creation of collaborative governance. The paradox is that while the federal government has made substantial progress – in terms of the allocation of financial resources to cities and metropolitan areas – and while the participatory and institutional mechanisms at all levels of government have been strengthened, they have not become the building blocks of a robust metropolitan development agenda for the country as a whole.

Perhaps this is one of the lessons that emerge from the recent Latin American experience. While performing a key role within the national spatial economy – concentrating the bulk of the social deficit and economic opportunities – the intense process of economic, territorial and regulatory restructuring of the last decade has struggled to mobilize multi-scalar strategies which could have resulted in more cohesive and socio-spatially inclusive metropolitan areas at different scales. On the ground, social and institutional innovation is indeed ongoing, but this has not been embedded into broader governance structures that recognize the role of city regions and metropolitan areas within national development policy. Thus, while the spatial Keynesian model of the 1970s, with uniformly established metropolitan institutions as key instruments within national strategies, has gradually faded away, no alternative regime has been put in its place. For Latin America, this 'multi-scalar vacuum' will continue to limit the positive impacts of local innovation at the metropolitan scale.

THE CULTURES OF THE METROPOLIS

Gareth A. Jones

AUTHORITY IN THE FAVELAS

Street life in Latin America reflects the hunger for social structure in a world in which gang culture can have as much impact on the daily lives of the dispossessed as the preconceptions of the official establishment.

Georg Simmel would be both fascinated and alarmed.[1] On the first evening of each month, the streets of Tepito in downtown Mexico City are full with thousands of people moving excitedly in anticipation of seeing and possibly touching La Grande, a life-size statue of the Santa Muerte or saint of death. The pavements are packed with traders offering Santa statuettes – red for love, gold for wealth, black for protection – powders for the devotions, as well as charms and sweets. Walking through the bustling crowd, the sunken sockets of the Santas follow one's progress, the glow from the hundreds of candles giving the moment an eerie feel. For outsiders who think of Tepito as the 'barrio bravo', the archetypal marginal space associated with the *piratería* of fake DVDs and fashion labels, with *fayuca* or contraband from China, child trafficking and drugs, just mingling to get a glimpse of La Grande is exhilarating and nerve-racking. Jostling for space with a heavily tattooed youth who gives every indication of being a hardcore gang member; how long before one sees that he is carrying a baby? These nights mark an unannounced truce between the local gangs, whose members bring their children to see La Grande, placing a cigarette at their babies' lips to cast smoke over the shrine.

La Santa's devotees are identified in the media as drug addicts and dealers, prostitutes, bankrupts and former prisoners, but she also draws trades people, bus drivers, mechanics and government employees. As a 'crisis religion', the Santa Muerte provides the victims of the neo-liberal economy and the escalating violence caused by 'public security' measures with some form of social attachment. The Santa provides the individual in the crowd with one way to make sense of private heartaches, financial worries, and the anxieties that come with families who are trying hold together with 12 million Mexicans in the United States and Canada. These people are what the Mexican writer and critic Carlos Monsiváis once called the city's 'radical optimists'.[2] As he puts it, faced with an urbanism that 'signifies above all else the superabundance of people', a city in which the 'multitude that accosts the multitude imposes itself like a permanent obsession', making the 'urban vitality a relentless grind', the residents avoid the temptation to seek 'the perfection of solitude' and embrace the city as an 'aesthetics of multitude'.

The Place of Religion in Social Life

For the inhabitants of Mexico City, the *chilangos*, read the *porteños* (those from Buenos Aires), the *cariocas* (from or living in Rio de Janeiro), *limenhos* (from Lima) and *los managuas* (from Managua). The scenes are a little different but essentially the

same. In a Maceió *favela* located on a rubbish dump a *mãe-de-santo* (Mother of Saints) receives visitors to divine their life-paths through interpretation of cowrie shells. The old woman has a steady stream of clients, keen to understand their futures but also grateful that believing in something provides the necessary motivations to be 'healthy'. In a *favela* riddled with drug addiction, alcoholism, tuberculosis, dengue fever or 'nerves', this concern with health extends beyond the spiritual.

In São Paulo, religion is also central to the animation of social life. Neo Pentecostalism is the fastest growing religion in Brazil, with 24 million faithful (four times as many as in the United States). The March for Jesus organized by the Renascer em Cristo church recently brought together over 1 million people for a day-long festival of faith. Many of those in attendance are drawn by the messages of hard work, family, moral integrity – disseminated by the Record Network of television and radio channels run by the Igreja Universal do Reino de Deus (Universal Church of the Kingdom of God). Churches with broad denominations have sprung up in prime city sites and disused factories, in elite enclaves and the most recent squatter settlement. Despite the scandals surrounding many churches, the demand for 'faith' seems to exceed supply in today's metropolis.

Religion offers salvation in many forms. Among Latin America's numerous gangs, the 80,000 or more members of the *maras* in San Salvador or Guatemala City, or the *parche* in Bogotá and *malandros* in Caracas, conversion to Protestantism is one of the few ways to leave your *jombois* (home boys), and avoid the 'exit beatings' dished out to people requesting to become *calmado* (quiet one). Even then the decision is not taken lightly. In many cities gangs are the principal form of social engagement among young people. Members congregate on vacant plots or street corners, swapping stories, drinking, dealing drugs, discussing the latest styles of dress that might identify them as punk, hip-hop crew or *skatos*. Young people even in the most pressed of circumstances, such as surviving on the streets of Mexico, are acutely aware of their dress, bodily appearance and smell.

Youth and City Governance

The relations of gangs and groups of young people with community leaders, the police and rival gangs define the feeling of the *barrio* (neighbourhood). Tagging and graffiti mark the territorial limits, often drawing from 'scripts' through American and Japanese spray styles of cartoons and popular imagery, and give neighbourhoods particular aesthetics. Music plays an important role. Rio's soundscape gives assurance or warning to the initiated, an audio signal of which *Comando* controls the *favela*. The *baile* funk dance nights attract people from across the city, across class and 'race' divides, but limits are taken seriously. A *baile* in a Comando Vermelho *favela* is not the same as one overseen by Amigos dos Amigos, and the choice is either/or.

Gangs are deemed anti-social by politicians and the media, but to their members they are hyper social. In dense neighbourhoods there can be few secrets. Gangs know of the domestic violence, the adultery and alcoholism: they learn of the debtors and neighbours with disputes over noise, thefts or property lines. Although complicit in many of these problems the boss or gang leader is also the means of conflict resolution. In Rocinha, the archetypical *favela* holding on to a Rio hillside, the local drug gangs mediate disputes, sometimes working with NGOs. The Balcão de Direitos programme which organized f*avelados* to apply for registration papers involved the Rio Law School and the agreement of the major gangs. NGOs such as Sou da Paz and Viva Rio have worked with young people and gangs to reduce violence and the trade in guns. Though not always fair, people have no reason to believe that a gang's verdict will be any less just than a judge's, and it will be arrived at more quickly and compliance is recommended. In Rio it costs less to have someone killed than to get access to an illegal hook up to the electricity supply. Summary justice can be ruthless but gangs may impose norms to prevent *favelados* resorting to individual violence.

Public confidence in politicians, planners or the police is rarely very high, while the infidelities of area bosses and gang leaders may be condoned. As the saying goes, *ele rouba mas faz* (he steals but he gets things done). Neighbourhood leaders can offer many things – reciprocity, but also the organization of work programmes for drainage, water or the construction of a kindergarten, all of which require people to participate in collective action, known in different parts of Latin America as *faena*, *minga* or *rondas*. In Buenos Aires the block organizers, the *manzaneras* and *punteros*, create dense local networks often relying on fictive kinship to bond people to their community, and a party or politician. Patron-clientelism is a dirty word among political scientists and international agency 'experts', but on the streets it looks a lot like personalized mediation and problem-solving.

The Impact of Economic Crisis

Social and economic deprivation begets certain forms of social engagement. In Lima, the crisis of the 1980s motivated community groups to organize soup kitchens. By 1986 there were over 800 and by the late 1990s almost 10,000 providing half a million meals each day, as well as serving as meeting points to share childcare, medication and exchange clothes. With the support of the Catholic Church the committees drew the attention of the municipality that used the kitchens to distribute free milk to children through the Vaso de Leche (glass of milk) programme. One million children received milk through a committee structure involving almost 100,000 people. Threats to cut the Vaso budget brought widespread protests, especially from women, and obliged the government to back down. In 2010 a modified programme remains at the centre of public policy.

Argentina's repeated economic crises have prompted the formation of mutual solidarity and direct action groups. The best known are the *piqueteros*, organized groups of initially the unemployed and later with support from trade unions that blocked roads (*piquets*), charging a fee for safe passage. In 2003 there were over 5,000 *piquets* with maybe 360,000 members in the greater Buenos Aires area. The solidarity of the *piquet* was an intimidation to travellers and challenge to the state's legitimacy to manage the city. More benign, *clubes de trueque* (barter clubs) and *empresas recuperadas* (worker-occupied enterprises) sprang up to occupy streets, warehouses and factories. New union groups such as the Union of Seamstress Workers formed to protest at labour abuses in Buenos Aires' nearly 400 clandestine textile shops and urged the removal of the 100,000 undocumented immigrants from Bolivia, Paraguay and Peru. These diasporic groups, however, have held on and form substantial parts of areas such as the Bajo Flores and Villa 31.

The Formation of New Settlements

Opportunities to move to new areas are taken: extended families or groups of friends of co-nationals build houses in new settlements, often on the same plot. Elsewhere, in São Paulo for example, the Movimento dos Trabalhadores Sem Teto has used land occupations to extend poor people's access to land and housing. In 2003 the MTST mobilized 4,000 families to occupy land owned by Volkswagen. In Lima, around the fringes of Villa El Salvador, itself formed by a series of land invasions dating from the late 1960s and 1970s, and now a settlement with over 400,000 inhabitants, 'cooperative groups' are using the agrarian law to gain plots on the desert and sand dunes. At present just a series of reed mat houses, the community knows that the agrarian law affords them some protection from eviction.

Over time, the new area of Villa El Salvador will become a consolidated vibrant settlement. Established areas are full of billboards and vans with loudspeakers announcing the latest consumer items, and credit terms. The Avon ladies always do a good trade. There are small yards selling wood and concrete blocks, and stores selling kerosene, sewing workshops and plenty of mechanics. The settlement is host to 12,000 small- and medium-sized enterprises. There is no library that I know of but there are impromptu cinemas showing the latest films with rigged up screens and shaky DVD quality. With all this enterprise amid unemployment – 30 per cent of the district's population is permanently unemployed and 54 per cent have family incomes insufficient to cover basic needs – but with the police absent or bought off, crime is high. The residents of sub-districts such as Pachacámac have organized vigilante groups using either paid security guards or neighbour rota. In Lima there were over 700 reported cases of 'vigilante justice' in 2004, many in squatter settlements, and often meted out against the young people regarded as delinquents or gangs. In Villa El Salvador, 70 per cent of inhabitants are under 25 years old, but fewer than 15 per cent have access to some form of higher or technical education.

Alternative Finance Schemes

Sadly, funerals are an important feature of social life of cities with devotions to the dead bringing together family, neighbours and community leaders for days of mourning. Families may save in small groups, known as *cadenas de ahorro* (chain savings), for the funerals, costs of educating children or house construction. Until the 1990s, most savings clubs relied on circulating funds within the community. But with growing numbers of international migrants, the clubs have adapted to receive and circulate foreign remittances. Latin America may receive as much as US$70 billion (over €51 billion) via international remittances, according to the OECD. Quito, Guayaquil and Cuenca are built in large part with funds from the estimated 1 million Ecuadorians living abroad, in Europe and the United States. The picture is similar in Bogotá, Lima, San Salvador, and Tegucigalpa: the 20 million or so Latin Americans living abroad are connected by mobile phones, social networking sites, home-town associations, and – above all – by the offices of money-sending organizations like Western Union and MoneyGram.

Shifts in the 'money economy' have brought other ways of dealing with what Simmel would perceive as the punctuality, calculability and exactness of metropolitan life. A few savings clubs have joined with micro-finance organizations, some affiliated with larger banks or with NGOs. In Lima the largest is Mibanco, which specializes in small loans to micro-entrepreneurs; it acquired about 125,000 clients per annum in recent years. In Buenos Aires Progesar also gives small loans to members with limited formal savings histories, undercutting the major banks' and moneylenders' interest rates. The loans are usually devoted to the establishment of small shops or kiosks, selling everything from soft drinks to tins of tuna, toilet paper and candles. Inventory is limited, profits are small with so many competitors selling the same items, but risks are as low as possible.

The Importance of Affiliations

Contemporary social life is marked on the urban landscape. Driving through

Barranquilla's industrial and squatter areas en route to the airport, the view is punctuated by an enormous concrete stadium. Walking through Leblon in Rio in the aftermath of Flamengo beating Corinthians or near La Bombonera following a Boca Juniors victory over River Plate shows people spilling out of bars, impromptu meetings, the crowds on the pavement engaging with the shouts and horns of passing cars. The better off are wearing their authentic shirts, while others wear replicas. Car park attendants and vendors paint their faces to display team loyalty or to drum up a little extra business from the crowd. The rituals and chanting of songs give football a religious feel, just as well the Estádio São Januário in Rio has a church inside.

Emotions can get out of hand. The *tribus* and *barra brava* (supporter clubs) draw the attention of riot police and mounted patrols. Fights erupt inside and outside stadiums, leaving the injured nursing knife wounds or sometimes even dead. But organization is here too. The *barra* are linked to the clubs. Clubs anchor urban identities and connect neighbourhoods with social histories. Identifying with one team or another can mark people as local or an outsider, might indicate their political affiliation or class position – the Racing Club stadium in the working class area of Avalleneda in Buenos Aires is called the Estadio Presidente Peron. In Argentina, Brazil and Mexico which football clubs one supports might even be a reference to one's sexuality.

It is a dream of many policy makers to 'capture' and 'channel' all this social vitality to improve policy formulation, urban design and efficiency. Politicians in many cities recognize that people produce the city, its feel and excitement, and their reactions to the anxiety and fear of urban life will determine their sense of being 'citizens' or 'strangers'. As the experience of participatory budgets, now involving upwards of 2,500 city and district authorities in Latin America, and governance projects attest, 'city hall' can work with social complexity. Programmes such as 'Bogotá, cómo vamos' and the Compromiso Ciudadano movement in Medellín deserve recognition for opening dialogue with different urban actors. Such moves inform 'spheres' where people voice opinions in public, in conversations with neighbours or in the queues for the TransMilenio and Via Expresa. Cold infrastructure becomes animated.

Simmel considered how people would cope with the overstimulation of the metropolis. Presented with the fast pace of city life, the relentless drive of the economy and bombarded by media imagery and new technologies, he thought people's instinct would be to shut themselves off, to adopt a blasé attitude. Impulse and originality he feared would give way to order in which people would be 'cogs' in an urban capitalist machine. Scope for individualism would be limited, associational life would be functional. In Latin America we can still sense the dramatic variability of social life, the capacity for everyday life to hold on to the quality of contingency, and connection. Social form has changed in recent decades, not least as people have developed a broad range of strategies to respond to crises of various origins and effects. These responses range from the intimate and private to the public and occasionally extravagant revelations of anxiety, anger and positive proposal. Rallies and demonstrations involving hundreds of thousands are rarer than they once were and *ser radical* (being radical) is no longer a badge of pride. To the lament of some commentators, Superbarrio has given way to the Santa Muerte. But as Simmel reminded us at the start of the twentieth century, the task is not to complain or condone but to understand. At the start of the twenty-first century, the cultures of the metropolis need to be understood as spaces in which impulse and originality are retained.

LOOKING FOR A SHARED IDENTITY

José de Souza Martins

A SENSE OF BELONGING

The growth of cities in Latin America reflects the tension between city and nation-state. Brazil, like the United States or Mexico, grew from both voluntary and forced migration; first from Europe and Africa, then from the Middle East and Asia. Cohesion depends on building a shared identity for all of these migrants.

The city of São Paulo and its Metropolitan Region form without a doubt a multicultural whole. The list of cultural diversities that characterizes them is extensive and complex, which is not only due to waves of foreign immigration since 1870, but is also a result of the diversity that characterized this immigration.

The most significant of them, the immigration of Italians, was not actually 'Italian' per se. Theirs did not constitute an influx of tens of thousands of immigrants coming from Italy proper. They came from a newly unified Italy, a new state and nation, while they originated from many political realities, and hailed from regional cultures that formed the map of Italian diversity, unified by the *Risorgimento* in the course of the nineteenth century. They arrived in São Paulo speaking their regional dialects, bringing local customs and traditions with them. In some of the city's neighbourhoods people still speak Portuguese with a Neapolitan, Calabrian, Venetian or Mantuan accent.

They became 'Italians' in Brazil, through their children who went to Italian schools to learn their parents' native language. São Paulo became a city characterized by cultural duplications, where people would speak their mother tongue, whichever it was, at home, and speak Portuguese with a strong foreign accent on the streets. It is no coincidence, then, that the engineer Alexandre Marcondes Machado invented an ironic Italian-Paulistano dialect in his literary work, published under the pseudonym Juó Bananère, and that his first book, *La Divina Increnca*, published in 1915 – a parody on Dante's *Divine Comedy* – imagined multiculturalism as confusion instead of an encounter.

Since the beginning of the twentieth century, Portuguese with a foreign accent mixed with foreign words has been the language of comedy in the work of different authors in São Paulo. This was not meant to belittle the immigrants, but to provide an external point of view that could highlight, in a critical way, the municipal and political absurdities of the city, which was being transformed through the influx of money from the coffee export: money that would be multiplied in the financial world, in industry and in trade. This new money also changed social relations, especially social differences, as it took away prejudices and in a short time inverted relations of dominance and power.

In his book, Bananère traces a portrait of intense sounds, of the daily mentality of the population of São Paulo in the 1920s and 1930s, their ways of recognizing the city and living the contradictions of life. Immigrants didn't really become Brazilian until

AN IDENTITY FOR THE CITY

São Paulo established itself in a very brief period as a city that is able to drive Brazil as a nation in which a cosmopolitan culture can develop and thrive. It has become home to cultures from around the world, from Italy to Japan, and has created a very specific new voice for all of them.

the time they had grandchildren, through a process of slow migration to the culture of the society they had adopted – which itself was not a monolithic culture either, but a patchwork of contributions from various foreign immigrants, including Italian regional cultures. The work of an Italian descendant – João Rubinato – illustrates this. He made a move in the opposite direction of Bananère's, by adopting a Brazilian pseudonym: Adoniran Barbosa. His musical and popular compositions talk – equally ironically as Bananère– about the life of simple people and are written in a residual Brazilian language, mixed with traces of the Italian accent of the working-class neighbourhoods of São Paulo. Many people believe that this was a made-up language, like in Bananère's book. However, in reality Rubinato spoke exactly like that. When dealing with matters of daily life in the city, as in 'Saudosa Maloca' and 'Trem das Onze', he transformed the accent into a disguised ironic language that tells of the small daily dramas of workers and drunks, just like himself.

This diversity had countless other important manifestations that showed a kind of recognition and respect for multiculturalism, which separated the new generations of children from the generation of their parents (which involved just one or two cultures). Such was the case with a successful radio programme in the 1940s, the *Escolinha of Nhô Totico*. Nhô Totico was the nickname of Vital Fernandes da Silva, who was born in the countryside near São Paulo from an Italian mother and a Brazilian father from Bahia. He had a multicultural background as he was born into and educated in a third culture, the *caipira* culture, which was formed by old descendants of Indians and whites. In his radio school, Nhô Totico performed all the voices of its different characters: the Brazilian professor, as well as the Italian, Spanish, Syrian, Portuguese and Japanese students. He transformed the diversity of origins, so characteristic of São Paulo at that time, into a pluralist panel unified by the school and by the Brazilian teacher, turning it into an invitation to overcome cultural differences through education.

Later in the 1950s, the vast and intense stream of immigrants from northeastern Brazil, expelled by the crisis in sugarcane farming caused by episodes of drought, and attracted by the new industrialization developed by the automobile industry, made the culture of São Paulo even more diverse. Not only by the way they spoke, but also because of their kitchen and customs, the *Nordestinos* from northeastern Brazil added to the São Paulo culture specific traces of their own. Like there are typically Italian, Spanish, Arab, German, Jewish, Eastern, Russian and Ukrainian neighbourhoods, there are also typically *Nordestino* neighbourhoods in São Paulo. In recent decades Latin American immigration has added new colours to the city, particularly through immigration of Bolivians. This multiculturalism is evident to any tourist or local resident who samples the diverse culinary cultures available in São Paulo's restaurants.

The same can be said regarding its religious diversity, with buildings of worship ranging from synagogues to mosques, from Protestant and Evangelical temples to a great diversity of Catholic churches organized around different devotions which are all expressions of cultural diversity. You can follow a mass with Gregorian singing in the church of São Bento, or a popular mass in the shrine of Santo Amaro, an Orthodox mass in Vila Mariana, a Protestant worship in the city centre, a Muslim celebration on the Avenue of the State, a Jewish worship in one of the several synagogues, a session of the Pentecostal cult in a church in Vila Pompéia or in the Baixada do Glicério, a Protestant worship with the sound of balalaikas in a church of Russian immigrants in Vila Prudente, or even a Protestant worship in a Korean church from Luz.

However, São Paulo is multicultural not because it was historically open to diversity and tolerance. On the contrary, it carries the weight of two kinds of slavery in its history, together with the restrictions and prohibitions that all forms of slavery eventually resulted in. First, indigenous slavery, which was formally terminated in the early-eighteenth century, and subsequently black slavery, which was abolished in 1888. In a city with few slaves, one would anticipate slavery to end in several ways. However, it happened not as the result of a generous commitment to the idea of freedom and equality, but because slavery was an obstacle for a society hungry for cheap labour, which had already established a regular flow of immigrants and free workers that could fulfil its demands. In economic terms, slavery was a disadvantage.

Influences from those periods of slavery in the language remain in culinary and religious traditions and in other customs. There are even remnants of hybridizations from the time of indigenous slavery. Saci Pererê for instance is a mythical being of indigenous origin, which in its African version appears as a black boy with only one leg. As a regular appearance in children stories as a naughty character, he still inhabits children's imagination. His original name, Saci Pererê, is indigenous. He became a black character in the eighteenth century, when indigenous slavery was abolished and the flow of black slaves to São Paulo increased, especially to the sugar cane plantations that flourished within the Capitania, the state of São Paulo.

Studies by Renato da Silva Queiroz show the Saci Pererê was a mythical figure related to limits and boundaries, and therefore he usually appears in fences. In the eighteenth century he had crossed the boundaries and passed on to the side of the new subordinates, the black slaves, taking on their skin colour and identity while continuing to be an indigenous being in a society with social stratification, with more or less rigid boundaries between races, ethnicities and social groups. This cultural transgression of Saci Pererê was the first highly symbolic demonstration of adaptive multiculturalism in the region of São Paulo.

It is not strange that, at that time, the abbot of São Bento paid a black slave from his order, a magician, to remove the *banzo* (a mortal apathy caused by a longing for Africa) from his slaves. This means that a representative member of an emblematic Catholic order turned to voodooism to have his slaves freed from curses and spells. This is a demonstration of diversity and multiculturalism that do not converge, as if society was composed of a structure of specific and distinct cultural layers, each with its own logic, values and reach. Multiculturalism was, and somehow still is, experienced as a way of life in which people move through different cultures daily, depending on the roles they play in a fragmented life of slow and difficult convergences. This is something that persists in practices such as the attendance at shrines of *Umbanda,* and some people's adhesion to *Candomblé* and to traditions of African and black religious orientation, while at the same time moving in entirely different cultural and religious circles.

It is in religion and religiosity, indeed, where we find the most relevant signs of original traditions' survival, which is a very typical Paulistano way of continuing to be what one once was, rather than ceasing to be what one is. That is what makes São Paulo peculiar and multicultural. Not because it accepts the cultural diversity of those who arrive in it without conflict, but mainly because it ensures each example of diversity is allowed to be what it has always been, while the fact of their daily coexistence is embraced and leads to new forms and innovations.

It is therefore not strange to find a Japanese descendant singing Italian *tarantelas* in a canteen in Bras, still an Italian neighbourhood, or a black man from Bexiga spilling his sins into a priest's ear in Calabrian during confession. Or to have a Frenchman, such as the sociologist Roger Bastide, who is of Protestant and Calvinist origins, dive into African cultures so deeply that one could say that being black is not based on the colour of one's skin but on the structure of how one dreams. These are examples of how São Paulo's multiculturalism is, essentially, an invitation to continue to be what it always was, and to become someone new and different. It is a call for cultural creativity and for a free and constant move between different cultural standards.

In that sense, the multiculturalism of São Paulo and its surroundings can be better understood as a transitive multiculturalism, which makes it very different from

EXPLODING SÃO PAULO

In the period of its most rapid growth, São Paulo depended on attracting migrants from outside the country, and the opportunity it offered them in shaping the city's identity, as much as bringing in Brazilians from the rest of the country.

other multicultural metropolises that are characterized by the collage of a certain static diversity of cultures. In such cases, we are dealing with a multiculturalism of confinement, where diversity is accepted as an aggregation of cultural differences and not as a possible mode of communication and transit between differences. With this, I am not saying that multiculturalism should purely be seen as a transformative phenomenon, but that diversity can be considered from two opposing cultural angles.

Despite its historical references tending to confinement, the transitive multiculturalism of São Paulo ended up being imposed by the complex need for a multicultural transit in a city that was re-created in an urban, architectural sense and in terms of its population at least thrice in modern times: in the 1880s, 1910s and 1960s. These were culturally cataclysmic moments that added new characters to the scene, and, at the same time, cancelled out old conspiracies.

The rigidity of cultural traditions and customs softened to allow the new and reciprocal adaptation of the former residents and welcome the new ones. However, it would be wrong to say that Paulistanos are unconditionally open to multiculturalism. They are in relation to aspects of everyday life, in areas where plurality is inevitable, not failing to recognize that this plurality of coexistence is largely responsible for the breaking down of previous identities and the dilution of possible cultural resistance to change and adaptation. Simultaneously, they are not when it comes to aspects of their private life, family and community, where they will take care for certain elements not to become mixed up in a pluralistic re-socialization. As is the case of marriages in some of the cultures that persist in São Paulo, such as Japanese and Korean, which are reasonably protected from the outside, especially when they involve modes of behaviour between younger and older generations. More often though, these obstructions diminish over time, which is what characterizes the transitivity to which I refer, and there is a meaningful balance between maintaining the essential elements of the cultures of origin and a complete assimilation of what does not conflict with them or even complements them.

WORLDS SET APART

Teresa Caldeira

UGLY REALITY

The tension between São Paulo's economic success, its lack of investment in infrastructure, and its inability to control development has created a city at the limits of survival, whose very success could form a threat to its future.

One of the most iconic views of contemporary São Paulo, commonly used in international publications, is a picture in Morumbi showing the *favela* Paraisópolis on one side of a wall and a luxury building with tennis courts and one swimming pool per balcony on the other (see pp. 172–3). However, the scholarly literature on the city and several of its main instruments of urban policy insist on another image: one that contrasts a rich and well-equipped centre with a poor and precarious periphery. According to this view, the city is made not only of opposed social and spatial worlds but also of clear distances between them. Since these imaginaries are contradictory – one pointing to the obscene neighbouring of poverty and wealth and another to a great distance between them – can both represent the city? If so, how well?

Undoubtedly, São Paulo has always been a city marked by sharp social inequalities. However, in the last few decades, the multiple meanings of inequality, the quality of urban space, and the distribution of social groups across the city have changed considerably. The peripheries have improved and some of the physical inequalities between spaces have been reduced as the peripheries have improved. Yet the city that no longer believes in progress – as it did during the second half of the twentieth century – and where violence and fear came to occupy centre stage in citizens' lives, is now a city in which the markers setting social worlds apart are carefully and emphatically drawn. It is also a city in which the public space abandoned by most is reinvented as a space of contestation literally inscribed on its walls.

São Paulo is a complex city that will not be captured by simplistic dual models: neither of the proximity nor of the distance of its opposed social groups. Together, both pictures represent the city. In isolation, neither can capture the pattern of spatial and social inequality that structures the metropolis today. These images are the result of two historical processes that have now coalesced and their material expressions are superimposed in the spaces of the city. The view of the rich centre versus the poor periphery corresponds with the pattern of urbanization consolidated around the 1940s that dominated the city up to the 1980s. During this period, São Paulo's urbanized area expanded dramatically due to the spread of auto-construction. Workers moved to the city by the millions and settled in non-urbanized areas on the outskirts. They bought cheap plots of land in areas without infrastructure and spent decades of savings and family work to build and improve their dream houses. In São Paulo, as elsewhere in Brazil and in the developing world, workers have always

understood that illegality and precariousness are the conditions under which they become property owners and inhabit the modern city. The middle and upper classes remained in the centre and benefited from good infrastructure and services, as well as regularized and subsidized access to land. Thus, metropolitan regions have been marked by a dichotomy between the 'legal city', the centre inhabited by the upper classes, and the precarious peripheries.

However, since the 1970s this neat separation started to be transformed by processes affecting both the centre and the periphery. One of the main sources was the organization of social movements by residents of the peripheries. These urban activists, the majority of them women, were new property owners who realized that political organization was the only way to force city authorities to extend urban infrastructure and services to their neighbourhoods. These social movements contributed significantly to the democratization process and a new concept of citizenship. They also provoked a significant transformation in the urban environment of the peripheries. The state administrators responded to their demands and the city of São Paulo, among many others in Brazil, borrowed heavily to invest in urban infrastructure. As a consequence, the peripheries substantially improved road access, as well as sewerage, sanitation and electricity. These improvements sharply reduced infant mortality rates. As a result many neighbourhoods in the peripheries that began as 'bush' just a few decades ago have been completely urbanized. They have also been connected to networks of commerce and expanded forms of consumption. Although the urban social movements started to diminish in the 1990s, São Paulo remains highly organized. NGOs and associations of all forms, from religious to artistic – not to mention criminal – are everywhere. These heterogeneous associations signify the consolidation of democracy and the civic engagement of citizens.

A second process that transformed the centre-periphery pattern started in the centre. Beginning in the 1970s, wealth steadily moved away. On the one hand, a new business area was formed in the southwestern zone of the city along the Pinheiros River, which today concentrates high-end office complexes, shopping centres, media headquarters, hotels and new cultural centres. On the other, some of the middle and upper classes began to retreat from the centre and its public space. Fear of violent crime – which grew from the mid-1980s to the late 1990s – was their main justification for migration by the hundreds of thousands. Search for new lifestyles and modes of distinction combined to create a new aesthetics of security. These wealthy groups built fortified enclaves for home, leisure and work in areas where only the poor had lived before and from where they were not entirely expelled, as in the case of Paraisópolis. Thus, the dramatic proximity of wealth and poverty is a recent phenomenon caused by the voluntary displacement of the upper classes.

Although the image of the *favela* side-by-side with luxury apartments outside the centre captures a recent configuration of social inequality in São Paulo, it misses important factors. *Favelas* are not the type of housing in which the majority of São Paulo's poor live, and the heterogeneous peripheries cannot be described by the term *favela*. What distinguishes these is homeownership. Although there are many conditions of illegality and irregularity, the majority have bought the land on which they built their houses and have claims to ownership. *Favela* residents also own their homes, but not the land, which has typically been invaded. Moreover, the increase in homeownership in the municipality of São Paulo from 19 per cent in 1920 to 69 per cent in 2000 is due to high rates in the peripheries rather than in the central wealthy districts.[1] In many of the poorest neighbourhoods, it is more than 80 per cent.[2] Approximately 10 per cent of São Paulo's population lives in *favelas*,[3] while Rio de Janeiro and a few other Brazilian cities have an exceptionally high percentage of *favela* residents. Yet, if the view of the centre distant from the periphery misses the new developments that have brought people from radically different social conditions to live side by side, the picture that features this proximity misses the complexity of the peripheries and their significant urban improvement and incorporation into the consumption market.

Increased violent crime and fear have also provoked dramatic changes in the space and quality of everyday life across the city since the mid-1980s. The circulation of fear and discourses about violence that have exacerbated it together created new physical landscapes as well as new idioms under which polarized and dualistic and simplistic representations of inequality are framed.

Violent crime increased substantially from the mid-1980s to the late 1990s. With an overall annual murder rate of more than 60 per 100,000 people in the late 1990s, São Paulo became one of the most violent cities in the world. However, violence is distributed unevenly. Many of the neighbourhoods in the peripheries had a murder rate of more than 110 per 100,000 people, compared with less than 5 in the city's central districts. The main victims of murder are young men, especially black. Moreover, most of the outrageously high number of cases of police abuse and killings happen in the peripheries. In the 2000s, violent crime rates decreased from 57.3 per 100,000 people in 2000 to 11.3 in 2009, which includes decreases in the peripheries.[4] The distribution of violent crime continues to be unevenly distributed throughout the city and especially throughout the peripheries, which have also been transformed by the presence of organized crime and its main institution in São Paulo, the PCC (Primeiro Comando da Capital).

In spite of the decrease in homicide rates, the city still seems full of the chaotic feelings associated with the spread of random violence, which has been a common topic of conversation since the 1980s.[5] Amid the chaotic feelings associated with the spread of random violence people talk. Contrary to the experience of crime, which disrupts meaning and disorders the world, the talk of crime symbolically reorders it by trying to re-establish a static picture of the world, which is expressed in simplistic terms and clear-cut oppositional categories, the most important of which are good and evil. Such reductions and caricatures are central mechanisms associated with the talk of crime. Like other everyday practices dealing with violence, crime stories try to recreate a stable map for a world that has been shaken. These narratives impose partitions, build up walls, establish distances, segregate, impose prohibitions, and restrict movements. In short, they simplify and enclose the world, elaborating prejudices and eliminating ambiguities.

Fear and the talk of crime also organize the urban landscape and public space, generating new forms of spatial segregation and social discrimination. Their most emblematic form is the fortified enclave. These are privatized, enclosed and monitored spaces for residence, consumption, leisure and work structured by the discourse of security. They can be shopping centres, office complexes, residential gated communities and edge cities. They depend on private guards and high-tech security for protection and for enforcing exclusionary practices that guarantee their social exclusivity. They reproduce inequality both as a value and as a social fact. They treat what is enclosed and private as a form of distinction. As this logic becomes dominant, it spreads throughout the city. Walls are now everywhere, even in the most

Swimming pools that overlook streets with no sewers.

remote areas of the peripheries, not only to protect from crime, but also to distinguish neighbours from each other and express claims of social belonging.

It is in this context of simplifications and stereotypical interpretations anchored in the fear of crime that the heterogeneous peripheries of São Paulo started to be called *favelas*, a process that obscures their significant urban and social improvements. The tendency to homogenize the conditions and spaces of poverty and to identify them with their worst configurations is now widespread. It is found in several recent Brazilian films that make poverty and *favela*, blackness and violent crime coincide. The iconic example is *City of God*. It is also the procedure Mike Davis uses in *Planet of Slums,* to reduce the most diverse urban housing conditions of the poor worldwide to a single symbol of the worst: the slum.

This tendency is also reproduced by residents of the periphery themselves. In important ways, São Paulo's rap music elaborates a dichotomy between there and here and the denunciation of the inequality that exists between them. Rap articulates the experience of young men in contemporary peripheries growing up in a context of high rates of violence and few chances for inclusion in the formal markets. Hip-hop wants to save their lives and contain violence. By portraying the conditions of the poor in the peripheries, and critically incorporating the prejudices usually voiced against their young and black residents, rappers articulate a powerful social critique. They denounce racism, express an explicit class antagonism, and create a style of confrontation that leaves very little space for tolerance and negotiation. Their raps establish a non-bridgeable and non-negotiable distance between rich and poor, white and black, the centre and the periphery, and articulate a position of enclosure. They think of the periphery as a world apart, something similar to the American ghetto, an imaginary that has never been used before in Brazil in relation to the peripheries, whose residents have always considered themselves unprivileged but nevertheless an integral part of the whole city. As one of the most famous rap groups, the Racionais MC's, put it in the rap 'Da Ponte pra cá' ('On this side of the bridge'):

> *in the party with us you don't go*
> *We here, you there; each one in his place*
> *Did you get it?*
> *If life is like this, am I to blame?*
> *The world is different on this side of the bridge.*

As rappers' followers reflect on the conditions of life on the outskirts of the city, they transform the quite diverse peripheries into a symbol: a *periferia*. As this new symbol, the periphery is homogenized to represent the worst social inequalities and violence. This transformed space of despair contrasts sharply with the image of improvement and mobility that dominated its representation from the 1940s to the 1990s. It is also sometimes called *favela*, not to describe the peripheries but to refer to its poor conditions that are now re-signified to represent and denounce poverty in general.

The construction of clear and non-negotiable social separations, the circulation of imaginaries of despair, the construction of leftover spaces, and the use of stereotypical symbols to represent opposed social worlds is nowadays found on both sides of Brazilian society. Rappers' construction of self-enclosure is paralleled by upper-class practices of enclosure. Dichotomization, simplification and intolerance structure the imaginaries on both sides.

Fear, the talk of crime, and the adoption of walls and separations all transform the character of public space. Privatization, enclosures, policing of boundaries and distancing devices create a fragmented public space in which inequality is an organizing value. Even so, this leftover public space has not remained empty or unmarked. In São Paulo, in addition to walls and fences, graffiti and *pixaçãos* (a form of tagging typical of São Paulo, using calligraphy in straight lines and black ink) proliferate on almost every street. In fact, with the success of the Cidade Limpa (Clean City) law the removal of outdoor and control of commercial signage, *pixaçãos* became one of the types of signs most homogeneously distributed throughout the city, making uniform the most diverse spaces, in whatever direction one moves. These public inscriptions are usurpations that recreate a public domain in a city privatized by walls. Graffiti and *pixação* reclaim the streets, the facades and the walls as spaces of communication and contestation instead of separation. Most graffiti artists and especially *pixadores* are young men from the peripheries. Through their inscriptions, they transgress, ignore boundaries, and appropriate spaces to mark their discrimination. Obviously, many interpret these appropriations as vandalism, crime, and proof of the deterioration of the public space.

Although both graffiti and *pixação* have similar roots, they constitute different types of intervention in public space. Graffiti are large and coloured murals, frequently on large public surfaces such as viaducts and retaining walls. They are accepted as a type of public art, frequently authorized by the city, and occasionally sponsored by private institutions. Several graffiti artists from São Paulo are known internationally, and a few sell their art in private galleries for high prices.

But if graffiti can be assimilated into the imaginary of art and beauty, *pixação* has remained much more transgressive. It is conceived by its practitioners as an anarchic intervention and as a radical urban sport, an urban alpinism. *Pixadores* inscribe the most impossible of spaces, such as the top of buildings climbed from the outside, and are never sponsored by City Hall. Instead, they are targets of police harassment and the general population's disdain, who think that they deteriorate and deface, not improve, public space. For *pixadores*, though, their intervention signals the character of a public with few other forms of belonging. With *pixação* and graffiti, those who have been kept outside of the dominant cultural systems master writing and painting in the same way that rappers master rhyming. They invent new styles, spreading signs of their transgressions and powerfully transforming the character of public space.

Together, walls, fences, fortified enclaves, raps, graffiti and *pixaçãos* configure public space with unmistakable signs of social inequality and social tension. When the city was growing and violence was not an issue, the imagination that dominated the city was one of social mobility, improvement, expansion and incorporation. Distances embodied spatially and socially were relatively unmarked symbolically. They had to remain fluid to anchor the strong belief in social mobility. Nowadays, inequalities and differences are prominently produced and are rarely left unmarked. Exaggerated and simplified, they mask processes of transformation and of improvement, and inevitably amplify the tension among social groups. Inequality has become naturalized, the taken-for-granted of everyday life, the matter of social communication, even while it is denounced by unexpected interventions. Therefore, it is the tense and multi-layered production and contestation of inequality that we should look at to capture both the city's predicament and its vitality.

THE MIRAGE AND ITS LIMITS

Raul Juste Lores

THE ANONYMOUS CITY

For such a successful city, São Paulo has been curiously unable to produce an image of itself that provides a positive representation of the city to the outside world. There are no architectural icons or place-specific images that characterize the city, except the negative and generic ones of pollution and lawless *favelas*.

Every Friday afternoon, an insane race begins for millions of Paulistanos. Who manages to escape São Paulo first? The city's fugitives know they will face miles of congestion, that it will take up to four hours in a car to make a 150 kilometre (91 mile) journey, and that the same punishment awaits them on their Sunday return. Yet this breathless race is repeated every weekend and on national holidays, accompanied by bringing traffic in over 220 km (133 miles) of the city's streets to a halt.

São Paulo's biggest challenge is invisible, but it is both the cause and effect of its most renowned problems: security and traffic. This challenge is the feeling of being in an urban prison and the need to escape it. Residents complain about it daily, and even those who love the city say 'São Paulo is hopeless'. But how can such a young city, which only became important in the second half of the twentieth century, now be seen as an incorrigible old hand?

In this era of global competition, in which cities want to impress investors and tourists and recruit talented nomads and resources, São Paulo does not present an image of modernity. Missing are Shanghai's Maglev, Dubai's new skyline and Tokyo's high-speed trains. Old and insufficient infrastructure is everywhere: 60 km (35 miles) of metro lines compared with 200 km (121 miles) in Mexico City; hours-long connections between the airport and city centre that depend on taxis; and rivers that are dead and that stink, despite decades of investment to clean them.

Trying to assess where São Paulo went wrong or to identify solutions involves confronting questions that range from a lack of mobility to architectural ugliness and residents' feelings of insecurity – even in safe areas – on empty streets and during weekends. São Paulo needs to analyze itself, and correcting its future growth would be a good starting point. Over the last 20 years, the Berrini and the Nações Unidas Avenues have shown the greatest economic strength in São Paulo. Yet the area's expansion reveals a series of mistakes, especially in the inhuman, arid and unsustainable form the city is adopting – mistakes that were not due to a lack of money, as with other cities in the developing world. The roads that surround the area are only suitable for cars, never for public transport, and they send a clear message: use your car because you cannot rely on access via a metro line or bus.

Real estate speculation has transformed what was once a marginal area inhabited by slums into a series of so-called 'intelligent' high-rise buildings that shut out the city. In some cases, it is difficult to find an entrance other than the car park or the garage. Blocks are over-sized, there are no trees or public spaces, and the

ground floors lack bars, restaurants and shops. Even during the day this area seems uninhabited apart from the permanent traffic congestion surrounding it.

Property developers bought the area cheaply and built-up the last square centimetre. Subsequent lobbying on behalf of the corporations that settled there forced the government to bring in electricity and water supplies, as well as public transport and other public services, leaving the bill to be picked up by the public coffers. São Paulo has repeated this property market cycle now several times: first abandoning the centre for the Avenida Paulista in the 1960s, then Paulista for Brigadeiro Faria Lima Avenue in the 1980s and subsequently this western area in the 1990s. Rehabilitation and modernization of the city's architectural heritage is alarmingly rare – existing buildings are neglected while new financial districts are created.

São Paulo is, increasingly, an octopus whose tentacles stretch further and further outwards, making it impossible to provide efficient public transport. The tentacles head in all directions. To the west, where the corporate world, gated communities and high-rise buildings proliferate. To the north, east and south, where, despite the hundreds of empty pockets, abandoned buildings and waste land in the centre of the city, the poorest people seek housing on the edge of the city, polluting areas that should be environmentally preserved, and contaminating the reservoirs that provide the metropolis' drinking water.

In both the expansion of the suburbs and of financial districts, public powers arrive too late, and thus they institutionalize the errors made. And despite São Paulo's construction boom and unprecedented economic growth over the last 30 years, resources are not being directed to correcting previous mistakes. Both the mayor and the state government are required to act as educators and regulators for managed growth, and neither should be afraid to curb certain investments, put up barriers or impose conditions.

The unwelcoming character of the Berrini and Marginal Pinheiros areas can be addressed through demands to the property developers themselves. Buildings over 15 storeys high should allow for the creation of a square, a garden or a public space that enhances the street-front experience. Buildings along avenues need restaurants, bars, shops, pharmacies and bookshops on their ground floors. These functions animate street life throughout day and night, and provide the social surveillance that São Paulo so desperately needs.

Why is it, then, that Avenida Paulista is more secure 24/7 than other parts of the city? It is because its design embraces the city and mixed use. There is Trianon Park, there are public squares, wide pavements, medium-sized blocks and an eclectic occupation. Next to large residential buildings, such as Paulicéia, Saint Honore, the Nações Unidas and Três Marias, there are banks, schools, colleges, hospitals, pharmacies and pubs, newspaper stands and cultural centres such as the Theatre of SESI, Itaú Cultural and São Paulo Museum of Art (MASP).

Conjunto Nacional proves that São Paulo once knew how to build intelligent buildings. On its 33 floors, divided into three blocks, there are offices and apartments with separate entrances. The wide pavements outside the building are made of the same material as the floors inside, thus obliterating the boundaries between public and private. The ground floor hosts cinemas, shops, banks, chemists and restaurants. This varied use demonstrates how to inject modernity and new life in a 1950s building without damaging it. The result is that the Conjunto Nacional block is the liveliest on Avenida Paulista. Continuous streams of people walk in and around it weekdays or weekends. In a city that is a prisoner of the paranoia about safety, the generous and welcoming architecture of Conjunto Nacional offers coexistence and safety for thousands of people. Criminals, who prefer dark and abandoned places where they can be left alone, are unwelcome there.

Why have the postmodern buildings of the Marginal Pinheiros and Berrini never managed to repeat the success that the Conjunto Nacional, designed in 1953, still has now? If the current real estate market of São Paulo prefers repetitive and simple solutions, it is the responsibility of the public powers to make demands that can 'build the city'. Despite extensive literature about how malls damage the urban landscape the same permissiveness exists in the planning for shopping centres: large boxes of windowless walls require air conditioning and artificial lighting, create traffic congestion and vast car parks, as well as mountains of rubbish. They also kill street markets, a life-giving force for neighbourhoods. São Paulo now has nearly 80 shopping centres. In five years, the Daslu, Cidade Jardim and Vila Olímpia centres were built next to older ones such as Iguatemi, Morumbi, D&D and Market Place. The result is a chain of seven centres within 10 km^2 (3.9 square miles). Just as the mayor can veto building a hundred-storey tall tower because of its impact on the neighbourhood, or can prevent the demolition of a house built in the 1920s, permission for the construction of new shopping centres should require contractors to think about alternatives.

Any intervention that makes a Paulistano not use a car, but instead walk for a few hours on the street in public space, would already have educational value. Not only because the streets – like the ones in Manhattan, Buenos Aires, Paris or Rio de Janeiro – would be full of people, but also because if São Paulo's elite occupied the streets more often, there would be greater demand for the care of pavements, transit signs and urban furniture.

Designers of new shopping centres would do well to remember the trade streets that marked the Paulistano centre, such as the Barão de Itapetininga. The shopping mall typology that has dominated the past 40 years is not sustainable. Beijing has just inaugurated the Sanlitun Village mall, which features 19 low buildings up to four-storeys high designed by 16 different architects. The result creates diversity among the buildings, and allows for vast pavements and safe alleyways. It is, in effect, an open shopping centre. So why continue to allow projects that do not give anything back to the urban landscape?

In Tokyo, where real estate is more expensive and scarcer than in any neighbourhood of São Paulo, municipal regulations required the multifunctional complex of Tokyo Midtown to set aside 40,000 m^2 (430,556 square feet) of gardens, with an art gallery in the middle, as public space. Roppongi Hills sponsored the design of benches around the enterprise. In Berrini, builders have already demonstrated that they will not care for the city of their own volition. Regulations could force them to look after the design and maintenance of bus stops, benches and squares – investments that would only enhance their property values.

Palácio das Indústrias, Casa das Retortas, Memorial da América Latina, Casa and Parque Modernista and Parque Trianon, are all well-known names for Paulistanos, but what do they have in common? The first two are large historic public buildings that have been empty for years, waiting for a new use. The others are freely accessible public spaces that are empty during weekends. Meanwhile, São Paulo has built several theatres in recent years in a region beyond the Marginal Pinheiros and Berrini. For most of the public it takes up to an hour and a half by car to get to a concert or a play.

The public authorities have failed to create incentives to use empty and centrally located places that already have infrastructure and public transport.

The same waste occurs in the centre of São Paulo. In a city that has only a handful of buildings more than 150 years old, the heritage of the small town that became the largest metropolis in South America should make preservation and re-investment in the centre a priority. There are dozens of empty or underused 20 storey buildings. Yet despite the rhetoric about revitalizing the historic centre, the last remaining large companies and law offices have left in the last decade.

Residential projects in the centre do not succeed because either humble people without savings are installed in 20 storey buildings in which the lifts alone generate service charges expected of middle-class housing; or because the 'brand' of the centre still has a negative connotation. Buenos Aires with its Puerto Madero, Mexico City with its historical districts of La Condesa and Roma, and Bogotá with La Macarena prove that even cities poorer than São Paulo can recover derelict neighbourhoods and transform buildings of past decades into local versions of Soho and Chelsea in New York City or the fashionable Marais district in Paris.

São Paulo's centre has the highest concentration of museums and cultural facilities in the city, the most metro stops and bus stations, several squares, wide pavements and public buildings, and the police are more present there than in other areas. The centre is also strategically located in the middle of the city.

Why, then, has the revitalization of the centre not worked? The answer is that the boost given by the public authorities was too timid. Large construction companies building high-rises on the western fringes of the city could have been required to think about alternatives in the empty centre or even retrofit buildings whose historical charm is an added bonus. Photographers, visual artists, stylists, advertising executives, musicians and designers have never needed an explicit and direct invitation from the authorities to occupy these voids. The city quickly expropriates whole buildings to make room for viaducts, tunnels and other works, but it cannot allow new uses for empty buildings in the centre for professionals in the creative industries who are priced out of overvalued properties in Vila Madalena, Vila Olímpia or Jardins.

Even significant investments in the so-called 'revitalization of the centre' have been unable to 'build the city'. The Pinacoteca, the Sala São Paulo and the Museu da Língua Portuguesa, all excellent cultural institutions, suffer from a presupposed revitalization of their neighbourhoods. They remain isolated buildings, where users arrive and leave hastily by car, avoiding any intrusion into the areas beyond their walls. Nobody thought about creating offices, residential use or studios – subsidized or not – which could have provided a halo effect for the surroundings.

One of the recent examples of the contrast between public service inactivity and São Paulo's vitality can be seen at Roosevelt Square. A pile of concrete since the 1960s, when it was constructed to connect express roads and viaducts, Roosevelt Square was the locus of drug trafficking and prostitution until over five years ago. Its devalued residential buildings, however, now have new uses on the ground floor: cinemas and bars sit next to alternative theatre groups in search of cheap space. From the dramaturgic talent to urban opportunity, Roosevelt Square now hosts bars and seven theatres that offer plays throughout the day to pay for their overheads.

The courage of the pioneers and the growing movement in the area has driven away criminals. Roosevelt Square has thus turned into a small village in the city centre. But despite years of discussions and promises, a 'pentagon' of concrete prevents it from becoming a real square. A landscape design project would allow the Roosevelt 'movement' to spread to neighbouring streets, building even more theatres, pizzerias and bars and bringing even more lively youngsters to the area. Several other areas in the centre could host clusters of creative industries, such as the beautiful working class village next to Casa de Dona Yayá in Bexiga, the empty plot beside the Teatro Oficina, the large pavements with galleries from the 1950s, the beautiful Largo do Arouche, the Avenida Vieira de Carvalho and the abandoned Vila Itororó.

The success of the Cidade Limpa (Clean City) project, which focused exclusively on removing billboards and outdoor advertisements from the streets of São Paulo, shows how even very small interventions can have a strong impact on Paulistanos' perception of their city. This was not an expensive project, but it managed to counter the belief that 'São Paulo is hopeless'. That the project stopped working reinforces the idea of the timidity of São Paulo's public management. The billboards hid an ugly and grey side of the metropolis that is now visible, and the government's failure to improve the urban landscape only adds to Paulistanos' low self-esteem.

Twenty-two years ago, Barcelona changed its landscape with the 'Barcelona, posa't e guapa' project, which combined the withdrawal of outdoor advertising with concessions for temporary billboards. When renovating the facade of a historic building, the sponsors were allowed to put their logo on the protective mesh covering the work. With the ban on billboards, street advertising was thus transformed into something more valuable that gave the local authorities enormous bargaining power when it came to making better use of existing resources.

São Paulo has one of the world's largest collections of architectural Modernism: from the 1930s to the 1960s the city was what Shanghai is nowadays. Yet despite several works by Oscar Niemeyer, a cultural or tourist map does not utilize this heritage. Recovering the self-image of the city could start with these architectural landmarks. If it wants to be beautiful, São Paulo needs to dust off, polish and highlight its past glories as any old European city knows how to. That the facade of Copan is in poor condition, that the Esther building from 1936 has a decrepit front, and that historically important if not architecturally revolutionary buildings like Martinelli or Sampaio Moreira seem semi-derelict, show the challenges ahead for São Paulo.

São Paulo needs to re-embrace architecture, just as it did in the years of accelerated boom and confidence in the future – in the years when its elite created the MASP, the Biennale and the Museum of Modern Art. This could give its young talent the opportunity to build better than the repetitive and awkward custom of today's real estate market. It could ease the entry of talented foreign architects, who would bring new perspectives, new materials and sensibilities to the city. It could also allow the creation of social housing projects by local architects finding new forms rather than the hundreds of identical 'crates' on the periphery. Lastly, the city could create public-private partnerships and international competitions for the construction of major buildings, with prizes awarded by the public for projects that stimulate beauty and create collective spaces that, rather than frighten, attract the Paulistano.

LIVING ON THE EDGE

Fernando de Mello Franco

UNDER THE SURFACE

There are penalties for unfettered growth. São Paulo demonstrates the bleak outcomes, in terms of pollution, and dislocation of a city that finds it difficult to develop a way to control its growth and shape its own future.

The Movement

The architecture of inert materialities, of objects fixed in space and permanent in time, has proven to be inadequate to meet the changing demands that arise from the rapid process of the construction of the contemporary city. What makes architecture effective, more than striving for the permanence of monuments, is to activate its capacity to adapt to changing situations.

Thinking in terms of transformation requires other paradigms for architectural practice. One answer could lie in figuring out how to conceive the measures that can best support the instability of movement, this continuous process of change in the relationships that form the physical and social environment.

It is interesting to think that the city in transformation needs to be supported and leveraged in order to allow for movement in all its variations. Therefore, understanding its elements of support can help in formulating some hypotheses that can be applied in the formulation of strategies. It is useful to conceive projects that accept and allow for the reorganization of space, that support movement to take place in a dynamic equilibrium. However, once the instruments for driving and guiding movement have been established, what directions are they to be given?

In São Paulo, a vigorous process of transformation is under way that corresponds to a new productive cycle and which will lead to significant consequences for the urban fabric. It is highly necessary to consider the values that will guide these changes. In its spatial dimensions, São Paulo is a shapeless urban entity without defined outlines. It spills enormously beyond a specific geographic area with little control. It has been a continuously moving process in its temporal dimension since its brief modern history began, a little more than 100 years ago.[1]

Running counter to the current assumption of it being a chaotic, random and ineffective city, the Metropolitan Region of São Paulo's output accounts for 15.6 per cent of the country's GDP,[2] generated in the tiny part of 0.09 per cent of the county's territory.[3] Which leads us to explore the evident need of some level of organization that would facilitate the intense dynamics of this metropolis. The signs indicate that this organization arose as a response to the need to meet the demands of a modern industrial city undergoing intense development, without, however, any concern for safeguarding an adequate living environment for the city's inhabitants.

The founding of São Paulo dates back to 1554. The history of the original village, situated on a watershed plateau 720 metres above sea level, close to the Atlantic Ocean

yet isolated from it by a steep escarpment, is marked by its distance from the colony's political centre. São Paulo was never a capital like Salvador and Rio de Janeiro, and did not play a leading role in Brazil's economy until the late-nineteenth century.

Nevertheless, ever since its origins it has been a centre of influence that extended over a much larger territory than one would assume that small initial settlement to have. The reason is that the Upper Tietê Basin is the geographic centre of a waterway system of natural transportation routes provided by valleys and watercourses that radiate from it in nearly every direction. The indigenous peoples of the region knew how to take advantage of this exceptional condition and set up a network of overland paths, complementing the waterways, in order to provide for communication and trade routes between the diverse nations that populated South America.

The inverse direction of the Tietê River, whose waters first flow inland, then turn and run parallel to the coast, to eventually meet the ocean in the Prata Basin (at Buenos Aires, Argentina) was an important factor that favoured the exploration of and settlement in the hinterland. In the first centuries of colonization, the Portuguese and Jesuits soon recognized the potential of this pre-existing and well-organized system on the lands they were to explore. Departing from São Paulo, they used it to take possession of a vast territory. They trespassed the lines established by the Treaty of Tordesillas and thus defined Brazil's continental borders.[4]

São Paulo's process of modernization followed the same colonial trajectory as the exploration of its natural resources, especially in terms of leveraging the rivers' potential and taking advantage of the city's strategic geographic condition to enlarge its sphere of influence. If there was any logic in the ordering that structured this development, it should initially be sought in the transformation of the natural environment through the successive technical interventions in the area aimed at supporting capitalist modes of production.

Development of the area through multiple infrastructural projects only began here from the second half of the nineteenth century, when the late-arriving process of industrialization began. Large infrastructural systems, financed by foreign capital, above all British, were built to support the modernization of modes of production. When the centre of political and economic influence switched to North America in the twentieth century, new models were introduced, yet the proposal of transforming the marshes and floodplains of the city's watershed plateau to provide conditions that would drive the metropolis's development was reiterated. Railways, a structural motorway system, and canals for drainage, water supply and power generation provided the bases for an industrialization that defined the logic of the establishment of industrial parks and of the working class districts built in the lowlands along the rivers, the most fragile yet promising part of the watershed plateau.

São Paulo's structural logic derives, therefore, from the replication of a model structured by the practices prescribed by international capital. This logic is easily recognized in various other parts of the world, wherever a city is constructed primarily as a technical product.

The Change

The metropolis is currently facing a resurgence of developmental change. The process of productive restructuring is reconfiguring the city's industrial condition and opening up ways for São Paulo's reorganization. In the current context of a decelerating rate of population growth, upgrading of the urban environment becomes possible, theoretically, through the reconversion of the old industrial areas and the urbanization of *favelas* – both essentially linked to the structure of connecting waterways – in a process removed from the historical model of diffuse and unlimited expansion.

During the urbanization boom of the 1960s, the population of the metropolis grew at an average of 5.6 per cent per year.[5] Today we see a reversal of this demographic dynamic. The metropolis is growing at a rate of 1.21 per cent, with the average for the city of São Paulo proper being estimated at only 0.59 per cent in 2010.[6] The reversal of the migratory trend, which now presents negative balances for the city, was decisive in these changes.

However, the data demonstrate an imbalance in this growth. While the central area is losing population, the periphery continues to grow at rates of more than 5 per cent in some places.[7] Yet it is certain that the space available for this expansion is becoming scarcer and increasingly at odds with environmental policies with regards to the headwater protection zones that surround the metropolis. Particularly in the City of São Paulo, the renovation involves a transformation from within, which is now being made for the first time on a large scale and in a systematic way.

The productive restructuring began two or three decades ago, along similar lines as those of other industrial cities. At the moment, this process is gaining even more momentum with the current growth of the Brazilian economy, and is taking on unique aspects that enhance the interest for São Paulo.

The Emergency

Brazil is currently enjoying a prosperous cycle. The political institutions are still fragile, yet undeniably democratic, and there have been various successes in overcoming the traumas inherited from the military regime. Natural resources, positive macro-economic foundations and public administration over the past 16 years, marked by governments at least minimally committed to an agenda of structural improvements, have created the bases for economic emergence. Adding to this positive image are socio-economic governmental aid programmes such as the Bolsa Família (Family Grant),[8] and the increase of the minimum wage, as well as the extension of consumer credit to the middle classes, a new development in this country. All of this has resulted in a significantly higher standard of consumption among the population, the great engine of the internal market, which grew precisely at the moment when the global crisis reduced the volume of international trade.

Continued growth will require the expansion of the country's infrastructure in a short space of time, which is only viable with the support of large investments. In this scenario, the transformation of São Paulo's metropolitan territory will involve an upgrading of the infrastructure systems that run along the waterways. The conversion of 270 kilometres (164 miles) of urban railways, previously dedicated to cargo but now used for mass transit, is already showing significant improvements for the city's difficult transport situation. A new approach to the management of water resources, necessary in a context of water scarcity, could open up opportunities for new landscaping configurations. The renovation of the current and programmed uses of the vast productive area undergoing restructuring could promote new urban models. All of which suggests that this is an opportune moment to investigate other possible ways of organizing the city. But there is a great risk of losing this momentary chance, in light of the fragility of the values that have guided not only the city's construction, but the very idea of the city.

In the minds of the real estate developers, who are confident in their ability to interpret the consumers' desires and fears, 'the cities are becoming increasingly chaotic'.

And they foresee that: 'in the future, the shopping malls will be mini-cities, with offices, hotels, doctors' and dentists' offices [since] people want everything in the same place.'[9] The industrial areas offer the ideal space for the large-scale construction of these already disseminated gated communities. The true inventors of this process are the marketing professionals who follow the logic of market segmentation in line with consumer patterns. Factors such as social class, income and age, including sexual orientation, define the specialized character of the developments. The city is fragmented into specific marketing niches, which, in their intrinsic logic, group similar people and avoid the confrontation with different social values and modes of behaviour while dissolving the common forms of coexistence. The city tends to be configured as an archipelago of closed-off superstructures, reorganized as a sum of products ironically described as 'come and live in total freedom', 'all inclusive' and 'city free'.

The context of economic growth and the reduction of the crime rates, which would theoretically weaken the arguments in favour of the 'city of walls', leads us to infer that the city's crisis reflects a crisis of culture. This dynamic is being driven by the values of a population that demonstrates that it does not wish for urbanity, even when its promotion begins to be possible. Here there is an intriguing contradiction. On the one hand, the awareness that the city is the principal place from which one can imagine a future. On the other, it is a refusal of the city as it is presented today.

This observation compels us to take a closer look at the emergence of the new middle class, constituted by the transfer of the population from classes E and D to class C.[10] There are various assumptions about the cause of this social mobility, but they all fall around the significant number of 30 million Brazilians who have recently risen above the poverty line. It is important to underline that the key turning point between its rural and its urban condition took place in Brazil between 1960 and 1970. Therefore, it can be assumed that the new middle class within the cities can be found among the already urban population, which has been constructing an urban culture that is expressed, to a certain extent, by its own values. It is likely that the older generations still wish to return to their places of origin. But the younger people, born in São Paulo, have the notion of belonging to the place where they now live.[11]

Souza and Lamounier propose that: 'this phenomenon [the emergence of the middle class] tends to produce powerful impacts not only in the economy, but also in the governmental structure, by way of, for example, the demand for services, in the social values, in political life and even in the natural environment.'[12] The question is whether this phenomenon will lead to the construction of cultural values and forms of political organization that desire relationships with the city, distinct from those that are prevalent today. This question can only be answered in the future. But it already suggests to architects the need for critical revision of the approaches that drive design processes, given that this is an opportune moment for the proposal of new demands.

The logic behind the investments in infrastructure decisively influenced the historic process of São Paulo's urbanization. Today, it is argued that new investments in the expansion of infrastructure are fundamental for sustaining the city's future economic growth. This means that it is a strategic imperative that architects and urbanists participate in the process to redefine the paradigms that rule the construction and organization of infrastructure. Everything suggests that the transformation will be leveraged by the pre-existing systems, and that once it is differentiated by the strategic concentration of the infrastructural systems, the complex territory of the rivers and lowlands is the most appropriate area around which to structure the next stages.

In this process, the context of climate change presents a dilemma. Estimates indicate that the increase in temperature in São Paulo will be in the range of 2°C to 4°C by the end of this century. Long-term climatic analyses predict that storms accompanied by a large amount of rainfall will occur more frequently in the future.[13] Change in the rainfall patterns are already noticeable, and the city is suffering from downpours with greater frequency and intensity. The pocket of hot air above the city that is generated by the vastness of the urbanized area and by the scarcity of vegetation causes differences in atmospheric pressure, which divert moist air masses from the Atlantic Ocean towards the city, which then condense and turn into violent rain showers. The chronic problem of flooding will directly affect the lowlands along the waterways, where the streams, rivers and the metropolitan car traffic flow coexist with the old industrial areas now being restructured. One of the main questions facing the city is how to reconcile the development of these areas with the climatic phenomena; it requires a structural change of the values governing the usage patterns of the occupied space.

The rising levels of environmental awareness give urbanists the opportunity to present the population with new arguments in defence of a better city. The concept of sustainability presupposes a certain notion of dynamic balance, even though the term is worn out because of ill use. And, since the environmental and infrastructural issues are systemic, a redistribution of investments in the region that does not only prioritize the privileged areas is required. It will not be possible to solve flooding issues or to upgrade the water resources without solving the systemic problem of infrastructural encroachment of the streams and the advance of the city's informal areas into the headwater protection zones. The necessary mitigation of the serious environmental problems is one of the few arguments that can raise the awareness among those in political power in favour of reducing the city's inequalities.

The city's current dynamic phase is fully under way, and we need to effectively reposition our support and our tools for driving it. Like a saddle on a horse, the infrastructure is merely a tool with potential. A question to be considered in the design of infrastructure is the need for a strategy of agency between an environment that is everything but inert and a society in transformation, which assumes a critical reflection on the desirable directions to be given to the movement itself and, in essence, a different perception of the infrastructure. Normally seen only as consisting of technical artefacts, infrastructure should be considered also as a place of dwelling.

In São Paulo, the canals, avenues and bridges are not imagined as habitable spaces, just like the functional virtues of its elements are not perceived as ornamentation too. The trees, usually thought of as a landscaping element, could, if widely planted throughout the city, also improve the impact of the pocket of hot air that hangs over it and retain part of the rainfall in their leaves, operating as an efficient, diffuse water retention system. Besides their systemic functions of drainage, the artificial basins for rainfall retention can along with the channelled rivers and streams, also structure landscapes that reconnect the city with its waters, especially in a Brazilian city located at some distance from the ocean, without a beach.

A stopgap approach to solving the problems of the productive dynamics has proven to be insufficient for ensuring quality of life for an urbanized population over the last half-century. Actions should be planned within a consistent programme of spatial and programmatic agencies that add new values to the spaces available. Because there is an urgent need in São Paulo for the establishment of an affective relation with the city. This will require an embracing of the sense of territoriality: the feeling that we belong to that which belongs to us.

ISTA

NBUL

Two suspension bridges link Europe and Asia while a third is planned.

Much of this apparently historical city is younger than Los Angeles.

But even after decades of frenetic growth, the city centre still reflects its past.

High-density housing meets low-density shopping.

Despite the city's ferries, and mass transit, traffic is reaching a standstill.

Kanyon, designed by the Jerde Partnership and Tabanlıoğlu, is a new shopping centre on a former factory site.

A popular but derelict neighbourhood, Tarlaba ı is feeling the pressure of the city's new-found affluence.

Istanbul's heart still reflects an older form of urbanism.

THE CITY TOO BIG TO FAIL

Deyan Sudjic

Istanbul is a city as beautiful as Venice or San Francisco, and, once you are away from the water, as brutal and ugly as any metropolis undergoing the trauma of warp speed urbanization. It is a place in which to sit in the shade of ancient pines and palm trees for a leisurely afternoon watching sun on water, looking out over the Bosporus. But also, in some parts, to tread very carefully. Istanbul has as many layers of history beneath the foundations of its buildings as any city in Europe. In 2010 it was one of the European Capitals of Culture. Depending on how you count, Istanbul has been the capital city of three, or perhaps four, empires. It is still shaped by the surviving fragments of Greek, Roman, Byzantine, Venetian and Ottoman civilizations. It has Orthodox Christian churches, Sunni mosques and Sephardic synagogues. It has vast classical cisterns, ring upon ring of ancient fortifications, souks and palaces. It also has desolate concrete suburbs of extraordinary bleakness, urban terrorism and a rootless, dispossessed underclass struggling to come to terms with city life.

It is the largest city in a state that emerged in 1923 from the chaos of World War I and the Versailles treaty, and the vision of modern Turkey's founder, Kemal Atatürk, who, though he was born in what is now Thessaloniki, and so unmistakably a European, moved his capital to Ankara, a city created almost from nothing. For the first few decades of modern Turkey's existence, the state devoted most of its resources to the new capital and its infrastructure. For a while it looked as if Ankara and Istanbul might become twin poles: one a European gate, the other a counterbalance in the heartland of Anatolia. As Turkey's urbanization started to accelerate in the 1950s, the balance shifted overwhelmingly towards Istanbul. The rural poor poured into the big city and what used to be considered a cosmopolitan enclave, a demonstration of Turkey's tolerance of other ethnic groups and faiths, has also become the heartland of its most conservative constituency. It is a city in which 3,500 dispossessed Romas, descendants of a community that has lived in the Sulukule district in the shadow of the Byzantine city walls for centuries, have been systematically moved out of sight and out of mind in an operation that recalls Robert Moses' determination to drive federally funded highways through the black and Puerto Rican neighbourhoods of New York City.

Istanbul is the largest and most febrile urban centre in a country with an army committed to secularism, which, in some extreme cases, shades away from Atatürk's ideals towards authoritarianism. If the generals miscalculate, it has the potential for an insurgency that could make Turkey a kind of Algeria and Istanbul its Algiers.

1.2m

population of Istanbul in 1950

12.9m

population of Istanbul in 2010

But Istanbul is also what is driving Turkey towards Brazil, Russia, India and China, the new economic powerhouses. The collapse of the Soviet Union made Turkey in general, and Istanbul in particular, a vital new centre for services and expertise profiting from a rapid growth in the energy-rich former Soviet republics. It is a phenomenon that is reflected in the array of carriers at Istanbul's greatly enlarged airport, from Uzbekistan Airways, to Dniproavia, Tajikistan Airlines, Air Astana, Donbassaero and Tatarstan Airlines, their hulls painted in gaudy colours, more like buses than Boeings.

It is also visible in the stream of ships that clogs the Bosporus day and night, a continuous double file of tankers and freighters flows past the minarets and the suspension bridges that define the city. Istanbul is the base for the architects, the construction companies, the advertising agencies, and the banks that are reshaping Kazakhstan and Azerbaijan, and the Ukraine and even Russia. It has banks and television stations; it has manufacturers that are shooting rapidly up the value chain from generic products to designer label kitchen sinks.

Istanbul is Turkey's passport into the European Union. It sees itself as part of a group of cities on an axis running from Dubai to St Petersburg. If London is Europe's first global city, Istanbul sees itself as its second. It's a city whose influence is shaped by both culture and commerce. Istanbul has a thriving approach to contemporary art, although surprisingly perhaps, given the close personal interest that Atatürk himself took in architectural issues, importing Austrians to plan Ankara, it has not as yet developed a distinctive architectural culture of its own in the way that Mexico or Australia have. Its geographic size and population mean that Istanbul has a strong claim to being regarded as the largest city in Europe, even if it partly lies in Asia, where a third of its citizens now live. In the European suburb of Levent, one of Istanbul's main business districts where banks cluster, you can find facsimiles of smart London Chinese restaurants and mega shopping centres. But Istanbul also has settlements within its limits, in which Kurdish migrants from rural Anatolia tend flocks of sheep under the gaze of prefabricated concrete apartment blocks.

It is a city like no other and yet it is a city that has things in common with many other cities, even if it does not always recognize it. While Cairo's population has doubled, Istanbul's population, like Lagos, has quadrupled since 1980. It straddles two continents, in a way that is very different from, but inevitably also reminiscent of, the twin cities of El Paso and Ciudad Juárez straddling the Rio Grande, blurring Mexico with the United States.

Istanbul is home to 12.9 million people, governed in a recently adjusted unitary jurisdiction, which saw the city's land area nearly triple from approximately 1,800 square kilometres (695 square miles) to 5,300 square kilometres (2,046 square miles). Even now, it still pulls in another 1.5 million workers every day, swelling its peak time population to near 15 million. The city administration is attempting to limit its population to 16 million, fearing that if it is allowed to spread unchecked it will reach an impossible 25 million, in a country that has currently 72.5 million people. But this is really in the hands of the national government, rather than the city, given that the GVA of the poorest regions in Turkey is just 23 per cent of that of the richest areas of the country. With such an imbalance, it is no wonder that Istanbul has become a magnet for the rural poor. Turkey's internal migration has had the effect of making the inequalities of Istanbul grow more acute, rather than less, even as it has prospered over the last decades. And it is not the master of its own fate. There is the TOKI state housing programme, run by the Prime Minister.

Very few cities have such a compartmentalized geography. The vast majority of Istanbul's citizens never make the crossing from one continent to the other. But the 10 per cent who do cross from one half of the city to the other every day amount to a still huge total of 1.3 million. And to accommodate them, plans have been approved to build a third bridge across the straits. However, it is feared by some that this will destroy the reservoirs that feed the city. Ask civic leaders if there is an environmental problem for Istanbul. The first thing that they talk about is 17 August 1999, when a serious earthquake hit the city, causing 20,000 deaths. Natural resources, population growth and civil equity barely figure.

But there are ambitious plans to create linear sub-centres, both on the east and the west sides of the city, allowing the two sections to function better. The one on the Asian side of the city, at Kartal, is being shaped in its early stages by a dynamic masterplan prepared by Zaha Hadid. Among such privately financed developments, Istanbul has been investing heavily in its infrastructure. A metro system is gradually taking shape, the trams are being revitalized. There is a new rail tunnel under the Bosporus, which will allow the realization of the ancient goal of one of Europe's empires: to create a direct rail link from Berlin to Baghdad.

In a world in which an accommodation between competing power blocks is essential for both cultural and political reasons, Istanbul is a key bridge between them. It is a city with more than enough of the usual urban problems, but that also has the energy and the resources to stand a chance of addressing them. It's in nobody's interest that they should fail.

BRIDGING HISTORIES

İlhan Tekeli

EUROPE'S BIGGEST CITY

Istanbul is Europe's largest and one of its oldest cities; one which has deep roots, but that also points to the future of cities all over the world that are undergoing rapid development. It demonstrates the longevity and the significance of a city set against the timescale of a nation-state.

Assessed in economic terms, Istanbul is an international success story. It would be wrong to attribute this success just to policy makers or planners; much of it must be put down to the creative potential of the Turkish people and their ability to come up with new solutions; something that is often overlooked by the political establishment.

In terms of providing quality of life for its inhabitants, it is difficult to claim the same level of success. Life in this city is difficult. It is common for a city dweller to spend two hours a day commuting and one can waste up to eight hours a day in traffic jams, or just trying to get around. However, the city succeeds in creating a high level of quality of life for its wealthier residents; perhaps one of the reasons why the city has been able to accommodate a mass of nearly 13 million people over the last decades.

Using global city theories doesn't provide sufficient evidence for an evaluation of Istanbul's success story. The opinion of the city's residents on their perceived quality of life needs to be taken into account too. Global city theories assume that if a city has a larger population, its size impacts upon a larger amount of external economies. However, unless there are ways to measure the external economies that are effectively realized, it is impossible to argue that a 15-million Istanbul will realize more external economies than a 10-million Istanbul.

In this essay I wish to argue that urbanization is a complex socio-spatial process and will place equal emphasis on both dimensions of Istanbul's recent development at two scales. I will look at the macro level, focusing on the historical redistribution of Turkey's urban population; and I will take into account the micro level, focusing on the effects of the 'emergence' factor of the provision of housing on the city's built form.

Istanbul up to 1945

Like other countries of a similar level of development, Turkey did not expect the rapid urbanization that followed after World War II. During the war, Turkey assumed it would resume the Republic's project of radical modernization once the war was over. However, Turkey and Istanbul were confronted with the problem of an urbanization boom, one of the most deep-rooted transformations that a country can experience.

With the limited amount of experience in urban planning and management it had gathered during the 'radical modernization project' of the first 22 years of the Republic, Istanbul was not fully equipped yet to address the major issues. The regime's decision to move the capital from Istanbul to Ankara in 1923, to boost the construction of the nation-state, had major consequences for urban planning and

municipal administration across the country. The stakes were high in moving the capital from a historic and established city to a relatively small, centrally located town in a country with limited levels of capital accumulation. The new Republic assumed this risk and quickly gained considerable experience in developing and administering the functions of a new city.

During the 1930s, Turkey institutionalized this knowledge by passing legislation on urban governance, national health care, infrastructure and even architecture. The 'modernist project', it could be argued, provided a framework of 'modernist legitimacy' to support the growth and development of Turkey's cities. This framework was based on two principles: the preparation of city plans that would be explained to the public, ensuring compliance from property owners and residents and avoiding a situation in which people would be faced with faits accomplis. It was during this period that urban planning courses were set up in architecture and political science departments of higher education institutions in Ankara and Istanbul.[1]

Istanbul's population of 1.2 million before World War I halved to 600,000 when it lost its status as the capital city in 1923.[2] It faced problems that city planners of the day, accustomed to dealing with expanding cities, were not able to comprehend. It was not easy to boost the city's economy or to implement processes that would reconstruct large areas of the city that had been abandoned or were devastated by fire. As part of its modernist drive, the state launched new initiatives to extend public works in Istanbul in the 1930s, which was still Turkey's largest city. The French town planner Henri Prost was appointed to develop an expansion plan for the city in 1936. Prost's all-encompassing, detailed masterplan (designed at a 1:5000 scale), was the first step towards the concrete realization of the nation's modernist project. Although Prost's masterplan was not fully implemented, it nevertheless gave a sense of direction at a time when the city was experiencing a lull in rapid growth.[3]

The Turkish state developed an aggressive industrialization stance that was both protective of the national economy and promoted the development of small Anatolian cities along major railway routes across the country. Little state investment was channelled to Istanbul. However, Istanbul was the only Turkish city with a university, and it possessed a dynamic import-export activity driven by the private sector, mainly by small and medium enterprises. As part of a national programme of nation-state building, the city's non-Muslim population lost its significance and the city began losing its cosmopolitan character.

Shifting its status from a world city to the biggest city of a nation-state in the making, Istanbul rallied its economy. And, following Prost's masterplan, its population was redistributed across new, sought-after residential neighbourhoods. The areas around Taksim, Harbiye, Maçka, Nişantaşı and Şişli, spread alongside the newly designed Atatürk Boulevard, became the residential location for the wealthy middle and upper classes on the western side of the Bosporus. On the Asian side, Kızıltoprak, Göztepe, Erenköy, Bostancı, Maltepe and Suadiye, all located between Kadıköy and Pendik, transformed from seasonal recreational zones into permanent residential areas over the years.

Re-establishing Istanbul's Significance 1945–1980

After World War II, Turkey's government switched from a single-party to a multi-party regime, bringing a strong populist character to the Republic's project of radical modernity. The country aligned itself with the West during the Cold War and embraced a mixed economy that favoured import substitution and industrialization.

As a result, as the private sector grew, Istanbul's economic significance increased. None the less, the city's development was driven by a rapid urbanization that assumed a certain measure of autonomy.

The industrialization of agriculture and subsequent demise of subsistence farming led to the creation of strong national and international markets after World War II.[4] While Ankara was the only city to have grown at an annual growth rate of 6 per cent during the post-war period, there was a staggering urban growth rate in subsequent years across the entire country, with a peak of 6.1 per cent annually between 1965 and 1970.

Istanbul's share of the national population steadily increased thanks to internal migration, especially from the Black Sea region. In 1945, 4.5 per cent of the country's population lived within the municipal boundaries of Istanbul. By 1980, Istanbul was an urban metropolis consisting of 32 municipalities hosting 10.4 per cent of the nation's entire population. This trend alone had a greater impact on Istanbul's development than the economic policies of the state. The city generated its own economic core by expanding its domestic markets and export economy, as well as getting the most out of its human capital. Istanbul's historical benefits, alongside its exceptionally favourable geographical features, catalyzed growth and development in these dynamic years.

The emerging form of a rapidly expanding Istanbul was the result of a socio-spatial process that required large investments in the industrial and service sectors to provide employment for the city's new residents. A similar large-scale investment in housing and urban infrastructure was needed to accommodate people in an environment that adhered to the principles of the modernist project. However, the scale of capital accumulation in Turkey at the time was woefully inadequate to realize this ambition. Many of the new urban dwellers were villagers who lacked the sense of urban culture that was required to inhabit the city in a contemporary way. The housing problem was not resolved by the state or municipal authorities. The new wave of urban settlers took on the issue themselves, building informal housing (*gecekondu*, or 'built by night') across the expanding city, without official permission or any form of legitimacy. Informal housing became a *habitus* that gained public approval. The autonomous nature of the solution became a fait accompli that transgressed all notions of the modernist, efficient state. Informality spread from housing to other aspects of urban life, including work (street hawkers), transport (shared minibuses or *dolmuş*), music (arabesque), construction (*yap-satçılık*).

But the lack of housing provision affected the middle classes just as much as the city's swelling underclass. The law permitted ownership rights for a single home on a single parcel of land, but the steep rise in land prices meant that the middle classes could no longer afford to own their own homes. The construction of multi-level apartment blocks on parcels that had previously contained single houses became the obvious solution for the city's bourgeoisie, leading to the adoption of the *yap-satçı* mode of supply, which allowed ownership of a single development plot to be shared. Small-scale contractors built multi-storey apartments on the land bought from the original landowners in exchange for a number of flats, rather than through exchanging cash. The remaining flats were sold on the free market, allowing the contractor a return on investment and the landowner a long-term interest in their original parcel. This mechanism opened up almost the entire city to apartment housing development – an emergent solution, as radical and informal as

CHANGING URBAN LANDSCAPES

Quasi-rural living conditions of the earlier phase of *gecekondu* informal housing have been gradually replaced by post-*gecekondu* apartment blocks, built on the land of uncertain ownership.

the *gecekondu*, even though it met with the fundamental regulations of the state to promote capital accumulation as part of the realization of its modernist project.

But neither Prost's masterplan, nor the creative, informal responses to the real estate situation gave a definite steer to the direction of this rapidly expanding city. As a result, the authorities adopted a new strategy that recognized the speed of urbanization and the cultural make-up of its new residents based on the principle of legitimization of informal dwellings. The existing city masterplan became ineffective as a result of the process of plot-sharing outlined above. Increased and unplanned densification led to inadequate municipal services and traffic congestion. Large-scale development could only be implemented with high-level intervention, often from the prime minister himself. Centrally funded resources were poured into some initiatives, which required legal boundaries to be significantly stretched. Negative public reactions and lack of resources led to the formulation of a new masterplan that gave some legal framework to previously informal solutions. But these new plans failed to obtain public support or establish a clear vision for the city's development. As a result, Istanbul's expansion progressed apace with a hybrid form of development that was half planned and half unplanned, despite the highly centralized nature of its municipal governance.

What followed has been described by planners as an 'oil spill', that spreads across a sheet of rough paper. The city grew along the inter-city road axes but became squashed at the centre. Central business districts became denser while high-income neighbourhoods sprawled outwards to the periphery of the city. Much

CONFRONTING NEWNESS
Remnants of Istanbul's ad-hoc development sit next to the emerging world mass housing built by the central government agency TOKI.

needed investments in infrastructure meant that the city became a permanent construction site. The *yap-satçı* mode of supply promoted the destruction of much of the city's original fabric with high levels of private-sector investment in industrial and commercial zones, often cheek-by-jowl with working-class *gecekondu* neighbourhoods. In the time span of a few decades, Istanbul did not become a metropolis, but a monstrous industrial city, covering the entire area around the Bosporus and the Golden Horn.[5]

Regaining World-City Status: Istanbul Since 1980

In the 1980s, the Turkish government abandoned the mixed economy model and adopted a private-sector-led liberal policy. Import substitution gave way to an export-oriented economy. Turkey's economy became increasingly influenced by globalization; it transitioned from an industrial society to an information society; from a Fordist accumulation regime to a form of flexible accumulation.

The collapse of the Berlin Wall in 1989 and the adoption of market economies by Eastern Europe and Russia offered a new opportunity for Istanbul to regain its 'world city' status, lost after World War I.[6] A consensus among politicians and the business elite, who shared the vision of Istanbul as a 'liveable world city', was achieved by the mid-1990s. Turkey's application for full membership of the European Union has strengthened this vision.[7]

In this respect, Turkey can claim success in promoting Istanbul in a competition between world cities rather than nation-states. By becoming a world city, Istanbul did not only organize and supervise its own international economic hinterland, it became at the same time capital exporting financial centre for this expanding hinterland. The city also began to invest heavily in art and culture, and major international corporations moved their regional headquarters to Istanbul. Economic development policy based on the growth of Istanbul can be considered as evidence of Turkey's socio-spatial understanding of a national development process.

It is difficult to have a clear grasp of the exact population size of an urban region with vague borders. The most recent census, which stands at 12.9 million people, covers the province of Istanbul. When neighbouring provinces of Kocaeli and Tekirdağ are also taken into account, the total population of the urban region approaches 15 million people. In 1980, Istanbul represented 11 per cent of the country's population, and by 2010 the urban population constituted around 20 per cent of the nation's. Although Istanbul is not yet among the top-10 most influential cities of the world, it sits comfortably in international rankings between 20 and 25. There is no other city within Eastern and Southern Europe, the Caucasus and the Middle East that can compete with it.

As Istanbul continued to establish its primacy, its spatial structure transformed from a monstrous industrial city to an urban region. The main reasons for this transformation can be attributed to the replacement of the Fordist type of production with a system of flexible types of production. The dominance of flexible production has changed the mode of integration from vertical and hierarchical ones to one based on horizontal relations. These new modes of integration created a tendency to transform the city from single-centred to a multi-centred one. Another important factor was the creation of strong actors that have the capacity to intervene in this process of transformation. In addition, the construction sector became one of the top three in the world, reflecting the importance that the development industry had acquired. The real estate market opened up to foreign investors as the city regained its world city status, inviting external agents to take part in the transformation process. The role of the public sector also grew in significance. Apart from the massive increase in political and fiscal power of the Istanbul Metropolitan Municipality, the national Housing Development Administration (TOKI), based in Ankara, was set up by the prime minister with special powers to deliver millions of residential units for the country's emerging low to middle classes.

As a result, mass housing has played a key role in the reshaping of Istanbul. Although private sector developers and cooperatives found niche opportunities for investment, it has been TOKI's gargantuan housing programme that has determined the city's development, both in the residential and the commercial sector. In addition, large-scale industrial zones, storage depots, wholesale trade centres, specialized manufacturing hubs and free-trade zones emerged alongside a new generation of transport services.

Since the 1980s, Istanbul has been transformed by the actions of large-scale actors and institutions, unlike the previous phase of piecemeal development that was mainly driven by smaller scale developers and contractors. A new central business district, complete with a slick cluster of skyscrapers, was established along the axis stretching between Mecidiyeköy and Maslak. As the old districts of Eminönü and Beyoğlu were unable to meet the demand and were subjected to a degree of planning control, the city sprawled along its western side with high-income residential neighbourhoods. As a result of this mobilization of large amounts of accumulated capital, Istanbul slowly transformed into the multi-polar city we experience today.

During this process, services and production facilities that had previously been located in the centre moved out to these new areas. The remaining voids became the focus of a process of gentrification in neighbourhoods like Kuzguncuk and Cihangir and the re-structuring of historic areas such as Sultanahmet with hotels and tourist facilities. In parallel, a number of regeneration projects were initiated by the political establishment, which had not been attempted during previous phases of the modernist regime. Improvements of *gecekondu* neighbourhoods and earthquake-prone areas became part of this renewed urban strategy, reflecting a real need to tackle these severe problems. None the less, a further set of initiatives has been implemented with the objective of preserving the unique identity and historical characteristics of some central areas, driven mainly by an obsessive ideology of the city's political actors. A generation of buildings in 'Neo-Ottomanesque' style were readily granted planning permission, replacing the typical modern architecture of Istanbul. The redevelopment of the Istanbul Manifaturacılar Çarşısı industrial complex and the imposed regeneration of Sulukule, a traditionally Gypsy neighbourhood inhabited for centuries by Roma people, are examples of this new wave of what I would call non-consensual, pseudo-regeneration projects.

Istanbul may need a new planning and governance system to address its new reality. However, Istanbul's policy makers do not seem to embrace this prospect. Advanced democracies have discovered that it is impossible to control a city with outdated plans that do not reflect the real boundaries of the city. Metropolitan growth can be carefully steered with strategic plans that have gone through some process of public consultation and participation. However, these transparent processes are lacking in Turkey today, and planning decisions still reflect the top-down nature of municipal government, with the mayor firmly in charge. The demand for greater participation and devolution of power are often the subject of political exploitation, reflecting the fact that municipal governance is still not fully democratized and that power is mediated through parochial feudal chiefs rather than at a city-wide level. Despite the lack of success of the planning process, there is no doubt that the creation of a modern world city has occurred as a result of the popular adherence to ad-hoc strategies and emergent solutions. Today, unregulated development is commonplace not only in *gecekondu* neighbourhoods but also in the modern areas of the city.[8]

Observations

Istanbul has taken important steps in becoming a world city in the last 20 years and continues to do so. The city is able to host great events that attract the world's attention. It has transformed itself from an overgrown industrial city to an urban region. It offers an attractive lifestyle to the international community and high-income groups. Istanbul has performed well, impressing its visitors with its energy. However, it is difficult to claim it has succeeded in providing the same quality of life for low-income groups and the poor. Istanbul will continue its dynamic growth in the years ahead, but new conceptual frameworks will be required to address these fundamental urban problems.

THE HINGE CITY

Richard Sennett

AT THE CENTRE OF TWO WORLDS

Istanbul's hinge city status comes from its physical setting and geographical context. It is a combination that gives it a continuing significance, a focus both for Turkey and its neighbours. New migrants from Anatolia bring rural customs to its suburbs.

It is often said that a Europe of cities has emerged in the last generation, cities whose ties to each other weaken the bonds of each city to its own nation-state. This proposition is both true and untrue. And just to make the matter more complicated, new memberships in the European Union, as in those of Poland and Hungary, did integrate cities like Warsaw and Budapest into the network of European cities; economic and political integration, however, also stimulated social and cultural withdrawal *from* Europe.

The background to a Europe of cities lies in how most European cities dealt with the huge damage done in World War II. Recovery meant, largely, restoring the central-city fabric that existed before. New buildings filled in an old grain: one usually established before the Industrial Revolution, which meant in turn that the periphery of cities became the key site for new forces, the thinly populated or unbuilt periphery the receptor for new immigrants, new forms of industrial production and offices. Profound consequences followed: the human settlements on the periphery became isolated from, and invisible to, those who lived in the centre, while the economic activities at the edge followed a different path from economic renewal in the centre. The seats of national power were restored, following an old European pattern, to the compact city centre – a matter of re-linking centralized power to the fortunes of the urban centre.

This path of restoration in London, Manchester, Frankfurt, Hamburg, Warsaw and Milan contrasted with the post-war decades in American cities, whose middle classes abandoned the central city; again, in a different way, with São Paulo and Johannesburg, places which in the growth years that began half a century ago developed patchwork enclaves of race and class, cities which became archipelagos of poverty and wealth.

The Urban Age conference in New York addressed the hollowing out of the central city.[1] William H. Whyte first plotted the movement of executive jobs from the city streets to isolated corporate campuses in the 1960s and 1970s, and he explored the worrying tendency of such companies to implode shortly afterwards. Ex-urban locations, he suggested, had the effect of isolating corporations from the face-to-face economy of the city, and thus further weakened companies that were already vulnerable. In Johannesburg, the work of the Urban Age found an equal hollowing out of its urban core. Here the driver was exclusively racial and the economics of large-versus-small business playing a weak role.

ANOTHER KIND OF STREET

Istanbul's core now represents the urban setting for little more than a tiny fraction of its exploding population. It has yet to find an equally distinctive contemporary version for its new settlements, and relies on local translations of American models.

These very different ways of evacuating the centre contrast with the European city in the last half century. Rebuilding the distinction between centre and edge, privileging again the centres, marked Europe's path of urban growth. The image of a 'Europe of cities' concerns the networking of those centres, not of the cities as a whole. Movements of populations from one periphery to another are quite rare: few Turkish families pushed to the edge of Frankfurt are prompted to make a beachhead migration to the edge of London. There is also little movement between the peripheries of London and Paris. Whereas the centres grow ever more tightly bound: the financial trade routes between the City of London and Frankfurt are stronger than, and largely divorced from, the financial activity each city does with its own nation. Similarly, the trade route of foreign tourism – a principal source of central-city wealth – is marked by a fixed London-Paris-Rome path rather than by dispersal from the monumental urban centre into the rest of the nation.

These are familiar facts that many working for the European Union hoped to alter. In the 1990s, Brussels' officials in both the labour sector and in urban planning wanted cities in new member states, particularly Poland and Hungary, to break the post-war pattern of Western European growth. Through investment policy and the application of a common labour-law, Brussels sought to create more internally cohesive cities, less segregated from and more integrated with smaller towns in the same nations. This has not happened, at least not in financial services, high-tech and creative industries – the drivers of the new economy; more integrated into Europe, Warsaw and Budapest are increasingly withdrawn from their nation-states.

Many would argue that global capitalism is the source of centralization and withdrawal, that this pattern of urban growth can be seen also in Mumbai, Tel Aviv or São Paulo, that it is not distinctively European. At the Urban Age conference in São Paulo, Saskia Sassen argued that the rebuilding of central areas in cities, whether downtown or at the edges, is part of their new, global economic role. Rebuilding key parts of these cities as platforms for a rapidly growing range of global activities and flows, from economic to cultural and political also explains why architecture, urban design and urban planning have all become more important and visible in the last two decades. And more standardized. Related to this sweeping economic change is the fact that modern urban development has homogenized building forms, the poured-concrete and glass box becoming ubiquitous.

One reason standardization has progressed lies in the fact that such buildings can be globally traded: like money, they are equally the same in all places. The social consequences of standardization can also be taken to be global rather than European: homogeneity in built form abets segregation – that is, it becomes much quicker and easier to erect entire communities destined for particular social groups, to sort people out, than if planning has to adapt to the quirks and complexities of local buildings. This marriage of homogenization and segregation is an issue Urban Age addressed in Mumbai. If true, then the prospect for Istanbul as a city in the European Union would mean that the machinery of the Union – its codes of labour and building practice, its banking rules on investment, its assertion of citizens' rights of free movement – abet the process of inclusion in a capitalist rather than a European order. 'Europe' lays down just a marker of how this larger inclusion will occur through accentuating the distinction between centre and periphery.

But that distinction matters in large measure because it is not static. Exclusion is not a fact that people accept passively. Much of the dirty work of rebuilding and maintaining European cities was done by immigrant labour; immigrants worked on building sites, cleaned the streets, staffed hotels and hospitals. Now, in the second and third generation of these immigrant families, continued existence as peripheral peoples is no longer acceptable. Nor among 'native' Europeans has the concentration and withdrawal occurring in the centres of cities become naturalized as a fact of life. The resurgence of cultural nationalism in the last decade signals in part a refusal of people outside the centre to be sidelined, their invisibility taken for granted, the local seen as mere decor. The centre/periphery distinction generates profound social dissonances. This is a large issue, one faced by any city like Istanbul entering a period of expansion.

The dissonances of centralization appeared in places as diverse as Mexico City and Shanghai in our study of global cities. But a more focused version of this problem might appear in Istanbul because it is a 'hinge city', an urban form that has had a particular shape in Europe. Venice is the European prototype of the hinge city. Renaissance Venice was built on trade with very distant places, dealing in spices from India, slaves from what is now Morocco, cloth and rugs from the countries along the Asian Silk Road, and sending goods finished in Europe to the East. Filled with foreign traders, Venice sought to contain them through the most rigid residential segregation, confining Jews to the three ghetto islands, Turks, Germans and others to *fondaci*, gated communities in which people were checked out for the day and checked in at night. The *fondaci* failed as containing institutions: foreigners gradually installed themselves everywhere in the spaces of Venice.

What makes Venice the prototype of a hinge city is the impermanence in time of these foreigners inhabiting a cosmopolitan space. They seldom stayed more than a few years. And this has been largely true of hinge cities around the Mediterranean. We imagine that places like Izmir, Barcelona or Casablanca are cities where different groups lived together generation after generation, but the statistical reality is that the internal composition of each community shifted from generation to generation. The Mediterranean hinge city earned its reputation for mutual toleration only because much of its population used the city as a transit camp, a site for deals and work, by peoples of an entrepreneurial bent who were willing to move whenever they sensed opportunity elsewhere. Mutual ethnic tolerance thus rested on a lack of permanent identification with local life. The hinge city is a city of migrants rather than immigrants, a place of location rather than a destination, a city of mobilities.

During the era when Venice dominated the Mediterranean, Constantinople had something of this character as well. In the wake of historical research by Fernand Braudel and William H. MacNeill, we now understand better than previous generations did – which viewed the Sultanate as a closed society – just how dynamic the movement of people as well as goods was through Constantinople, along the eastern and southern rim of the Mediterranean, even as Europe had sought to seal the northern rim from the sixteenth century onwards.

In function, the urban 'hinge' addresses a basic problem in most crossroads cities. This is that the strength of commercial activity attracts more in-migrants than the cities can provide with jobs or opportunities. Rather than rooting misery to one spot, the contacts and information flows that the hinge generates allow people to look and to travel elsewhere. In urbanistic terms, this means that public spaces for sociability acquire great importance: talk in the café or in the market is how people find work or opportunity.

It is sometimes thought that the advent of cyberspace communication will replace the physical public spaces of the classic hinge, but economically the case has not been proven. Face-to-face contacts and connections remain vital, because they generate personalized trust in what is being communicated, and such personalized trust is especially necessary for poor people to be able to act on information. Without fat bank accounts or institutions to support them, the knowledge they have to act upon resides largely in how they assess the people who impart it.

If the 'informal' public realm is crucial for survival in the overcrowded, under-resourced crossroads city, a great planning tragedy is occurring today in cities around the Mediterranean. The hinges are, as it were, beginning to rust. Along the northern European rim, informal movement and informal labour are becoming criminalized. In my view, the European Union has wrongly conspired with rather than contested the nationalist impulse to make informality illegal. Along the eastern and southern rims of the Mediterranean, the hinge of mobility is rusting due to issues that more directly concern us as urbanists.

Much of the urban development occurring in Lebanon, Egypt, Algeria and Morocco is eliminating or weakening informal public space. In Beirut, for instance, post civil-war reconstruction has forced small-scale enterprises away from the seafront. In Alexandria, the renovation project around the library is replacing

COPING WITH DENSITY

For generations Istanbul has balanced the intensity of its residential neighbourhoods with a diverse and dynamic public realm that acts as a conduit for social engagement.

informal places usable by poor people with clean, controlled public space meant mostly for tourists. Some of this erasure and expulsion can be traced to economics, but basic issues of urban design are also involved in the weakening of the informal public realm. Informal public space requires under-determined urban planning, that is, an architecture that allows flexibility of use and admits physical gaps and indeterminate relationships between buildings. It is in these liminal spaces that informality can flourish – the café built into a parking lot or the market stall outside a loading dock. The virtue of informal public space in hinge cities requires us, in other words, to challenge ideas that emphasize spatial order and purpose in urban design; ideas realized in practice, produce an over-determined environment.

Whether this is also a danger Istanbul is facing, we ought to explore what we, as policymakers, planners and architects, can do to protect and promote informal public space. Both the challenges of centralization and informalization could be put as a question: does Istanbul in the future want to look more like modern Frankfurt or Renaissance Venice?

IT'S ISTANBUL (NOT GLOBALIZATION)

Hashim Sarkis

CENTRE NOT PERIPHERY

Istanbul's position and heritage have given it a new significance in its regional context, a magnet for both European and Asian cultures, a centre rather than a periphery that recalls its older role at the centre first of the Byzantine and then the Ottoman empires.

In July 2008, I could not find a seat on a plane from Beirut to Istanbul. Fearing that I would miss a meeting with Mayor Topbaş, I asked a travel agent to find me alternative routes via Damascus or Amman. She laughed and explained that tourists were flocking to Istanbul from all over the Arab world because of *Noor*, a highly popular Turkish soap opera, dubbed in Syrian Arabic dialect and broadcast across the Arab world via a Saudi satellite network.[1] Travel agencies were organizing guided tours to the villa and to the different neighbourhoods where the series was shot. Some 100,000 Saudis visited Istanbul in 2008, up from the 30,000 the year before.[2] Their itinerary included the city's historic monuments, but the Byzantine churches or the Ottoman palaces were clearly not the main attraction. The Arab public may have finally rediscovered the capital of an empire that controlled the region for more than 500 years, only their focus has been diverted.

The 'Noormania' of 2008 represented more than a fleeting infatuation. The Arab audiences were drawn to the blissful rendition of Istanbul, to a higher level of social tolerance within Islam, to the glitz of a city with 35 billionaires, and to the cosmopolitan lifestyle of a young couple living beyond the confines of their traditional values.

Whereas the soap operas of Hollywood, Brazil and Mexico have already disseminated their own portrayals of glamour and passion to Arab satellite televisions, observers of the 'Noor' phenomenon contend that the Turkish soap operas unfolds too close to home to be dismissed. The love between a young Muslim couple, a woman's career drive supported by her husband, and the possibility of moving from a village in Anatolia to a villa on the Bosporus within the span of one lifetime, captivated about 80 million Arab viewers in the last episode. This also unleashed visceral reactions from religious leaders who wanted to ban the show.[3]

While social scientists are still debating the gender, class and ethnic reverberations of the Istanbul-based soap opera on the Arab world, the spatial and geographic terms of this relationship may be worth exploring too. Apart from the nostalgias of an older generation and of Sufi or pan-Islamic revivals, how could it be possible that Istanbul's pull has not been felt until now in the Arab world despite the physical proximity, the historic connections and the large overlap between the Arab and Turkish traditions, languages, cuisines and music?

From Hollywood, the answer would be 'What is the difference?' A video clip of the famous tune 'Istanbul not Constantinople', rendered by the Tiny Tunes animators,

confounds the stereotypes of Istanbul with those of the Arab world. Deserts and tents form the backdrop to the city's minarets and domes. Lumping together everything east of the Marathon plains is not a new mistake in American popular culture.[4] However, Orientalist prejudices notwithstanding, cultural similarities are always expected where there are geographic proximities. In this case, the recent Arab attraction to Istanbul may have more to do with the city's ability to shun such affinities. Along the lines of David Harvey's analysis of the spatial underpinnings of globalization, I will rely on the historic evolution of these geographic relationships to explain Istanbul's cosmopolitan posture.[5] In turn, and wherever applicable, I will also use spatial models based on Mediterranean historiography to analyze the city's ambivalent relationship with its larger context.

The dynamics behind Istanbul's exponential growth in the past 20 years have been consistently ascribed to the advent of globalization. Whether describing the financial and gold markets, the textile and fashion industries, or construction and real estate, these accounts emphasize that the city is increasingly reaching beyond Turkey's immediate geography and the confines of national territory to a second ring of regional, geographic proximities (Central Asia and the Balkans) and then on to the rest of the world.

As is the case with many global cities, Istanbul's economic exchanges turn out to be rooted geographically and historically.[6] As an example, the construction industry link to Central Asia is based on geographic proximity, but also on the affinities with the reawakened Turkic cultures in these former Soviet nations. However, in the globalization discourse, emphasis is placed on transcending these connections and attaining a role, scale and scope that situate the city somewhere else, outside its immediate geography. Again, Istanbul dutifully obliges in this respect. This act of transcendence has been performed by the city in the past, when it was capital of the empire that ruled over the extended territory. The city best illustrates the continuities between empire and global city through its ambivalent relationship with its first (national) and second (regional) territorial rings.

In this transition from geographic confines to a regional and then global role, it is significant to recognize which geographies have been suppressed. The connections to the Balkans, to Central Asia, and even to Western Europe have all been played out in explaining its ascent to a global city.[7] The European standards (and aspirations) guide its transportation, infrastructure and environmental standards. Its urban workforce is increasingly Balkan. But its location in the eastern Mediterranean region has been mostly ignored. Whenever mentioned, this connection is described, for the most part and until recently, primarily as an accident of geographic proximity. It may very well be the case, as some historians have argued, that this transcendence of immediate context is characteristically Mediterranean, but there is also more to an imperial capital like Istanbul than the worldly aspirations of a port city would allow.[8]

Admittedly, the eastern Mediterranean remains quite troubled by the many tensions that flare up between Greeks and Turks, Arabs and Israelis, Turks and Armenians, Cypriots and Cypriots, Turks and Arabs, Arabs and Arabs, etc. This has no doubt hindered free trade and stronger cultural connections between Turkey and the Arab world. (Lebanon, for example, has always had good trade relations with Turkey, but until recently and because of prejudices against the Ottoman past and of the strong cultural and political presence of Greek Orthodox and Armenian communities, this connection has not been nurtured to a more conspicuous cultural exchange).

Throughout the period of Ottoman rule, which lasted from 1516 until 1918, Istanbul has exerted its influence on cities in the Arab world to varying degrees. Different models have been used to describe different epochs. The most frequently used are the triad of cities (Istanbul, Cairo, Aleppo), in the sixteenth and seventeenth century, and the network of ports (Istanbul, Izmir, Haifa, Beirut, Thessaloniki and Alexandria) in the nineteenth century. In either model, Istanbul held primacy as a distant first, but not one that was obsessed with its centrality. The early sixteenth- and seventeenth-century relationship between imperial centre and provinces extended from the earlier Ottoman nomadic state apparatus that maintained strategic distance as a means for exercising power.[9] Even when Istanbul prevailed over administrative organization and institutional buildings in sixteenth-century Aleppo, the structure of *waqf* organization, the religious holding, tended to reflect more the local practices and elite rule.[10] The nineteenth-century interpretations of a network of ports supported by discrete train lines that did not form a network in the hinterland also reaffirmed a nonchalant link between centre and territory. Ethnic groups, merchants and bazaars traded heavily with each other across the Mediterranean and exchanged goods and ideas, but they held on to their respective hinterlands with loose reins.[11]

According to recent scholarship, a structural shift in the spatial organization of the empire occurred in the late-nineteenth century, particularly after its loss of the Balkans, when Istanbul sought to impose a more centralizing presence in the Arab provinces. This translated into heavy investment in agricultural and irrigation reforms, new road networks, the introduction of railroads, tramways and waterworks into the major cities in the eastern Mediterranean. Many of these projects were financed through private concessions to European companies heralding their respective countries' growing interests in the region. Still, the image of the city-empire somehow prevailed over the equalization efforts. The clock towers and fountains planted in the centres of many Levantine cities, the fascination of many historians, have been interpreted both as signs of modernization and the establishment of decentralized networks of trains and public spaces and as signs of the ubiquitous image of the centre, the Sultan of Istanbul.[12] Despite these large investments aimed at equalizing the regional territories through modernization, despite a widely held sentiment that somehow centre and periphery were in this together, the disparities between Istanbul and the eastern Mediterranean remained vast at the time the Ottomans fully withdrew from the region in 1918.

The subsequent creation of Arab nation-states under European mandates, complete with exclusionary identities and prejudices, exaggerated the severance from the Ottoman past.[13] The Arab states also equated this part with the Turkish presence. The perceived contradiction between Arab and Turkish nationalism widened the cultural rift.[14] Despite recent joint efforts between the governments of some Arab countries and Turkey to revise the history books, this past continues to be portrayed in school text books as a long, dark era.[15] Another main point of divergence was the international politics of the 1950s when Turkey joined the Baghdad Pact and the sphere of American influence, while Egypt led the Arab world towards a non-aligned position.

Between the world wars, Istanbul lost its ethnic populations to the nascent nation-states around it and its political primacy to Ankara. In 1927, the year of the first national census, Istanbul counted about 690,000 residents, whereas Turkey counted 13.6 million.[16] That same year, the second city of the Ottoman Empire, Cairo, had reached 1 million, superseding Istanbul.[17] Cairo would continue its rise as the

A CITY OF SURVIVAL

Cities are shaped by both political and economic shifts. Istanbul survived Atatürk's creation of Ankara, then flourished as regional competitors such as Beirut went through turmoil. It combines a manufacturing base with a booming service economy.

regional political and demographic centre. Likewise, the independence of the Arab countries after World War II would lead to a period of rapid urbanization around the main, usually capital cities. Beirut, Baghdad, Kuwait, Amman and Abu Dhabi, and the list goes on, witnessed exponential growth during this period and achieved primacy each in their own national territory with varying degrees of concentration. Riyadh would have to wait to the mid-1970s to surpass the port city of Jeddah.[18] While maintaining political and cultural hegemony, only Damascus as a capital city would remain rivalled in its demographic and economic primacy by the regional capital of Aleppo.

When Istanbul picked up again as the centre of industry and trade in Turkey, particularly after World War II and the liberalization period under Menderes between 1950 and 1960, it set itself on a different path of growth and development than the Arab capitals. Istanbul faced the challenges of building motorways to link the expanded metropolis, of the growing 'misery belts', and of the stagnation of the inner city ahead of many cities in the region.[19] It also went through the processes of urban renewal and building edge city centres earlier. The Istanbul historic preservation movement achieved immense powers in the 1980s, leading the city to become enlisted as a World Heritage Site in 1985. Significantly, this came six years after Cairo and Damascus, but the scope and depth of preservation policies far exceed those of either.[20] Istanbul has also managed to address and curtail the growth of its informal sector in a more successful way than the other metropolitan centres in the

A CITY OF VIEWS

region. While some of these practices have been criticized for their selective exclusion of certain ethnicities, they have nevertheless attempted to edify the multi-ethnic character of the city from a spatial point of view. Amman, Beirut, Damascus, and even some of the wealthier cities like Jeddah, continue to struggle with the presence of large informal sectors. As much as 75 per cent of Cairo's residents lived in informal housing in 1996.[21]

Despite the growing rift, the Arab world and Turkey shared some of the planning and design templates that were being circulated at the time, even before the Bretton Woods agencies, the United Nations and individual experts started distributing their new models under the umbrella of development. The French planner, Henri Prost, who had worked in North Africa on the plans of such cities as Fez and Casablanca, brought his skills to bear on the planning of the city in 1938. He is credited with the consolidation of its depopulated areas and the introduction of industry inside the city. So too the Swiss architect-planner Ernst Egli worked between Ankara and Beirut in the 1930s and 1950s and proposed administrative reforms to correspond to the new metropolitan order of these cities.

Perhaps one of the main commonalities between Istanbul and the region lies in the urban administration of cities with mayors and cities with *valis* (or governors). This residue of the *Tanzimat* period is based on a bizarre reporting system that frequently produces tensions and conflicts among the different levels of a city's administration. Since 1984, Istanbul has managed to create a metropolitan municipality with an elected and relatively powerful roster of mayors to lead the city. The urban improvements that the city has undergone since then, including the control over informal development, could be attributed to the strengthening of the local government. In contrast, central administrations continue to exercise relatively strong control over the budgetary and administrative responsibilities of mayors in most of the Arab cities, many of whom continue to be appointed, not elected.

In the 1970s a significant overture between Turkey and the Arab world took place when, blocked out of the European market, Turkish workers found their way to the Arabian Gulf. Today, this labour force, which counts about 100,000 Turkish workers in the Middle East, about 95,000 of them in Saudi Arabia, has grown in significance, particularly as Turkish engineers and construction companies have also begun to move in, specifically to the Gulf area.[22]

Political scientists studying the rapprochement between Turkey and the Arab world attribute the twenty-first-century turnaround, which culminated in the 'Noormania', to the takeover of power in Turkey by the Islamic Justice and Development Party. Interestingly, they explain this as both an overture towards the Islamic world in defiance of continuing European snubbing, and as an expansion of the regional markets and powers in order to strengthen their European bid. One unambiguous indicator of such improved relationships is trade. Exchange between Turkey and the Arab world went up from US$11 (€8.1) billion in 2002 to US$62 (€45.5) billion in 2008. In 2005, a Turkish Arab Economic Forum was established with Istanbul as its permanent home and in 2006, Turkey was invited to become a permanent guest in the Arab League. Since 2002, Arabs have invested about US$30 (€22) billion, most of which is in Istanbul.[23] In 2010, a Free Trade Agreement was signed between Turkey, Syria, Lebanon and Jordan, which opened the borders between the countries' peoples and goods and delineated a new geo-economic entity within the eastern Mediterranean that transgresses older nationalist and cultural boundaries. Beyond the trade exchanges, the political rapprochement has accelerated during the past eight years and Turkey has graduated from nervous neighbour to trusted mediator and peacekeeper between Arabs and Israelis. Talks about sharing electricity and water via under-sea conduits between Turkey and Israel and Turkey and the Arab World have taken this cooperation to a futuristic, sometimes not-so-naively utopian, level.

During this period, exchanges in real estate and construction know-how and investment between Turkey and the Gulf countries have materialized around a particular Turkish brand of large-scale project management and construction in relation to the finance and development models from the Gulf.[24] These brands have created an unusual margin of excess in the development of these cities. The United Arab Emirates has tried to build towers that bear its name over the precious skyline of the Bosporus. The British-Iraqi architect Zaha Hadid is designing the new district of Kartal on the southern Asian tip of the city. Most of these projects are private developments, but they are sponsored and supported by the city's government. Timothy Mitchell suggests a similar phenomenon of excessive iconic megaprojects in Cairo, with projects such as Dreamland in the 1990s, which operate outside the sphere of governmental fiscal restraints but which grew out of selling cheap public land in order to generate a real estate market that in turn supports public expenditure on infrastructure.[25]

The gentrification and rebuilding of historic centres in cities such as Riyadh, Beirut, Aleppo, and now Jeddah and Doha has increased interest in the Ottoman architectural heritage, not without transliterations and occasional misinterpretations. The developers of downtown Beirut preserved very few of the Ottoman era buildings but they countered that with an overblown Ottomanesque revival style, including a new mega-mosque that dominates the city's skyline. The restoration of Ottoman Aleppo has fared much better in terms of preserving the Ottoman urban fabric and monuments and linking them with an economic revitalization project. In 2002, the Saudi authorities destroyed an Ottoman fortress in Mecca to build a housing project, causing the ire of Turkish officials and reminding of the deeper ideological tensions that exist between the two countries. The rage against *Noor* by the religious leaders was the latest expression of these tensions and it may have temporarily threatened this niche of tourism in Istanbul. Moderation finally prevailed and the flights to Istanbul continued to be full.[26]

I finally found a seat on a plane to Istanbul. A few days late, but the mayor was kind enough to reschedule the meeting. While waiting for him in his summer offices, in the Malta Kiosk in the Yıldız Palace gardens, a member of his foreign relations staff addressed me in perfect Arabic. He and other staff members had studied Arabic in Jordan at the University of Zarqa as part of an exchange programme. The mayor did not speak English and I did not speak Turkish, but it must have felt contorted for him to go through his translator in order to speak in English to an Arab professor from the United States while his foreign relations staff spoke Arabic to me.

From the Yıldız gardens, the seat of power in the nineteenth century, endless panoramas spread open, and you can see across the Bosporus deep into the heart of the city. Some of these vistas resemble edge cities and gated communities everywhere else in the world, including Dubai, Beirut, Cairo and Riyadh, but so far, they have not overwhelmed this city's unique beauty and its ability to seduce. Unlike these other cities, Istanbul has managed to maintain, albeit in a manicured way, a unifying geography over historic epochs and to display synchronicity among its historic layers, (a quality that Fernand Braudel has attributed as typically Mediterranean).[27] No city in the world exhibits as much face as Istanbul. The expanse and extent of visibility weave a world of their own, inviting and forbidding at the same time.

How insignificant Beirut and Cairo must have been to Abdul Hamid II, the main occupant of Yıldız, against this opera of seduction. How unattractive they still fare in comparison. During our conversation, the mayor repeated after Napoleon that if the world were one country Istanbul would be its capital. Napoleon was no doubt exuding strategy, the mayor pride. I was trying not to be distracted by the beauty of the place and not to make much of the fact that my family name, Sarkis, was the same as the first name of the Armenian architect, Sarkis Balyan, who designed the Malta Kiosk in the nineteenth century. The mayor must have known this, having been in charge of the restoration of the city's palaces in his earlier career. What he did not know was that on these same grounds as we were having tea, Mithat Pasha, my wife's great-great-grandfather, was tried for treason against Abdul Hamid II in 1881. Whether Arabs, Armenians, or Turks, we seem to be perpetually returning to this place, to project our renewed desires on the Empire's unfolding geographies.[28]

THE VIOLENCE OF CHANGE

Asu Aksoy

A CITY OF TOWERS

The new Istanbul is marked by three principal housing types: clusters of high-rise towers, ranks of apartment slabs, and suburbs of individual homes.

In the context of Turkey's accelerating membership negotiations with the European Union, and the popularity of the neo-liberal outlook within the Islamic AKP (Justice and Development Party) government, a more confidently outward-oriented, globalizing and liberal-minded Istanbul has been emerging over the last decade. This changing mood and orientation in Istanbul is a positive sign for the rest of Turkey, as Istanbul has not only effectively become the country's leading city in terms of wealth and influence, it is also once again a cosmopolitan capital with its predominantly migrant population from all over Anatolia (and increasingly from neighbouring countries, Europe and Africa). Thus, if this megalopolis of 13 million can hold on to its perspective of what might be termed 'worldliness' – a combination of openness, liberalism, pragmatism, democratic culture, and global 'embeddedness' – then this momentum would help Turkey become more centrally and deeply engaged with, and implicated in, world affairs. Turkey would finally leave behind the remnants of the inward-looking modality that has hitherto marginalized the country and condemned its people to provincialism and isolation.

The murder of Hrant Dink in early 2007 put the tentative and fragile nature of this new cultural orientation into perspective. The murder of this Istanbul-based journalist, writer and civil rights activist of Armenian origin – by a youth with ultra-nationalist connections in front of the office of the newspaper he edited – demonstrated that if there has been a certain opening up, diversification and reinterpretation of the mental maps of Turkey over the last two decades or so, this has been accompanied by a simultaneous convergence of reactionary positions whose common denominator seems to be precisely the fear of openness. What became apparent was the precariousness of this culture of worldliness, now increasingly being challenged by the very tensions it has given rise to. Therefore, how the public culture of Istanbul develops is central to the position that Turkey will adopt in the global world order. Istanbul's insistence on the virtues of openness, over and against regressive and nationalistic calls for defensive closure, will make all the difference.

Istanbul's pull into the force field of globalization is affecting deeply rooted ways of thinking and acting. With its new spaces and cultures of consumerism, its expanding and deepening financial flows in the real estate and service industries, and its new mechanisms for the global integration of local cultures through commodification, globalization is making irreversible entries into the daily life of the city, forcing change in urban spaces and on public culture. But it is far from

clear how this process of globalization might translate into an orientation towards cosmopolitanism in the city's public cultural life. As the city opens itself up to the contemporary global order, the issue confronting Istanbul should not be the choice between openness and closure, but a choice about the kinds of openness and whether the urban culture can harbour a cosmopolitan disposition. Crucial to this debate is the city's potential to articulate a counterweight to fundamentalist neo-liberalism by enhancing a democratic modality of worldliness. In the face of the uncompromising forces of urban globalization now assaulting Istanbul, openness could be diminished to the status of a market-driven and market-shaped culture of self-interest. In this context, Istanbul's choice should be for a kind of openness that deepens democratization through empowerment of the excluded and the disadvantaged.

Istanbul, in fact, has thrown itself open to a new round of urban globalization. When the Directorate of Privatization Administration sold 100,000 m^2 (1,076,391 square feet) of National Highways Authority land in Zincirlikuyu to a Turkish business group for US$800 (€587) million in 2007, the price of land in this central business area increased substantially. Shortly thereafter, the Istanbul Metropolitan Municipality finalized the bidding process for a 46,000 m^2 (452,084 square feet) warehouse space belonging to the Istanbul Transport Authority, situated immediately adjacent to the Highway Authority's land. It was sold to a Dubai-based real estate company for US$705 (€517) million, with plans to build the Istanbul 'Dubai Towers', Istanbul's tallest building, at an estimated cost of US$5 (€3.7) billion (the project has now been cancelled). With this municipal sale, the value of property in the area had risen to US$15,000 (€11,009) per square metre (US$1,394 or €1,023 per square foot) – surpassing average values in the central business districts of London and Tokyo. The price of land almost doubled between these two sales with shocking speed, indicating the appetite of global real estate investors for sites in Istanbul.

And there is plenty of land. The transfer of land to global commercial interests is no longer limited to one particular area of the city, as was the case in the mid-1980s. Public spaces located around the city are coming up, one by one, for large-scale privatization and development initiatives. Public authorities and municipalities are not wasting any time to facilitate the sale of public land. Massive stretches of land around both the Galataport and Haydarpaşa zones, situated at the two key entrance ports from the Anatolian and European sides of the Bosporus, are now being considered for redevelopment. Considering that there is also the political will to support privatization – Prime Minister Erdoğan declared that his duty is to market his country – Istanbul is going to witness more and more global capital pouring into its beleaguered urban space.

Thus the new round of globalization in Istanbul is primarily real estate driven. As Çağlar Keyder has remarked, 'land has finally become a commodity'.[1] It is within this context that the recent political initiative to push through large-scale urban regeneration programmes targeting neighbourhoods with low-quality housing or derelict but historically valuable properties should be evaluated. Policy makers at both the local and central levels are now frantically drawing up metropolitan-scale visions and plans to put in place the infrastructure required for the next round of investments. Cash-strapped municipal authorities are finding solutions through large-scale projects undertaken by powerful investment and construction companies.

The head of TOKI, the Mass Housing Administration, declared that half of Istanbul's housing stock (approximately 3 million buildings) would have to be replaced over the next 20 years;[2] work would begin in 20 slum housing areas.

Istanbul's residents – whether in Sulukule or in Süleymaniye within the historic centre's city walls, in Tarlabaşı in the Pera district or Zeytinburnu to the west of the city – have been subject to municipal programmes involving the expropriation of private properties in return for cash compensation or relocation to new developments in the far periphery. Thus, the historic Tarlabaşı district in Beyoğlu, with its abandoned Greek Orthodox churches and its streets of dilapidated nineteenth-century houses – now occupied by Kurdish populations from the southeast of Turkey living side by side with local Gypsy populations and illegal African immigrants – is targeted for clean up. This will entail turning the houses into 'attractive' residences with parking spaces and shopping areas and facades being one of the few remnants to be retained of the area's unique character. Across the city, construction companies have been pulling down entire neighbourhoods. This work is carried out on the basis of an explicit regeneration and redevelopment agenda to turn expansive city spaces into money-making assets: sites to accommodate the demands of the city's newly expanding nouveaux riches or for tourism, for heritage, shopping, entertainment and large-scale events.

In this new round of globalization, global investments invade the most profitable areas, the ones that are no longer associated with the industrial profile of the city. Investors are attracted to the skyrocketing consumer demand for high-quality housing, recreational and retail facilities, and, not surprisingly, for cultural tourism. Even though manufacturing still accounts for over one-third of employment in the city, its image is now no longer associated with industry. There is a very clear policy, in fact, to de-industrialize the city; as the metropolitan mayor, Kadir Topbaş argued, the aim is that: 'Istanbul should shed its industrial profile ... Istanbul should, from now on, become a financial centre, a cultural centre, and a congress tourism centre.'[3] Results of this shift can already be seen in Kartal, a heavily industrialized area with over 100 factories occupying 550 hectares (5.5 km^2 or 2.12 square miles) of land along the Anatolian seashore. The mayor of the Kartal municipality announced plans to attract US$5 (€3.7) billion from foreign investors to develop a project designed by Zaha Hadid for a marina for 1,000 boats, plus hotels, residences and plazas. In response, companies with factories in Kartal are moving their production base and getting ready to turn their sought-after land into shopping and recreational centres.

The project of globalizing Istanbul initiated in the mid-1980s is now being realized fully. But this is a new round of urban globalization. In the 1980s, and throughout the 1990s, the global vision achieved partial and piecemeal results. This earlier phase distinguished itself through real estate developments (shopping centres, residential complexes and commercial headquarters) that did not touch most of the city, and that did not have a large impact on the daily lives of its citizens. They remained sequestered projects of the city's globalizing elite, driven mainly by the Turkish-origin conglomerate capital. Istanbul thus entered the new millennium as a 'dual city'.[4] Now every part of the city is exposed to radical change, as more and more land is pulled into the market sphere, catapulting the whole of Istanbul into an irreversible process of large-scale urban development. It is an overwhelming and all-encompassing transformation resulting from the alliance of national and local political will as well as, of course, powerful economic interest, local and global.

The New Role of Culture

But this new round of urban globalization is not driven by real estate alone. It is also associated with an ambitous cultural project. As public spaces fall one by one within the ambit of spatial design and estate management projects (invariably through the involvement of global property development companies), the city's public space has become a business proposition conceptualized in terms of consumption and recreation. The Kanyon shopping centre, opened in Istanbul's central business district of Maslak, illustrates how public space has been incorporated into the culture of hyper-consumption. In as much as it covers a nearly 38,000 m² (409,029 square feet) plot of land, the centre literally transforms a huge public space into an affluent middle-class consumption arena; and it is not just a mere shopping experience. Four floors wrap around a canyon-like open-air environment to evoke the sense of being in a street lined with upmarket retail outlets, where well-groomed street vendors sell traditional food from designer carts, surrounded by arty street lighting and furniture. The publicity material boasts, however, that most walking areas are covered and climate controlled with natural light and open air allowing visitors to enjoy every season without suffering its excesses. What Kanyon offers, then, is a new interpretation and a new culture of the experience of the city and its variety of streets.[5]

In similar fashion, local authorities are initiating large-scale urban regeneration programmes using city image and style as arguments for legitimizing their often radically uprooting interventions. The Beyoğlu Municipality was the first to allow private developers to turn an entire street in a run-down part of the old Pera district into a themed area, based on the French lifestyle. Changing the street's name from Algeria Street into French Street, everything, from street furniture, sculptures and wall paintings to the design of the restaurant interiors, was styled to evoke a certain image of Montmartre. Once a public thoroughfare, the street is now a commercial area managed by a business association that dictates the outdoor music, the architectural features and the advertising. At one point, there was even an attempt to install security guards at the entrance to the street in order to monitor the flow of 'customers'. Especially in the central parts of the city, neighbourhoods are being 'cleared' of their old fabric of workshops, repair yards, and other informal service properties in the name of style, image and quality. This is what the Mayor of Beyoğlu boasts about when he explains how he has pushed for the transformation of the old Tamirhane district in Taksim: from being an area for shops specialized in car parts to becoming a centre for tourism with hotels, cafés and restaurants for the genteel.

New urban regeneration projects and residential developments all come with a desire to inculcate a certain sense of urban culture. Culture, in this new context, has come to be associated with 'lifestyle'. According to the marketing concept for one massive residential development project on the Anatolian side of Istanbul, My World Ataşehir, the new urban culture is informed by a dream of a world perfectly and completely thought through: here, they say 'you will find the life you are looking for.' Residents live happily within their own self-contained environments, alonngside their own kind of people, without having to rub shoulders with others (not even their next-door neighbours); they only need to leave their enclaves to go to work, and on weekends, if they so wish, to have a 'lite' heritage or arts experience.

In Istanbul, culture and its various meanings are shifting: culture in its anthropological sense as a way of life; in its economic sense as a business opportunity; and in its symbolic sense as a locus of power and status. Culture is seen as an essential ingredient of the new kind of urbanity that is being brought into existence, a vehicle to promote the image of the city, to attract tourism, and to 'civilize' its citizens. Investing in art and culture has become the fashion of the day, and major business conglomerates and their foundations are competing with one another for suitable spaces to build arts and cultural centres. After the opening of Istanbul Modern, founded by the Eczacıbaşı family, one of the city's prominent business families, came the proposition from another major holding-company-backed arts foundation, the Suna and İnan Kıraç Foundation, to turn the centrally located Tüyap area – owned by the metropolitan municipality – into an international centre for culture and arts with a US$60 (€44) million cultural complex designed by Frank Gehry and funded by the Kıraç Foundation's US$500 (€369) million for arts and culture (although the project has failed as yet to be realized). For the first time, foreign involvement in the traditionally closed off arts and culture sector is occurring through joint-venture agreements and collaborations; a five-year agreement for artistic and scientific collaboration between the prestigious Sabancı Museum and the Louvre is bringing cultural assets in the form of exhibitions, know-how and networking to Istanbul.

Culture is implicated in everything now. Companies use culture to enhance their image as sponsor, aware that investment in arts and culture also brings with it a higher profile and stature – and in turn helps to boost the city's overall visibility to investors, visitors and residents alike. The central government, as well as local municipalities, are now undertaking huge cultural infrastructure projects. In the centre of the city, the Atatürk Cultural Centre (AKM) in Taksim and the Muhsin Ertuğrul Theatre Hall in Harbiye both illustrate the trend of targeting existing cultural facilities for demolition in order to build super-modern, prestigious and multi-functional cultural spaces. The latter has now been rebuilt, while the fate of the more nationally symbolic AKM still remains unclear.

Central government and local authorities of the AKP have instigated a number of key initiatives – an example is the Istanbul 2010 European Capital of Culture project – explicitly aimed at using Istanbul's cultural assets and resources to improve the global image of the city (and thus of the country). The Istanbul Metropolitan Municipality's recently approved masterplan makes a great deal of its competitive aspirations through investing in culture in order to project a 'contemporary' image of the city.[6] Issues of 'city branding' and 'image marketing' have now entered into the city's political vocabulary. Neo-liberal strategists use culture as a tool for revenue generation as well as tourism. Although initiated by the private sector, this cultural renaissance derives support from the government in the form of legal and regulatory changes, including a controversial law for the 'renewal' of historic areas (Law 5366), in addition to well-financed programmes for the development and promotion of the city's cultural and tourism infrastructure. Central government has committed an investment equivalent to the Ministry of Culture and Tourism's annual budget towards the restoration and regeneration of the city's rich cultural heritage as part of the Istanbul 2010 programme. Istanbul's bid to become a global 'open city' involves transforming its image, creating what Mayor Kadir Topbaş refers to as 'a city with a different attitude towards the world.'[7]

The Need for a New Politics of Openness

So, what has changed in Istanbul? The answer lies in the shift of perspective that has taken place, away from an inward-looking stance: globalization is forcing open the city's urban and cultural practices, and bringing with it a parallel process of cultural transformation. This turn towards possible greater openness and interconnectedness, however, happens ultimately in close alliance with the city's gentrification. The 'projected city' is a collection of gentrified spaces, and the cultural imaginary is increasingly being shaped by this project of gentrification. For the ruling AKP government the programme of gentrification is very much linked to their desire to use Istanbul as a stage to demonstrate their modernity and globalism. The local and central governments are compelled to tidy up this stage, to eradicate what seems pre-modern, and to construct the decor of gentrified spaces according to the norms of global cities. In this city of the future, there is no more room for squatters and their 'peasant', and by the same token 'primitive', culture. Squatters should be 'modernized' – radically 'integrated', we could say. They should be encouraged to give up their 'squalor' and accept a new life in the mass-housing schemes that are being developed for them and their modernization needs. As many media columnists have openly argued, the squatters should not be allowed 'to occupy our common land and build illegal and ugly constructions…' [8] The city is urged to 'stop migrants damaging the city's quality of life and its image'.[9] Behind these expressions of 'official aspiration', we find a previously unanticipated – and 'unanticipatable' – coalition of urban elites. This coalition of interests – which is really only a semblance of coalition – involves an instrumental alliance between the so-called 'North-Istanbul elites' (the westernized, secular middle classes) and a new rising middle class made up of commercial and business elites of the Islamic-oriented 'traditional' circles.[10] Until recently, these two elite groups had remained polarized: now, for the moment at least, they share an aspiration and a vision for Istanbul as a globalized and gentrified city with clean, orderly public spaces and residential quarters, as well as an attractive global image.

What I have described so far is the global opening up of Istanbul according to an unfolding and relentless neo-liberal dynamic. In so far as the ruling AKP government has helped open up Istanbul to market-driven global forces, the city's transformation has been a state-led project. This process of restructuring suits the aspirations of its globalizing elites, but also, significantly, its expanding base of property owners. Considering that 58 per cent of the households (out of around 2.5 million from the 2000 census) live in their own property, a significant proportion of the urban population is directly implicated in the changing economy of the city. What is more, according to the Istanbul Governor's office, quite a sizeable proportion of this property-owning category consists of those living in recently legalized squatter settlements (*gecekondu*). In other words, as the squatters of yesterday turn into the property owners of today – however unplanned and run-down their properties might be – the scale of market activity is extended.

Perversely, this process aligns quite different constituencies of interest and self-interest: the result is a strange coalition of Islamic communities, secular elites, large capital, small and conservative business interests, legalized squatter owners, and even so-called bobos (bourgeois bohemians). All these different groups may, in different ways and in different combinations, tactically join forces – awkwardly and ironically – in their jostle to benefit from Istanbul's profit-generating transformation. Save for a few civil society activists and organizations, Istanbul's citizens seem to watch on as the poor, the informal self-employed, and the marginalized migrants are pushed out of the civic space as a result of urban regeneration programmes.

If not actively taking part in the displacement of these disadvantaged groups, the general response of Istanbul's more privileged strata is indifference and resignation. As was the case with Sulukule, for example, one of the oldest Roma neighbourhoods in the city, where all the inhabitants were recently evicted from their properties, and then relocated to far-flung destinations, despite the fact that they had been residents in this area for generations. The reason for this was a municipality-led renewal project, which proposed to turn the neighbourhood into an upmarket housing area. The same fate now awaits the local Roma population and the recent Kurdish immigrants from the southeast of Turkey in the Tarlabaşı district. These residents are very poor, but, more significantly, without title to their properties, and therefore unable to take part in Istanbul's increasingly market-oriented housing economy. It seems that those lacking title will be quietly relegated to the status of the invisible, no longer heard in the public sphere, except when they become junkies, dealers, or criminalized youths.

Insufficient welfare-state structures, alongside the collapse of informal and identity-based mechanisms of inclusion in the city, have created exclusionary dynamics that operate on a much larger scale than ever before. With high levels of unemployment, an unqualified labour force and the continuing influx of immigrants from the rural areas of Turkey, as well as from neighbouring countries and Africa, social exclusion finds fertile ground in Istanbul.[11] The scale of the social problem becomes clear when considering that Istanbul's official population increased from around 10 million in 2000 to over 12 million in 2007. Almost all of this growth can be attributed to new inward migration. And, crucially, Istanbul lacks a social vision to engage the mounting exclusionary dynamics of market-based relations. Unchecked, they may eventually find expression in social fracturing, division and conflict. In a context in which the division between the excluded and the included is sharpening dramatically, and where the familiar mechanisms of incorporation are increasingly being weakened, religious and ethnically-informed identity positions can become ready vehicles for venting frustration and anger.

There is the real danger that urban culture will lose its public nature as market-led consumerism overwhelms discourses about the collective interest. This represents a fundamental challenge for civic and participative urbanism. The reality is that, through global openness, a logic of cultural secularism and pluralism is inevitably put into motion. A possible consequence, then, might well be an increased political conservatism and even authoritarianism.[12] In the face of this scenario, there is clearly a need to argue and campaign for a new politics of openness – a perspective based on the notion that 'a different global model is possible'.[13] This is a project that requires, above all, a prolonged process of negotiation, with an explicit agenda about the kind of globalization and openness that might enlarge public spaces of interaction, engagement and mutual responsibility – against the fragmentation and commercialization of city spaces, which only serve to underline growing social inequality, exclusion and homogenization. This project insists on the imperative need to escape the powerful spell exerted by the apparent radiance of the new Istanbul.

Is this all just a dream? Will Istanbul come to terms with the choices it faces? In a context in which the commissioning of internationally renowned architects for public projects faces mounting anger, with protestors posing the issue as a confrontation between the local (read Turkish) and the international (read outsider), the vulnerability of even the neo-liberal project of openness becomes clear. Defensive and fearful responses to urban globalization slip easily and seamlessly into an exclusionary language and a rejection of difference and diversity. Ultimately this may fuel nationalistic mobilization. On the other hand, the neo-liberal outlook seems oblivious to the dynamics that render the glister of the city dull. The challenge, then, is to deepen and secure the continuation of any existing public experiences of cosmopolitanism – to not lose sight of the real choice that Istanbul needs to make. We have to hope that Istanbul's worldliness can help maintain a democratic basis of social solidarity, where the city is imagined once again as a public space for all.

THE CONTOURS OF CONCRETE

Ömer Kanıpak

ALONE IN THE CROWD

Its long intellectual history has given Istanbul a dense literary tradition that serves to map its shifting identity and character. Most recently, Istanbul's secular culture has had to accommodate an administration formed by Turkey's religiously orientated ruling political party.

It's hard to evaluate a city in which you have resided for years. Too accustomed to every detail that makes it beautiful as well as evil, as a resident of this huge organic mechanism you know which things don't work well, but also which of the city's characteristic features make it unique and interesting, and that almost personify it.

A member of the global megacities league, Istanbul is counted as one of the major business, transportation, cultural and tourist hubs in Europe as well as the Middle East. Like any megacity, its exact population cannot be determined; even the official number fluctuates between 12 and 14 million, a figure greater than the populations of 40 European countries. It is a metropolis so large that it extends more than 100 kilometres across and almost joins with Tekirdağ and Izmit, the cities of the two adjacent provinces, to form the Northern Marmara megalopolis. Since the rural exodus in the 1950s, Istanbul's rapid population growth has caused problems because of illegal settlements (*gecekondu*), which in turn have triggered deforestation, and transport, health care and education challenges, among other urban issues.

Istanbul currently lacks an executable strategic masterplan to coordinate development between the elected 39 municipalities. Even so, foreign investors are continually looking to enter the city's thriving property development market. This is partly because Istanbul remains a magnet for new residents from within the country and from abroad, as well as for global companies opening their eastern European and Middle Eastern headquarters. But Istanbul is not counted as one of the most liveable cities in the world. Quality of life in Istanbul falls well below that in Vancouver, Copenhagen or London. According to the 2008 Mastercard 'Worldwide Centres of Commerce' report, Istanbul ranks 57th of 75 cities compared for liveability, despite having one of the lowest crime rates. And for over 50 years, Istanbul has not been able to prevent illegal settlements emerging on the outskirts of the city, although clean water, electricity and the sewage system reach almost the entire population, including these illegal settlements. So what is working in Istanbul has still not been answered in a convincing fashion.

One of the most obvious of Istanbul's unique features is its geography. Specifically, it is the city's topography that is the strongest factor differentiating Istanbul from other global megacities. Steep hills, valleys and the sinuous curves of the Bosporus dramatically shape the city's urban pattern, its settlements and transport and even its ecology. In Istanbul, the terrain creates the notion of orientation, almost inscribing a three-dimensional mental map of the city in the

RESPONDING TO TOPOGRAPHY
The geographical constraints of a city, framed by water and steep hills, emphasizes the verticality of Istanbul's urban structure.

minds of its residents. Living in Istanbul one is constantly aware of water, which is always in close proximity or just within view. One knows that the slopes of the valleys lead to the Bosporus or the Golden Horn. It is this presence of water and the city's rising landscape that make the scene an omnipresent feature in the everyday life of Istanbul's citizens, an urban feature accessible by the majority irrespective of their social or economic class. And it is not a single scene but a collection of scenes from numerous vistas, thanks to the city's dynamic topography.

The ability to experience the city with the visual senses creates an awareness of the whole, as if the entire city were an enormous stage or collection of screens. This is possible without an Eiffel Tower, a London Eye or similar iconic structure. So we can easily assert that its geographical condition is the major factor that makes Istanbul unique, even though it creates many problems for mass transportation. However, this distinguishing feature is not quite appreciated by the municipalities when drawing up the regional plans or building codes; it's as if the city is as smooth as a blank piece of paper. Where building height restrictions are linked solely to the plot area, topographical differences are not taken into account or are seen as obstructions to be overcome or erased.

Another unique aspect of Istanbul is less obvious and harder to explain. In order to analyze the city, I offer a metaphor that may at first seem awkward: Istanbul is a piece of wrinkled cloth pinched in the middle by a blue string. From a distance this piece of cloth appears to have a homogeneous pattern and colour of its own. However, upon close examination one realizes that it is not a simple sheet but an assemblage of many different pieces of fabric, each with slightly different colours, hues, textures and shapes. Yet, it is not a patchwork of similar orthogonal shapes, a metaphor frequently used to describe any metropolis where diversity is a defining feature. It is more like a cloth that has a camouflage pattern, where the shapes are amorphous. One of the layers of these amorphous shapes may correspond to the social strata of the city, while another overlaps with its topography, and yet another corresponds to the characteristics of its built environment. These layers and shapes do not have a specific rule. Against all expectations, Istanbul becomes a surprising and dynamic city.

At the northern end of the Taksim-Harbiye axis, for instance, is one of the city's most exclusive areas. It borders the Nişantaşı neighbourhood, a predominantly residential area featuring high-end shops for luxury foreign brands. Steps away in the adjacent Feriköy-Pangaltı neighbourhood, located on the slopes of the Dolapdere valley, are rows of apartment buildings and a rectilinear street grid, which differ greatly from the interwoven streets and built forms found elsewhere in the city. The social pattern of this area is also marked by lower income groups and strong neighbourhood relationships. And yet, at the lower end of the Taksim-Harbiye axis sit the congress centre, five-star hotels and cultural facilities – the 'jewels of the valley'.

The same kind of juxtaposition can be found in any part of the city; in the gentrified urban grain of Cihangir, located near the low-income residents of Tophane and its neighbouring coastal business district. It is the relatively short distances between these unique areas that make the city unpredictable in every sense. The changing architectural styles, street patterns, topographical features, neighbourhood sizes and densities do not adhere to a rule that can be aligned to the social and economic characteristics of the inhabitants of these regions. Perhaps that is why the city lacks an executable strategic masterplan: until recently, analysis of this camouflage pattern has never been considered by the municipalities.

The Physical Reflections of Psychological Patterns

The reverse engineering approach should be applied as a method to understand a certain pattern or a certain region of the city that is being analyzed. However, the spatial and visual clues on their own will not lead us to a logical cause and effect scenario. We need to factor in human behaviour, and the psychological conditions of the people using that part of the city. We will need to use social psychology to analyze the effect of how certain groups of people behave on the physical environment.

For instance, in Istanbul you see the agglomeration of certain types of commercial activities in certain neighbourhoods. The Perşembe Pazarı district in Karaköy is famous for its hardware shops, whereas the Merter area is the area where textile outlet shops are all gathered together. If you want to buy cheap imported junk, Tahtakale is the place you should visit. Low-income families know that the cheapest garments can be found in Mahmutpaşa. For photography equipment or electronic gadgets, you need to go to Sirkeci. Even places to eat are clustered together in most neighbourhoods. The entrance of Istiklal Street welcomes you with numerous döner or hamburger shops, whereas the top of Ortaköy is filled with baked potato sellers lined up next to each other.

This clustering of the same commercial goods doesn't seem to make sense, since if the merchants would like to make more money they should sell something different than their neighbours. However, they prefer to be together and settle for a small slice from the cake. This seems to be a conscious and planned decision in order to create a more convenient environment for potential customers. However, the underlying reason might be totally different.

Like in many Middle Eastern countries, the level of tolerance people show to each other in Turkey is not as highly developed as in Western countries. The level of confidence in society is one of the lowest compared with many other countries in the world. Surveys conducted by, for instance, Professor Yılmaz Esmer's team, as part of the World Values Survey research, show that Turkish people do not have a great level of trust in each other or in the governing systems. According to Professor Esmer, intolerance and distrust are embedded into the genes of the population.[1]

This is quite visible in people's daily lives. Bargaining has become almost standard because people fear being cheated while shopping. Doubt about the trader's trustworthiness or the quality of the goods force customers to make comparisons before deciding to buy anything, whether it's a TV set or a hamburger. Even in a restaurant people will want to check the bill to see if the waitress has added it up correctly. This insecurity surrounding daily economical activities has resulted in similar goods to be sold in clusters of shops, which on the one hand enables customers to easily compare and decide and, on the other hand, allows the traders to control each other. Similar clusterings can be seen in many Middle Eastern and less developed countries in the world, where the same distrust of other people can be a common social pattern.

Citizens' distrust of the governing systems is also reflected in the urban patterns in Turkey. Built environment patterns in Turkey are highly fragmented and derived from the shape of the lots owned by individuals. After the death of the owner, larger lots are divided between their inheritors into smaller parts. Instead of uniting smaller lots all together to make larger plots for larger buildings, people prefer to own smaller plots individually and settle for a less convenient building. Today a short flight over Istanbul shows how the entire city is covered by small irregularly dispersed apartments. Large perimeter blocks, long rectilinear housing units or terrace house typologies do not exist in any city in Turkey. Even in the newly developing gated communities and TOKI (Turkey's Mass Housing Administration) applications, the same pattern is visible: large areas are punctuated by the same kind of square prism blocks.

Building regulations enhance this approach, since every clause in the building codes is created to avoid possible violations of the allowed limits, as if all of the citizens are potential lawbreakers. Thus architects who wish to create different typologies of residential units are restricted by very strict building codes that have resulted in the fabrication of the same shape all over the country.

The Liveliest City

However, not everything in urban life in Turkey is negative. It has often been said that public space does not exist in Istanbul and that there are no squares or similar open spaces where people can get together. This is actually a myth, as one can easily argue that Istanbul is one of the liveliest cities in the world with its ever-crowded streets. It is true that it does not have public spaces with well-defined borders, as we are used to seeing in central European cities or in urbanism handbooks. Nevertheless, the use of urban voids by the public in Istanbul is unique, mostly improvised and unplanned, but at the same time very well-coordinated and lively. In Istanbul, public space does not take the form of a static public square. It is defined as the axes along which people move through and intersect in the city. All they need is a more walkable surface redesign, since Istanbul is one of the worst cities in the world for pedestrian movement.

Orthogonal zoning principles used in Western cities cannot successfully be applied to the urban fabric of Istanbul without understanding the psychological motivation of its society. The widely accepted Western urban terminology proliferating in academia is not sufficient to explain 'the Istanbul condition'. Instead, Istanbul should develop an urban language of its own. And it should do so using its inherent features and codes – the elements that have not yet been comprehended or critically analyzed. Deciphering the aforementioned camouflage pattern is a crucial investigation, which can only be accomplished through the coordinated efforts of many disciplines brought together. The built environment is just a fraction of the whole of the experience of city making. Sociologists, economists, and, more importantly, social psychologists should work together to analyze how these seemingly incongruous neighbourhood patterns can live side by side. The tension between the amorphous shapes and different shadings of the social, economic, architectural and topographical strata are the binding forces of this camouflage-patterned piece of fabric called Istanbul.

Four Dimensional Urban Life

The interest of intellectuals in urban conditions comes with a danger. The knowledge we have and the new information we produce through our intellectual and academic studies does not directly penetrate the various levels of administration of our cities. We still cannot communicate well enough with the governing bodies, municipalities and developers that shape them. Thus our analyses are rarely grasped by those in positions of power; our solutions or suggestions are hardly ever realized, and more often than not end up on the shelves. We still haven't managed to create a successful interface to transfer our knowledge to those who govern.

The inherent metabolic rate of cities is also much faster than our reactions. While we as architects and urban planners are working to improve urban conditions, we mostly try to fix something broken instead of preventing the breakdown. Thus we find ourselves in a reactive position rather than a proactive one.

The increasing interest on urbanism in various intellectual circles creates its own popular culture as well. Think about the Oscar-winning film *Slumdog Millionaire* or the Oscar-nominated *City of God*. The whole set of real-life problems of these cities, and, most importantly, the problem of the people living in them, may become a kind of enchanting visual display. The real four-dimensional urban life can easily be flattened into the attractive looking graphs, surveys, numbers and images leaving the people in the streets with their own problems. We have to think more precisely and carefully about the consequences of our intellectual interest in urban issues, since the actual problem may easily become a spectacle, pulling it into the realm of the exotic, which is very dangerous.

Like in Istanbul, every city needs its spatial DNA to be deciphered by decoding its physical texture and by taking its social and psychological aspects into account as well. Not only Istanbul, but every city needs to create its own urban terminology in order to create better living conditions for their citizens. And if we want our researches and forecasts to be used effectively by the governing bodies of these cities, we also need to devise the communication interface for our studies.

MEASURING SUCCESS

Çağlar Keyder

THE VIEW FROM THE TOP

The development of new business centres is marked by high-rise architecture that serves to advertise and celebrate the corporations, many family-owned, that build and inhabit them.

Most observers will agree that Istanbul is on its way to success in terms of acquiring a prominent position in global economic, cultural and political circuits. From the point of view of the project that Turkish statesmen embarked upon in the 1980s, the former imperial capital has fulfilled the promise of spearheading the country's entry on to the global stage. Istanbul has become the undisputed portal to Turkey's opening up to the world, and has far outshone its potential rivals in terms of its presence in the contemporary scene.

This success, however, cannot really be dated to the more distant past than the first decade of this millennium. Throughout the 1990s Istanbul's evolution as a global city was stymied by a less than cooperative stance in Ankara. Governments were suspicious of policies that fully embraced pro-market tendencies and they refrained from subscribing to their polarizing implications. Hence, globalization occurred piecemeal and inadvertently. In the 1990s the impact of globalization was an undeniable social fact; there was, however, no coherent policy as yet, and conflicting signals from Ankara meant that the initiatives of the local government in Istanbul could be scuttled at any time, making it difficult for the urban elite to decide on committing their resources to the globalizing project with confidence. By the end of the twentieth century, there still was no resolution to these tensions, and it was fitting to describe what was going on as 'informal globalization', a process that made it impossible, especially for foreign capitalists, to trust the environment sufficiently to be able to invest in the sectors that needed to develop to enable Istanbul's transformation. If there was any doubt that Ankara's politics could undermine Istanbul's path, it became clear once again in 2001, when a spat over pro-market policies between the prime minister and the president triggered a currency crisis and led to a severe economic downturn, with Istanbul losing half a million jobs and witnessing rising poverty levels.

Istanbul's success in the global-city rankings, which has only become apparent subsequent to the 2001 downturn, should in large measure be attributed to the coincidence of political and economic expectations from the city, and thus to the coherence of the urban coalitions which aimed to upgrade the city's image and marketing potential in the eyes of a footloose global demand – whether for investment, for culture, or for leisure.

At the end of 2002 portentous change started to become visible in Turkey, which signified a qualitative break with the past, and which fully transformed Istanbul's

prospects as a global city. The social conservative Justice and Development Party (AKP), led by the former Mayor of Istanbul, Tayyip Erdoğan, won the elections and formed a one-party government. This meant that they would not have to make any concessions to coalition partners; and since Erdoğan had already declared himself to be a true believer in 'the market', they would be in a position to advance neo-liberal reforms to a much greater extent than before. When he was elected mayor, Erdoğan had declared his intention to close Istanbul to poor immigrants: his plan was to make the city expensive, by instituting a tax, or an entry visa. He also had made it clear that he was aware of the global-city 'buzz', and that he thought Istanbul's position to be crucial in order to secure Turkey's successful entry into world markets. In other words, Istanbul had to serve as the port for Turkey's opening up.

With Erdoğan's new government, political commitment to boost Istanbul's ranking by capturing a greater share of global flows of capital, tourism, and high-end services, was declared unambiguously. The central government in Ankara and municipal politicians in Istanbul were now on the same page. More important, however, was the signal sent to Istanbul's bourgeoisie that they no longer had to hedge their bets by maintaining good relations with the nationalist and anti-globalist statesmen of Ankara. They could now commit themselves fully to the global (and liberal) agenda. In fact, they did so by joining in with the investment decisions of foreign capital, by participating in partnerships with the municipal government, by funding museums and festivals, and acting as a volunteer development corporation in the quest to raise Istanbul's profile in the world market.

There were institutional changes that had to be undertaken at the level of central government in order to facilitate the transformation in the direction of global-city status. A city like Istanbul, aspiring to become more central in intensified transnational networks, needs to overhaul its physical aspect; it has to create an entire new level of built environment. New spaces have to be produced through the interaction of politics, economic flows and social experience. This production of space obviously requires the availability of land as a malleable commodity. Urban growth means urban development, in the sense that developers who open up new spaces on which to build have to participate in the activity. As more sophisticated and differentiated functions are called for, a greater commodification of land becomes a necessity. Land has to be seen as a commodity that can be bought and sold, considered as private property, developed according to known rules, and speculated with as an asset whose price fluctuates. It is crucial to trace the process of this commodification in the case of Istanbul, because, as in many peripheral environments, the property structure on land was often irregular, vague, uncertain and risky. Except that it was perhaps even more so, due to both the legal history of the Ottoman Empire and to the demographic upheaval of the city during the last century.

Legal history suggests that private property of land (as opposed to houses and other buildings) was always problematic in the Empire; no claim to ownership was ever properly respected by the authorities. In other words, private property was a suspect notion. Population dynamics added to the ambivalence with which property was regarded. Istanbul's population increased rapidly during the decades before World War I, to reach almost 1 million. At the time, around one-third of the population were Greek and 15 per cent held foreign passports. By 1923 Istanbul had lost a third of its population due to the departure of foreigners, to the compulsory Exchange of Populations with Greece, which required all those Orthodox Christians who could not prove residence in the city to leave, and the end of the imperial feeling of cosmopolitan accommodation. A lot of property was abandoned, then and subsequently, because of the homogenization of the population. The city's population, which had declined in the inter-war period, climbed back to the million-mark by 1950, from which point on the dynamics of third-world urbanization took over. In 1970 the population was 2.8 million, in 1990 6.5 million, and in 2000 9 million. Now, it has surpassed 12 million. The huge increase over the second half of the twentieth century had to be accompanied by a geographical expansion of the urban space. It was through the course of this expansion that the legal structure of property claims on land became even more involuted. There was land that was abandoned by the departing foreigners and non-Muslims whose property rights could not be defended; there was large-scale occupation of public land adjoining the inhabited spaces; and there was agricultural land that was held in usufruct that was 'sold' to immigrants. On all these different forms of land, informal development (*gecekondu*) took place. As a result of political bargains, the holders of housing plots in these areas obtained various forms of recognition of their ownership over time. The effect was that many of these *gecekondus* became legalized.

The point here is that the history of Istanbul's spatial expansion was not straightforward – in the sense that the accommodation of population growth required ad hoc arrangements regarding land ownership. When capitalism was deepened under the impact of global liberalism, more predictable categories were needed in order to allow investment at a new scale by businesses requiring new sorts of safeguards. In other words, the creation of space in accordance with the new requirements called for a new confidence in the legal arrangements for property. The story of the mutual understanding between the central government and the Istanbul municipality revolved around the establishment of these safeguards.

TOKI, the Mass Housing Administration, was entrusted with the urban regeneration policy pursued by the AKP government. It became the instrument through which the reforms required to restructure urban property were made somewhat palatable, especially in Istanbul. As is often the case, urban regeneration translated into slum clearance in the visible parts of the city.

Istanbul's municipality announced that it would use a variety of legal means (including assessment of earthquake preparedness, protection of cultural heritage, environmental regulations and clearing of green zones) in order to establish grounds for razing informal neighbourhoods and congested areas in the inner city which might be regenerated to contribute to the formation of investment- and tourism-ready spaces. TOKI was the agency through which this process was implemented, since the clearing of households always involved the relocation of the displaced population to mass housing in remote urban areas. In other words, TOKI became the generator of private property both on the outskirts of the city, through the construction of new residential areas, and closer to the city centre by removing the population with ambiguous claims over the land they lived on. TOKI was also able to take over and develop state-owned land unilaterally, and through this power opened up large zones of the city to developments such as residential quarters, business districts, and educational and health service campuses. This clearing of the city, creating development opportunities through privatization of public land, and formalizing land tenure patterns, has meant that the city is finally ready for the kind of property expansion needed for the creation of new social spaces. Land has finally been commodified, lifting the barriers for full capitalist development, investment and speculation.

While the direct impact of TOKI on capitalist development was evident through the emergence of a new property regime, it has also become a crucial agency of social policy that has contributed to the establishment of a housing policy. In Istanbul, as well as in other cities, the poor were left to fend for their own under a benign neglect, permitting them to build illegally on land that was not theirs. Housing has now become a major concern, as a result of the clearing of areas that are being opened up for gentrification, development, and in general for middle-class habitation and tourist enjoyment. A greater dominance of the market goes hand in hand with a 'modern' social policy to replace traditional populist and basically pre-capitalist arrangements.

A second condition, which might explain Istanbul's achievement as a global city that attracts capital and people, has been its image. As in all marketable commodities under competitive capitalism, branding of the product is a requirement for its successful sale. While it would be an exaggeration to attribute the secret of success completely to judicious branding, a coherent narrative that resonates with the prevalent global flavour would seem to be a definite plus. In the attempt to convert history and culture to marketable commodities, Istanbul has an embarrassment of riches. The new urban coalition – the city government, real estate concerns, the bourgeoisie in its manifold manifestations, and the top echelons of the civil society, including the media and the city-boosting foundations funded by businessmen – aimed to consolidate the city around an image of gentility. The marketing of Istanbul has proceeded along expected lines: the historical wealth of the city as well as its nightlife and culinary diversity are highlighted, along with the promotion of dozens of music, art, and film festivals, new museums and exhibitions, which all attempt to reference the master narrative of Istanbul's heritage.

On their own, these achievements do not provide a dominant theme, as all self-respecting cities try to excel in similar areas. The distilling of a defining theme is a tricky process, in which the archaeological layers of the city's many incarnations are alternative candidates for foregrounding. Various projects and imaginaries whose aim is to represent the city in a particular manner, highlighting specific features of a complex history, vied for providing the key to the narrative. The Byzantine city of the classicists who wanted to emphasize the land's geographical heritage competed with the Islamic city of the devout. According to the latter, Istanbul was the capital that the Prophet had promised to the believers. In the attempt to mobilize its cultural heritage, the Turkish city of the Republic was too narrow a reference and would not have much pulling power, especially since the Republic treated Istanbul with some coldness, if not disdain, until the 1980s. The secular elite would not play along with an agenda to reconfigure the Ottoman heritage into Islamic sites of visitation, and the classicist vision had no social support.

The compromise that was reached had the advantage of accommodating competing claims: Istanbul was presented as the Ottoman city of many cultures. An inclusive Ottomanism was concocted, a re-imagined rubric encompassing the multifarious heritages that the city could boast of. The elite were happy to display their mansions and *objets* dating from the Empire, while churches and synagogues were carefully restored along with mosques and civil architecture. Ottoman art of the nineteenth century became a staple in the new museums, where exhibitions helped establish that the multicultural Ottoman elite had been very much engaged with European art, music and literature. Gentrifiers lovingly restored Istanbul's nineteenth-century, Westernized neighbourhoods. This was a new representation of the city in which the peripheral modernity of the Empire seamlessly flowed into an aspired status in contemporary global space. What it achieved was a narrative that could easily be appropriated by the global media, the art world, and tastemakers who helped put Istanbul on the map – of investors, discerning tourists, exhibition curators, real estate developers, buyers of residences in 'in' cities of the world, and sundry consumers of culture.

Istanbul's success in this enterprise of acquiring a commanding position in the hierarchy of cities, which has become more apparent in the new century, can be attributed in large measure to the cooperation of political and economic powers. This cooperation made for the coherence of the urban coalitions aimed at upgrading the city's image and marketing potential in the eyes of a rising global demand – whether for investment, culture or leisure. Success in this sense refers to the objectives of the global city project itself. It does not imply a normative preference for the polarization and exclusion that often accompanies the process whereby segments in the social structure of the globalizing city find social, economic and cultural niches to align themselves with new transnational networks. The ensuing transformation in the social structure is often one of division and stratification where social spaces are re-defined to mark exclusive use. The city begins to attain a divided appearance where local cultures come to be branded as 'defenders of old spaces' while global actors – investors, professionals, businessmen and even tourists – define the criteria that will determine the new modalities of urban living.

In an important sense the ramifications of globalization, hence success in the global city project, are no more than the expected effects of deepening capitalism. As such the city becomes less ambiguously capitalist, because there is no more room for populist protection as it existed, for instance, during the period when new arrivals were implicitly granted the right to squat on public land. The groundwork allowing the city to accommodate flows of finance and investment (institutional frameworks, and the emergence of a growth coalition between the politicians and businessmen) accelerates the process of capitalist development. Successful marketing of the city to investors and tourists, through the branding of the product to allow it to become a desirable consumption artefact, increases the flows that reconfigure the urban space.

I edited a book on Istanbul in 1999, which contained a collection of articles on the global and local in Istanbul. At that time there was a real sense of struggle and tenacity of the local in the sense of old spaces, cultures and political mores both resisting and being defended. In people's habits and expectations there was resistance to the incursion of the global market and to dilution of the populist traditions of the nation-state. It seemed then that the contest was still ongoing and it was not clear how it would resolve. The acceptance of the global seemed to be temporary and provisional. Globalization was taking place in a way in which informal development in Istanbul also did – locating itself in places where there was least resistance, where the rules did not really impede but did not permit either. This process could be called an informal globalization in the sense that it was proceeding in the absence of proper rules, without the regulations and guarantees and the kind of infrastructure that more proper globalization would call for. All these requirements are now there and seem to work as expected. Istanbul's geographical and historical advantages can now be deployed through the mediation of politics and culture; and the marketing effort emboldened by this marriage of projects seems to have yielded the results expected from a successful deepening of capitalism, with the attendant social polarization and spatial segregation.

URBAN FOOTPRINT: MAPPING PEOPLE AND POWER

These maps identify the built-up area, shown in dark grey, of nine Urban Age cities drawn to the same scale (100 x 100 km) and also indicate the administrative boundary of the relevant municipality. They have been generated from 'heat-sensitive' GIS technology that captures the precise location of any built form, giving an accurate account of the real shape of the urban footprint in these global Metropolitan Regions.

They show that in some cities there is a misalignment between the administrative boundaries and where people live and work, highlighting the fact that cities are dynamic while urban governance is static. As cities expand they outgrow their municipal boundaries, which can become outdated and unrepresentative of the functional extent of the city. While this is not the case for Istanbul and Shanghai, whose vast administrative boundaries encompass nearly all the continuous built-up area, or London, which is contained within its administrative 'green belt', most of the built-up areas of the Urban Age cities spill out beyond their municipal boundaries. The extreme cases are Mexico City, New York City, São Paulo and Mumbai, where the municipal boundaries contain only 44, 46, 57 and 65 per cent respectively of their metropolitan populations. In addition, the maps reveal the variation in 'land-take' in response to geographic constraints and population densities. While Mumbai and Istanbul are constrained by natural contours and the sea, São Paulo, Shanghai and New York's Metropolitan Regions have expanded horizontally across a wide area. Berlin's built-up land within the city's administrative boundary covers an area of 570 square kilometres (220 square miles), twice as large as Mumbai, which holds three times the population of the German capital.

Urban footprint

City boundary

Metropolitan Region boundary

MUMBAI
11,710,000 people

Chhatrapati Shivaji Terminus

NEW YORK CITY
8,090,000 people

Central Park

MEXICO CITY
8,580,000 people

Zócalo

SÃO PAULO
10,400,000 people

Praça da Sé

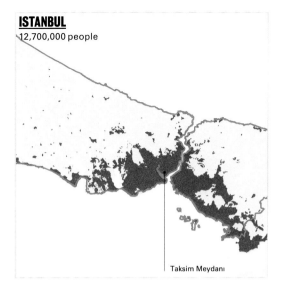

ISTANBUL
12,700,000 people

Taksim Meydanı

100 km

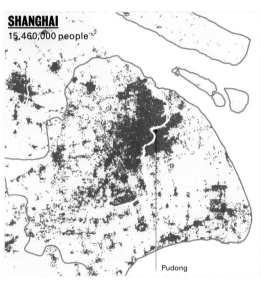

SHANGHAI
15,460,000 people

Pudong

100 km

LONĐON
7,560,000 people

Trafalgar Square

JOHANNESBURG
3,230,000 people

Downtown

BERLIN
3,330,000 people

Brandenburger Tor

POLITICAL METABOLISM: FROM THE REGIONAL TO THE LOCAL

Cities have strong economic and political interdependencies with their regional hinterlands and are accountable to their electorate through different systems of local representation, which guarantees or frustrates democratic engagement. While London and New York contain roughly eight million people, the former is divided into 33 boroughs and the latter into five, ranging from a population of 500,000 in Staten Island to 2.5 million in Brooklyn. While London's boroughs vary between 200,000 and 300,000 people, New York City has a further level of local government with 51 district councils that give its residents considerable local power. At the regional level New York operates within the wider Tri-State area (with the neighbouring states of New Jersey and Long Island), while London does not have a regional equivalent. For the Urban Age cities that exceed 10 million residents, Mumbai has 24 local wards, São Paulo 31, Istanbul 39 and Shanghai 18, reflecting very different systems of local governance and regional accountability. The State of São Paulo encompasses a wider metropolitan area of over 19 million people, and includes many of the decentralized industrial areas and *favelas* that form part of the city's functional infrastructure. At the other extreme, Shanghai includes extensive areas of agricultural land as well as built-up space and large industrial complexes. Johannesburg and Berlin, with populations above three million, are subdivided into seven and 12 local districts respectively, but both sit within robust structures of regional governance – Gauteng Province and the Brandenburg Metropolitan Region. Mexico City is very much a special case, given that less than half of its 20 million residents live in the Federal District, which is subdivided into 16 districts, while the rest of the population lives in the neighbouring State of Mexico.

Metropolitan region
Administrative city

———————————— Administrative unit boundaries

MUMBAI
24 Wards

Mumbai Metropolitan Region
Greater Mumbai

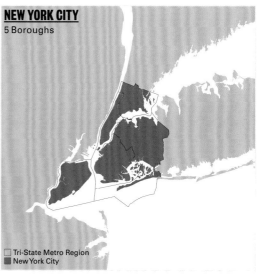

NEW YORK CITY
5 Boroughs

Tri-State Metro Region
New York City

MEXICO CITY
16 Delegaciones

Mexico City Metropolitan Region
Mexico City Federal District

SÃO PAULO
31 Subprefeituras

☐ São Paulo Metropolitan Region
■ City of São Paulo

ISTANBUL
39 İlçe

■ Istanbul Province

100 km

SHANGHAI
18 Divisions

■ Shanghai Province

100 km

LONDON
33 Boroughs

■ Greater London

JOHANNESBURG
7 Regions

■ Province of Gauteng
■ City of Johannesburg

BERLIN
12 Bezirke

☐ Berlin-Brandenburg Metropolitan Region
■ Berlin

CITY GOVERNANCE COMPARED

These charts illustrate how government structures are organized in Mumbai, São Paulo and Istanbul. They are designed to give a crude impression of how the basic responsibilities are arranged, identifying the key functions carried out at central, state and local government level. While they offer a useful comparative overview, they are not intended to give an accurate account of the detailed systems of accountability, which can only be explained on a case-by-case basis.

▓ National level
▒ State level
▒ City level
░ Borough level
— Executive power including the right for regulatory overwrite
--- Some limited powers

Mumbai
Reflecting India's highly centralized political system, national government has a strong say in Mumbai through a number of powerful departments. The Maharashtra State government, headed by a chief minister, operates many services within the city including roads, housing, education, health care, environmental services and policing. The city government is headed by an elected mayor with limited powers, and there is an absence of significant borough-level representation. The real executive power lies with the state, which controls the Mumbai Metropolitan Region Development Authority (MMRDA) and coordinates the development of Greater Mumbai.

São Paulo
The municipality of São Paulo is led by a directly elected mayor who works closely with the governor of the State of São Paulo. The state plays an important role in setting the strategic development framework for the wider Metropolitan Region, including integrated transport planning, housing, military and civilian forces. The municipality is responsible for local transport, housing, and utilities, and controls the local police force. A third, decentralized level of 31 *subprefeituras*, the main point of contact for the electorate, manages local public services and has limited planning and transport responsibilities.

Istanbul
Istanbul's government functions within a unitary national framework with federal ministries, based in Ankara, providing health care, primary education, policing and some housing and transport infrastructure – co-ordinated by a centrally appointed governor in Istanbul. The directly elected mayor of the Istanbul Metropolitan Municipality (IMM) shares executive power with a Municipal Council formed by selected members of the city's 39 District (*İlçe*) Municipalities and their respective mayors, who operate at the local level. The Mayor enjoys extensive powers and a significant budget for providing citywide services. The recently established Istanbul Development Agency co-ordinates work between the local, regional and national bodies.

MUMBAI

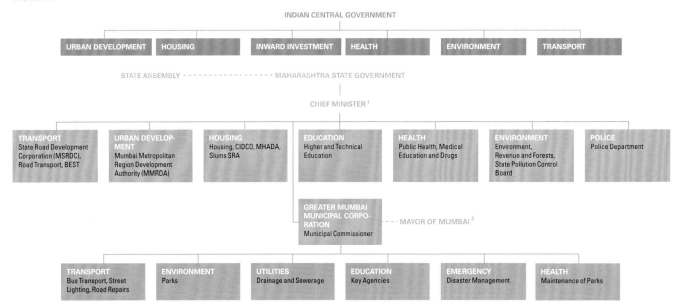

1 Elected by state assembly
2 Mayor elected by councillors of the Municipal Corporation

SÃO PAULO

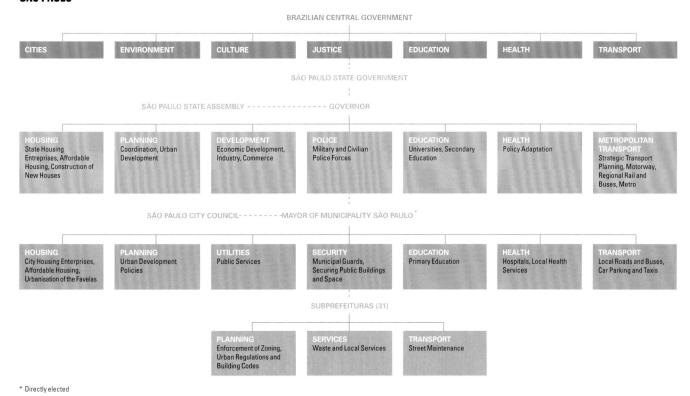

BRAZILIAN CENTRAL GOVERNMENT

| CITIES | ENVIRONMENT | CULTURE | JUSTICE | EDUCATION | HEALTH | TRANSPORT |

SÃO PAULO STATE GOVERNMENT

SÃO PAULO STATE ASSEMBLY - - - - - - - - - - - - - - - - - - GOVERNOR

| HOUSING
State Housing Entreprises, Affordable Housing, Construction of New Houses | PLANNING
Coordination, Urban Development | DEVELOPMENT
Economic Development, Industry, Commerce | POLICE
Military and Civilian Police Forces | EDUCATION
Universities, Secondary Education | HEALTH
Policy Adaptation | METROPOLITAN TRANSPORT
Strategic Transport Planning, Motorway, Regional Rail and Buses, Metro |

SÃO PAULO CITY COUNCIL - - - - - - - - MAYOR OF MUNICIPALITY SÃO PAULO *

| HOUSING
City Housing Enterprises, Affordable Housing, Urbanisation of the Favelas | PLANNING
Urban Development Policies | UTILITIES
Public Services | SECURITY
Municipal Guards, Securing Public Buildings and Space | EDUCATION
Primary Education | HEALTH
Hospitals, Local Health Services | TRANSPORT
Local Roads and Buses, Car Parking and Taxis |

SUBPREFEITURAS (31)

| PLANNING
Enforcement of Zoning, Urban Regulations and Building Codes | SERVICES
Waste and Local Services | TRANSPORT
Street Maintenance |

* Directly elected

ISTANBUL

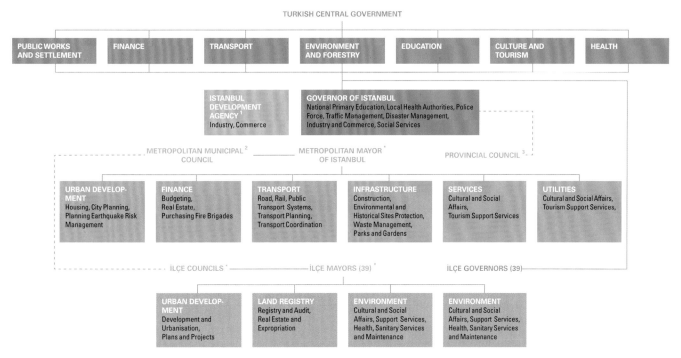

TURKISH CENTRAL GOVERNMENT

| PUBLIC WORKS AND SETTLEMENT | FINANCE | TRANSPORT | ENVIRONMENT AND FORESTRY | EDUCATION | CULTURE AND TOURISM | HEALTH |

| ISTANBUL DEVELOPMENT AGENCY [1]
Industry, Commerce | GOVERNOR OF ISTANBUL
National Primary Education, Local Health Authorities, Police Force, Traffic Management, Disaster Management, Industry and Commerce, Social Services |

METROPOLITAN MUNICIPAL [2] _____ METROPOLITAN MAYOR *   PROVINCIAL COUNCIL [3]
COUNCIL   OF ISTANBUL

| URBAN DEVELOP-MENT
Housing, City Planning, Planning Earthquake Risk Management | FINANCE
Budgeting, Real Estate, Purchasing Fire Brigades | TRANSPORT
Road, Rail, Public Transport Systems, Transport Planning, Transport Coordination | INFRASTRUCTURE
Construction, Environmental and Historical Sites Protection, Waste Management, Parks and Gardens | SERVICES
Cultural and Social Affairs, Tourism Support Services | UTILITIES
Cultural and Social Affairs, Tourism Support Services, |

İLÇE COUNCILS * - - - - - - - - İLÇE MAYORS (39) *   İLÇE GOVERNORS (39)

| URBAN DEVELOP-MENT
Development and Urbanisation, Plans and Projects | LAND REGISTRY
Registry and Audit, Real Estate and Expropriation | ENVIRONMENT
Cultural and Social Affairs, Support Services, Health, Sanitary Services and Maintenance | ENVIRONMENT
Cultural and Social Affairs, Support Services, Health, Sanitary Services and Maintenance |

* Directly elected
1 Recently established, not yet fully implemented
2 Formed by selected members of District Council and all District Mayors
3 Headed by the centrally appointed Governor of Istanbul, it is the council of the Provincial Special Authority

SIGNS OF AGEING

The age distribution among urban populations reveals a considerable variation across the Urban Age cities, one that closely mirrors national and global demographic trends. European and North American cities reflect a more mature average age compared to cities in developing countries, even though New York and London, and to a degree Berlin, have younger populations than rural areas in their respective countries. The age pyramids for these cities reveal a 'middle age spread', where residents between 30 and 50 years old constitute the majority, in line with declining birth rates and longer life expectancy experienced in these more advanced economies. The story is different in contexts of rapid urban growth. The age pyramids of Mumbai, Shanghai, Mexico City – and to some extent Istanbul and São Paulo – show the dominance of younger rural-to-urban migrants, with many residents below the age of 30 providing a broad base for the labour force and the large informal sector they work in. Shanghai graphically represents the ageing structure of its population, reflecting China's one-child policy and heavy in-migration from rural areas. The remarkable drop in life expectancy, especially among men, of people above the age of 50 to 60 is noticeable in Mumbai, Istanbul and Johannesburg, indicating limited access to health care, high levels of poverty and poor environmental quality.

MUMBAI

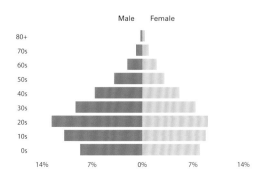

NEW YORK CITY

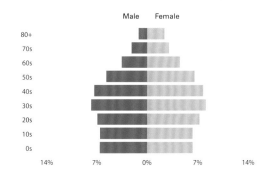

MEXICO CITY

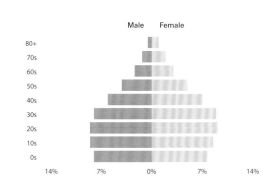

SÃO PAULO

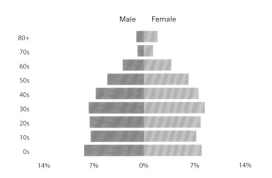

ISTANBUL

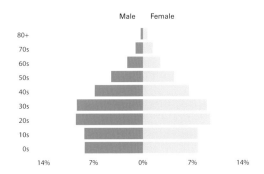

SHANGHAI

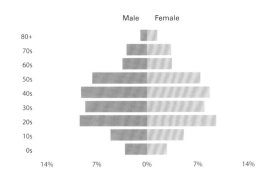

LONDON

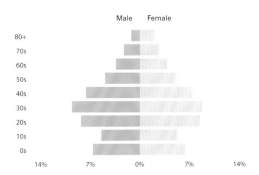

JOHANNESBURG

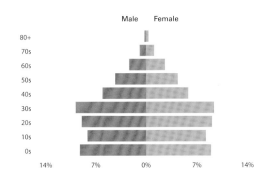

BERLIN

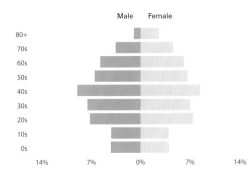

MAPPING SOCIAL ORDER

While economic theory goes some way towards explaining the distribution of social groups in different cities, the pattern of social disadvantage varies significantly across Urban Age cities. São Paulo and Johannesburg demonstrate extremes of peripherilization of exclusion, with higher levels of unemployment pushed outwards towards the city's edges that suffer from low levels of social and transport infrastructure. Despite the presence of inner-city slums, Mumbai presents the same pattern when measured by literacy rate, a proxy for social disadvantage. Mexico City reveals a more chequered pattern with well-educated neighbourhoods sitting cheek by jowl with more excluded groups, often living in slums – a pattern unexpectedly repeated in Berlin, whose recent history has skewed the classic social evolution of such a fundamentally bourgeois city. London and Istanbul display a contrary trend, with large concentrations of socially disadvantaged clustered in relatively central areas – locked into the inner city. Shanghai takes this model to an extreme with many inner-city areas still inhabited by the city's less affluent classes who have been living in state subsidized housing for decades, next to areas that are experiencing dramatic social and economic change. New York displays a complex spatial pattern of social exclusion that correlates closely with the city's ethnic minorities: Afro-Americans in Harlem, Hispanics, Puerto Ricans and Afro-Americans in the Bronx and Queens, white affluent classes in central Manhattan. London, instead, has little or no correlation between ethnic diversity and affluence, representing a more flexible pattern of social integration at a city-wide level. In all cities, areas with high shares of disadvantaged groups are poorly serviced, fuelling the spatialization of social difference.

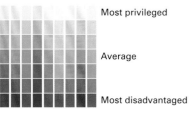

Most privileged

Average

Most disadvantaged

Administrative boundaries

MUMBAI

Chhatrapati Shivaji Terminus

NEW YORK CITY

Central Park

MEXICO CITY

Zócalo

SÃO PAULO

Praça da Sé

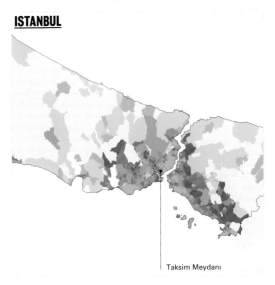

ISTANBUL

Taksim Meydanı

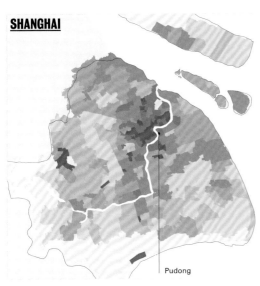

SHANGHAI

Pudong

LONDON

Trafalgar Square

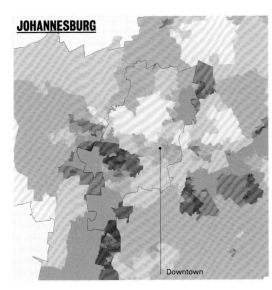

JOHANNESBURG

Downtown

BERLIN

Brandenburger Tor

THE CHANGING NATURE OF URBAN WORK

The nine Urban Age cities are at different stages of a transition from an industrial to a knowledge-based economy. The employment figures presented here show that London and New York have advanced the furthest towards this economic transformation, although neither city has an economy based exclusively on financial and business services; retail, leisure, social and personal services continue to be major sources of employment in both cities. Most of the other Urban Age cities retain 10 to 20 per cent of their secondary sector employment – dominated by manufacturing, industry and construction. In some cases, a small agricultural sector also remains. Istanbul's situation closely mirrors that of Shanghai – both cities have retained an extensive manufacturing base (around 40 per cent). With respect to the other Urban Age cities, this difference originates from the fact that they are municipalities with large territories where manufacturing and agricultural activities still dominate. In terms of formal employment Mexico City, Mumbai, São Paulo and Johannesburg all show over 70 per cent of the workforce employed in some level of service-based activity. But, these statistics do not show the importance of informal employment in most cities of the developing world. Mumbai's informal urban economy, for example, engages more than 60 per cent of the workforce often made up of low-skilled rural migrants who live and work in slums.

MUMBAI

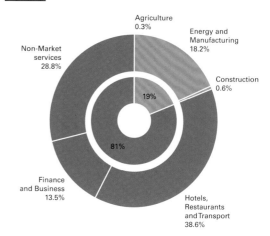

NEW YORK CITY

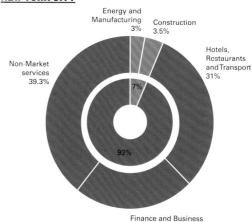

MEXICO CITY

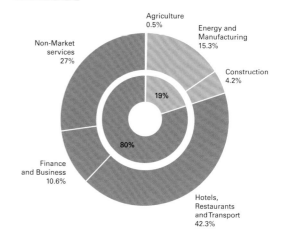

Primary sector
Secondary sector
Tertiary sector

SÃO PAULO

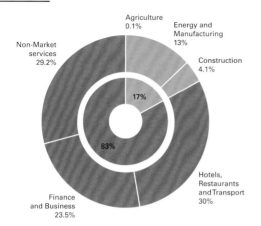

Agriculture 0.1%
Energy and Manufacturing 13%
Non-Market services 29.2%
Construction 4.1%
17%
83%
Hotels, Restaurants and Transport 30%
Finance and Business 23.5%

ISTANBUL

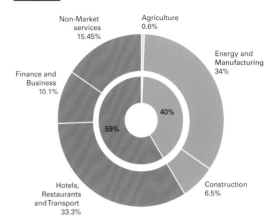

Non-Market services 15.45%
Agriculture 0.6%
Energy and Manufacturing 34%
Finance and Business 10.1%
40%
59%
Construction 6.5%
Hotels, Restaurants and Transport 33.3%

SHANGHAI

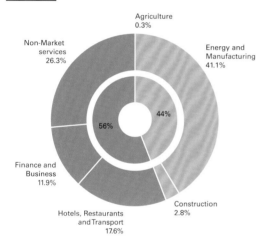

Agriculture 0.3%
Non-Market services 26.3%
Energy and Manufacturing 41.1%
56%
44%
Finance and Business 11.9%
Construction 2.8%
Hotels, Restaurants and Transport 17.6%

LONDON

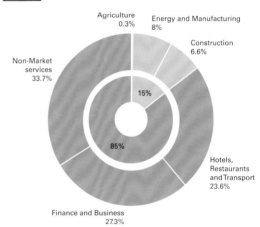

Agriculture 0.3%
Energy and Manufacturing 8%
Construction 6.6%
Non-Market services 33.7%
15%
85%
Hotels, Restaurants and Transport 23.6%
Finance and Business 27.3%

JOHANNESBURG

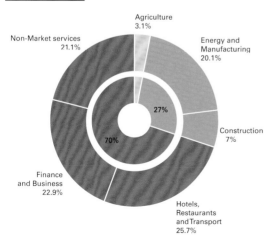

Agriculture 3.1%
Non-Market services 21.1%
Energy and Manufacturing 20.1%
27%
70%
Construction 7%
Finance and Business 22.9%
Hotels, Restaurants and Transport 25.7%

BERLIN

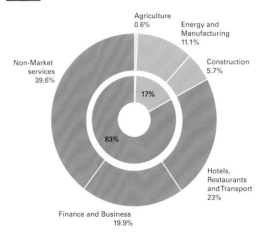

Agriculture 0.6%
Energy and Manufacturing 11.1%
Non-Market services 39.6%
Construction 5.7%
17%
83%
Hotels, Restaurants and Transport 23%
Finance and Business 19.9%

CAPTURING URBAN DENSITY

Residential urban density measures how many people live in relative proximity in cities. The diagrams below show the number of people living in each square kilometre of an urban region that extends 100 x 100 kilometres in the nine Urban Age cities, with tall 'spikes' indicating peak densities and low gradients indicating low densities. On the right, a 'figure-ground' illustration of the areas of peak density in each city is identified. More detailed information on these areas and the density distribution diagrams are given on the following pages.

Residential density is largely driven by topographical constraints and the location of public transport and other infrastructure, but also by each city's inherited traditions of urban culture and development. Urban Age cities demonstrate a wide range of differing density patterns – from the very high densities in the centres of Mumbai, Istanbul and Shanghai to the much lower density development patterns of Berlin and London. Johannesburg shows

MUMBAI
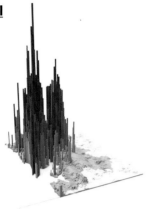

SÃO PAULO
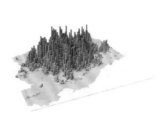

ISTANBUL
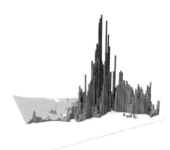

NEW YORK CITY
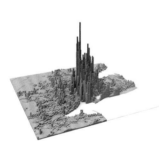

SHANGHAI

LONDON

MEXICO CITY
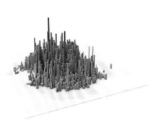

JOHANNESBURG
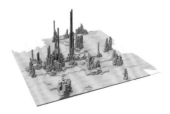

BERLIN

limited areas of high-density set around a downtown that no longer has a residential population, in the midst of a very low-density sprawl. The pattern displayed by New York, on the other hand, shows how the constraints of waterways drive densities that rise to a 'spike' in Manhattan and parts of the Bronx, Brooklyn and Queens, while the rest of the Metropolitan Region has a lower density. São Paulo is multi-centred and similar in its overall density pattern to Mexico City. This is a striking comparison given that the two cities are very different in terms of their urban form – São Paulo's skyline is dominated by high-rise apartment blocks, while Mexico City's is consistently low-rise. These similar density profiles confirm that high-rise buildings do not necessarily create higher density in comparison to more tightly planned low-rise development, especially when individual towers are surrounded by large areas of tarmac or unused space.

MUMBAI

SÃO PAULO

ISTANBUL

NEW YORK CITY

SHANGHAI

LONDON

MEXICO CITY

JOHANNESBURG

BERLIN

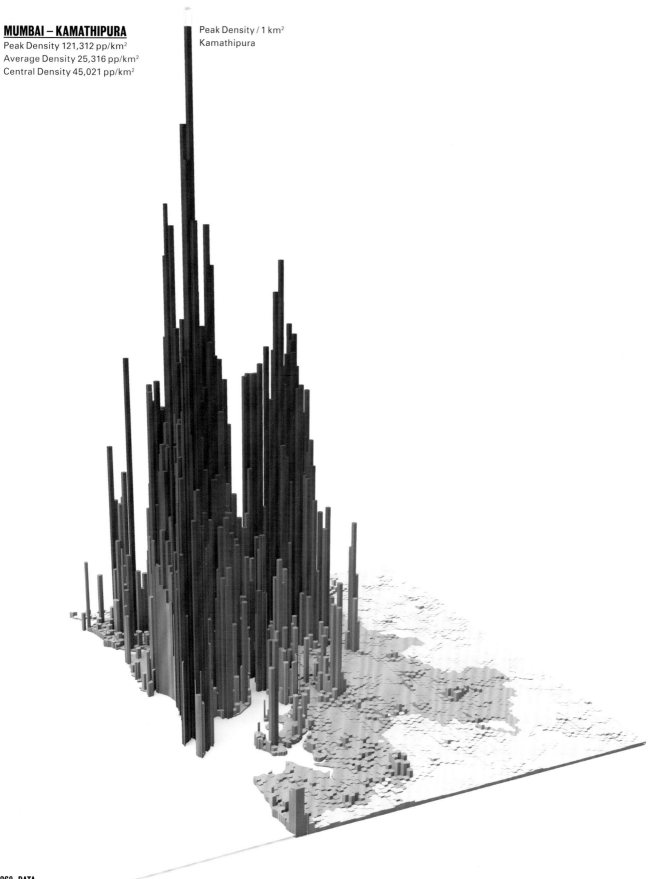

MUMBAI – KAMATHIPURA
Peak Density 121,312 pp/km²
Average Density 25,316 pp/km²
Central Density 45,021 pp/km²

Peak Density / 1 km²
Kamathipura

The densest part of Mumbai, Kamathipura, is situated in the southern portion of the island city, 1.5 kilometres (less than a mile) northwest of the city's most dynamic areas. It features a mix of traditional one-storey structures, multi-storey apartment blocks and high-rise towers. Known as Mumbai's oldest and Asia's largest red-light district, it is nonetheless a vibrant residential area with many small-scale commercial and manufacturing activities and shops creating an uninterrupted, active edge along congested alleys and major streets. The constrained nature of the city and escalating land values have made the area desirable for redevelopment; many of the low-rise structures are being replaced by taller buildings with a larger footprint that is transforming the fine urban grain of the area.

Peak Density / 1 km²
Kamathipura

SÃO PAULO – SANTA CECÍLIA

Peak Density 29,704 pp/km²
Average Density 6,832 pp/km²
Central Density 10,376 pp/km²

Peak Density / 1 km²
Santa Cecília

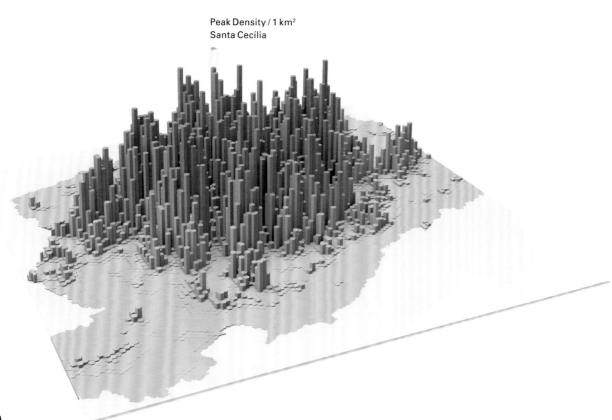

Santa Cecília, the densest residential neighbourhood of the city, is located in central São Paulo, 2.5 kilometres (1.5 miles) northwest of the Praça da Sé, its historical centre, and 2.5 kilometres (1.5 miles) to the north of the Avenida Paulista, now the city's main commercial and business district. Eight- to ten-storey apartment blocks and some residential towers (around 20 storeys high) are the dominant building forms that define a loosely structured rectilinear urban grid, which is not characterized by a continuous street wall. Once the favoured location of the coffee barons who dominated the early-twentieth-century Brazilian economy, the area decayed as a result of the 1930s coffee production crisis, which saw the transfer of many of the city's core business activities to the more 'modern' Avenida Paulista. The neighbourhood is witnessing a renaissance as middle- and upper-class residents move in from the more expensive areas to the immediate south, with newer and taller apartment buildings rising within the dense urban grid.

Peak Density / 1 km²
Santa Cecília

ISTANBUL – GÜNGÖREN

Peak Density 77,267 pp/km²
Average Density 2,380 pp/km²
Central Density 20,128 pp/km²

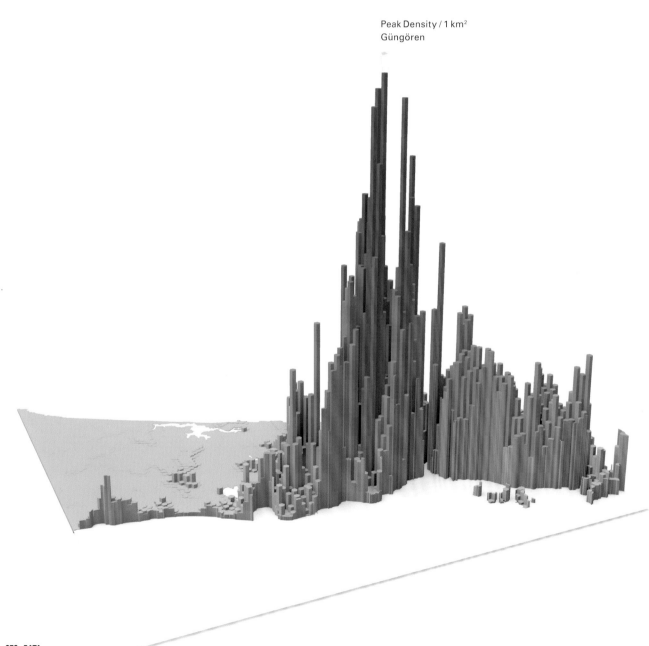

Peak Density / 1 km²
Güngören

The tightly packed urban structure of Güngören, a working class residential district 10 kilometres (6 miles) west of the Golden Horn on Istanbul's European side, reflects its status as the densest residential neighbourhood in the city. Fuelled by immigration from Anatolia from the mid-1950s onwards, the small urban village has become home to nearly 250,000 people. Six- and seven-storey apartment buildings create a strong edge to the main streets and narrow alleyways that form a hybrid grid – part rectilinear, part organic – announcing their origin as *gecekondu* informal housing. The area stands out for its lack of green or open spaces, typical of a dense, compact city like Istanbul. Nevertheless, it is occupied by large families and its residents are often employed locally in the area's dynamic commercial and manufacturing economy, defined by small stores and workshops along the busier wider streets that connect to the city's road network.

Peak Density / 1 km²
Güngören

NEW YORK CITY – UPPER EAST SIDE

Peak Density 58,530 pp/km^2
Average Density 9,272 pp/km^2
Central Density 15,353 pp/km^2

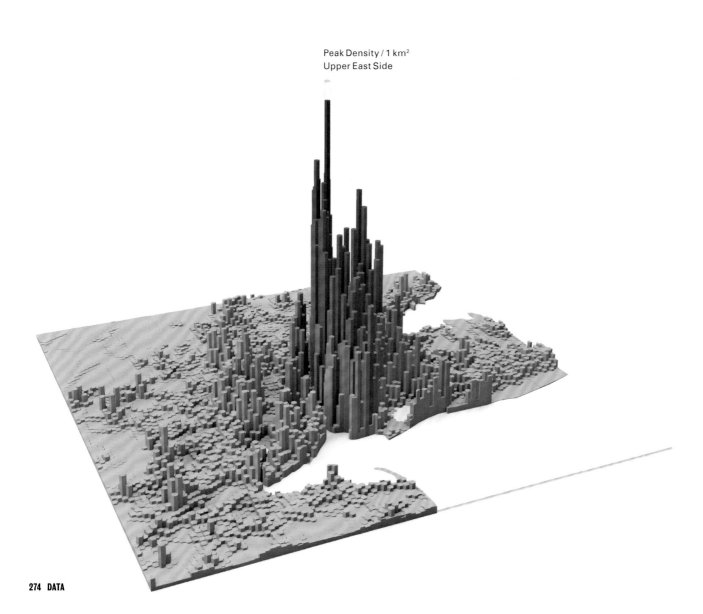

Peak Density / 1 km^2
Upper East Side

The Upper East Side is located between Central Park and the East River in Manhattan, one of New York City's five boroughs. Located 3 kilometres (1.8 miles) northeast of Times Square, it contains some of the densest and most expensive real estate in the city, home to some of its most affluent residents who benefit from the proximity to Central Park and views across the East River. Like the rest of Manhattan, the area has a regular rectilinear street grid, defined by wide north to south avenues (from 1st to 3rd Avenue) and narrower east to west streets (roughly from 73rd Street to 85th Street) with continuous street frontages often lined by shops, bars, cafés, restaurants and convenience stores. Very tall residential towers – some 40 storeys high – stand next to traditional late-nineteenth-century town houses and eight- to 10-storey apartment buildings from the mid -twentieth century, creating a very diverse typological landscape which none the less possesses a clear sense of spatial cohesion at street level.

Peak Density / 1 km²
Upper East Side

SHANGHAI – LUWAN

Peak Density 74,370 pp/km²
Average Density 3,136 pp/km²
Central Density 23,227 pp/km²

Peak Density / 1 km²
Luwan

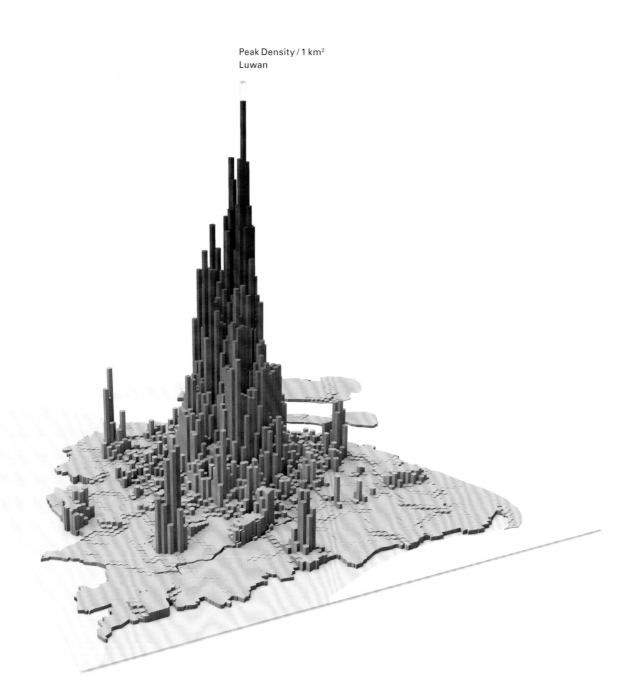

Luwan District, the densest of the city, is located in central Shanghai, 1.5 kilometres (less than a mile) south of People's Square and 3 kilometres to the southeast of the Pudong financial district. While Pudong is the city's new business and financial centre, Luwan is its historical, commercial and residential hub, well known for its boulevards, international fashion shops and high-class restaurants. Originally part of the French Concession, one of the most prestigious sections of the city in the early-twentieth century, the area reflects the fast pace of Shanghai's urban change. Its major thoroughfares define a central zone of rectilinear urban blocks, which are made up of tightly packed low-rise traditional Chinese houses accessed by extremely narrow alleyways. The edges of the district instead reveal the presence of large scale, high-rise residential building typologies inhabited by China's growing urban middle class, that encroach upon and break up the subtle grain of the older urban fabric.

Peak Density / 1 km²
Luwan

LONDON – NOTTING HILL

Peak Density 17,324 pp/km²
Average Density 4,497 pp/km²
Central Density 8,326 pp/km²

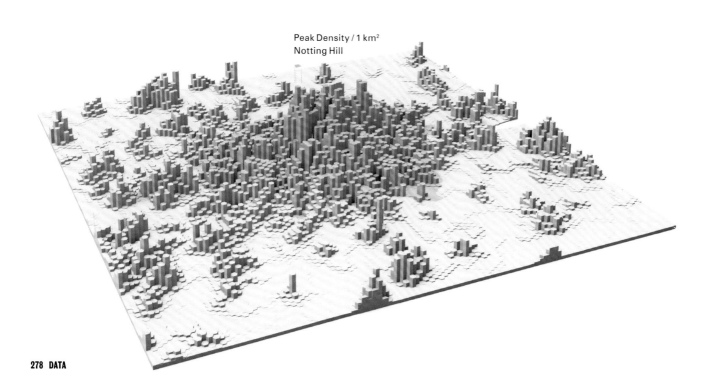

Peak Density / 1 km²
Notting Hill

Most Londoners would be surprised to learn that the genteel, leafy and affluent neighbourhood of Notting Hill is the densest residential district in this large, relatively low-density city. Located 5 kilometres (3 miles) west of Piccadilly Circus, Notting Hill is just north of Hyde Park. Much of the area was developed in the early- to mid-nineteenth century as a real estate venture to house London's new urban bourgeoisie, a key part of the westward expansion of the world's first megacity of nearly 10 million people. The unique typology of five- to six-storey townhouses that enclose a private communal garden has proved a lasting and much admired urban form that has adapted to changing lifestyles and socio-economic change over the last two centuries. Many of the original townhouses were turned into multi-occupancy rentals in the mid-twentieth century, attracting Caribbean immigrants and students to the area. By the 1980s, many of the properties were converted back into single-occupation houses, attracting professional and creative classes who value the generous internal spaces and presence of green, next to some of the city's most desirable shopping districts.

Peak Density / 1 km²
Notting Hill

Peak Density 49,088 pp/km²
Average Density 5,786 pp/km²
Central Density 12,880 pp/km²

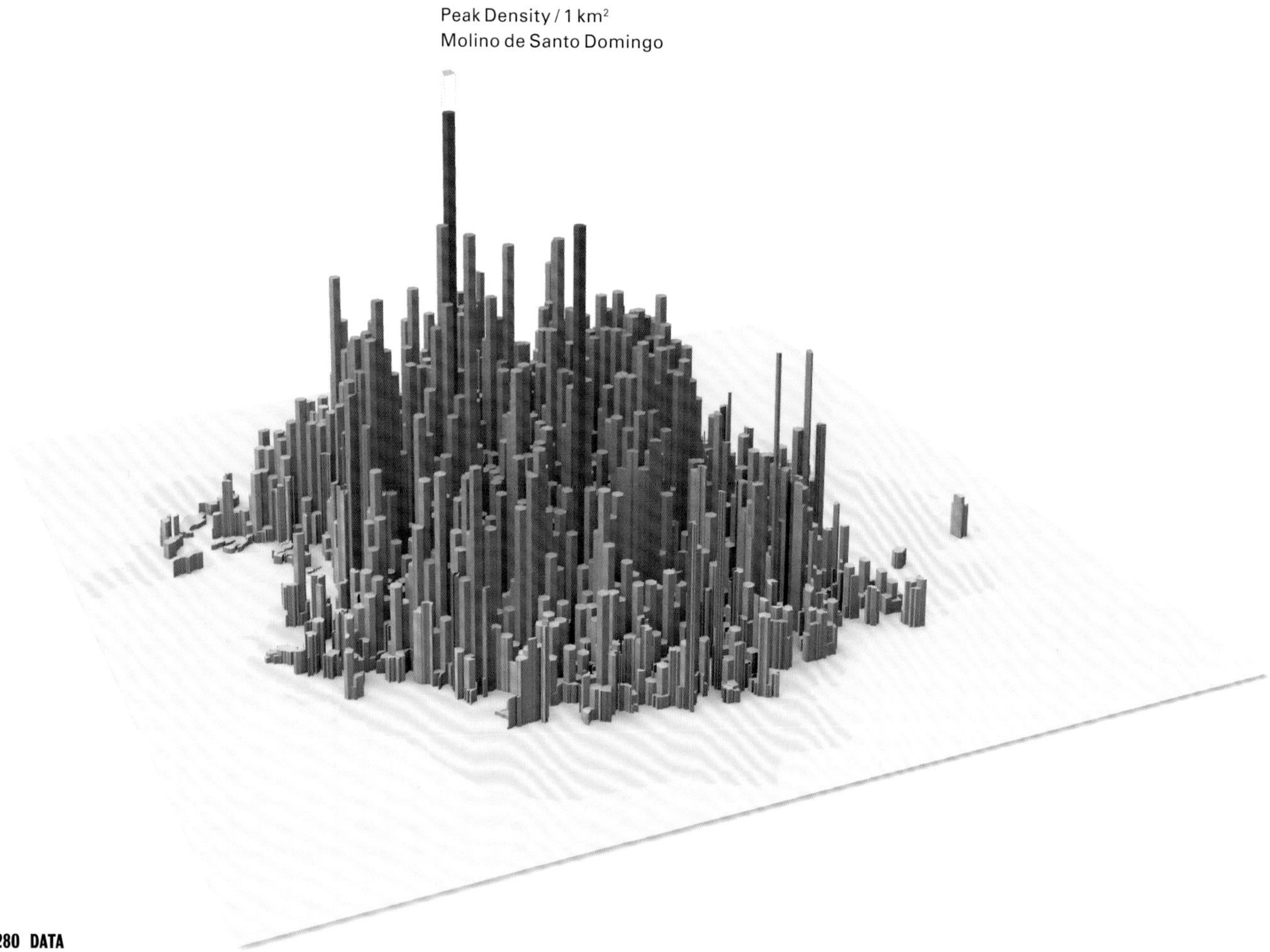

Peak Density / 1 km²
Molino de Santo Domingo

Molino de Santo Domingo is located on Mexico City's western fringe, 10 kilometres (6 miles) to the southeast of the Zócalo, the main central square of the city. Originally an informally planned area situated at the foot of one of the city's distinctive mountains, the residential buildings are spread over a shallow valley on either side of a major road thoroughfare that connects to the city's extensive traffic network.

The urban character of the area, with many one- or two-storey buildings neatly arranged in streets that run perpendicular to the slope of the valley, belies the very high levels of residential density determined by the lack of open space and the large families who live in relatively constrained accommodation. A series of public housing blocks and industrial units define the edges of the main road,

while the bulk of the small homes are knitted together in a tight urban grain that gives a degree of visual cohesion to an otherwise fragmented area, which takes advantage of its gateway location to the city, acting as a trading and exchange point for people and goods between Mexico City and the neighbouring states of Mexico and Michoacán.

Peak Density / 1 km²
Molino de Santo Domingo

JOHANNESBURG – BEREA

Peak Density 42,398 pp/km²
Average Density 1,963 pp/km²
Central Density 2,203 pp/km²

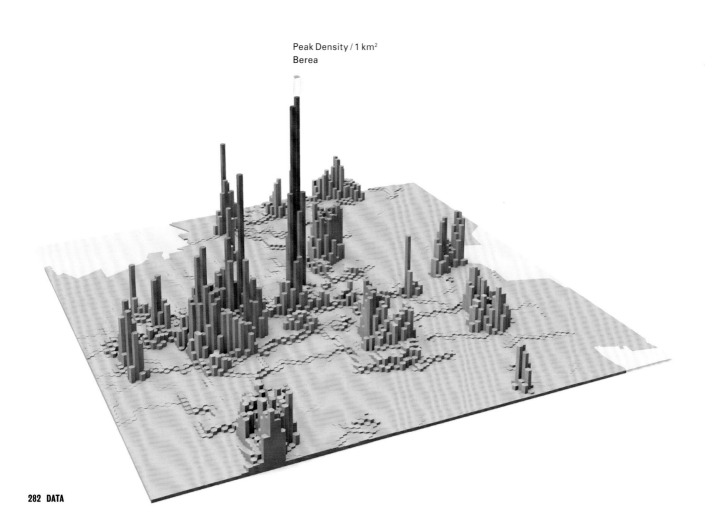

Peak Density / 1 km²
Berea

Berea is an inner city neighbourhood, 2 kilometres (1.2 miles) northeast of downtown Johannesburg, close to Hillbrow and other areas that have experienced intense change over the last tumultuous decades of South Africa's post-apartheid history. This high-density area is dominated by large apartment blocks, many over 20 storeys high, which create a fragmented urban landscape with little continuity of street frontage and a poorly defined public realm. There are clusters of tightly packed single-family houses in the eastern and northern sections. In the 1970s it was an apartheid-designated 'whites only' area, but soon became a 'grey area', where people of different ethnicities lived together and acquired a cosmopolitan and politically progressive feel. In the 1980s, poor planning, low investments in infrastructure and rapid population growth caused an exodus of middle-class residents and the decay of major buildings. Today most of the residents are migrants from townships, rural areas and the rest of Africa, many living in extreme poverty.

Peak Density / 1 km²
Berea

BERLIN – SCHILLERKIEZ
Peak Density 24,186 pp/km²
Average Density 3,737 pp/km²
Central Density 6,683 pp/km²

Peak Density / 1 km²
Schillerkiez

Schillerkiez, the city's densest residential quarter, is located in the less affluent part of West Berlin, 4.5 kilometres (2.7 miles) south of Alexanderplatz. Part of the former American Sector under the four-power occupation of the city, it is close to the better-known, lower-end but Bohemian district of Kreuzberg. Though the urban fabric of the quarter is varied by Berlin standards, it is principally composed of large five-storey perimeter blocks from the early- to mid-twentieth century with internal courtyards that create a continuous edge to the main roads and avenues. The area has one of the highest proportions of migrants in Berlin, and has a very diverse and socially mixed community. The area lacks some of the more generous parks and open spaces of more typical Berlin neighbourhoods and is bordered by large office complexes and the nearby recently decommissioned Tempelhof airport. Gentrification has started spreading from Kreuzberg, further exacerbating the split between the wealthier north and more deprived south of this gritty urban quarter.

Peak Density / 1 km²
Schillerkiez

INFRASTRUCTURE OF MOBILITY

Transport infrastructure is a critical driver of urban form, enabling centralization of economic functions and the accommodation of a growing population along public transport routes. Where public transport infrastructure is not in place, space-hungry motorways dominate, usually resulting in more sprawling forms of development and congestion as private car use persistently runs ahead of road building. The most extensive metro, bus and rail systems have been realized over more than a century in London, New York and Berlin, creating a wide and dense web of accessibility that connects central districts with the wider Metropolitan Region. Mumbai and Istanbul are constrained by natural geography but have efficient and affordable public transport, with Istanbul investing heavily in extending the existing metro and Bus Rapid Transit system. Though not affected by natural constraints, São Paulo and Mexico City still possess a rudimentary rail-based transport system, wholly inadequate to the size of their working populations, which suffer long commuting times. Shanghai is instead investing heavily in metro and rail transport, but has a significant way to go to upgrade its infrastructure in line with the global aspirations of its economy. Johannesburg has a significant under-provision of affordable public transport, and relies heavily – as other Urban Age cities in the developing world – on informal and unregulated forms of transport like collective taxis and services to connect to underserved areas typically inhabited by the urban poor.

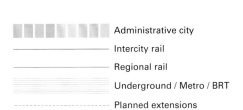

Administrative city

———————— Intercity rail

———————— Regional rail

≡≡≡≡≡≡≡ Underground / Metro / BRT

------------------------- Planned extensions

MUMBAI

Chhatrapati Shivaji Terminus

NEW YORK CITY

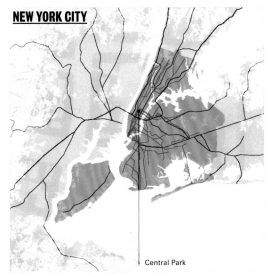

Central Park

MEXICO CITY

Zócalo

SÃO PAULO

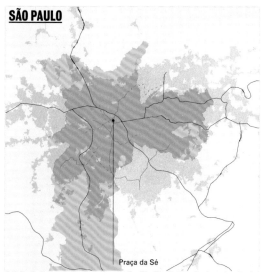

Praça da Sé

SHANGHAI

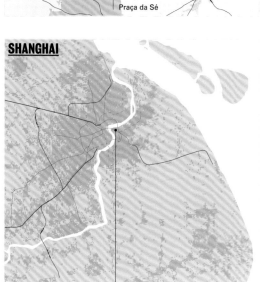

Pudong

JOHANNESBURG

Downtown

ISTANBUL

Taksim Meydanı

LONDON

Trafalgar Square

BERLIN

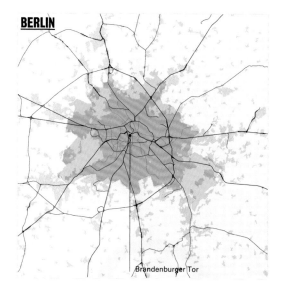

Brandenburger Tor

TRAVELLING TO WORK

How people travel within cities – the 'modal split' – reflects the level of provision of public transport infrastructure, but also local economic development, climate and urban form. Almost 60 per cent of all trips to work in New York are made by public transport – a share that remains unmatched in any other Urban Age city, even though London and Berlin reach about 40 per cent. Despite very different economic profiles, nearly as many people drive to work in Johannesburg as they do in London, and nearly a third of all commuters drive in São Paulo and Mexico City, while in Mumbai the level drops to 1.6 per cent. The usage of non-motorized travel is high in less developed but denser cities: 45 per cent of work trips are made on foot in Istanbul, and in Mumbai and Shanghai more than half of the trips are on foot or by bicycle. Again, São Paulo and Johannesburg occupy the middle ground with shares of walking significantly higher than in the wealthier cities. Around 40 per cent of residents in New York's Midtown Manhattan walk to work and over 90 per cent of affluent business workers use public transport in journeying to London's financial hub. Shanghai has experienced rapid growth in public transport use, while cycling remains prevalent. Although Berlin has high rates of cycling, its relatively uncongested roads allow high levels of car use – despite the presence of a high-quality public transport system. In some other cities, even where there is a good metro system like in Mexico City, informal transport often dominates, reflecting a mismatch between commuting patterns and infrastructure as well as the relatively high cost of public transport.

Non-motorized transport
Public transport
Private motorized transport

MUMBAI

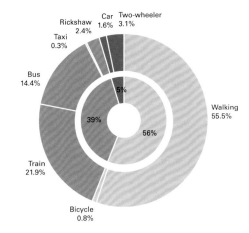

NEW YORK CITY

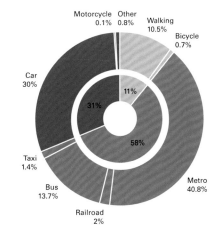

MEXICO CITY

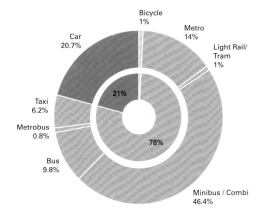

*There is no data available for 'walking' as a mode of transport for Mexico City. The share above is over all other modes of transport.

SÃO PAULO

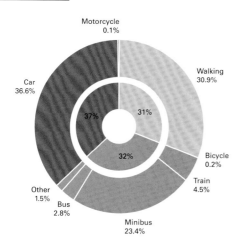

Motorcycle 1.9%
Other 0.2%
Car 27.2%
Walking 33.1%
29%
34%
37%
Taxi 0.2%
Bicycle 0.7%
Metro 5.8%
Train 2.1%
Bus 28.5%

ISTANBUL

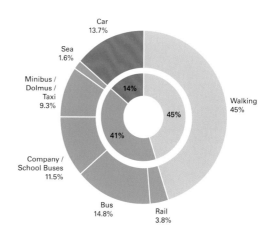

Car 13.7%
Sea 1.6%
Minibus / Dolmus / Taxi 9.3%
Walking 45%
14%
45%
41%
Company / School Buses 11.5%
Bus 14.8%
Rail 3.8%

SHANGHAI

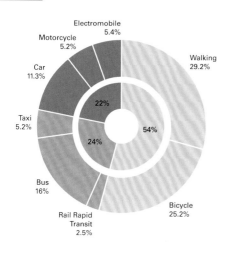

Electromobile 5.4%
Motorcycle 5.2%
Car 11.3%
Walking 29.2%
22%
54%
24%
Taxi 5.2%
Bicycle 25.2%
Bus 16%
Rail Rapid Transit 2.5%

LONDON

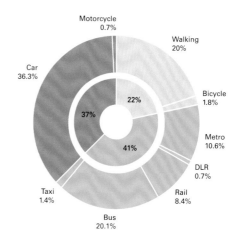

Motorcycle 0.7%
Walking 20%
Car 36.3%
22%
37%
41%
Bicycle 1.8%
Metro 10.6%
DLR 0.7%
Taxi 1.4%
Rail 8.4%
Bus 20.1%

JOHANNESBURG

Motorcycle 0.1%
Car 36.6%
Walking 30.9%
37%
31%
32%
Other 1.5%
Bicycle 0.2%
Bus 2.8%
Train 4.5%
Minibus 23.4%

BERLIN

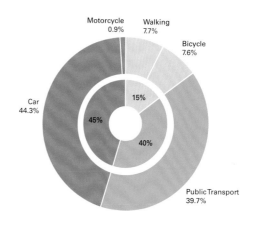

Motorcycle 0.9%
Walking 7.7%
Car 44.3%
Bicycle 7.6%
15%
45%
40%
Public Transport 39.7%

CONNECTING DENSITY TO PUBLIC TRANSPORT

The more mature Urban Age cities – London, Berlin and New York – show how investment in public transport has a close relationship to patterns of residential density over time. The most connected areas are where one finds the greatest concentration of people, justifying century-old policies that have prioritized rail-based public transport linking the wider Metropolitan Region with centralized employment zones. Mumbai, perhaps, offers the most effective model where residential densities reach their peak along the two railway lines that link the centre of the city to its extensive quasi-rural hinterland, bringing a large workforce to its places of work on a daily basis. These correlations can be found with highly integrated over- and under-ground rail services in Berlin, as well as the extensive rail systems in London and New York. In Mexico City, São Paulo and Johannesburg, rapid urban growth has outpaced transport infrastructure, privileging the expensive private car over public transport. Nonetheless, Shanghai is investing heavily in underground transport and Istanbul has made the most of its informal and extensive *dolmuş* (shared-vehicle) system to complement its patchy public transport system. Johannesburg shows a misalignment between public transport availability and residential density, where car ownership (expressed as the number of cars per 1,000 residents) has far lower levels of ownership than in Mumbai, Shanghai and Istanbul with 36, 73 and 139 cars per 1,000 residents respectively. This is in stark contrast to 368 in São Paulo, 360 in Mexico City, 345 in London and 319 in Berlin.

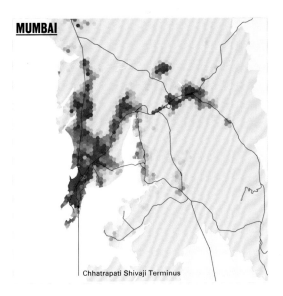

MUMBAI

Chhatrapati Shivaji Terminus

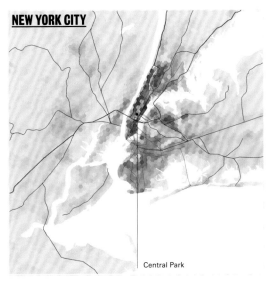

NEW YORK CITY

Central Park

MEXICO CITY

Zócalo

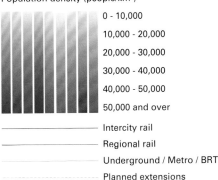

Population density (people/km²)

0 - 10,000

10,000 - 20,000

20,000 - 30,000

30,000 - 40,000

40,000 - 50,000

50,000 and over

——— Intercity rail

——— Regional rail

——— Underground / Metro / BRT

---------- Planned extensions

SÃO PAULO

Praça da Sé

ISTANBUL

Taksim Meydanı

SHANGHAI

Pudong

LONDON

Trafalgar Square

JOHANNESBURG

Downtown

BERLIN

Brandenburger Tor

UNDERSTANDING
THE NUMBERS

Justin McGuirk

COMMON TERMINOLOGY FOR
MEASURING URBAN DATA

GVA
The Gross Value Added measures the domestic output of a wider region around the city.

GINI coefficient
Measures the inequality in income distribution, where 0 expresses total equality and 1 total inequality.

HDI
The Human Development Index measures the composite level of social and economic development, with values closer to 1 meaning higher levels of HDI.

Given the sheer amount of data that Urban Age has amassed between 2005 and 2010, and given how clarifying it appears to be to see them all laid out in neat tables, it is tempting to put them to the test. Can they be used to judge the health of a city? Could they even enable us to establish the characteristics of an ideal city? Imagine each number – whether it's GDP per capita or the murder rate per 100,000 inhabitants – as a gene sequence of urban DNA. If you swapped the strands around, choosing the most advantageous numbers, you could perhaps clone an urban paradise: a city that is not too crowded, not too poor, and altogether green, clean, safe and happy. Or, if you prefer a more perverse creation, you could splice together all the most negative traits and give birth to a modern Gomorrah. Either way, you will have created a freak, an impossibility. And yet, if you look at the table comparing all the essential data of the Urban Age cities, one of those impossibilities already exists. It's called Mumbai.

Mumbai may not be the perfect city, but it is certainly an extreme city. The highest and lowest figures in that table almost always belong to it. If you only look at one half of the data, you might indeed think that you have a latter day Shangri-La on your hands. After all, Mumbai is the very model of a green city. It has by far the lowest carbon emissions rate, the lowest energy consumption, the lowest water consumption and produces the least waste. Add to that the fact that it has the lowest car ownership rate, the highest incidence of walking and cycling and the cheapest public transport and you have – on paper – one of the most sustainable big cities on the planet.

However, Mumbai also suffers the highest population densities in the world, with, at its peak, 121,312 people crammed into a square kilometre. And despite already having the most populous metropolitan region of the nine Urban Age cities, its population is also now the fastest growing, having recently overtaken Shanghai, with a projected population increase of 44 people per hour between now and 2025. To make matters worse, it is also the poorest city, with by a long stretch the lowest GDP per capita. With the largest, poorest and fastest growing population of the Urban Age cities, Mumbai would seem to be sailing into a perfect storm.

But if the city were a living organism, all you would have to do is swap two of Mumbai's traits – say, those for density and GDP per capita – with those of New York and you would have what, statistically, looks like the perfect city. But this is not a game, and cities, judging by Mumbai, cannot have it both ways. They cannot achieve Mumbai's apparent sustainability with New York's affluence. What's more, statistics will only tell you so much about the nature of a place. Scanning Mumbai's numerical

	Current population in the city GIS-based	Current population in the metropolitan region	Central area density (people per km²) GIS-based	Projected growth 2010–2025 (people per hour)
MUMBAI	11,710,000	19,280,000 2005	45,021	44 2009
SÃO PAULO	10,400,000	19,220,000 2007	10,376	11 2009
ISTANBUL	12,700,000	12,700,000 2008	20,128	12 2009
NEW YORK	8,090,000	18,820,000 2007	15,353	9 2009
SHANGHAI	15,460,000	15,460,000 2006	23,227	26 2009
LONDON	7,560,000	7,560,000 2007 - Greater London	8,326	1 2009
MEXICO CITY	8,580,000	19,240,000 2005	12,880	10 2009
JOHANNESBURG	3,230,000	3,890,000 2007 - CoJ Metro Municipality	2,203	3 2009
BERLIN	3,330,000	4,300,000 2002	6,683	0 2009

extremes will not tell you how the city looks and smells. The difficulty of giving data a tangible form was on display at the 2006 Venice Architecture Biennale, where density models for a number of cities were transformed into polystyrene foam towers to dramatic effect, but some visitors misinterpreted them as actual high-rise landscapes.

The purpose of this essay is to probe the data, to question them. By which I do not mean the accuracy of the numbers – although not every government census can be taken at face value – but, rather, asking: what do the data really tell us? What follows is a guide to finding interpretations and readings in the wall of numbers.

What Does Density Look Like From The Street?

In London, density was an ambition in the first decade of the 21st century. After decades of urban flight and suburbanization, the city centre – the hole in the doughnut, as every downtown was understood in the 1960s – suddenly started growing again. Life in the city centre became an aspiration for those who could afford it, but also an instrument of municipal policy. Density was understood to be one of the means to an efficient, vital city, and to a fair city where the poor and the rich rub shoulders. Density, it would be fair to say, was a virtue. And yet, clearly, it is relative. Low-rise London, with its terraced housing and Victorian suburban grain, is the least dense of the Urban Age cities. Compare it with Mumbai, where densities can reach an unfathomable level of over 120,000 people per square kilometre, and suddenly you have too much of a good thing. The question inevitably arises, is there such a thing as an optimal density?

To answer that question, you would need to look at quality of life, applying a range of cultural factors to the density figures. And even then it might be difficult to pin down precisely. New Yorkers may not expect the same degree of personal space as Londoners, but they would balk at the number of times their body would be touched walking down a street in Mumbai. Equally, London may be the least dense of the Urban Age cities but the West End can be so congested that there have been calls to introduce slow and fast pedestrian lanes just to keep the flow moving.

Density models have a tendency to be more ambiguous than they at first appear. First of all, we should be clear that we are talking about residential density and not workplace density. Also, the computational termite mounds in the data section are topographies of people rather than physical landscapes. But what kind of people are they? Does a soaring peak represent a poor or a rich neighbourhood? Are its residents stacked in high-rises or crammed into informal shanty towns?

We tend to associate extreme density with poverty, and yet the densest quadrant of New York is on the Upper East Side, that bastion of old money and privilege. Admittedly, in the last decade developers have been throwing up condominium towers that combine mean floor plans with upmarket addresses and 'spectacular views'. But here the well-off live at closer quarters than even the poor do anywhere in Mexico City. If you can sustain a wealthy Manhattanite's quality of life at 58,530 people per square kilometre then perhaps high density is not such a bad thing after all – even if Upper-East-siders need to escape to the Hamptons over the weekend.

You would still have to more than double that figure, however, to reach the peak density of Mumbai. This is to be found not, as one might have expected, in Dharavi, often somewhat misleadingly described as Asia's largest slum, but in Kamathipura, Asia's largest red-light district. Here, in the heart of the city, 121,312 people occupy one square kilometre of decrepit three-storey buildings. Originally a brothel district established for British troops under the Raj, today the sex workers of Kamathipura trade in some of the most cramped conditions on the planet. Just as a point of comparison, Dharavi, made notorious by *Slumdog Millionaire*, only reaches 82,000 people per square kilometre. But even outside of these spikes, the majority live in dreadful conditions. Three quarters of the city's housing stock is made up of chawls, which Mike Davis describes as 'a one-room rental dwelling that crams a household of six people into 15 square metres; the latrine is usually shared with six other families'.

One of Mumbai's closest competitors in the density stakes among the Urban Age cities is Shanghai. In Luwan, just across from Pudong, density reaches an impressive 74,370 people per square kilometre. And yet the streetscape is rather different from Kamathipura. This is a planned, formal neighbourhood made up of a mixture of high-rises and tightly packed medium-height residential blocks hugging broad avenues. Indeed, Shanghai has taken steps over the last decade to reduce density, moving people towards the edge of the city and enlarging the minimum apartment floor plan – as in Mumbai, sharing a 15-square-metre apartment with three generations of your family makes for a difficult life.

The comparison of low-rise Kamathipura with the mixed grain of Luwan suggests that high density is not intrinsically linked to particular urban forms. This would seem to disprove the argument that high-rise living is the most effective way to achieve density in the city – that is, unless you consider the conditions in which the residents of Kamathipura live. Perhaps a better example of this case is a comparison of São Paulo and Mexico City. They have similar levels of density that are consistent throughout the city (there are no spikes along the lines of Mumbai or Shanghai), and yet São Paulo is made up of residential towers while Mexico City is a largely low-rise sprawl. This pattern is consistent even in their densest neighbourhoods, which in São Paulo is not a favela but the centrally located Santa Cecília, and which in Mexico City is the slums of Molino de Santo Domingo on the western edge of the city.

This raises an interesting question: does informal housing result in the highest densities or is it planned housing? If you took the two extremes, Mumbai's Kamathipura (121,312) and London's Notting Hill (17,324) you would appear to have your answer. Similarly, informal Molino de Santo Domingo (49,088) is significantly denser than high-rise Santa Cecília (29,704). And yet Shanghai and New York, with their market-driven tower blocks, disprove the notion that slums are denser than developers' high-rises. Even Johannesburg's Soweto township is nowhere near as dense as Berea (42,398), a run-down formerly white enclave that consists mainly of apartment blocks, including the notorious 54-storey Ponte Tower.

What is clear, however, is that the densest parts of these cities are the repositories of recent migrants. In Istanbul, the peak is to be found in Akıncılar, in the Güngören district on the European side of the city. This is a classic post-*gecekondu* neighbourhood where rural migrants who arrived since the 1980s have gradually upgraded their single-storey homes into dense four- and five-storey neighbourhoods. With its large numbers of Anatolian migrants, Güngören has its own ethnic and political tensions, and in July 2008 two synchronized bombings killed 17 people there and injured more than 150. London and Berlin are the two anomalies on the chart, with the lowest densities, yet the pattern of recent migration and density is the same. The most crowded neighbourhood in Berlin is Schillerkiez in Neukölln district, a heavily Turkish neighbourhood. Even London's Notting Hill, a byword these days for a particular kind of boutique affluence, has for the last half century absorbed waves of West Indian migrants occupying rabbit-warren conversions of the otherwise quite grand Victorian housing stock.

	City as a percentage of national population	GDP per capita (US$)	City as a percentage of national GDP	Average annual growth in GVA 1993–2010 2010
MUMBAI	0.9 2006	$1,871 2006	2.9% 2006	4.09%
SÃO PAULO	5.8 2006	$12,021 2006	11.9% 2006	1.73%
ISTANBUL	17.8 2008	$12,856 2007	22.0% 2007	1.80%
NEW YORK	2.8 2008	$55,693 2008	3.3% 2008	2.15%
SHANGHAI	1.0 2005	$8,237 2005	5.0% 2005	9.35%
LONDON	12.4 2007	$60,831 2007	3.4% 2007	2.19%
MEXICO CITY	8.4 2006	$18,321 2006	21.5% 2006	1.65%
JOHANNESBURG	8.1 2005	$9,229 2005	14.8% 2005	1.58%
BERLIN	4.2 2007	$34,017 2007	3.4% 2007	−0.10%

Perhaps what the density models tell us most about the Urban Age cities is how evenly or otherwise their populations are distributed. Johannesburg, for instance, is a collection of disparate nodes with one extreme spike at Berea and nearby Hillbrow. São Paulo, on the other hand, with a much larger population spread over a much greater urban footprint, has a relatively low and even density. This is a young city that has grown incredibly fast. Mexico City, too, is fairly consistently populated, without extreme peaks. It is Mumbai, Shanghai and Istanbul – three of the fastest growing cities – that have the most dramatic spikes, suggesting that migrants are simply arriving faster than provision can be made for them. Some cities have made attempts to lure or uproot poorer residents away from the centres that they rely upon for their livelihoods. Mexico City and Mumbai built satellite cities to siphon people into. In the case of Navi Mumbai, built across the Thane Creek, the strategy failed, instead luring the wealthy middle classes. In Istanbul, moving people has occasionally been a matter of enforcement rather than enticement. This was the case for the Roma population of Sulukule, whose ancestral neighbourhood inside the old city walls was rather too prime a piece of real estate for their own good.

Accessing the City, With or Without Transport

Given the tendency to equate density with civic virtue among a generation of architects, it could be assumed that high residential density was a sign of good public transport. In fact, it is the opposite. The cities with the most developed metro and regional rail networks, London and Berlin, are the least dense of the nine cities. Istanbul and Shanghai, two of the densest cities, have the smallest public transport systems, while Mumbai, the densest, has no metro service at all and relies entirely on its rail network.

What does this tell us? Is it that extreme density prohibits effective public transport infrastructure, or that a lack of transport encourages cramped living conditions, forcing people to live and work in the same part of a city? Mumbai is a case in point, as ever in the extreme. Fifty-six per cent of all journeys there are made on foot, with most pedestrians reaching work in 15 minutes. Many Western cities would love to achieve that statistic, but in Mumbai it comes at a huge cost to quality of life. For instance, well over a million people live on the streets (according to 1995 estimates in Mike Davis' *Planet of Slums*), many of them street vendors, rickshaw drivers or market porters who are forced to stay close to their work in the city centre. In the pursuit of a livelihood, access to the city is the chief priority for most Mumbaikars and, as Suketu Mehta memorably put it, their discomfort is an investment.

With the highest walking rates comes the lowest incidence of car ownership, a negligible 36 cars per 1,000 inhabitants. Though car ownership is rising, there is no corresponding increase in the road network, and traffic is severe. In any event, cars are the preserve of the rich in Mumbai, with 70 per cent of them being chauffeur-driven. In terms of public transport, Mumbai relies almost exclusively on its suburban rail network, which ferries 6.4 million commuters a day. However, trains are appallingly overloaded, and though passengers may literally cling on for their lives, a shocking 13 people die every day in accidents.

Istanbul is another dense city that has limited public transport and high walking rates, with 45 per cent of journeys made on foot. Does this mean that residents' experience of this 100-kilometre- (nearly 61-mile-) wide city tends to be limited to their immediate localities? That depends which side of the Bosporus you live on.

Seventy per cent of Istanbul's white-collar workers live on the Asian side, crossing the Bosporus every day to Europe, which holds 85 per cent of the office space. They are presumably the ones sitting in the traffic jams. In fact, car ownership is relatively low in Istanbul (138 per 1,000 people, behind only Mumbai and Shanghai), yet the city's road network cannot cope with it. With 420,000 vehicles crossing the Bosporus' two bridges each day, it is all too predictable that the municipality has its eyes on a third bridge, which will inevitably only make the traffic worse. What is less clear is why the city's new metro system appears to be so underused, although that may be simply down to its rather limited range – Istanbul's varied topography is awkward for underground networks.

It is perhaps obvious that car ownership should be lowest in the three densest cities, Mumbai, Istanbul and Shanghai. It also makes sense that it would be highest in the two cities with the largest urban footprint, Mexico City and São Paulo (not counting the New York Metropolitan Region). But was it sprawl that demanded the car, or the car that created sprawl? The answer is different in different cities.

São Paulo has the highest car ownership rate (368 per 100,000 people), with 4.2 million cars. There are metro and rail lines but these are not adequate for the city. Buses are more popular, but even the dedicated bus lanes, the Corredores de Onibus, have limited reach. The municipality plans to add 300 kilometres (182 miles) to the system by 2025, but there is no hiding the fact that the city's public transport systems are massively under-invested. Mexico City's car ownership is almost on a par with São Paulo's, but it also has a more effective and cheaper public transport system. It is difficult to break down Mexico City's transport usage exactly because we lack the data for how many journeys are made on foot, but public transport appears to be heavily used, especially given the high car ownership rates. That may be because there is a strict anti-pollution law that restricts car use to certain days of the week based on licence plate numbers. And then, perhaps drivers have noticed the road death figures, which at 20 per 100,000 are the highest of the Urban Age cities.

It is also interesting to observe that although London's car ownership is lower than São Paulo's and Mexico City's, the UK capital records the highest number of car journeys, accounting for 36 per cent of all travel. And that is in spite of the Congestion Charge, which was supposed to discourage residents from using their cars. Perhaps this has something to do with the price of a tube ticket, which is 37 times more expensive than in Mexico City. Indeed, this raises the question: is there a correlation between ticket price and public transport uptake? As yet we have no accurate figures for this – only the metro ticket price is recorded for each city, rather than an average transport cost that includes buses.

Of the nine cities, Shanghai is by far the most popular with cyclists, despite its past efforts to deliberately reduce the torrents of bikes. Indeed, Shanghai achieves a unique balance between the different forms of transport – public, walking, cycling and driving – each accounting for roughly a quarter of journeys. The only other city where cycling registers with any meaningful popularity is Berlin, where it accounts for 8 per cent of journeys. With its new cycle hire system, however, and its bicycle-loving mayor, we can expect to see two-wheel transport to be taken up more enthusiastically in London.

Governance and Urban Footprint

The maps showing the urban footprints of the nine Urban Age cities read like negatives of cities seen from the air at night. What do these tell us? At a glance they give a rough sense of the relative sizes and shapes of these cities. But it's not until you compare the municipal boundaries with their actual urban footprints that a more complex picture starts to emerge. In Mexico City, for instance, more than half of the population lives outside the federal city boundaries. In São Paulo it's a little over 40 per cent. And this is not just a symptom of urbanization in developing countries; even in New York, more than half of the inhabitants of the Metropolitan Region live outside the five boroughs demarcated by the city border. Cities clearly have minds of their own. They expand irrespective of borders, often existing across separate administrative jurisdictions. This raises a number of questions. First, how do we organize and bind together cities that sprawl beyond their administrative borders? As cities expand, how do we govern them? And can a city become too big to work?

When half of a city lies outside the municipality's jurisdiction, there are obvious implications for the provision of basic services, or, say, for collecting taxes. How do you achieve coordinated decision-making in the name of the public good? How power is divided between the city and regional or national government will reflect the relative political strength of these various constituencies. But it can also be an administrative tangle. In Istanbul, for example, transport matters are the ultimate responsibility of the Ministry of Transport and the Istanbul Metropolitan Municipality. Yet a 2002 study found that there were in fact 17 local and national authorities responsible for the planning and running of the city's transport system. In São Paulo, which has grown by a factor of twenty in the last two decades, the local government did little to control or indeed cater for the proliferation of informal settlements around the edges of the city. Transport is a huge problem (evinced by the city's high car ownership), but even more serious is the lack of infrastructure bringing clean water to the millions of people living not just outside the municipal borders, but apparently outside of the municipality's field of vision.

In theory, infrastructure such as transport or running water should be regulated by public authorities established by the state, with control over the actual, entire city rather than a legal definition of it. Of course, that is a highly political question – how do you define the 'actual' city? One solution is to expand the boundaries all the way out to the regional border, so that the municipality has authority over the entire metropolitan area – a move made by both Shanghai and Istanbul. This tactic ought to make administrative decisions easier, giving the municipality greater control over its own suburbs and hinterlands, and thus over the future expansion of the city.

Expanding the boundaries might arguably make those cities more powerful – the mayor of Istanbul, for example, may be the most influential politician in Turkey after the prime minister. It may also be a move that requires a certain ruthlessness to achieve, bearing in mind that Shanghai and Istanbul are controlled by highly centralized, if not authoritarian political systems. It's not so easy in affluent North American cities, where, for instance, wealthy taxpayers on the periphery of Los Angeles fight hard to avoid incorporation, and the tax to pay for downtown that comes with it. Whether, in the end, the concentration of civic authority in a single jurisdiction is effective depends of course on the mayor, and there is an argument that the checks and balances provided by, say, New York – where the mayor has to negotiate with the five borough mayors and the state governor – are good for the democratic process. As for the idea of Istanbul and Shanghai becoming more powerful, it is worth pointing out that policy in both places is set by the national government, and that they remain under the watchful gaze of Ankara and Beijing. Both mayors are members of the ruling party and, as such, must be team players.

Indeed, the mayor of Shanghai may have less actual power than the municipal Communist Party chief.

Cities that can't claim control over their entire populations would certainly seem to be at a disadvantage when it comes to governance. This becomes an issue, for instance, as the urban footprint of São Paulo extends beyond the boundaries of city of São Paulo to its metropolitan region that includes several different administrative authorities. Mumbai's municipal authorities are at the mercy of the state of Maharashtra. The city is also weakened by being surrounded by urban areas – often independent towns – that account for 7 million people in the Metropolitan Region. Indeed, the state has sometimes sought to undermine the pull of Mumbai as a deliberate strategy. With overcrowding such a problem, it was decided in the 1970s to build a twin city, Navi Mumbai, across the Thane Creek. It is the largest planned city in the world and it is strategically positioned outside Mumbai's municipal boundaries so that it can compete. But although it now has a population of over 2 million, it did little to lure people away from Mumbai.

Can a city be too big? Too big, in other words, to work properly? It seems unlikely. Tokyo has one of the largest municipal areas, and consequently one of the largest municipal governments, in the world. Its boundaries were expanded in the 1940s precisely to aid the efficiency of the war effort. But national governments can also decide to limit a city's size, as the UK did by creating a green belt around London (Tokyo actually tried, and quickly abandoned the idea of a green belt). It is true that the UK capital had already experienced runaway urbanization in the nineteenth century and is unlikely to go through anything similar again, yet it was a radical and effective move. Indeed London has several advantages: a well-defined border that is consistent with the actual shape of the city, a footprint that is entirely under the aegis of a central municipal body – the Greater London Authority – and meaningful local government by the 33 boroughs.

There is another question worth asking: how powerful are the Urban Age cities in relation to their states? The only means we have of measuring this are economic, in terms of the percentage of national GDP that each city accounts for. It is attempting to assume in those percentages a corresponding cultural power but that would be spurious. You have only to look at the low contributions to GDP made by New York and Mumbai to realize this has no bearing on the sheer presence of those cities at the forefront of their national psyches, or indeed in their international image. In fiscal terms, Istanbul is the most powerful city relative to its nation, driving 22 per cent of the economy. This is closely followed by Mexico and then, at 16 per cent, London. Although Istanbul is not a capital, those three cities are the most significant metropolises in their countries. For one thing, they lay claim to the highest portions of the national population – Istanbul accounts for 18 per cent of Turkey's population. By comparison, New York holds only around 3 per cent of the US population and contributes about the same fraction to the economy. Economically, Mumbai looks like the least powerful city within its nation, behind New York, contributing less than 3 per cent of GDP. However, it is staggering to be reminded that its population of 12 million is less than 1 per cent of the national figure, but then India is a country of over a billion people, and still largely rural.

Citizens and the Urban Economy

Studying the urban workforce figures, for the first time one can start to form a mental picture of who actually lives in these nine cities. They tell us in which industries the

	 Percentage of the population under 20	Income inequality (measured by the GINI index)	Human Development Index	Murder rate (homicides per 100,000 inhabitants)
MUMBAI	**36.3** 2001	**.35** 2004	**.86** 2001	**3.0** 2005
SÃO PAULO	**31.0** 2010	**.61** 2005	**.88** 2000	**21.0** 2006
ISTANBUL	**32.1** 2009	**.43** 2003	**.90** 2000	**3.0** 2007
NEW YORK	**25.7** 2008	**.50** 2007 - New York-Northern New Jersey-Long Island, NY-NJ-PA (MSA)	**.99** 2005	**6.3** 2008
SHANGHAI	**16.0** 2005	**.45** 2001	**.89** 2008	**1.4** 2005
LONDON	**23.8** 2009	**.32** 1995	**.98** 2006	**2.2** 2007
MEXICO CITY	**32.9** 2005	**.56** 2005	**.87** 2005	**13.2** 2007
JOHANNESBURG	**34.6** 2010	**.75** 2005	**.75** 2003	**15.7** 2007
BERLIN	**16.5** 2008	**–**	**.95** 2006	**1.2** 2007

populations are most likely to be employed and what the largest age groups are. More than that, if we assume an evolutionary progression from industrial activity to a service or knowledge economy, the charts are revealing indicators of the stage that the cities have reached in their economic cycles. Thus nineteenth-century powerhouses such as London and New York, which industrialized more than a century before some of the other cities here, are clearly the furthest along in that transformation.

New York has the most advanced economy, with 93 per cent of its employed population working in the service sector and only 6 per cent in secondary sector activities such as manufacturing and construction. In this instance 'services', or what's known as the tertiary sector, includes everything from retail to finance, real estate and even public services. London is close behind New York, with 85 per cent of its economy represented by services, but even in London 15 per cent is dedicated to construction and manufacturing, which is only slightly less than São Paulo. Indeed, apart from New York, the portion of these urban economies taken up by the secondary sector is fairly consistent. There are, however, two clear exceptions: Istanbul and Shanghai. These are still predominantly manufacturing cities.

What does it mean to be a manufacturing city in the twenty-first century? At first glance, there are some rather enviable characteristics associated with it. First, there is the economic diversity that makes these cities less susceptible to fiscal crisis – suddenly an asset in the post-credit crunch era. Secondly, looking at the factors on the DNA chart, these are cities where people are more likely to walk or cycle to work, and that have cheap public transport, negligible car ownership and low crime rates. Sounds good, doesn't it? Except that these are also relatively poor cities, with a low GDP per capita and some of the highest density and pollution levels. Life expectancy is likely to be lower than in the other cities, with the exception of Mumbai and Johannesburg. It is no wonder that both Istanbul and Shanghai are busily reinventing themselves as globalized service cities. And with former manufacturing giants like Detroit offering salutary reminders, cities have to keep reinventing themselves or die.

However, it's worth looking at the figures more closely. Because the extremely high percentages of people working in manufacturing in Istanbul (40 per cent) and Shanghai (44 per cent) are in part achieved by including their large industrial hinterlands in the count. Both cities now consider their regional border as the outer limit of the city. And if Mexico City were to do the same then its figure of 19 per cent manufacturing would likely rise to similar levels as Istanbul's. Shanghai also has a burgeoning services sector (56 per cent of the economy), yet it is significantly behind other cities in the developing world. Mexico City, for instance, the capital of one of the world's fastest growing telecommunications industries, has an economy that is 80 per cent tertiary. Mumbai's is 81 per cent dedicated to services, a figure that may reflect its new position as a global outsourcing hub.

As London and Mexico City prove, though, the shift to a service economy can have unfortunate consequences on what Saskia Sassen would call 'cityness'. The demand for office space – indeed the speculative building of office towers beyond projected demand – often leads to sterile business districts removed from city centres. This was the case with Canary Wharf in London and Santa Fe in Mexico City. Such high-yield, portfolio developments have an insidious effect on urbanity, promoting social segregation and often draining investment from traditional city centres.

Interestingly, economic development seems to have corresponding effects on the youthfulness of these urban populations. If you look at the age pyramids, you'll notice that the less developed cities – for instance, Mumbai, Istanbul, São Paulo and Johannesburg – have broad bases, meaning that they have young populations. They are characterized by high birth rates and significant percentages of under-20s (Mumbai is the youngest, where 36 per cent are under 20 years old). In these cities, the largest population segment consists of 20-somethings. By contrast, London and New York are older cities, where the largest segment of population is in their 30s. It is in Berlin, however, with its static growth rate, where the population is ageing fastest – its largest percentile is in the 40-something bracket.

Given what we already know about these cities, these are fairly obvious patterns. In general, a young population seems to go hand in hand with poverty, high density and rapid population growth. The only real anomaly is Shanghai, which, despite having similar densities to Mumbai and an industrial economy like Istanbul's, has an ageing population like Berlin's. A disproportionate fraction of the population is in its 40s, and it has the lowest percentage of under-10s of any Urban Age city. But then China has enforced a one-child policy for the last three decades in the interest of controlling the size of its immense population.

The Unfairness of Climate Change

We know that the world's richest countries are responsible for the majority of the carbon emissions that cause global warming. But at city level, allocating responsibility for greenhouse gases becomes rather more complex. At a glance, the Urban Age graph of carbon emissions per capita reveals exactly what we would expect: the countries with the largest GDPs – the United States, Germany, China and the UK – are also the largest emitters of CO_2. Correspondingly, developing countries such as India, Brazil and Turkey, are the lowest carbon emitters. A New Yorker emits 20 times the amount of CO_2 of a Mumbaikar.

And yet that leads us to a paradox. It is a matter of orthodoxy that cities are responsible for the majority of carbon emissions – the figure most often cited is 75 per cent. If that's the case, then why is it that in most cases the city CO_2 levels are so much lower than the national averages? New Yorkers, for instance, produce just over a third of the CO_2 of a typical American. Londoners and Berliners, meanwhile, emit just over half that of the average Briton and German. The reason might be obvious: cities, with their compact lifestyles and public transport, are simply more efficient than suburban and rural communities. However, there is also a discrepancy in terms of how the carbon emissions are allocated. For instance, carbon fuel burning power stations tend not to be located in cities, even though it is urbanites that are consuming most of the energy they generate.

Only Shanghai and Mexico City have higher emission rates than their respective countries. Indeed the rate in Shanghai is more than double that of the average Chinese, but that is what marks out an industrial powerhouse whose administrative boundaries include its industrial base in a still predominantly rural nation (a fact reflected in its pollution levels, which are the highest of the nine cities). As for Mexico City, the explanation is less forthcoming. Does it have to do with the high car ownership and the expansive urban sprawl? Probably not, since Paulistanos own even more cars and are responsible for much lower emissions.

Nevertheless, the example of Mexico City raises the question of how much an effective public transport system reduces a city's carbon footprint. London, Berlin and New York have the most extensive metro and rail systems, but their emissions rates are still nowhere near as low as those in the cities in developing countries. No, it is quite clearly energy consumption that is one of the biggest factors. There is an

	 Percentage of daily trips on foot or by cycle	Rail Network System Length (km) GIS-based	Metro ticket price in 2010 (US$) 2010	Car ownership rate (per 1,000 inhabitants)
MUMBAI	56.3 2007	477	0.2	35.9 2006
SÃO PAULO	33.8 2007	275	1.6	368.0 2007
ISTANBUL	45.0 2008	163	1.0	138.5 2008
NEW YORK	11.2 2008	579	2.3	209.4 2008
SHANGHAI	54.4 2006	169	1.5	72.6 2006
LONDON	21.8 2008	1,393	7.1	344.7 2008
MEXICO CITY	N/A	353	0.2	360.0 2007
JOHANNESBURG	31.1 2004	581	–	205.7 2000 - Gauteng Province
BERLIN	15.3 2004	950	3.8	319.0 2008

obvious correlation between annual electricity use and greenhouse gas emissions, with New York and Shanghai at the top and Mumbai and São Paulo at the bottom. In the case of Shanghai, a large portion of that usage will be for industrial purposes rather than personal, whereas it is a rare New Yorker who will put up without air conditioning. It is a truism that higher standards of living demand more carbon. The only exception to this rule appears to be Johannesburg, which has one of the lowest GDPs of the Urban Age cities – second only to Mumbai – and yet an emissions rate almost on a par with London's. Is that because it is a city of extreme social divisions where the wealthy make up in energy consumption what the poor have little access to? That would be consistent with its position at the top of the income inequality chart, with a GINI coefficient of .75, and a rate of electricity use that is almost equal to Berlin's. But it's hard to draw any conclusions because, again, the numbers never tell the whole story.

However, one indisputable fact is the inverse relationship between a city's carbon emissions and its vulnerability to the effects of global warming: the lower the emissions, the more susceptible a city is to freak phenomena like floods and droughts. The clearest examples are Mumbai and São Paulo, both at high risk of flooding because of erratic rainfall and deforestation. Flooding in Mumbai killed 5,000 people in 2005 and brought the entire city to a standstill. To make matters worse, those most affected by these tragedies are the disadvantaged, living in informal areas without proper drainage and no infrastructural protection against flooding or landslides.

The Social Equity Question

Taking all of the Urban Age data together, what could one say about the social equity in these nine cities? This is a rather nebulous and no doubt relative notion, and yet there are ways of measuring it. One tool is the Human Development Index (HDI), which examines a range of factors: life expectancy, literacy, education enrolment and GDP per capita. We should be clear that HDI is not the same thing as quality of life – it's an index of development – and yet it is as quantifiable an indicator as we are likely to find. And the first thing to point out on the HDI chart is that all the Urban Age cities, except for Berlin, maintain a higher quality of life than the national averages. This reinforces the idea of cities as the natural cradles of humanity, as magnets of opportunity and social interaction. Despite all the factors taken into consideration by the HDI, it is predictable that, in the end, overall quality of life comes down to wealth. The cities with the highest GDP per capita – in order: London, New York, and Berlin– are also those with the highest HDI. Again predictably, the poorest city, Mumbai, has the lowest index of development. For those cities in-between, different factors come into play. For instance, Istanbul has a lower HDI than its GDP would lead you to assume, and this is because of the lower education and literacy rates among women. Education may also be the prohibiting factor in Johannesburg. However, there are other factors not measured by the HDI that one would think should come into play: the high murder rates in São Paulo and Johannesburg, for instance, or the fact that breathing Mumbai's air has the equivalent effect of smoking two and half packets of cigarettes a day.

There is also another telling variable in the Urban Age's DNA data, and that is income inequality. This is measured using the GINI index, and one would think that the cities with the most extreme inequality would be those with the lowest Human Development Index. At first that appears to be true, given that the most socially inequitable cities, Johannesburg and Mumbai, also have the lowest indices of human development. But, again, New York disproves the pattern. The city with the most billionaires in the world is socially divided (with a GINI index figure of .50) and yet it has the second highest HDI on the chart. Can one in fact argue that social inequality is a good thing for cities? In some sense the very idea of a vital city relies on extremes of wealth and poverty, and it is the aspiration of moving from one to the other that keeps it vibrant. This is a self-consciously provocative point, and yet it is no doubt true that Mumbai is a more important city since it is starting to lure back India's best and brightest with the promise of an economic boom. Global cities will always be made up of yin and yang. Conversely, it is surely true that the least inspiring cities are the monocultures.

Interestingly, for those of us who live there, London comes out top not just in human development index, but also in income equality, in the lack of presence of data available for Germany at the city level, in which case, Berlin would most likely to be top ranked. If this is surprising that London does come out on top, it is because the one thing that most people know about London – that it's expensive – is precisely the thing that makes life hard for its residents. With exorbitant rents and the growing unlikelihood that young couples will ever be able to get on the property ladder, sometimes the advantages of living in the capital can feel rather academic. But then it is also the richest (by per capita GDP) of the Urban Age cities, and so perhaps the equanimity comes from everyone being in the same boat. Or, then again, perhaps it is that the latest GINI figure we have is from 1995. There is no doubt that the period between 1995 and 2010 has seen the UK become a more divided society, and at the national level income disparity has been rising steadily. It would be interesting to see whether London is following the same trend.

A City of Many Qualities

Now that we have probed the data, are we any closer to imagining a theoretical ideal city? Would the urban geneticist perhaps choose to splice together the DNA of London and Mumbai? The characteristics of this city – let's call it Lonbai – would include London's wealth, its equitable society (based on its GINI coefficient), its low pollution levels and its extensive public transport network. On the other hand, that transport would have to be priced at Mumbai rates. A shrewd Dr Frankenstein would also choose Mumbai's compact urban footprint, its high incidence of walking, negligible car ownership and phenomenally low CO_2 emissions. Throw in Berlin's murder rate and New York's peak density and you have a wealthy, fair, safe, green, efficient and compact city.

Of course, one could also choose to create the antithesis. Based on what we've seen, that might be an amalgam of Johannesburg's social division, Mumbai's density and poverty, São Paulo's murder rate, urban footprint and car ownership, Shanghai's pollution and CO_2 emissions, and London's transport prices. That is a city in the process of self-destruction. But cities are not isolated Petri dishes on a laboratory table; they exist as part of a continuous system. House prices in London affect the decisions made by affluent Mumbaikars. The National Health Service's recruiting policies may strip Johannesburg's hospitals of nurses, and rising crime may push its professionals to move to safer cities. In the global urban ecosystem, one city's loss may be another's gain.

	Annual waste production (kg per capita)	Daily water consumption (litres per capita)	Annual electricity use (kWh per capita)	Annual CO$_2$ emissions (kg per capita)
MUMBAI	193 2001	90 2005	579 2007 - Maharashtra State	371 2000 - Maharashtra State
SÃO PAULO	504 2007	185	1,954 2006	1,123 2003
ISTANBUL	383 2006	155 2008	2,267 2007	2,720 2005
NEW YORK	529 2005	607 2005	6,603 2007	7,396 2007
SHANGHAI	343 1999	439 2005	6,357 2005	10,680 2003
LONDON	459 2005	324 2005	4,539 2000	5,599 2005
MEXICO CITY	228	343	–	5,862 2000
JOHANNESBURG	558 2007	378	3,388 2007	5,025 2007
BERLIN	497 2007	171 2000	3,880 2005	5,821 2005

UNDERSTANDING WHAT PEOPLE THINK

Tony Travers

Public opinion was tested for the Urban Age conferences in each year from 2007 to 2010. The international polling firm Ipsos MORI undertook major surveys in São Paulo, Mumbai and Istanbul to create an information base about the attitudes and aspirations of the residents of those cities. This work built on a series of polls undertaken in London by Ipsos MORI, testing people's opinion about the city's government and other issues. This essay brings together the findings from these polls in the four major metropolitan areas to compare and contrast the opinions of people living in cities that are in some ways similar, but in other ways very different.

Major metropolitan areas often have common interests. Their residents are more likely to be concerned with traffic congestion, pollution, crime and the need for improved infrastructure than those who live in rural and other non-urban areas. Having many millions of people live within a relatively small geographical area creates conditions that are very different from those experienced in smaller cities and in the countryside. London, São Paulo, Mumbai and Istanbul, though at different stages of development, are similar in this regard.

On the other hand, there are characteristics that are unique to each city, or at least much more important to their residents, than the same characteristics elsewhere. The polling undertaken for the Urban Age started off with a small exercise to determine which issues were of particular importance to each city. Thus, for example, transport was explored in greater detail in Istanbul and climate change impact in Mumbai. However, this chapter will consider those polling results that are available for all the cities, to allow 'compare and contrast' similarities and differences to be explored.

Population Stability and 'Churn'

Urban Age research has produced many comparative data about the population and other demographic detail of the cities it has studied. But the Ipsos MORI polling makes it possible to consider aspects of the population that are not observable from the overall totals. Questions were asked about how long people had lived in each of the four cities and also about how long people had lived at their current address. The responses reveal very different levels of stability and 'churn' from one city to another.

In London around one-seventh of the population has lived there for less than five years, suggesting a substantial level of in-migration within a very short period. The figure was lower, at 7 per cent, in São Paulo and Istanbul and close to zero in Mumbai (even though this result may be strongly affected by methodological inconsistencies). The clear implication is that the government and residents of London need to be prepared to cope with a significantly larger flow of migrants than in many other cities.

This finding is borne out by the figures for the proportion of the population who have lived in a city for over 20 years. In Mumbai, 96 per cent of the population have been in the city for at least 20 years, compared with 78 per cent in São Paulo, 64 per cent in Istanbul and 58 per cent in London. The London finding is remarkable: given the speed of in-migration it seems likely that soon under half of the city's population will have lived there for 20 years. London and Istanbul also have relatively low proportions of their populations born in the city: 40 per cent in Istanbul and just 30 per cent in London. In the case of London, migration from within the UK and overseas (both of which have been substantial in the past 50 years) means under a third of its population was born locally. The importance of these figures is that they provide clues to the movement of people in, out and within the city. Large movements of people in and out (particularly if they are international migrants) and 'churn' of population within the city are likely to add to public service costs and may weaken cohesion. A very settled population, particularly if born locally, might be expected to share values and would be easily understood by local politicians and officials. On the other hand, a city where there was massive in- and out-migration and where residents moved around the city from address to address would be likely to be less cohesive and also be more difficult for city government to manage.

Of course, characteristics such as the stage of economic development, openness to trade and national history will affect the extent to which people will have been resident in a city for a long time and also their likelihood to move homes. In Mumbai, the city is still growing significantly as India becomes industrialized. The population is relatively young, as it is in Istanbul and São Paulo. London, by contrast, is an old city with a slower rate of growth, though it has a tradition of international trading and historical links with many Commonwealth nations.

In terms of the implications of these results, New York or Toronto would be similar to London, while Shanghai is likely to be more like Mumbai or Istanbul. Policy makers in all metropolitan areas must face up to issues such as migration, the need for new housing and the costs of population movement. These numbers suggest the range of experience and difference will be very great from city to city.

Good and Bad Things about the Cities

Ipsos MORI's research examined the things people like and dislike about the cities in which they live, starting with a general question about levels of satisfaction or dissatisfaction. Of course, people may answer a question of this kind from different cultural starting points. However, it is likely the differences revealed show something real about the contentment or otherwise people feel with different cities.

Graph 1 summarizes the results. Mumbai achieves the highest level of satisfaction, closely followed by London, while Istanbul and São Paulo register the highest levels of dissatisfaction. The scale of the difference between 'satisfaction' figures in Mumbai and London and those in Istanbul and São Paulo is large enough to be significant. Residents of Mumbai and London show very high levels of satisfaction, with over 70 per cent being either 'very' or 'fairly' satisfied with their city. In Mumbai, only 2 per cent of people are dissatisfied, which is remarkably low given the stresses and strains of urban life. Even in London, capital of a notoriously pessimistic nation, only 13 per cent were either 'very' or 'fairly' dissatisfied. As a

Graph 1: How satisfied or dissatisfied are you with your city as a place to live in?

very satisfied
fairly satisfied
neutral
fairly dissatisfied
very dissatisfied

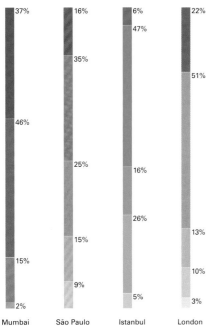

Mumbai	São Paulo	Istanbul	London
37%	16%	6%	22%
	47%		
	35%	47%	51%
46%			
	25%	16%	
		26%	13%
15%	15%		10%
	9%	5%	3%
2%			

result, the residents of both Mumbai and London show extraordinarily positive satisfaction levels.

The significantly lower net 'satisfaction' levels in São Paulo and Istanbul stand in stark contrast to the figures for London and Mumbai. It is impossible to be certain why exactly such a difference exists. Both São Paulo and Mumbai have millions of people living in informal settlements. Istanbul and London have existed as major cities for many centuries. It is possible, as figures in Graph 3 suggest, that concerns about crime and personal safety have eroded residents' satisfaction levels. But there can be no doubt that people in London and, in particular, Mumbai, are significantly more satisfied with their city than those in São Paulo and Istanbul.

The question of why people like or dislike the city in which they live will be influenced by many factors. Ipsos MORI asked people to list the 'best' and 'worst' things about living in their cities by showing them lists of possible issues that might affect their lives. In some of the research, they offered people the opportunity to choose as many factors as they wished, while in others they limited them to two or three. The results suggest distinct 'likes' and 'dislikes'.

In London and São Paulo 'range of shops' was selected as the most popular thing they liked about their city, though in the Latin American city it tied with 'job opportunities', which were a close second in London. Such a finding is perhaps unsurprising for the consumerist British, but perhaps rather more so in Brazil. Shopping did not feature in the 'top three' for either Mumbai or Istanbul. Indeed, 'range of shops' was a low 'best things' factor in Istanbul. 'Job opportunities' appeared in the top three in all four cities, emphasizing the economic importance of each city within its country. London, São Paulo, Mumbai and Istanbul are major agglomerations of economic activity, providing opportunities for people from elsewhere in the country and from other countries. It is clear from the answers to the researchers' questions that people are aware of this economic dynamism. It is unlikely that the residents of smaller cities or rural areas would see employment as a key benefit of the place where they lived. 'Schools' appear as one of the top three 'best things' about living in São Paulo, Mumbai and Istanbul. In Mumbai, schools are top of the list, suggesting that the city is seen as having a good education system by national standards. The same appears to be true of 'health', which comes a close second in Mumbai and also in Istanbul. Indeed, public education and health care provision is clearly held in greater esteem in Istanbul and Mumbai compared with London.

As an older and more developed city, London is today seen as having public services that are often overstretched and generally worse than in smaller towns and rural areas in Britain. In rapidly developing Mumbai, Istanbul and São Paulo it is likely that services have the potential to be better organized and more universal than in rural parts of the country. Thus, one of the drivers of in-migration into such cities will be the promise of decent public provision. A growing economy creates additional tax resources to pay for improved health care and education services, which, in turn, make the city even more productive – and attractive. As London developed into a megacity in the late-nineteenth century it was able to expand public provision that would have been unavailable except in other rapidly industrializing cities.

That the high cost of living in a megacity is an issue is clear from the responses to the 'worst things' question, shown in Graph 3. Both the 'cost of living' and the 'cost of housing' feature as issues in Mumbai and London, with Londoners citing the cost of living as the top of their 'worst' factors. Only the residents of São Paulo did not

Graph 2: What are the 2 or 3 best things about your city?

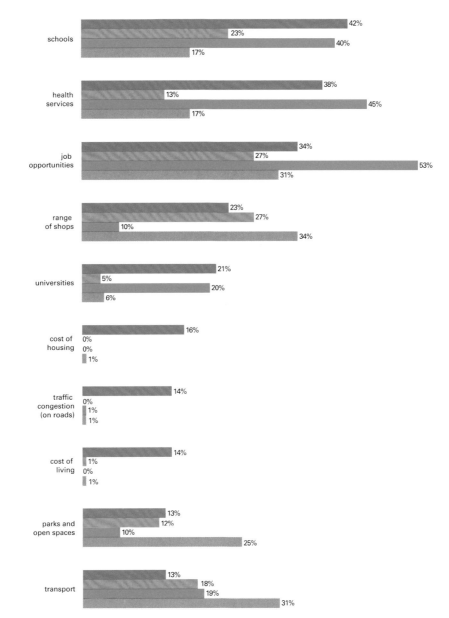

Mumbai
São Paulo
Istanbul
London

schools
Mumbai 42%
São Paulo 23%
Istanbul 40%
London 17%

health services
Mumbai 38%
São Paulo 13%
Istanbul 45%
London 17%

job opportunities
Mumbai 34%
São Paulo 27%
Istanbul 53%
London 31%

range of shops
Mumbai 23%
São Paulo 27%
Istanbul 10%
London 34%

universities
Mumbai 21%
São Paulo 5%
Istanbul 20%
London 6%

cost of housing
Mumbai 16%
São Paulo 0%
Istanbul 0%
London 1%

traffic congestion (on roads)
Mumbai 14%
São Paulo 0%
Istanbul 1%
London 1%

cost of living
Mumbai 14%
São Paulo 1%
Istanbul 0%
London 1%

parks and open spaces
Mumbai 13%
São Paulo 12%
Istanbul 10%
London 25%

transport
Mumbai 13%
São Paulo 18%
Istanbul 19%
London 31%

put living costs in their top three concerns. 'Crime' and 'safety', unsurprisingly, were selected as key 'worst' factors in London, Istanbul and São Paulo. Research conducted in advance of the Urban Age conference in São Paulo had suggested crime and personal safety were significant concerns in the city, leading to in-depth questioning on the issue. Interestingly, in the light of the amount of publicity given to crime in São Paulo and other Latin American cities, 'health services' were citied by Paulistanos as the single worst feature of life in the city.

Mumbai and Istanbul residents put 'traffic congestion' as their number one complaint about the city. Virtually all big cities suffer from over-used roads and the pollution and safety problems this causes. By not selecting this option, people living

Graph 3: What are the two or three worst things about your city?

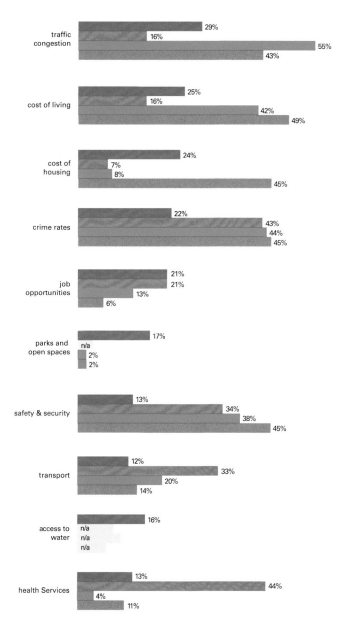

Mumbai
São Paulo
Istanbul
London

traffic congestion
Mumbai 29%
São Paulo 16%
Istanbul 55%
London 43%

cost of living
Mumbai 25%
São Paulo 16%
Istanbul 42%
London 49%

cost of housing
Mumbai 24%
São Paulo 7%
Istanbul 8%
London 45%

crime rates
Mumbai 22%
São Paulo 43%
Istanbul 44%
London 45%

job opportunities
Mumbai 21%
São Paulo 21%
Istanbul 13%
London 6%

parks and open spaces
Mumbai 17%
São Paulo n/a
Istanbul 2%
London 2%

safety & security
Mumbai 13%
São Paulo 34%
Istanbul 38%
London 45%

transport
Mumbai 12%
São Paulo 33%
Istanbul 20%
London 14%

access to water
Mumbai 16%
São Paulo n/a
Istanbul n/a
London n/a

health Services
Mumbai 13%
São Paulo 44%
Istanbul 4%
London 11%

in London and São Paulo are suggesting that, for them, traffic is less of a problem. It is possible that in London the introduction of congestion charging has affected perceptions about the problems caused by vehicles.

The City's Image

In the years since the 1980s, leading cities have increasingly seen themselves as part of a system of 'global' cities. Academic and professional researchers have evolved a literature about these leading metropolitan areas and their functions. The Urban Age programme is itself a product of this heightened interest in global or 'world' cities. In this context, the self-image of a city is an important feature in the development

Graph 4: 'My city is a place I identify with'

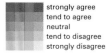

- strongly agree
- tend to agree
- neutral
- tend to disagree
- strongly disagree

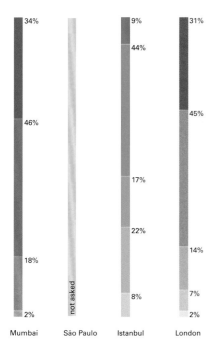

Mumbai: 34%, 46%, 18%, 2%

São Paulo: not asked

Istanbul: 9%, 44%, 17%, 22%, 8%

London: 31%, 45%, 14%, 7%, 2%

of its international, external, image. With this in mind, Ipsos MORI asked residents in London, Mumbai and Istanbul about the extent to which people identify with their city. New York City's early 'I♥NY' branding during the 1970s and the 'Glasgow's Miles Better' campaign during the 1980s were exemplary in setting the pace for other cities in attempting to make their own citizens as well as outsiders improve their perception of the city.

In Mumbai, 80 per cent agreed with the contention 'My city is a place I identify with', with only 2 per cent disagreeing – producing a remarkable +78 per cent 'agree' rating. London had a 76 per cent 'agree' score and just 9 per cent disagreeing, leaving a +67 per cent positive rating. Istanbul produced both a weaker 'agree' score and a stronger 'disagree' one, leading to a positive score of +23 per cent.

Answers to the first question suggested that both Istanbul and London had a larger immigrant population (domestic and international together) than São Paulo and Mumbai, so it is perhaps unsurprising that Istanbul has a lower 'identify' reading than in a city with a population where people were more likely to have been born locally. But London, which has also seen very high levels of immigration (particularly from other countries) in recent years, shows very high levels of civic identification. It is possible that many new migrants who arrive in a new city from overseas feel a strong sense of belonging in the place they have chosen to make their home. It is possible (though this research did not probe this issue) that international settlers in London identify more strongly with the city than people born in the UK.

A strong sense of identification with a city is an important element in the place's capacity to assent to be governed. If residents feel they are strongly linked to the city, and possibly proud of it, they are more likely to accept changes made by mayors and city councils to the way the city operates. In this sense, identification with the city is a potentially important tool for city government in seeking an agreed agenda for progress. Barcelona, in particular, has used complicity of this kind to alter itself and its international offer radically.

Public Safety and Crime

Public safety and crime are issues that all city governments have to take seriously. The concentration of millions of people, often including a significant proportion of deprived and immigrant residents, creates the potential for violence and crime. Big cities are generally more prone to criminality than smaller towns and rural areas. In addition, capital cities and other metropolitan centres in countries facing a threat from terrorism are generally a prime target.

On the question of safety, as Graph 5 shows, the polling produced startlingly different results in all four cities. People were asked 'How safe are you walking in your neighbourhood in the evening by yourself?', with the option of answering 'very' or 'fairly' safe or 'very' or 'fairly' unsafe. In three of the four cities, a significant majority of people did not feel safe, with 76 per cent and 66 per cent in Istanbul and São Paulo stating they felt unsafe. By contrast, in London 61 per cent felt safe and only 33 per cent unsafe. As a result, it appears Londoners feel substantially safer in their city at night than the inhabitants of the other three cities. These polling results are supported by data from the International Crime Victim Survey, where Londoners were far less likely to expect a burglary to occur within the next year than the residents of São Paulo or Istanbul. Given media-driven perceptions of crime in most big cities, the London result suggests that people have made a realistic assessment of the very low risk of violent crime in their city. Polling in São Paulo in particular implied residents see crime and public safety as a key issue for improvement.

The pollsters went on to ask more detailed questions about why people felt threatened in their neighbourhoods. 'Fear of attack/mugging' was seen as important in London, São Paulo and Istanbul, while 'fear of burglary' was the top problem in Mumbai and second most important in London. Five issues appeared only once among the top three for the cities: 'pickpockets' were seen as a key issue in Istanbul, while in Mumbai 'fear of sexual harassment' and 'fear of attack due to race/religion' were very important. In London, 'teenagers hanging around on streets' was the third most cited 'unsafe' issue, yet it was well down the list of concerns in São Paulo and Mumbai, though a medium-scale concern in Istanbul. In São Paulo, lack of police presence was regarded as an issue. It is evident from these findings that particular problems surface in some cities but not others. 'Gun crime' was just behind the top three in Istanbul, suggesting a heightened sense of public concern there that was not present in the other cities. Fear of young people has evidently been a growing challenge in Britain in recent years, while inter-ethnic and religious violence can be a problem in parts of India. Having said this, many of the reasons why residents feel 'unsafe' are common to the three cities and, without doubt, most others.

Graph 7 shows the results of questioning about what would make residents feel safer in their home neighbourhoods. A 'faster/more severe justice system' was seen as a key factor in Mumbai, Istanbul and São Paulo, implying people do not have full confidence in the courts and other parts of the criminal justice system. In São Paulo, 'better street lighting' was the most favoured way of improving safety. Like the expressed desire for improved health care services shown in Graph 3, it appears Paulistanos have a powerful desire for strengthened municipal interventions to drive up basic service standards. 'More police on patrol' and 'more security cameras' were seen as important in both Istanbul and London.

In Mumbai 'improve employment possibilities' was believed to be a way of increasing safety, suggesting people see a direct link between under-employment and

Graph 5: How safe are you walking in your neighbourhood in the evening by yourself?

very safe
safe
unsafe
very unsafe
✳ ✳ ✳ ✳ not going out at night

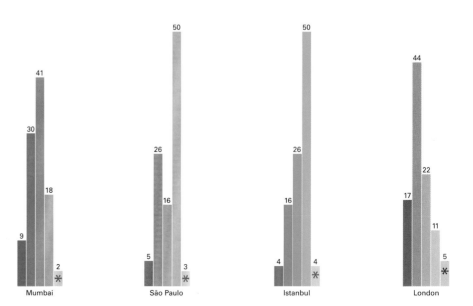

Graph 6: What makes you feel unsafe in your area?

Legend:
- Mumbai
- São Paulo
- Istanbul
- London

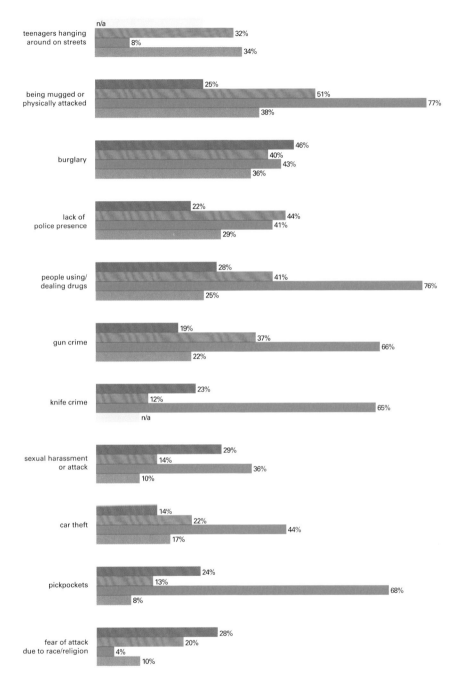

teenagers hanging around on streets
- Mumbai: n/a
- São Paulo: 32%
- Istanbul: 8%
- London: 34%

being mugged or physically attacked
- Mumbai: 25%
- São Paulo: 51%
- Istanbul: 77%
- London: 38%

burglary
- Mumbai: 46%
- São Paulo: 40%
- Istanbul: 43%
- London: 36%

lack of police presence
- Mumbai: 22%
- São Paulo: 44%
- Istanbul: 41%
- London: 29%

people using/dealing drugs
- Mumbai: 28%
- São Paulo: 41%
- Istanbul: 76%
- London: 25%

gun crime
- Mumbai: 19%
- São Paulo: 37%
- Istanbul: 66%
- London: 22%

knife crime
- Mumbai: 23%
- São Paulo: 12%
- Istanbul: 65%
- London: n/a

sexual harassment or attack
- Mumbai: 29%
- São Paulo: 14%
- Istanbul: 36%
- London: 10%

car theft
- Mumbai: 14%
- São Paulo: 22%
- Istanbul: 44%
- London: 17%

pickpockets
- Mumbai: 24%
- São Paulo: 13%
- Istanbul: 68%
- London: 8%

fear of attack due to race/religion
- Mumbai: 28%
- São Paulo: 20%
- Istanbul: 4%
- London: 10%

a challenge to safety. Mumbaikars, more than others, believe traffic restrictions have a role to play in improving safety, presumably because of the chaotic nature of the city's streets. Londoners saw 'more things for young people to do' as a key way of improving safety. It is clear that Londoners, more than inhabitants of the other three cities, view the young as a major problem and key challenge to personal security.

According to the residents of the four cities the improvement of safety and personal security require significantly different problems to be tackled.

Graph 7: What two or three things would most
improve safety in your area?

Mumbai
São Paulo
Istanbul
London

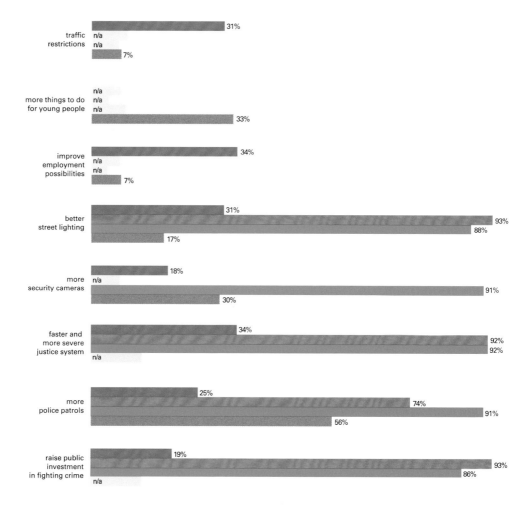

traffic restrictions	31%	
	n/a	
	n/a	
	7%	
more things to do for young people	n/a	
	n/a	
	n/a	
	33%	
improve employment possibilities	34%	
	n/a	
	n/a	
	7%	
better street lighting	31%	
	93%	
	88%	
	17%	
more security cameras	18%	
	n/a	
	91%	
	30%	
faster and more severe justice system	34%	
	92%	
	92%	
	n/a	
more police patrols	25%	
	74%	
	91%	
	56%	
raise public investment in fighting crime	19%	
	93%	
	86%	
	n/a	

Improvements to the justice system and additional police are widely seen as important, though there are other issues that are crucial in some places but not others. The possibility of transferring lessons and implications from one city to another may therefore be somewhat more difficult in the sphere of law and order than elsewhere. People in each city appear to have particular needs and expectations that may not be seen as particularly important elsewhere. 'More police' is a simple slogan in relation to personal safety, but it appears local demands are more complex.

The Environment

The Urban Age programme has taken a particular interest in environmental sustainability and the quality of life in cities. Liveability is a key issue in mega-cities and as concerns have developed about the need to make more efficient use of natural resources many city leaders have been encouraged to improve environmental quality by tackling the detrimental factors affecting urban life. Graph 8 shows the issues cited as constituting each city's major environmental problems.

Unsurprisingly, 'pollution from traffic' and 'air quality' proved to be significant negative environmental factors in all four cities. In Mumbai and Istanbul,

Graph 8: Considering the quality of the environment, which are the city's major problems?

Mumbai
São Paulo
Istanbul
London

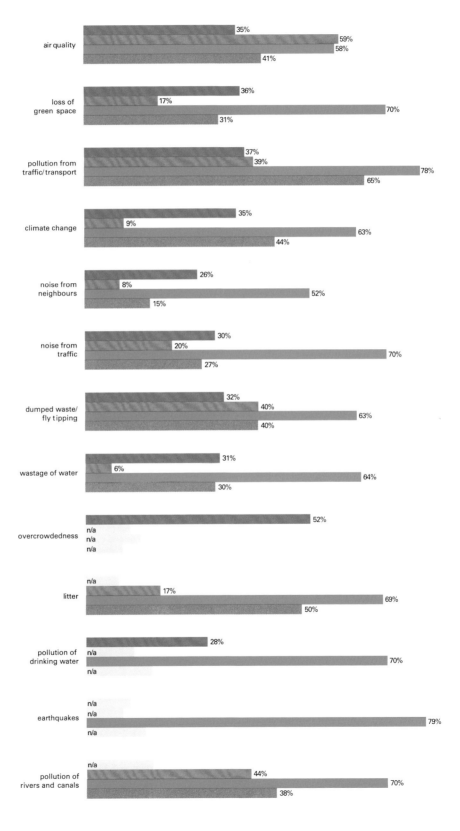

air quality
Mumbai 35%
São Paulo 59%
Istanbul 58%
London 41%

loss of green space
Mumbai 36%
São Paulo 17%
Istanbul 70%
London 31%

pollution from traffic/transport
Mumbai 37%
São Paulo 39%
Istanbul 78%
London 65%

climate change
Mumbai 35%
São Paulo 9%
Istanbul 63%
London 44%

noise from neighbours
Mumbai 26%
São Paulo 8%
Istanbul 52%
London 15%

noise from traffic
Mumbai 30%
São Paulo 20%
Istanbul 70%
London 27%

dumped waste/fly tipping
Mumbai 32%
São Paulo 40%
Istanbul 63%
London 40%

wastage of water
Mumbai 31%
São Paulo 6%
Istanbul 64%
London 30%

overcrowdedness
Mumbai 52%
São Paulo n/a
Istanbul n/a
London n/a

litter
Mumbai n/a
São Paulo 17%
Istanbul 69%
London 50%

pollution of drinking water
Mumbai 28%
São Paulo n/a
Istanbul 70%
London n/a

earthquakes
Mumbai n/a
São Paulo n/a
Istanbul 79%
London n/a

pollution of rivers and canals
Mumbai n/a
São Paulo 44%
Istanbul 70%
London 38%

'polluted drinking water' was considered problematic, reflecting different levels of development than in London where the issue has no salience. Mumbaikars were uniquely worried by 'overcrowdedness' and Istanbulites by 'earthquakes', reflecting particular problems in those cities that did not appear elsewhere. Similarly, 'dumped waste/fly-tipping' was in São Paulo's top three, but not in the other cities. 'Climate change' was significantly important in London. As with crime and safety issues, there are some problems that appear common to the four metropolitan areas and others that are relevant in only one.

City governments are often judged in relation to their environmental performance. Originally, this meant specifically their capacity to keep streets clean and ensure air pollution was tackled. Latterly, the populations of megacities have come to expect local policy makers to contribute to wider efforts to tackle environmental sustainability issues. It is possible that it is because the consequences of some kinds of environmental detriment are particularly visible in big cities that the pressures to find solutions are most developed there.

Transport

Public transport is possibly the single most important form of provision used by cities to promote economic growth while reducing air pollution and improving quality of life. Older centres such as London, Paris and New York have extensive rail, metro and bus networks that allow them to generate high levels of output and productivity with relatively reduced reliance on private cars. Typically 75 to 85 per cent of central business district employees in older, developed, cities travel to work by public transport each morning. Rapidly developing megacities are in most cases building commuter rail, metro and/or rapid bus systems to allow a shift from cars to public transport.

Graph 9 shows the three things people told Ipsos MORI they believed would most improve roads or reduce traffic. Investing in metro, rail and bus systems was seen as important in São Paulo, Mumbai and Istanbul, while in São Paulo and Mumbai there was support for more road building. By contrast, in London it was believed that maintaining existing roads and better planning of roadworks would improve things. There is little support in London for new roads, largely because the city has already been very fully developed and it would be impossible to create new motorways without knocking down homes or businesses. Earlier campaigns to construct major new roads in London during the 1950s and 1960s produced an anti-roads backlash that still affects policy.

In Mumbai and São Paulo, where there is likely to be a continuing increase in car ownership as economic development occurs, a demand for more road space seems logical. Istanbul residents showed a willingness to follow London in introducing congestion charging.

Governance

The quality and effectiveness of urban government was a regular theme of the Urban Age research and events. As part of the polling undertaken in Istanbul, Mumbai, São Paulo and London, people were asked how satisfied they were with the way each mayor is doing their job. For Mumbai, where there is no elected mayor, the question was asked in relation to the Chief Minister for Maharashtra.

In Istanbul and London, around half the population were satisfied with the mayor, with a particularly strong positive balance in Istanbul. In São Paulo, more

Graph 9: Which two or three things would most
improve roads/reduce traffic?

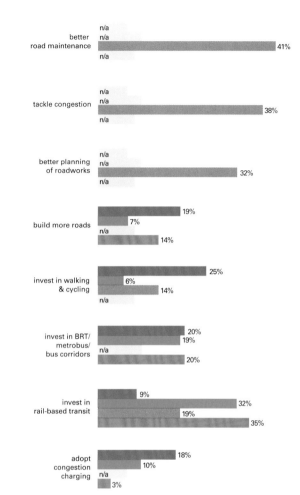

■ Mumbai
■ São Paulo
■ Istanbul
■ London

better road maintenance — n/a / n/a / 41% / n/a

tackle congestion — n/a / n/a / 38% / n/a

better planning of roadworks — n/a / n/a / 32% / n/a

build more roads — 19% / 7% / n/a / 14%

invest in walking & cycling — 25% / 6% / 14% / n/a

invest in BRT/metrobus/bus corridors — 20% / 19% / n/a / 20%

invest in rail-based transit — 9% / 32% / 19% / 35%

adopt congestion charging — 18% / 10% / n/a / 3%

people were dissatisfied than satisfied, leading to a net 'dissatisfied' reading. In Mumbai, there appeared to be weak approval of the chief minister, but the polling did not ask about disapproval. The numbers from Istanbul and London suggest it is possible to be civic leader of a major city and retain public approval, though it is worth noting that the London mayor at the time of the polling went on to lose the next election. As Graph 10 shows, approval is not sufficient to assure re-election.

Conclusions

Opinion polling is now an established element of the operation of most democratic states. The research undertaken for the Urban Age programme used Ipsos MORI's extensive network of offices to test how urban residents in four of the world's leading cities felt about the places they live. Given the well-publicized strains on urban life, the results suggested a reasonable degree of happiness with city life, in both older, developed cities and newer, rapidly industrializing ones.

Polling of this kind is important for mayors and local governments in testing what people do and do not like about their neighbourhoods and cities. Personal safety is a key issue in major metropolitan areas and the polling makes clear that in

Graph 10: How satisfied are you with the way your
elected representative is doing his/her job?

Mumbai: Satisfaction levels with the Chief Minister of Maharashtra

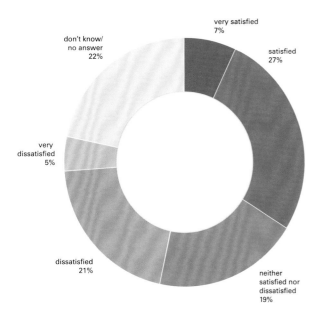

don't know/
no answer
22%

very satisfied
7%

satisfied
27%

very
dissatisfied
5%

dissatisfied
21%

neither
satisfied nor
dissatisfied
19%

São Paulo: Satisfaction levels with current city government

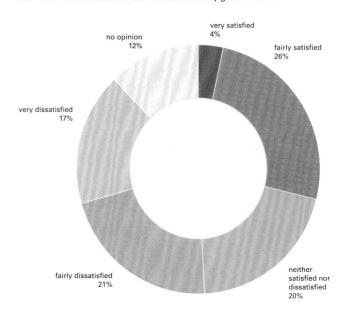

no opinion
12%

very satisfied
4%

fairly satisfied
26%

very dissatisfied
17%

fairly dissatisfied
21%

neither
satisfied nor
dissatisfied
20%

Istanbul: Satisfaction levels with the Mayor of Istanbul

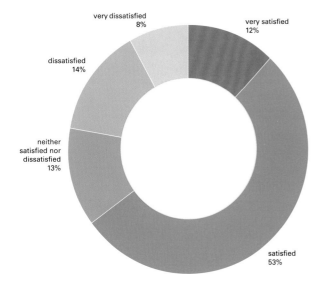

very dissatisfied
8%

very satisfied
12%

dissatisfied
14%

neither
satisfied nor
dissatisfied
13%

satisfied
53%

London: Satisfaction levels with the Mayor of London

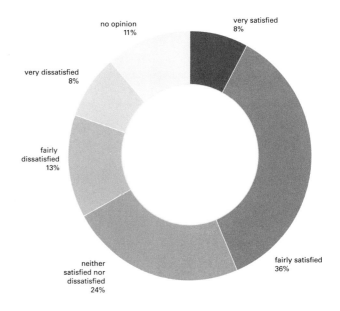

no opinion
11%

very satisfied
8%

very dissatisfied
8%

fairly
dissatisfied
13%

fairly satisfied
36%

neither
satisfied nor
dissatisfied
24%

São Paulo and Istanbul there is a significant issue here. Health care and other public services are seen as poor in some developing cities, while the 'range of shops' can be an important reason for residents liking where they live.

There is no overwhelming feeling within the four cities that life is bad. The fact there is growth within the population and economy of London, São Paulo, Mumbai and Istanbul implies these are relatively successful places. Each has a higher GDP per head than their country as a whole. Migrants to the city are, to a significant degree, 'volunteering' to live there. As long as mayors and city councils are capable of ensuring that public services are good enough to allow 8 or more million people to live in close proximity, the cities will be likely to register broadly positive poll ratings. But, where the polls show dissatisfaction, there will be a need for public policy action.

REFLE

CTIONS

BOUNDARIES AND BORDERS

Richard Sennett

SLUMS AND GHETTOES

The ghetto in Venice has long been a picturesque attraction for tourists. Its structure is not so far removed from that of a settlement in Mumbai that is too easily described as a slum.

The cities everyone wants to live in would be clean and safe, possess efficient public services, support a dynamic economy, provide cultural stimulation, and help heal society's divisions of race and ethnicity and class. These are not the cities we live in. This is in part because the city is not its own master; cities can fail on all these counts due to national government policies or to social ills and economic forces beyond local control. Still, something has gone wrong, radically wrong, in our conception of what a city itself should be.

It is fair to say that most of my professional colleagues share the fear that the art of designing cities declined drastically in the course of the twentieth century. The vernacular environments of earlier times have proved more flexible, sustainable and stimulating than those designed more recently – which is a paradox. Today's planner has an arsenal of technological tools, from lighting and heating to structural support to materials for buildings and public spaces, which urbanists could not begin to imagine even a hundred years ago. We have many more tools than in the past, but we don't use these resources very creatively.

One way, I believe, to moving forward in making truly modern cities lies in re-conceiving where the important spaces of the city lie. Traditionally, the centre has been the most important place in the city; we might now want to think about edges within the city – the lines and zones which separate different ethnic communities, economic classes or functional activities. How can these zones be brought to life?

Edges in Nature

Edges come in two forms, as borders or as boundaries. This is an important distinction in the natural world. In natural ecologies, borders are the zones in a habitat where organisms become more interactive, due to the meeting of different species or physical conditions. The boundary is a limit, a territory beyond which a particular species does not stray. For instance, in the border-edge where the shoreline of a lake meets solid land there is an active zone of exchange; here organisms find and feed off other organisms. The same is true of temperature layers within a lake: where layer meets layer defines the zone of the most intense biological activity. Whereas the boundary is a guarded territory, as established by prides of lions or packs of wolves. The border has more energy than the boundary.

Not surprisingly, it is at the borderline where the work of natural selection is the most intense, because exchange among different kinds of organisms is heightened;

to the ethologist, a borderland is full of time. By contrast, the boundary is a static space in time, because there is less exchange – it is marked by things petering out, not happening.

This spatial distinction in natural ecologies relates to a difference in the structure of cells themselves. It is the difference between a cell wall and cell membrane. A cell wall serves as a container holding things in, while the membrane is at once porous and resistant, letting matter flow in and out of the cell, but selectively, so that the cell can retain what it needs for nourishment. This is an ambiguous distinction at the cellular level, in part because cell linings can sometimes switch function; again, a wholly sealed wall would cause any cell to die. But the difference, in degree, between wall and membrane is important for our understanding of what nature might tell us about making cities.

The essence of a cell membrane is that it combines porosity and resistance. That is, in nature – either at the cellular or ecological level – 'open' does not mean pure, free flowing; nature requires differentiation in spatial as well as in physiological form. Living territories and individual organisms cannot survive if their constituent elements are subject simply to chance; resistance conserves the value of these elements, yet porosity nourishes them by exchange and influence from the outside. Thus a living edge, whether membrane or border, will make exchange possible yet resists simply dissolving into formless flux.

The natural distinction between borders and boundaries applies to human communities, and matters particularly for the practice of urban design. In the twentieth century, planning tended to define and enshrine boundaries; it created static territories in cities, which diminished exchange between social, economic, religious and ethnic groups. The technologies of transport, the gated communities, the articulation of vertical buildings, all tended to seal off and isolate differences. The planning of the last century was hopeless at creating or promoting borderlands; when urbanists thought about the alternative to the sealed boundary, the dead edge, they could imagine only stripping away all distinctions, creating amorphous 'open' public space. They did not know how to bring edges to life by combining porosity and resistance.

We need, then, to re-think the morphological elements that mark an urban edge: the most important of these elements is the wall.

The Wall

The walls around traditional cities would seem an unlikely instance of the border/membrane condition. Until the invention of artillery, people sheltered behind walls when attacked; the gates in walls also served to regulate commerce coming into cities, often being the place in which taxes were collected. Yet the massive medieval walls such as those surviving in Aix-en-Provence or in Rome furnish a perhaps misleading visual evidence. On both sides of the Aix-en-Provence wall sites for unregulated development in the city were to be found; houses were built on either side of these medieval walls; informal markets selling black-market or untaxed goods sprung up nestled against them; the zone around the wall was where heretics, foreign exiles and other misfits tended to gravitate towards, again far from the controls of the centre. In social practice, then, such walls functioned as membranes, both porous and resistant.

Solid walls are replaced in the modern city by spaces, by voids, which tend much more to the boundary condition. Motorways cut through cities are the obvious example: crossing through six or eight lanes of traffic is perilous; the sides of motorways in cities tend to become withered spaces; these invisible walls infamously have been used to mark off the territories separating the rich from the poor, or race from race. Porosity is lacking. Put as a general rule, in the twentieth century planning motion has served as the instrument for making boundaries rather than borders.

Three cities form an instructive contrast in the solid/void, border/boundary difference in making walls.

The built fabric of modern Istanbul is full of solid walls, but its planners have for the most part kept these walls porous. They allow activities from inside a building to spill out into the street, and encourage the combination of different functions at street level. The street wall of compressed buildings is thus an active edge between inside and outside. Crime levels in Istanbul are relatively low because there are innumerable 'eyes on the street'. Though history and geography erected two seemingly unrelated parts of the city – a European part on one side of the Bosporus, an Asian part on the other side – each contains a mixture of peoples and activities, and the edges between these communities are sites for both economic and social exchange.

By contrast, São Paulo's planners have largely sought to deaden the edges within the city. This planned deadening begins with the physical street wall of buildings; 'development', they have thought, should do away with the porous/resistant qualities of compressed buildings in the city's *favelas*; 'development' means separation and distinction of individual buildings; separation and distinction lead to isolation. The gated community is justified as a necessity to ward off crime, even though in fact the dead walls surrounding these communities provide little real security – São Paulo's property and violent crime rates are much higher than Istanbul's. Planning in São Paulo, as in modern Los Angeles and Beijing, has used traffic flows on huge motorways to deaden contact and exchange at the larger macro-level of urban form.

London sits uneasily between these extremes. Due in part to the post-war effort to spread social housing throughout the city, economic and social mixture occurs in some rich areas like Kensington; gentrifiers in poor sections of the city, particularly in the East, have eschewed turning these districts into bourgeois shopping centres. London is full of local membranes. Yet motorway development in the post-war period has done its terrible work of boundary-making here too; the development of new housing along the eastern reaches of the Thames has sealed off the river ever more from those not living on its banks, and the social housing estates themselves, as they have aged, have become ever more places where the poor are gated-in, sealed off from daily contact with other Londoners.

There are obvious remedies for boundary making, some of these remedies simple, others technologically advanced. The simple solution is pedestrianization – perhaps too simple, as banishing traffic tends to homogenize urban space, pedestrian zones becoming shopping centres rather than serving the complex needs of production and work as well as consumption. Experiments in mixing complex activities within pedestrianized space in Stuttgart and Bogotá have seen the steady, necessary return of traffic. A more promising way of avoiding motion-walls makes use of sophisticated technology like computerized bollards, mechanical pistons dug into the street that remain down when service and commuter traffic needs to flow, but go up around lunchtime and at night, when pedestrian use makes more sense. This is but one example of how technology could be used in the future to convert boundaries into borders within the city. Much of what now passes for 'smart city' design is not as smart as it should be, at least from this perspective. By binding the activities of the city together electronically, so that there is more coherence, efficiency,

THE FORMAL AND THE INFORMAL

Nowhere is the boundary between the formal and the informal settlement more clearly visible and as sharp as in Latin America, as seen in this example from Caracas.

and order, 'smart city' design risks reducing chance encounter, open exchange, and mutual discovery. The whole point about a porous/resistant membrane is that it allows mutual stimulation in exchange; fixed mechanization inhibits this social process. We want smart cities in which the technology encourages flexibility and innovation, just as our medieval ancestors discovered that a solid object – the massive stone wall – could be adapted in time, without mechanical predetermination, to become an active scene of exchange within the city.

The design of buildings is likely to prove a tougher case. Take the wall made of plate glass, a ubiquitous material in modern architecture that allows architects to deliver walls of framed glass, used now almost universally in office construction. On the ground plane you see what's inside the building, but you can't touch, smell, or hear anything within; the plates are usually articulated so that there is only one, regulated, entrance to the inside. Plate glass walls thus make for boundaries rather than borders. As with the sides lining motorways, nothing much develops on either side of these transparent walls; as in Norman Foster's new City Hall for London, dead space develops on both sides, but here the political activities within the building are invisible outside. By contrast, the nineteenth-century architect Louis Sullivan used much more primitive forms of plate glass more flexibly; as invitations to gather, to enter a building or to dwell at its edge. His plate glass panels functioned as porous walls.

The View

To make living borders in cities, we need to change our habits of seeing, to revise critically the way we compose the city as a visual landscape. This is not an abstraction; it is implicated in how we make urban sense of natural elements like water.

Water plays a particular role in defining the difference between boundaries and borders. Up until the 1950s, the existence and shape of waterways has supported the economy and determined the shape of cities like Mumbai, Shanghai, Istanbul, London and New York – water, the material, was an urban medium for trade and circulation. But the docks and warehouses and water itself held little aesthetic interest for urban designers; water was just the utilitarian substance of the trading city.

In the early-nineteenth century functional watery scenes began to be valued aesthetically, as when the *European Magazine* described the original West India Docks in London in 1802, of which Canary Wharf now forms a part '... nothing can be conceived more beautiful than the dock. The water is of the necessary depth; its surface [thanks to the locks is] as smooth as a mirror, presents to eye a haven secure from storms.' This view expressed, if you like, a porous joint between commerce and aesthetics. But the joint came to be contested among urban designers, expressed by the American urbanist Daniel Burnham in 1909: 'the viewing of water is a solitary act, the regard of nothingness; in viewing water man turns his back, literally, on the conditions which support his life.' Burnham realized this view in the design he made for Chicago's lakefront in that same year; the places where water meets land are visually important but socially neutral; Burnham put parks, promenades and other low-density uses at the joint of water and land.

This watery aesthetic provides insight into how inert boundaries are created in cities: viewing space becomes opposed to working space. The divorce between art and work is hardly unique to architecture. The two aesthetics appear in painting during the late-nineteenth century, Impressionist painters frequently depicting the Parisian suburb of Argenteuil in scenes that mix factories with people picnicking or promenading, while post-Impressionist painters removed scenes of pleasure from the industrial landscape. Still, the privileging of the view has a profound social consequence; the messy mixture of activities is expelled from a scene for the sake of clarifying the view.

New water-edge projects in Mumbai propose, for instance, to evict a mass of small-scale businesses and pavement dwellers from the waterfront; the justification offered by the developers is in part visual, that of 'cleaning up' the view by reducing the density of people and complexity of uses. The offer of visual pleasure at the cost of mixed social and economic use afflicts similar proposals in Buenos Aires and London – all descendants in form of Burnham's Plan, all leading to social exclusion in the name of visual order and pleasure.

The unobstructed view governed the economics of high-rise, residential building in New York throughout its modern history. Originally the view focused inward, towards the centre, as at the heart of Manhattan around Central Park; today the same logic of the unobstructed view dictates the cost of residential housing at the edges of all boroughs that give on to water. The unobstructed view, the visible absence of other people, is New York's reward for wealth. The unobstructed view is the consummation of the boundary as a socially inactive condition.

We need to add a caveat: in New York, age moderates this general proposition. Young New Yorkers buying flats often want to see the life of the city outside their windows; rich young New Yorkers are willing to pay for such views, as long as what they see is below them, safely at a distance. And whereas the absolute logic of the empty view operates in new cities like Dubai, researches done for Urban Age in London, Istanbul and São Paulo show that, in these cities too, the elite's taste for cosmopolitan stimulation can counter the isolating logic of the view – like the remnant memory of being once young and alive. Correspondingly, we found that relatively few young members of the São Paulo elite equated a gated community with community itself.

The socially-minded planner wants to examine the way they see: we concentrate too much on visual legibility, and so on making 'legible landscapes' through framing street corridors, or imaging public spaces without 'unsightly' obstructions; this way of seeing naively follows the capitalist logic which now exploits the view as an isolated condition. The planner should counter the logic, by looking in another way. What need to be put on display are scenes of social mixture, in all their messiness and vitality.

Centre and Edge

Because exclusion and eviction are so deeply rooted in capitalism, it may be beyond the humane planner's power to make boundaries at a mega-scale. At a smaller scale, the urbanist may have more freedom to manoeuvre, but here again they need to be self-critical in order to achieve membrane/borders.

When we imagine where the life of a community is to be found, we usually look for it in the centre of a community; when we want to strengthen community life, we try to intensify life at the centre. In reflecting on my own planning experience, I know why projects at the local scale should have dwelt on establishing a centre for community life: most poor people in cities suffer for lack of it. In the history of immigrant communities in London, for example, central places like coffee shops, restaurants, money-transfer shops, or even mosques weaken their hold if immigrants remain in one place for more than one generation. So finding or establishing the centre becomes a planner's recipe for creating social cohesion.

Emphasis on the centre, however, may lead the designer to neglect the edge condition, treating it as inert, lifeless – as a version of the boundary. This strategy means that exchange between different racial and ethnic, or class communities is diminished. By privileging the centre, community-based planning can thus weaken the complex interactions necessary to join up the different human groups the city contains.

This danger has a sociological frame: how important is preserving identity in the life of a city? The centre of a homogeneous community will reinforce local cultural identities, but this may be disabling for poor people in a city; to survive the city's complexity, they need to deal with people *unlike* themselves. The centres of poor, ethnic neighbourhoods can serve the rich for a kind of tourism, known in New York as 'slumming', but there is no real encounter.

The word 'identity' has a double meaning: it denotes something like a brand, a label, a social classification; it also connotes a negotiation between self and circumstance. The psychoanalyst Erik Erikson probed identity in this latter sense;

'who I am,' he wrote, 'is the product of negotiations the ego has with its environment, not simply an "ascription" as a label put on the self.' Most of us have multiple identities depending on different negotiations we have with the different spheres of our experience: a gay man has experiences as a worker or religious believer which cannot be crammed into the single ascription 'gay'; that too is the case with racial, class or religious ascriptions.

The urbanist's issue is how and where these multiple negotiations should occur: the centre of a residentially homogeneous community may discourage the development of a more complex identity in Erikson's sense. Yet in twentieth-century planning, we did just that, in the name of strengthening communities.

Let me give as an example just such a failure of my own in my professional practice. Some years ago I was involved in plans for creating a market to serve the Hispanic community of Spanish Harlem in New York. This community, one of the poorest in the city, lives above 96th Street on Manhattan's Upper East Side. Just below 96th Street, in an abrupt shift, resides one of the richest communities in the world, running from 96th down to 59th Street, comparable to Mayfair in London, or the 7th Arrondissement in Paris. In this case, 96th Street itself could function either as a boundary or a border. We planners chose to locate La Marqueta in the centre of Spanish Harlem, 20 blocks away, in the very centre of the community, and to regard 96th Street as a dead edge, where nothing much happens. We chose wrongly. Had we located the market on that street, we might have encouraged activity that would have brought the rich and the poor into some daily, commercial contact.

Wiser planners have since learnt from our mistake, and on the West side of Manhattan sought to locate new community resources at the edges between communities, in order, as it were, to open the gates between different racial and economic communities. Our imagination of the importance of the centre proved isolating, their understanding of the value of the edge and border has proved integrating.

I don't mean to paint, in sum, a Panglossian picture of the value of borders over boundaries in cities. Particularly in cities where the poor are under attack, resistance is the countervailing strategy for expulsion; under the sway of modern pressures to banish the poor, the dead borderland may be a tool for resisting 'development'. Moreover, borders can serve as tense, combative zones rather than friendly sites of exchange – evoking some of the predatory activities along borders in natural ecologies. All this said, planners still have to make a hard choice: is isolation and segregation better than the risks entailed in interaction? It is worth bearing in mind that a cell membrane is resistant and porous in equal measure. In cultural terms, this means communities have to decide what they can't share with others as well as what they can. But this is a decision that, in my view, should result after the experience of exposure to difference, rather than flight from contact.

The smart city of the future, therefore, will choose the living edge over the dead edge; it will use technology to make the city a more open and flexible, less routinized system. In practice living-edge urbanism means thinking about where buildings are sited, the claims buildings make to views, and that the experience of identity translates into different values for the centre and for the edge. Our goal should be no more and no less than stimulation in the midst of others, the stimulation of difference, and this goal is the purpose cities should serve in culture.

NO FRILLS AND BARE LIFE

Alejandro Zaera-Polo

LOSING THE MIDDLE

Air travel brought about a second revolution when it moved from the elite era of the jet set, to the mass mobility offered by no-frills airlines. It is a model that architects could learn from as they seek to operate within an economic model that challenges tailor-made individualism.

Now that we inhabit the hangover of neo-liberal capitalism and globalization, and everybody is looking towards the political leaders for redemption, it may be an ideal opportunity to consider what the real transformative capacities for architecture are and could be in the twenty-first century. Looking with some perplexity at the incredible burst of urban development that capped several decades of uninterrupted expansion of global capitalism, and at the scale with which those bland and sanitized projects took shape all over the world (more so in the developing world), one wonders if the qualities of what was produced fit within what we generally understand as a city, as a locus of collective and democratic life. Are these developments just a device to efficiently organize rapidly growing urban populations and submit them to certain protocols that enable their integration into new productive orders in a way that causes the least amount of tension and conflict? Or do they represent the rise of an entirely new form of urban assemblage, with its own political dynamic? Despite their ruthless efficiency, do these urban topographies contain a possibility for the emergence of political life, with its own mechanisms of opinion, dialogue, dissent, resistance, and even subversion? Or has this new brave world done away with the customary forms of citizenship altogether?

As much as the phenomenon of rampant urbanization may inspire doubts about the possibility for a truly democratic life in these new communities, there is none the less something liberating about them: the possibility for anybody's access to urban life; the escape from the haphazard and often despotic regimes of rural life and the clutches of small communities; the freedom to move across these metropolitan communities; and the access to an ever-expanding range of services and commodities.[1] Urban inhabitants are substantially wealthier than rural ones, hence the massive migration towards cities that is currently taking place. On the surface there seem to be potential openings towards new freedoms by engaging with the protocols of urban life. For, if anything, urbanization is giving an increasing population access to what is arguably the most desirable commodity on the planet: urban life and the choices it offers. The question is whether there is a possibility for the urban agglomerations that result from these developments to embody a sustainable democratic life, and, if so, how?

Perhaps there is the possibility for these material accretions to become politically charged: both the global phenomenon of the rise of the swing electorate, focused on concrete decisions rather than on ideological consistency, and the emergence of new

political constituencies through informational technologies are crucial changes in contemporary democratic protocols.

Beyond urban development and architecture, there are other contemporary products that have already become vehicles of political constituencies without having to resort to political ideology or political discourse: low-cost airlines have effectively de-classed the aeroplane cabin and de-rooted large populations, exposing them to other cultures. Low-cost fashion and furniture have been made widely available to the emerging urban population, providing a physical self-confidence among the urban lower-middle classes that did not exist before. Yes, perhaps at huge ecological cost and perhaps by exporting the lower classes to developing regions, but every revolution comes with its own problems …

While it may be dangerous to assume that access to goods and services can be equated with the accessibility of rights that characterizes a democratic community, it is important to understand where the political agencies of the market reside within the framework of urban growth, because the market economy is its predominant milieu. Rather than enforcing the independence between economy and politics, it is crucial to understand how these new products of global capitalism might constitute political constituencies; how, without being mediated by the more conventional forms of mainstream political discourse, they might regain some political agency for architectural practice.[2]

The political discourses that set the benchmarks for modern democratic societies – irrespective of how successful any of these were at implementing social justice or political advances in the communities in which they operated – were primarily based on political realism and reached maturity in the second half of the twentieth century. Most of these ideologies explored the notion of equality as a political objective: Mao Zedong enforced the equalization of class, Che Guevara that of geopolitics, Betty Friedan the equalization of sexual pleasure, Malcolm X that of race and Daniel Cohn-Bendit the equalization of age.

The intensification of global practices in the 1960s made those ideological formulations seem irrelevant. Why equalize geopolitics when economies and technology can do the very same without the attendant ideological battles? Why equalize class, when class has transcended politically and geographically determined communities? One might conclude that the 1960s economic boom was the death knell of political ideology as an effective mechanism to transform society.

As the world was leaving the first oil crisis behind in 1975, Bill Gates founded Microsoft Corporation, and Amancio Ortega founded Zara, the largest clothing manufacturer in the world. Two years later, Steve Jobs founded Apple Computers. Ten years later, in 1987, Alan Greenspan became Chairman of the Federal Reserve and implemented a policy of cheap borrowing that triggered unprecedented investment and growth worldwide. Other paradigmatic corporations among this new breed of agents, like EasyJet and a reborn Monsanto, emerged in 1995 and 2000, profiting from the consolidation of global regulations and the opening up of markets. Despite the apparent lack of a politics per se across their practices, what links such players as Greenspan, Haji-Ioannou (EasyJet), Ortega (Zara), Kamprad (Ikea), and Gates (Microsoft) is a political programme without political office. Their political agenda is implemented through the role of the global entrepreneur – providing products or services at relatively low prices by optimizing the supply routes. The milieu of the politics of globalization became primarily mediated by the abundant supply of capital to facilitate and service ever-growing markets and the political ideology of equalization was replaced by a strategy of cheapness. Leaving aside the potential impact on global warming, social ossification, and other unpleasant side effects of neo-liberal economies, the capacity for social transformation in many regions of the world has been nothing short of remarkable. If we owe the ideological framing of neo-liberal capitalism to some of those earlier visionaries, even those who might be said to have been ardent anti-capitalists, it appears as if our everyday life is now fundamentally determined by the actions taken by this second generation of late-twentieth-century, non-ideological visionaries.

Given the impact on the growth of cities fostered by the monetary policies of Greenspan (Federal Reserve) and other central bankers (ample capital chasing 'pliant' urban populations), changes both in the workplace and in private life – made possible by the new affordability of communication, information technology, foreign travel and fashion – seem symptomatic of a larger shift in the demos, which marks the implicit ideology of technological innovation: re-subjectivization coupled with an increase of productivity.

What is new about these prospects is the relationship between production and political ideology. If vision was traditionally a value added to a product, these new agencies base their performance primarily on the reduction of costs. The political effects of this strategy are particularly interesting when considering the goods and services most related to the body: clothing and air travel. If Chanel or Issey Miyake were supposed to be adding a wholesome aura or lifestyle to the body and were duly priced upwards, some of the low-cost operators have resorted to a radical minimization of production costs, which in turn produces their identity. In this mode of operation, the relationship between style, price and value is inverted and the political agency of production is reframed, emptying the product of any explicit ideological ambition, jettisoning the spectral surplus value of the commodity. This is delivered either by tracking the market by the week – as if the designer had been replaced by popular taste – like Zara and Topshop, or by cutting down everything unnecessary, the so-called frills, and synthesizing a new style, freed from conventional expectations. (See for example, the no-nonsense character of EasyJet or Muji.) As with the new local government policies of David Cameron's Tory coalition government in the UK, the political model of cheapness replicates the business strategies of the low-cost airlines, and success is measured by its ability to deliver services at minimal cost to the taxpayer.[3]

Within a market economy we could probably substitute 'low cost' for the Italian philosopher Agamben's double-edged term 'bare life' (from the Greek, *zoe*). Bare life is the ultra-quotidian, sacrificial life of the dispossessed, a form of abject citizenship that inhabits a non-qualified political nether-region. 'The political system no longer orders forms of life and juridical rules in a determinate space, but instead contains at its very center a dislocating localization that exceeds it and into which every form of life and every rule can be virtually taken.'[4] In other words, exceptions are the rule in the contemporary city, and the state of exception (when all rules of citizenship are suspended) is its foremost materialization.[5] Agamben's term connotes a perverse economy of absolutism working in both markets and politics.

And if life in neo-liberal capitalist terms can be reduced to consumption and markets (with their constantly shifting horizons), economic fortunes are made in the reduction of plentiful life (*bios*) to bare life (*zoe*) by focusing on the biopolitical horizon of life at the expense of all else and conceptually reducing, in turn, citizens to mere biological units. All citizens in such a model are now de facto outcasts, insofar

GENERIC TOWERS

The mass produced high-rise, high-density apartment blocks of Shanghai, which have succeeded in giving its citizens a substantial rise in personal living space, can be seen as the architectural version of a budget airline: not pretty but of huge social importance.

as all citizens operate within a narrowing field of deterministic economic and political functions. But, as in Agamben, bare life acquires a new dignity when taken out of this schematic and placed in a semi-sacred free state: a non-use value as irreducible as the fact of (bare) life. A politics based on the concept of bare life – an ancient juridical term – is not necessarily the automatic enslavement by socio-economic means, nor the totalitarian assault on subjectivity it might become. And perhaps, most importantly, it unfolds several possibilities all at once and illuminates multiple approaches to urban design and architecture as possible means without ends, or projects without addresses. Is it really beneficial for architects to keep producing grand visions, or is it perhaps a matter of exploring concrete, technical aspects of a project as the origin of urban or architectural expression? Mobilizing a political expression of the prosaic or the banal and addressing its multiple attachments may enable us to frame architecture not merely as a representation of an ideology or an image of utopia, but as concrete and effective political agency able to assemble and mediate the interests of the multiple stakeholders that converge on the contemporary project. It is perhaps the most basic, bare, technical and pragmatic questions that enable us to explore the discipline as a source of effects

TAILOR-MADE
The highly specific sculptural object, with a distinctive architectural signature, is perhaps a predictable response to the anonymity of generic no-frills building.

that may actually destabilize power regimes rather than function as their vehicle of implementation or as their mere representation, whether of the status quo or its resisting parties. The opening up of power structures is better served by focusing on the means to ends, while voiding the project from within of all-too-obvious ideological and utopian content. Rather than aiming at revolution, a political practice of architecture is perhaps shifted to explicitation by means of reduction to a 'bare state', a mode where political practices are attached to artificial environments in which we co-exist, and where concrete aspects become the primary source of political agency – in other words, an enlightened materialism.[6]

The implicit resetting of relations between value and style was explored by a group of artists just a few years before Zara and Microsoft were founded. In 1967, the Italian art critic Germano Celant – currently senior curator at the Guggenheim in New York and director of the Prada Foundation, which is due to open a new landmark museum in Milan in 2012 – coined the term *Arte Povera*. He used it to describe a group of young Italian artists experimenting with non-traditional and politically charged art as the Italian economic miracle of the immediate post-war years collapsed into economic and political chaos. Under the title of Arte Povera –

which literally means 'poor art' – there was an exploration of a wide range of artistic materials and practices demolishing the aesthetic of the quasi-precious traditional ones (primarily painting and sculpture), which questioned the 'value' of art per se – plus the art market and the burgeoning politics of the so-called art world (a term only then coming into common use). Arte Povera sought for an art made without restraints – a laboratory situation in which any theoretical basis was rejected in favour of complete openness towards materials and processes. The movement promoted the notion of a revolutionary art – free of convention, power structures and the marketplace by virtue of austerity. Arte Povera was a relevant precedent to some of the strategies of cheapness that began to emerge only a few years later as effective business models, as well as an alternative to ideological formulations in the pursuit of a democracy inevitably mediated by production and artificiality.

It is precisely the notion of frills – ornamental, and contingent excrescences on the surface of clothing (conventionally used for female clothing to elicit a sensual response or arousal) – that low-cost airlines and similar downmarket entrepreneurs use to describe all services that are not part of the core product that suggests an intriguing metaphor for architectural praxis; that is, a new means for negotiating the relationship between economy, value and style. In this sense, bare life might equal no frills, or an elective avoidance of all things unnecessary. While such a model contains the seeds of its own destruction (as it might eliminate its own market), it also signals a possible escape route from overweening, abject consumerism.

It may be precisely in the articulation between value, economy and style in architecture that we may find the opportunities to retrieve political agency within a market-driven economy. In the triangulation of style, price and frills, which is by no means a simple matter or stable formula, it is worth trying to define these relationships by tracing a small history of this equation since Modernism, when for the first time economy enters into the theory of architecture and urbanism as affect.

Recent explorations of cheapness can be found in Koolhaas's infamous statement, 'no money, no detail', in which the project's economy becomes the source of its aesthetic approach, making a virtue out of a necessity. This concept of an aesthetic of cheapness was explored in OMA's Lille masterplan, with a proposal to specify low-grade concrete for all buildings in it. The plausible excuse was that the character of Lille was intended to be markedly different from Paris, more rough and tumble. This strategy of intensifying the material grain by downgrading the material quality recalls Brutalism. This qualitative cheapness was supposed to automatically emerge from the lower material specification, rather than by design. In this case, the no frills strategy of bare life produces a sort of deep *rusticato,* which goes deeper than the skin, into the structure of the buildings. This is a sort of neo-Rousseauian approach where, if desirable, the social contract and the so-called 'rights' of citizens that come with it are voluntarily suspended (the consumer's rights to quality) as a critique of the status quo and the premiation of natural traits – rights – antecedent to it.

As the celebrity model of the 1990s and 2000s – which in architecture translated into the star system – draws to a close, the elastic relationship between style and economy becomes an intriguing issue, particularly in light of what is happening in the emerging low-cost markets. There are spatial and temporal implications associated with these models of cheapness that may be worth considering in their translation into architectural practice. There is a geopolitical model associated with the production chain of these companies: while the high-end boutiques are traditionally built according to a recipe of high design, exclusivity, lots of marketing and a decentralized production, retailers such as Topshop and Zara have defied many of these premises by co-locating design and production. In a typical fashion house, design and marketing are often located in a world capital – Paris, London, New York or Tokyo – while production is located in emerging economies, where the designs are executed. The goods are then shipped back to metropolitan centres to be sold at artificially inflated prices.

Alternatively, some of the new low-cost emporia operate on the model of 'vertical integration' – a term famously central to American Apparel's public relations strategy, which states that the company keeps jobs in downtown Los Angeles by pursuing novel production techniques where the company's design and production are deeply integrated and co-located.[7] Most of Zara's production is done in La Coruña, Spain, where design and marketing headquarters are also located, while the Topshop lines are purchased from small design-production units.

Unlike previous common mercantilism, this type of centralized operation, even at the expense of higher production costs, is capable of providing retail advantage: a relationship between design and production. Operating in this manner, these companies enable a much more intense and direct feedback loop between the different phases of the project's procurement. This logistical framework for ultimately measuring a product's immediate effectiveness (in industry parlance, its 'turn') provides a type of index for a marketing model that focuses on means rather than ends – the product seems almost expendable in a chain of relationships that maximize liquidation (and liquidity). It is one of the potentials of cheapness – cheapness as a powerful antidote to excess – that makes it the nemesis of both utopian and visionary alternatives.

Finally, it is in the feedback loops across the procurement route where the temporal implications of this model lie: the distance and time lag between design and production of garments has been reduced to such a degree that such companies can now churn out new designs as rapidly as they can conceive them. Zara and Topshop's competitive advantage is that design and production are so intimately connected, they can change their collection every two weeks, short-circuiting the tempo of fashion and the seasonal collections: they are, in fact, turning the market into an evolutionary continuum. Again, this may be an indication that a project without a definitive target, one primarily focused on its means, may be a vital tendency within cheapness.

Precisely by suspending ideological judgement and relying on production, the cheap frills model of Zara and Topshop provides the largest diversity of products to the broadest audience at any given time. As an ecosystem, these models have an advantage driven by a reverse econometric, a result of trends in globalization – speed, mobile labour, heightened- and micro-production facilities, plus a perceived anomie of faceless multinational clothiers. Such post-neo-liberal business models and brands mutate rapidly, as they are not constrained by a history of the brand, nor by the need to create an ideology, a signature style, or a comprehensive *Weltanschauung* to justify their existence. When Karl Lagerfeld took over Chanel, or Tom Ford took over Gucci, the first task was to reinvent the history of the brand, interpreting it for a new audience. What were the classic designs of the brand? And how can that brand be expanded and connected to the contemporary market? New low-cost brands have shed the weight of the past, producing an in-born, half-mythological history. They have no identifiable style beyond the generic ubiquity they breed and covet. They can go anywhere, anytime they identify an opportunity. Style consistency and brand stability are evidently not an asset in the low-cost markets, but a liability. Can they remain an asset in the future of architectural practices, as they have been through the starchitect period?

Across these low-cost practices, and beyond these general tendencies of re-localization, integration between design and production, and overcoming of the fashion cycles and stylistic inconsistency, we can identify two basic models of operation. One option is the enforcement of no frills as the origin of a new style with a better value. In this case, cheapness becomes the origin of a new style: this is the model we can see emerging from EasyJet's no-frills airline, and from Muji's no brand goods (a brand paradoxically reversing Naomi Klein's *No Logo* strategy to build up a brand). In these models, a new aesthetic leap of the cheap emerges from a careful consideration of how to eliminate excess, the exceptional, the precious, the over-priced, and the exclusive. A certain acceptance of the 'generic' is implied in this model, which includes brands with similar political ambitions, such as Ikea and American Apparel, where a certain purification of style is enforced, albeit perhaps without the rigour of the bargain-bin models of EasyJet and Muji.

We can see a second alternative in other markets where the use of cheap frills is the economic driver of choice for the product: in this case, cheapness is the result of sophisticated procurement techniques that allow the product to access style while remaining reasonably priced. Such is the strategy of brands like Zara, Topshop, Primark – or even the haute-bohemian airline Virgin Atlantic – where combining cheapness with a certain level of hedonistic extravagance produces a very marketable approach. In such instances, the concept of brand crosses back over the threshold of elitism to bend the product closer to affordability, without losing its semi-prestigious cachet. Such approaches are made possible through very shrewd tactics capable of both lowering the retail cost of the product while maintaining some of its qualities or services (often the most idiosyncratic).

Different forms and modalities of citizenship also produce different forms and modalities of urbanity: there is the hyper-city of law and order (like New York or London's urban police state) and there is the no-frills Modernist city, typically sprawling, where economy and optimization are part of the manifestation of law and order (of the qualified life), and the source of a no-frills aesthetic. The latter cities are on the rise. Then there is the postmodern city where law and order have been replaced by a city of exceptions (states of permanent emergency and contingency) and frills, with diminished constitutional rights in return for endless diversions.

The question here is whether these models could be potentially used to challenge the status quo and operate as a powerful transfer device, much like Agamben suggests bare life can be turned into a powerful political weapon. Architecture by the likes of Lacaton & Vassal is loaded with an implicit critique of the star system and architectural consumption. Short of a new Brutalism, one can only imagine that cheapness in architecture (*sans* ideology) might come back as an architecture that is quite simply architecture, and not a brand. Political agency means, often, to do only what is necessary. In the case of Lacaton & Vassal, if the buildings are partly planted in the earth and open to the environment, despite their cheapness, there is also the economy of natural forces at work – recall that Thoreau opens *Walden* with a disquisition on economy. Not far from Thoreau's Walden Pond, in Cambridge, Massachusetts, is Le Corbusier's Carpenter Center. One thinks immediately, then, of Le Corbusier's dream for the Carpenter Center: that nature would provide the finishing touches, a dream made slightly absurd by French artist Pierre Huyghe in his *This is Not a Time for Dreaming* (2004).[8]

The notion that politics and economics can be neatly divided into *polis* and *oikos* – either in the sense that the markets should be entirely freed of political intervention or that political action can be effected without careful consideration of economic inputs – is ludicrous. In parallel to the increasing level of governmental intervention in the markets that we are starting to witness, we will also see the growing effect of economies on political discourse. (The UK Prime Minister David Cameron's Easy Council is paradigmatic.)

It is in the exploration of the types of citizenship that are increasingly mediated by economics that we may be able to find solutions for the cities of the near future, and where cheapness and its aesthetic implications may prove a fruitful field of investigation. Democracy, in its global neo-liberal form, is expensive, often inefficient, and consumes a substantial amount of resources. We live in an age in which the limitless capitalist system has come across the limits of the planet's natural resources, which will increasingly make economy – rather than excess – the engine of all processes: economies of urban land, as global populations flock to the cities; economies of energy and carbon emissions, as 3 billion people will enter the global middle classes in the next four decades and claim their legitimate rights to air conditioning, private vehicles and air transportation; economies of money, as credit becomes reattached to real assets, ad infinitum.

As we move forward, the crucial question is how to preserve true democracy, whatever that might be, and its corollary 'actual capital' – real estate – within the emerging landscapes of cheapness that proliferate everywhere, as cheapness may deliver democracy on the ground (bare life as egalitarian global ethos) or do away with it once and for all. A materialist approach to political agency might seem an ancient artifice, a founding act of *polis*. But bare life, as free, political-economic agency, implies that the luxury of the many resides in a model that bridges not wealth and poverty per se, but multiple economies given to benefiting some when they might benefit all. Cheapness may become this potential bridge, not as a cheapening agent as such, but as a form of recalibrating the engines of production and consumption, of which architecture is a principal component.

CITY SOLUTIONS TO GLOBAL PROBLEMS

Nicholas Stern, Dimitri Zenghelis and Philipp Rode

SYSTEMS FOR BUSES

Organized traffic management systems for public buses send a powerful signal of the attractions of civic society in sharp contrast to the highly visible anarchy of a free-for-all motorway.

Cities have clearly played a major role in the creation of the problem of anthropogenic climate change and they will form a central part of any solution. No global collaborative agreement to tackle climate change can be delivered without the full involvement of cities. Yet the evidence suggests that measures that make cities work better in terms of emissions and sustainability, are also the measures that make them work better as prosperous and attractive places to live and work. Some cities are already demonstrating strong leadership in putting forward ambitious plans for carbon emissions reductions. Many more have joined networks and partnerships to address climate change collaboratively.

Less than 2 per cent of the earth's surface is occupied by urban areas, but this land accommodates half the world's 6.7 billion population and accounts for 70 per cent of the world's GDP. By 2050, the share of urban dwellers is projected to exceed 70 per cent of the global population. Cities are well placed to lead the process of low carbon innovation. They combine a mix of specialization and diversity derived from a concentration of people and economic activity that generate a fertile environment for innovation in ideas, technologies and processes. They produce and distribute the resources that provide better livelihoods for urban and rural residents alike. Their size and economic complexity mean that city-specific problems such as congestion, waste, education and crime require considered, city-specific public intervention. At the same time the high population density and compactness can allow for economics of scale and collaboration.

Carbon emissions are directly related to income. Per capita incomes are generally higher in cities than in surrounding rural areas, leading to a generally higher average per capita demand in all the major emissions sources. But not all cities are the same. There is an enormous variation in emissions among cities with similar per capita incomes as a result of local climatic conditions, their energy mixes and industry shares as well as the extent to which they simply export their emissions. It is the last point that tends to make most urban areas look far better than they actually are by ignoring emissions linked to their material consumption and embodied energy occurring elsewhere. But carbon emissions have also been associated with differences in settlement patterns, leading to an underlying tendency to lower average per capita emissions in denser, more compact cities. Consequently, even when appropriately acknowledging that cities are not self-sufficient entities and ought to share responsibility for carbon-intensive activities beyond their boundaries, some world

RELATING POLLUTION TO AFFLUENCE

While cities and countries of the developing world tend to produce fewer CO_2 emissions (with Shanghai standing out as an outlier with respect to China), some affluent cities like Tokyo, Paris and New York are weak polluters in comparison to the average comsumption patterns of their respective nations.

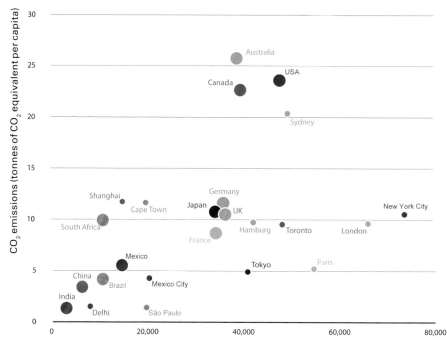

metropolises seem to be relatively energy- and carbon-efficient, whether measured by unit output or per capita. Paris, São Paulo, London, Dhaka, Hong Kong and Tokyo have among the world's lowest levels of energy intensity – about one-quarter of that of the five highest scoring cities and less than half of the 50-city average.[1]

Cities with limited urban sprawl and integrated urban transit systems have in many cases become affluent with low emissions per head. Compact, well-managed cities with intelligent infrastructure can be more attractive to footloose workers than suburban or rural communities. Inner-city Paris, Rome, Barcelona and London, together with New York, Singapore and Tokyo provide examples of creative, growing city centres with access to a variety of amenities, including green space. Hoornweg found dense cities tend to have lower per-capita emissions provided they are also served by good public transport systems.[2] Their relative resource efficiency is mainly a result of greater transport energy efficiency due to reduced distances and greater shares of green transport modes, greater heat and cooling energy efficiency in buildings due to lower surface-to-volume ratios of more compact building typologies and lower embedded energy demand for urban infrastructure due to greater utilization. But compact, well-managed cities such as Vienna or Madrid have significantly higher population densities and higher public transport use than sprawling cities such as Atlanta and Houston, with correspondingly lower emissions per capita. The same applies, to a lesser extent, to cities such as Portland and Vancouver, which have had their scope for spatial sprawl limited by the constraints of oceans and mountains, as well as strong public policy and local interest.

With shorter transport networks and less diffuse utility infrastructures, denser cities generate significant savings in operating costs running to thousand of dollars per year for the average household.[3] But suburban living remains popular, so dense cities need to be carefully planned to attract wealth-creating individuals who can choose other options. Without coordinated planning, cities will be at risk of 'locking in' to long-lived, high-carbon capital infrastructure that will be costly to reverse.

Implementing greenhouse gas reduction strategies can pay economic dividends. It can drive efficiency and allow cities to reduce waste and cut costs. Cities offer a unique environment to innovate, develop and scale-up new ideas and processes. These promote the growth of clusters of expertise in knowledge-intensive green production sectors. Cities have become laboratories for action on climate change where learning and experience induces further innovation and falling cost in new technologies. Integrated recycling networks, methane capture and combined heat and power have relied on ready access to new technologies as well as skilled engineers and installation experts, all of which are easier to access in a compact urban environment. Scale economy benefits of urbanization mean that cities can capitalize in developing 'green' investments, such as integrated public transit, sewers and water systems, congestion pricing, smart grids, smart buildings and decentralized energy networks.[4] Urban regions already produce 10 times more renewable technologies patents than rural regions.[5]

Climate policy also yields collateral benefits at the local level, while investment in attractive and successful cities will yield climate benefits. Reduced particulate pollution reduces health care costs, increases city attractiveness, and promotes competitiveness, while reduced waste makes for a more attractive environment (for example through reduced use of landfill) and enhanced energy security by limiting reliance on imported energy and raw materials.[6] This means policies must be well-planned, for example, efficiently reducing congestion and emissions requires complementary measures on public transport, cycling, electric and shared vehicle infrastructure, urban planning, zoning and carbon pricing. During economic downturns, such programmes can boost job creation and stimulate activity, especially in 'shovel-ready' sectors such as building efficiency retrofits, broadband infrastructure and retooling manufacturers. Policies to increase vegetation and green spaces not only reduce the heat island effect, but also improve resilience to flooding.

Implementing Bogotá's TransMilenio bus system was primarily motivated by an urgent need for cost effective, high-capacity urban transport, congestion reduction and improving the quality of life locally rather than aiming to reduce global carbon emissions. However, this scheme has not only reduced emissions, it has shortened travel time and lowered congestion at peak times by 40 per cent.[7] Seoul's car-free day has succeeded in taking 2 million cars off the road every year, decreasing traffic volume by 3.7 per cent, and CO_2 emissions by 9.3 per cent. Overall, health benefits in cities as a result of green transport strategies are particularly high as they combine emission reduction, increase physical activity levels and road safety. Health and safety benefits have been estimated as five to 20 times greater than the cost for integrated non-motorized and public transport measures in diverse cities such as Bogotá, Morogoro and Delhi.[8]

Transport contributes around 22 per cent of the world's energy related greenhouse gas emissions. Until now, many aspects of commuting and transport design have been wasteful and inefficient. In the UK, the cost of public transport relative to private transport has risen sharply over the past 20 years, compounding the waste from congestion. Congestion of roads in the UK causes estimated annual losses of around GB£7 to 8 billion (US$11 to 12.6; €8.1 to 9.3).[9] Costs are even higher in developing countries with rapidly growing cities unable to catch up with population growth and motorization. The costs of congestion in Buenos Aires are estimated at 3.4 per cent of local GDP, in Mexico City 2.6 and in Dakar 3.4 per cent.[10]

POWER AS IT ONCE WAS
Once the visible sign of electrification and modernization, the cooling tower has turned into a symbol of a high-carbon footprint, bringing with it the threat of climate change.

Time losses, wasted energy, higher accident risks and the negative impact on the quality of life make a powerful case for strategies to reduce congestion. London's congestion charge reduced congestion by an estimated 30 per cent between February 2003 and February 2004, in comparison with the same period in previous years[11] and CO_2 emissions from traffic inside the charging zone were cut by 19.5 per cent.[12] Mexico City and Bogotá have introduced number plate restrictions with measurable impacts on congestion and air quality.[13] Efficient, affordable and reliable public transport alternatives further reduce the appeal of the private car. In recent years, more established cities of the global North like Copenhagen, Amsterdam, London and New York have consistently invested in pro-cycling and walking strategies.

Electricity and heat production contribute 37 per cent of global energy related emissions.[14] Some cities have invested heavily in clean electricity and heat production such as photovoltaic (PV) systems located on building roofs and facades, or in dedicated open areas. In Freiburg, PV systems cover 13,000 square metres (139,931 square feet) of the city's building surfaces – including the main railway station – while San Francisco operates the largest city-owned solar power system in the United States.[15] Further opportunities are offered by wind energy, with turbines typically located outside city boundaries. The 'London Array' offshore wind-turbine system is projected to produce 1,000 MW, enough to power 750,000 homes.[16]

ANOTHER SHADE OF GREEN

Years of under-investment in simple technological systems have given India's cities the highly visible pollution levels that have created a demand for a new approach capable of dealing with the health and environmental challenges.

Copenhagen's district heating system, which captures waste heat from electricity production, normally released into the sea as hot water, has helped reduce emissions and shaves €1,400 (US$1,907) off household bills per annum. It is estimated that people in metropolitan Portland, Oregon, save US$2 (€1.47) billion annually through coordinated changes in land use and transport policies over the last three decades. These include modest increases in building density, light rail transit schemes and policies to encourage walking and cycling. In many European cities, recycling levels are in the region of 50 per cent of domestic waste, while Copenhagen sends only 3 per cent of its waste to landfills.[17] Buildings contribute 21 per cent of the world's energy related greenhouse gas emissions.[18] The imposition of tough building standards and mandatory energy certificates, as well as the provision of tax incentives and loans, has also had a measurable impact on energy demand in a number of European and American cities.[19]

Integrated technologies will help make dense complex cities work efficiently. Cities provide a critical mass of potential users for a wide range of IT-based services, which build upon complex physical infrastructure systems (such as roads, rail, cabling and distribution systems buildings). A broadband digital infrastructure can connect people to people, people to city systems and city systems to city systems, allowing cities and their residents to respond to changing circumstances in near real-time. Improved monitoring and measurement of resource flow patterns will allow more informed infrastructural investment decisions.[20] In addition, smart transport systems are being used to tackle congestion, facilitate road user charges or supply real-time information on traffic problems – examples include Stockholm's congestion tax and Singapore's electronic road pricing. Amsterdam currently trials smart work centres that allow workers to use local office facilities rather than having to commute to their main office.[21]

From a policy perspective, therefore, this is not only about the construction of the infrastructure for roads, buses and railways; it is also about their pricing and management, regulations applying to the location of homes, the use of cars and the design of cities. It concerns the structure of workplaces and practices affecting conventions for physical attendance. Many, or most of these involve networks in some shape or form in which the decisions of an individual on where to live, how to move, how to interact and how to commute have powerful effects on others.

Given the growing evidence of a virtuous circle associated with green cities and prosperity, the question arises why do more cities not commit to green growth? Firstly, the payback from investment in energy efficiency is not immediate and often requires an additional upfront investment. Liquidity constraints and limited access to capital may therefore preclude profitable investments. Secondly, the gains to energy efficiency and renewable investment may not yet have been recognized. As fossil fuel and other scarce resources continue to rise in price, and as the policy environment clamps down on waste, this should change. However, even where clear gains have existed in the past, there have been a number of barriers preventing optimal investment in resource efficiency.

There are often split incentives where the benefit of energy savings do not accrue to the individual or group making the investment (the landlord, construction firm or property seller, for example). Energy efficient equipment is often more expensive than more wasteful alternatives, and even where payback periods are short, many face financial constraints in making the initial investment (for example for low income residents). There are often costs associated with managerial and decision making requirements which can be saved through aggregation – the time cost of a million individuals working out the payback period for a boiler or domestic appliance can be slashed at a stroke by legislation on minimum efficiency standards which closes off markets for wasteful products. Weak monitoring and measurement systems make it hard to manage and monetize the gains from efficiency investments – for example the general absence of smart metering alerting consumers to energy use and waste-reducing the incentive to invest. RD&D in renewable energy is often long-term and speculative, carrying many risks, with knowledge spillovers which are hard to monetize or patent. Consequently, innovation often has fallen short of the social optimum. Finally, a lack of capacity and expertise often increases the costs of transforming the urban environment. A recent energy efficiency drive in Australia had to be scaled back due to a shortage of appropriately trained skilled installation engineers. Overcoming all these barriers requires a mix of policy tools and a clear and unambiguous public sector commitment to green transformation.

Nevertheless, cities increasingly lead the field in popular will in favour of sustainable policies, often influencing or driving the agenda at the national level. Examples include congestion charging in London, car sharing in Berlin, while planning and policy leadership in Barcelona, Portland, Bandung, Brisbane, Guelph and Nanjing often set the standard within their countries. Central and local government agencies are often best positioned to prompt behavioural change by engaging a well-informed population.

Surveys suggest urban populations place a higher premium on sustainability; initiatives like recycling or the take up of new technologies through behavioural change tend to originate in, and spread from, cities. Public intervention with a popular and clearly understood mandate is essential for addressing market failures associated with urban sustainability. To avoid a patchwork of uncoordinated targets, goals and programmes, and to allow the most cost-effective emissions reductions opportunities to be exploited, national governments should lead on the coordinated design and implementation of policy instruments. Targeted procurement affords cities a chance to shape markets and incentivize innovation on low-carbon products and services. But transport and urban design policies must also:[22]

- Charge for greenhouse gases.
- Price congestion properly so that we make much better use of our infrastructure, while at the same time encouraging shared transport – for example, traffic lanes for cars with multiple occupancy.
- Seek out ways of improving energy efficiency, especially by use of standards and regulations.
- Invest more strongly, with due care to cost and efficiency, in public transport.
- Encourage local work practices, which allow people to travel less and at more efficient times and make cycling easier and safer.
- Regulate the expansion of cities and improve design, with still greater focus on the ability of people to use them with as little private transport as possible.
- Make it easier for people to generate their own electricity and sell to the grid.
- Look at the potential within a community of combined heat and power – local energy structures are important.
- Encourage recycling by making it easier.
- Support research and demonstration for new, clean technologies.

These points all require public or collective action. As well as being more efficient, many, or most of them will draw communities together and make cities more pleasant and safer. Successful cities can generate economic prosperity as well as an improved quality of life. Increasingly, cities are competing on quality-of-life measures to attract the most important economic resources – people, ideas and skills.

With supportive policy, innovative businesses can avail themselves of growing new business opportunities in low-carbon investment, estimated to be worth US$500 (€367) billion a year, and rising, with clean energy investments in 2008 totalling US$177 (€130) billion.[23] A broad range of successful cities will increasingly specialize in higher-end business services, which can include activities such as environmental consulting and intermediating carbon.

Further empirical investigation is required, and this demands the development of a consistent urban database and improved assessments of best practice. Yet cities should not wait for perfect information before taking into account the latest understanding of climate change when making long-term planning decisions. How cities develop is part of the climate problem, but it can also be part of the solution. All cities have opportunities to guide urban planning and prevent the expansion and lock-in of high-carbon infrastructure, especially in the developing world. The investments and strategic decisions made over the next few years will determine where the winners and losers will be in rising to the challenge of a sustainable future.

DEMOCRACY AND GOVERNANCE

Gerald E. Frug

POLITICAL ENGAGEMENT

Some political cultures such as the one in London, above right, expect their politicians to walk to meet their electorates, and to be able use their bicycles as a means of transport. Others believe in a degree of armed protection that may reflect status issues as much as security.

In his groundbreaking article, 'The World City Hypothesis', John Friedmann claimed that globalization has enabled 'wealthier "world cities" … to operate like city-states in a networked global economy, increasingly independent of regional and national mediation.'[1] Others have made similar claims.[2] I shall argue the opposite proposition: national, state and regional governments continue to maintain control over global cities. Every Urban Age city could be used as an example of this control. After all, in 1986 the national government in the UK abolished the London-wide government altogether. And, when Parliament established the new city-wide government, the Greater London Authority, after a 14 year absence, it gave it only limited, albeit significant, functions. Similarly, the refusal by New York State to allow the City of New York to implement congestion charging is only the most well-known of the state's wide-ranging restrictions on the city's power to control its own future. Rather than focus on these cities, however, I will concentrate here only on the last three Urban Age cities: Mumbai, São Paulo and Istanbul. The power of each of these cities is significantly limited by centralized government, but each is limited in its own way. This variety of mechanisms of control is illuminating, because it helps demonstrate the range of methods that enable national and state governments to ensure that global cities are not 'independent'.

It's not that decentralization of power is thought to be a bad idea in India, Brazil and Turkey, quite the opposite. Both India and Brazil have amended their national constitutions in recent decades in order to enable the exercise of more local power. Turkey abandoned its commitment to the direct centralized control of its cities in the 1980s, and vastly expanded the territory governed by the Istanbul Metropolitan Municipality in 2004. The extent of centralized control over these cities also cannot be explained by the absence of local democracy. All three countries are democracies, and all three have locally-organized elections for municipal officials. The reason for national or state control of these global cities is much more fundamental. National and state governments have overriding policy objectives – transforming the three cities into global cities being one of them – and they are not about to let the city governments, however democratically organized, frustrate these national goals. Legal authority is organized to ensure that this doesn't happen.

Mumbai is an example of a city globalizing pursuant to national and state policy objectives. But the way it is organized is quite unusual. The most important constraint on Mumbai's power comes from the state in which it is located, Maharashtra. It is

THE NATURE OF HOUSING

From Istanbul to Mumbai by way of São Paulo, a new kind of high-rise concrete vernacular has taken shape, creating superficially interchangeable suburbs, even if they result in buildings with different meanings and purposes.

important as a background to have in mind that although Mumbai is a major world city, with a population of more than 12 million, Maharashtra is vastly bigger, with a population of almost 100 million. As a result, state policy, quite reasonably, takes into account the interests of the majority of people who live outside the city. The city government in Mumbai itself is called the Municipal Corporation of Greater Mumbai. It is made up of a local legislature, a mayor chosen by the legislature, and a municipal commissioner. Of the three, the key policy figure is the municipal commissioner; he is the executive head of government. The commissioner, however, is appointed by the state government, and not (like the local legislature) elected by the residents of Mumbai. He therefore is a vehicle for the implementation of state policy. In addition, under the Municipal Corporation Act, which established this city structure, the Maharashtra government retains considerable authority over the city, including the ability to direct Municipal Corporation policy and even to dissolve the Corporation altogether. And that's not all: regional planning in Mumbai is governed by the Mumbai Metropolitan Region Development Authority, which is a state agency. Other important functions – in particular housing and slum redevelopment – are managed by other state agencies. The mayor, by contrast, serves as the ceremonial head of government.

In 1992, the Indian constitution was amended by the so-called 74th Constitutional Amendment. This amendment created, for the first time, a constitutional status for municipal government. (The 73rd Constitutional Amendment, which was adopted simultaneously, sought the same goal for local governments in rural areas.) The 1992 Amendments sought to decentralize power from the states to localities, and they included a detailed list of functions for local governments. Prior to that, local governments in India functioned as agents of the states. One might have thought – the sponsors might have thought – that the 74th Constitutional Amendment would change the state-city relationship in Mumbai that I have just described. But it did not have this effect. The critical constitutional provision provided that the states 'may, by law, endow' municipalities with more power. The meaning of the word 'may' in this provision can be, and has been, debated. But it has been interpreted, in Maharashtra and elsewhere, as allowing the state to decide not to devolve power to cities. This is the course Maharashtra has followed. It should not be surprising that a national constitution can be interpreted in a way that does not radically change the state-city relationship. The reluctance to do so would exist anywhere where there is a federal or other three-tiered system of government. This reluctance would certainly be experienced in the United States (which has no federal constitutional protection for cities from state power at all).

São Paulo is organized very differently from Mumbai. In 1988, after the end of the military regime, Brazil adopted a new national constitution. The constitution established for the first time a Federative Republic, with the three constituent governments – national, state, and municipal – each declared to be autonomous. In other words, unlike in India (and the United States), state governments in Brazil do not have the power to create or control the local governments within their borders. This constitutionally granted municipal authority has enabled São Paulo to exercise significant aspects of local self-government. Even so, the limits on the city's power are very real. One limit stems from the fact that the population of São Paulo, like of Mumbai, is only somewhat more than half of its region: São Paulo is surrounded by 38 other municipalities. The 1988 constitution gives these other municipalities autonomy, just as it gives it to São Paulo. As a result, although many of the issues facing the city are regional in nature, there is no effective metropolitan government mechanism to which it belongs. Indeed, ironically, because it would require a constitutional amendment to override the autonomy the 1988 constitution grants all municipalities, regionalism faces hurdles in Brazil that are more difficult to overcome than it does elsewhere.

Another limit on the power of São Paulo stems from functions the constitution delegates to the state government. Although the constitution grants the city autonomy from state power, it also gives the state authority over activities that play a decisive role in city life. One dramatic example of this state power deals with what many consider the major problem facing São Paulo and other important Brazilian cities – violence. The 1988 constitution empowers the state, not the city, to control the civilian and military police force. This leaves the city without authority to deal either with the street- and gang-related violence that threatens its development or with the ways in which the police force itself exacerbates this violence. Finally, federal power over city policy remains considerable. There are federally imposed limits on São Paulo's ability to initiate legislation and on its ability to spend resources. In fact, federal law requires that some local resources be spent on specific functions. The constitution also grants some tasks – importantly including urban development – exclusively to the federal government, although it permits the federal government to enable localities to play a limited role in this process. (Under the federally enacted Statute of the City, it has done so.) Other major urban issues are allocated to federal, state and municipal governments concurrently; on these issues, the federal role is often decisive. The combined impact on São Paulo of these other decision makers – the other municipalities in the region, the state government, and the national government – subject the city to considerable national and regional control.

Istanbul too is subject to formal controls imposed by the national government. From 1923 to the 1980s, municipalities in Turkey were directly run by national government appointees. In recent decades, however, decentralization has been embraced in Turkey as in India and Brazil. Even so, national ministries still provide many important services in Istanbul, and the Governor of Istanbul province, an appointed official, coordinates many of these federal functions. Moreover, the formal organization of city government is itself complex. Since 1984, responsibilities have been divided between the metropolitan government and (currently) 39 district governments, each with its own mayor.

Responsibilities are also divided between formal and informal settlements, between the government and private organizations or public-private partnerships, and between the city and independent public authorities. As a result, the Istanbul Metropolitan Municipality does not have the power to establish an overall urban policy for the city. 'Formal urban policy of local government,' Feyzan Erkip writes, 'is a mix of different models with different policy objectives and ideological standpoints as a result of incompatible urban problems and priorities.'[3] Istanbul, however, does not face one of the problems that constrain Mumbai and São Paulo: the city's relationship with its region. In 2004, the national government increased the geographic size of the city threefold, with the result that the Istanbul Metropolitan Municipality now has jurisdiction over most of its province. (Istanbul is more than 10 times the size of Mumbai and more than three times the size of São Paulo.)

There is another aspect of the national-local relationship in Istanbul of considerable importance. The dominant political party has become a principal vehicle for national control of the local agenda. The Justice and Development Party (usually referred to as the AKP) controls both levels of government, and the current Prime Minister, Recep Tayyip Erdoğan, is a former Mayor of Istanbul. Sema Erder describes the resulting power dynamic as follows:

[U]pon gaining power and its political advantages, the central AKP administration began turning down calls for decentralisation, and instead reinforced their centralist tendencies further. Thus when it comes to the making of macro-level decisions it is possible to say that the central government exercises a strong influence in Istanbul.[4]

The fact that the same political party controls both the national and local governments does not align their policies everywhere. In some countries, the conflict between the central government and the city continues whichever political party is in control. In countries with one dominant political party, however, the situation is often different. The party agenda both supplements and reinforces the formal power that the legal structure gives the nation over the city.

The preceding survey of the governance structures of Mumbai, São Paulo and Istanbul only begins to indicate their complexity. But it should suffice to make clear the extent of the power of national or state governments over urban policy in all three cities. What remains is a final, critical question: why does this exercise of centralized power matter? There are many reasons why it does, but I will focus here on only one of them: the impact of globalization on the three cities. Writers on globalization from the outset have emphasized the ways in which globalization fosters income polarization.[5] That polarization is dramatically in evidence in Mumbai, São Paulo and Istanbul. The vast informal housing complexes, *favelas*, and squatter settlements are a major feature of each of them. So is the quite visible wealth that other city residents have accumulated. The effort to remove the informal housing in large parts of central Mumbai, the violence in São Paulo, and the dramatic immigration into Istanbul, together with the secluded housing built for the wealthy, create the potential for a major political battle over the definition and future of the globalization process.

The battle is likely to be different depending on where this political conflict takes place. If the cities themselves were in control of their own destiny, the policy of globalization that is now embraced in all three cities might be contested and revised. The vast majority of the population of these cities is poor. One should recall that all three are democracies. City residents might demand that urban policy be clearly targeted at improving their own lives – and they might question whether the current embrace of globalization is adequate to this task. If so, they might use the local electoral process to ensure that their elected officials are responsive to their demands. Sometimes this might not work; sometimes city policy will be controlled by elites notwithstanding popular opposition. But sometimes it might work. Now, by contrast, local objections to government policy often take the form of street protests or organizing efforts by non-governmental organizations. Local residents seem to think that resistance to governmental power, rather than controlling it, is the best way to pursue their goals.

Local legislative officials intervene on individuals' behalf when they run into trouble, but that's not the same as their having the power to reverse current policies.

When major decisions are not in the hands of city residents, the politics of globalization changes. Control is in the hands of people elected by a different constituency, and the impact on poor city residents is evaluated by people influenced by many other considerations. Some of these influences derive from sources other than the electorate: the World Bank, business corporations, and the fear of losing out in what national and state leaders experience as the worldwide competition to be at the top of the list of global cities. No doubt, those who pursue current globalization policies will insist that it is in the interest of everyone to do so. But the debate over that contention is the critical political issue in Mumbai, São Paulo and Istanbul. It matters a great deal where this debate occurs and who can resolve it. No one thinks that cities should be able to control their destiny solely on their own. State and national interests will have to be taken into account. But governance is the mechanism for balancing local, state and national interests – it is the way decision-making power is allocated. Mumbai, São Paulo and Istanbul illustrate there is no one way to organize a governance system. But they also illustrate that there are a variety of ways to subject city policy – even in countries that have worked to foster decentralized power – to centralized control.

THE URBAN EARTHQUAKE

Anthony Williams

THE POLITICS OF THE CITY

The volatile nature of Parisian suburbs, excluded from the affluence of the city centre and where politicians fear to go, has become notorious. In America, the view from the mayor's motorcade is an essential aspect of political reality.

Another Urban Age meeting is wrapping-up. The beautiful site of the summit is being reconstructed for the next event, attendees have resumed their roles in the local community or have headed to the airport, and the local leader, the mayor, is no sooner back in her office managing the constant demands on her time. When she gets a moment, she stops to reflect on important lessons learnt. What are the practical takeaways? How does she implement them? How does she think about her role: as a leader of the government; as a standard-bearer of the overall community? What is this public realm she hears so much about in meetings with the planning staff and at the Urban Age? And forget about 'best practices'. How does she improve to a level of 'average' processes as a signpost towards these 'best' practices?

She thinks about her job and her oath of office. Clearly, she signed up to manage a government body. She realizes she's on board for something much larger, leading the public and private; the secular and the clerical; the owner and the worker. Not on all issues, but certainly on many important ones. What are they? How does she think of this authority?

Identity: The Global Local Distinction

Like most people, the mayor does a lot of thinking while driving and as she leaves the office this day is no different. She's thinking about this concept of the public realm as she travels down the latest addition to a great national motorway out of the centre city, past the international airport, and into the suburbs. She pulls off at a typical intersection. She realizes that things look more or less the same everywhere. Quick-stop service stations, strip malls, office parks, and other common features dot the landscape. She realizes she's seeing, stop after stop, a concrete example of the global versus local distinction. This global economy is one of impressive scale, standardization, speed and convenience. What it fails to do is give the mayor any indication of where she really is. What really defines this place? Was this parking lot once a historic battlefield or homestead? Does his global economy speak to the institutions, activities and traditions that really make a community unique?

Of course, the public realm is neither global nor local; in reality it is both. This brings her back to her demanding workflow. What if 70 to 80 per cent of what she does on a day-to-day level, is shared by thousands of other similarly situated cities? If it's global anyway and not really distinctive, is she taking advantage of global networking and systems to minimize the commitment of resources to these

activities? And for the remaining 20 to 30 per cent, is she prioritizing people's political capital and time on those activities that really distinguish their city as a place to live and to invest?

Unity: Bridging the Great Divide

Whether she's in New York, Chicago, Mumbai or Johannesburg, our mayor will most likely need this investment of time in addressing the problem of a divided city. Our colleague, Bruce Katz, has pointed out in his important work 'A Region Divided' (1999) that my own city of Washington, DC is the centre of one of the most divided regions in the United States. As this region struggles to make its way in this global economy, as the leader of its centre, Mayor Adrian Fenty attempts to improve the state schools, a crucial component of the public realm, a fierce debate rages over how we think of public benefits and how they are allocated. He makes difficult decisions to improve school performance and loses his mandate and hence his office, largely along race and class lines. While tragic, is this surprising in a city that hosts the most knowledgeable citizens in the country, but also a high level of illiteracy, that harbours the wealthiest residents but also a disgraceful level of poverty?

Cities must think at both the macro and micro level in approaching this endemic condition. The Urban Age Awards illustrate, in the micro, the power of local, tangible, sustainable projects to bring people together, to work together, and to succeed together. Positive examples command the respect of other citizens and stakeholders. It is no wonder that many of the successful public works projects we've seen, such as cycling corridors in Bogotá, Colombia, have been not only about public works writ small – new advances in mobility – but about the public realm writ large: conferring dignity onto groups and classes in society that were formerly ignored and disregarded.

And there's a larger component as well. While many mayors chase after the vision of the beautiful city, more and more acknowledge that this vision is realized through more than simple bricks and mortar. Where these projects have succeeded, local leadership has taken the time to make an initiative more important than another totem of prosperity. As we've seen in the Olympic Legacy in London, the Anacostia Waterfront in Washington, and the great work of Mayor Jaime Lerner in Curitiba, Brazil, public undertakings that embody enhanced and valued public ownership can integrate the physical and the social; the aspirational and the practical.

Trust: Accountability and Transparency

Many supposedly knowledgeable commentators will tell the mayor that her job is more than simply 'picking up the rubbish'. Take a stand on the great issues of the day, they say, whether they are about human rights or war and peace. And yes, to lead in the public realm it is necessary, but not sufficient, to manage the government well. None the less, what is necessary can be quite critical.

When we think of public trust, we often focus on the obvious factors: clear standards of conduct; consequences for success or failure; and institutional controls to protect the public purse. All of our cities are replete with examples of abuse of discretion, corruption large and small, and enormous amounts of public funding lost in ill-conceived schemes or worse. But public trust is also built on established expectations: the ability to do the small things reliably and well.

Take a typical day. When you awoke in the morning did the alarm clock ring? No electricity? Where's the mayor? Was there noise and commotion on the street last night? Call the mayor? You can't see the sunrise because your tree hasn't been pruned? The mayor again! My point is that our trust in government, and hence its ability to do great things, is founded on our established expectations. Our belief that our team can win is premised on our belief that it can reliably play the games that bring it the championship.

Faith: A Belief System

If our mayor can bring her city to understand what it is, who it is, whom it serves, and on what basis, she's well on her way on the road to getting citizens to believe in her city. Again, this is not based on the dream of a newly reconstructed beautiful city. It is based on the idea of a dynamic, sustainable, resilient city. And cities are resilient, if we believe in them. Unfortunately, immersed in the economic difficulties and pursuing projected economic benefits, facing many cities, leaders may be tempted to doubt themselves and embark on major works that do more harm than good. We have seen many ring roads, expensive underground railway systems and obsolete-upon-completion public works projects that illustrate a collective psychology of doubt and denial. To be fair, these examples are balanced by initiatives that recognize that the built form, in cities, produces an inordinate share of our carbon footprint, and conversely, that a substantial share of the solution is in initiatives such as transit oriented development, intelligent pricing of transit options, and green developments, not just green buildings.

Moreover, and perhaps most importantly, we've seen profound models of cities that prove they can be resilient and eternal. After all, national governments rise and fall; cities as great centres of civilization advance and move forward. Think, for instance, of Berlin, Mumbai, Shanghai, London and Mexico City. Indeed, during my time with the Urban Age, I've been amazed to see cities weather one calamity after another, ranging from wars and terrorist attacks to hurricanes, floods and epidemics. We may be in for a bumpy ride, and may have to fasten our seat belts, as Bette Davis once said, but we can believe, and yes, we can be confident, that ultimately, our cities and the public realm will not only survive but will prevail.

UNEVEN LANDSCAPES

Sophie Body-Gendrot

THE CULTURE OF TOLERANCE

By their nature, cities both demand and encourage tolerance, sexual and social: qualities that bring them under sometimes lethal attack from those who see open societies as a threat.

Throughout their histories, cities all over the world have attempted to find a balance between disturbances of the existing order, followed by periods of change and innovation, a subsequent return to order, and eventually sclerosis, to use an organic metaphor. Currently, urban situations of disorder reveal the crises in cities' ability to come up with appropriate solutions for the challenges they face. Some inefficiency, disorder and unpredictability may indeed be productive for their rejuvenation, but that sits in sharp contrast to the social damages that are the result of what may at first instance appear to be logical and functional propositions by the institutions and bodies that govern them.[1]

The changes brought about by globalization are accompanied by often extreme forms of vulnerability of large percentages of the population in the global cities of the South. They are subjected to terrorist attacks, gang wars over illicit trafficking, high rates of homicides, the occurrence of no go areas, etc. Here I want to focus particularly on Mumbai, São Paulo and Istanbul, on what they have in common and how they differ in respect to inequalities, social tensions and disruptions. We will also look at the lessons they have to offer through the responses they have come up with in dealing with these issues.

Several questions arise straight away: does the current phenomenon of globalization inevitably increase inequality, which in turn generates social tensions, hampering the economic, political and social well-being of cities? If so, are global cities in less-developed countries more vulnerable? How much do they lose if either external events and forces hit them, or if fragmentation happens from within?

Situations in which fear and feelings of insecurity converge can be seen in Mumbai, São Paulo and Istanbul, yet the types of disorder that confront each city differ from one another, and so do the responses.

Globalization, Inequalities and Urban Disorders

When we look at urban inequalities, it is not their increase that should attract our attention, as they certainly were just as pronounced in the past, but how the current phenomenon of globalization transforms our perception of them. Because of the large extent of global interdependence and the constant stream of information through our communication networks, they are fully visible and foster a sense of injustice. In the 1980s, it was mainly those at the bottom who were affected. Since the 1990s, the middle classes have started to feel the effects as well, while the higher

classes have benefited from the globalization and have been able to increase their assets more than proportionally. Today the CEO of Walmart earns 900 times the wages of his average employee.[2]

The classic tool for measuring inequalities is the GINI coefficient. It measures inequality across a society as a whole rather than simply comparing the extremes. The higher it is, the less equal the society in question is. In New York, it averages 50 (in 2007). In cities of the global South, it reveals higher inequalities in Johannesburg (75), in São Paulo (61) and in Mexico City (56) than in Istanbul (43) and Mumbai (35).[3]

Secondly, what we mean by globalization – the interconnection of mass communication, finance, knowledge institutions, administration and force in a power network – seems to express an agreed view of the world. The formation of transnational circuits, displacing national monetary flows, production processes and whole populations encounters fewer constraints, due to the fact that 'the dynamics engaged by the global do so inside the national'.[4]

The disconnectedness of numerous elites that move within their own self-referential spheres, who are in general the spokespeople in charge, and the disenchantment felt by large sections of populations – especially the young who feel abandoned and disrespected by those elites – is still the prevalent situation in a world largely devoid of in-betweens. The reactions to ad hoc and unnegotiated modes of operation at the local level generate social tensions, struggles and resistance, the nature of which changes according to the cities' history, institutions and policies.

The levels of inequality, however, should in no way lead to thinking that they are automatically correlated to urban violence. New York has a high level of inequality, but in terms of safety it has become a success story. Inequality does not in itself lead to violence, and the level of economic development does not in itself affect violence. And, according to Weede, who compiled data in 47 nations, the curvilinear relationship between the level of repression exercised by a regime and violence is rather thin.[5]

Situations of disorder that hit cities now are both an opportunity as well as an event. They often highlight issues that are being ignored in public discourse, like situations of injustice and people's emotions. They form a connection between the global and the local. 'Disorders are born out of silence, absence and omission, and from a paradoxical consensus that both stigmatizes and erases a part of society.'[6] In cities, they give globalization its confrontational dimension, without immediately resorting to political claims. The urban sites targeted by terrorists, dissenters and rioters symbolize what global cities (New York, Paris, London, Madrid, Mumbai) are: in terms of flux and wealth, but also of social failures. Situations of disorder are a mode of social expression: they reinterpret public space and organize a drama in the context of marked and contentious territories.

Cities are both the material support and the symbolic (and strategic) stake that situations of disorder need. Old forms of urban violence, such as ethnic hatred or caste tensions, for instance, are continuously revived under new conditions. As Appadurai has remarked, 'The fear of small numbers is intimately linked to the tensions produced by the forces of globalization.'[7] Situations of disorder reveal issues that have no political legitimacy and belong to the non-decision-making. The majority of them do not resonate beyond their immediate context, yet they do resonate in the imaginaries of youth cultures. The dispersion and disparity of such situations do not allow a convergence of local resistances into a global social movement. There may, however, be a correlation between macro-economic developments, rising inequalities, and the dialectics of order and disorder. Where income differentiation is high, so are social stratification and levels of distrust.

Cities are complex social sites and social order is more difficult to assert in very large cities, fragmented by a diversity of people's trajectories and status, and by growing individualist claims – not to mention class, age, race, gender and background. The urgent and complex challenges and the global risks and threats cities have to deal with, from terrorist networks to transnational gang activities to social secession, make them 'frontier spaces', in terms of vulnerability.[8] It does not necessarily follow that everything in cities is global: localized grievances and conflicts do persist. However, global dynamics and conditions can displace, submerge, erase and subordinate intense local conflicts and therefore the priorities of governance have to be shifted.

New Forms of Insecurity in Global Cities

Globally oriented developments that trigger urban violence are increasingly visible in cities throughout the world, but major differences obviously exist between them. A vignette from Mumbai, as revealed by Weinstein, displays how much the globalization of criminal activities transforms cities and what forms of responses they and their residents have to deploy to counter negative changes.[9]

Mumbai's organized crime groups have long had connections outside India. With the support of financial infrastructures, they amassed new forms of capital and established new sources of power in the 1990s. 'Extended now from the Persian gulf to Malaysia and with links identified in London, Johannesburg and New York, the strength of the city's large organized crime organizations result not only from their ties to political parties and embeddedness in antagonistic religious communities but also in their increasingly global reach.'[10]

The move of these groups into land development was a result of the local state's decision to make certain valued land plots available through a series of conversions, slum clearance schemes and deregulation of public lands. Prices spiralled in the mid-1990s, boosted by speculation. Resorting to violence, threats and bribes, the criminal organizations purchased numerous properties throughout the city directly or indirectly. Meanwhile, sub-standard housing and health conditions and deteriorating security, continued to characterize life for 6.5 million (around half of the city's population) in the slums of Greater Mumbai. Since the mid-1990s, however, local, national and international institutions have attempted to turn the city into a clean, efficient, 'world class' city, investing in major infrastructures.

A similar analysis connects globalization and the 2007 terrorist attacks. 'The available evidence thus far suggests that the masterminds of the attack exploited the fact of a long-standing, mostly low-intensity conventional conflict to achieve their own, perhaps separate concerns.'[11] The terrorist attacks have been attributed to inter-communal antagonisms, as well as to Muslim and Hindu hatreds, and to a geo-political rivalry between Pakistan and India. But, as pointed out by Sassen, the context is also linked to the segmented condition of the modern statehood's authority. Terrorists exploited a weak state and made use of highly visible and symbolic urban sites to destabilize the opinion of the elites and the world alike. Mumbai is a well-guarded city, yet its openness and complex interconnectedness in an array of key places make the city (or any large city) vulnerable to such attacks.

The attacks have been perceived and judged differently: the average Mumbaikar

LIVING IN THE CITY

Religious affiliations can serve to delineate territory in the city through iconography and architectural symbolism. They can bring support and welfare networks but also exacerbate social tensions.

is probably more concerned with the 10 commuters that are killed each day as a consequence of falling from trains, or they are concerned with crime and burglaries. The local and national elites as well as the Hindu and Muslim leaders and traders were shocked and worried. As elsewhere though, civic actions that alleviated the effects of terrorist attacks prevented the elites from extreme decisions of retaliation. The 'maximum city' demonstrated its capacity to contain and resist violence.

Another vignette is provided by São Paulo. The concentration of multinational companies, the presence of Latin America's most important Stock Exchange and the rapid development of a knowledge economy make it a global city with multiple circuits that connect it firmly to other parts of the world. But there is little relation between the city's spectacular access to global circuits of power and its level of social inclusion. For a majority of the city's residents, education and opportunities of mobility and to alter one's life prospects are slim. Trends in violence show that the poorest are hit disproportionately. Yet, as pointed out by Caldeira, only 10 per cent of the poor live in *favelas*.[12] Many of the wealthy have moved away from the centre and opted for gated communities at the periphery. So the picture of a dual city is somewhat of a distortion. The per capita average income of US$12,000 (€8,807) far exceeds that of Mumbai's US$1,800 (€1,321). The proportion of young people (one-third of the population) is the same in both cities. However, São Paulo distinguishes itself from the other two cities looked at here through its murder rate, which reached 21 per 100,000 (versus 3 per 100,000 in Istanbul and Mumbai) in 2006; if limited to the young, it reached 54.5 per 100,000. The intellectual challenge is therefore to understand what specific circumstances cause these exceptional numbers, ruling out terrorist attacks, of which the city has been spared. Is it another form of globalization that can explain this situation, or a specific culture within the city that tolerates such levels of violence? Or is it the inefficiency of organizations and the lack of political will to alleviate inequalities?

Fear has always played an important part in the imaginaries of the Paulistanos, all the more so as the city absorbed wave after wave of poor immigrants and territorial inequalities have over time become highly visible. After the transition to a democratic government, fear of crime became an excuse for the most affluent to lock themselves away. 'Fear, the talk of crime, and the adoption of walls and separations all transform the character of public space. Privatization, enclosures, policing of boundaries and distancing devices create a fragmented public space in which inequality is an organizing value.'[13] The reifying vision of stigmatized groups in disreputable areas, partly shared by their residents themselves, helps to maintain urban inequality, 'a process which in turn moulds reputations, reinforces stigma and influences the future trajectory of the area.'[14] One can understand why fear is so widespread: in the 2008 Urban Age survey, over 57 per cent of residents claim that either they or a close family member have been robbed, and half say that they know of someone who has been murdered, although violent deaths, assaults and rapes largely spare the upper and middle classes. The predictability of violence is even higher in poor areas if gangs dispute their boundaries and rule over parts of them.

A major criminal organization, Primeiro Comando da Capital, imposed its power over weak institutions, following an incident related to a transfer of prisoners to maximum security prisons: bank branches were vandalized, buses set on fire and a state of emergency was declared in 80 penitentiary institutions. Gangs in São Paulo govern public space and they worsen the territorial fractures that local authorities and committed residents attempt to alleviate. 'Besides their local criminal activities, … they are also increasingly taking over "government" functions: "policing", providing social services and welfare assistance, jobs and new elements of rights and authority in the areas they control.'[15] This explains why the Paulistanos' primary demands are for a faster and more severe justice system, for more security cameras on the streets and in public spaces, and for more visible policemen on the streets. They also want minors to be punished in the same way as adults are.

Research shows that much has been done already to improve security in sensitive areas, because, as a competitive global city, São Paulo has much to lose from being thought of as synonymous with danger. How to address inequalities and the segmented nature of public services is regarded as a low priority, whereas the concern for security intersects with the construction of the city's contemporary landscapes.

The last vignette comes from Istanbul, a city of 13 million people, 'too big to fail'. Its growth and job opportunities are a magnet for migrants in search of the realization of a dream. Here, the distribution of inequality is not as sharp as in Latin America. How is it then that the fear of crime (three-quarters of the residents expect to be burgled at some stage) is so much higher than that in many other global cities? Is it the cosmopolitan and fast-changing demography of the city, along with the uprooting of the newcomers that explains why only 20 per cent of the city's residents feel safe to walk outside after dark (compared with 31 per cent in São Paulo)? Challenge to urban order stems from mobile people and from those of no fixed address, who do not fit within the social and spatial hierarchy. A similar phenomenon has been observed with the floating population of Shanghai, migrants from neighbouring states in Johannesburg, those from the northeast of Brazil in São Paulo, and the Roma everywhere in Europe. Most of the first-generation newcomers tend to adjust to their new circumstances, but their descendants seem to experience more problems.

As with ghettoes, *favelas* and townships, the word *varo*, a term used in the 1990s to designate the characteristics of poor neighbourhoods at the periphery of Istanbul, is linked to poverty, enclosure and the concentration of marginalized populations, many of them rural Kurds. In common perception, these areas are associated with situations of disorder, violence, revolt, delinquency and the potential risks that the young men among them evoke for mainstream society. However, recent research carried out in Bağcılar, Güngören and Esenler reveals important differences.[16] Young Turks enter into the formal and informal labour markets at an early age and have less time to contest their circumstances than their counterparts in developed countries like France or the UK. The social capital retained by families and communities translates into a control of behaviour, all the more so as the public systems of redistribution are limited and do not allow young people to develop a large autonomy. However, they seem less isolated and less segregated than in other cities, because of the multiple communities within which they are embedded and because of their rural ways of living, even in Istanbul. Those with most difficulties are those who have to find their way outside the communities' networks, making a living as street vendors or shoe-shiners. They are the ones who may be tempted by opportunities in the illegal economy associated with trafficking and crime.

In the last few years, a new public policy has created 130 youth centres where social workers interact with street youths, thus attempting to alleviate the fear of crime that these young people experience and in turn generate among the general population. The local authorities also organize entertainment for all in these areas, and they distribute scholarships and offer after-school activities. These discrete initiatives are only a beginning and do not provide a strong support network for those that are socially excluded: that would require more determination and resources. But research points at a general mood for entrepreneurship, at trust and at a sense of support from families and communities, which may explain why the level of violence, compared with that of São Paulo, remains low.

As elsewhere, surveys among residents conducted by Urban Age show they would like their institutions to be more efficient. A faster and more severe justice system is perceived by a majority as an efficient way to improve safety. There is support for the notion of installing more cameras in public spaces, limiting the sale of alcoholic beverages, for better street lighting and the prohibition of the sale of guns to civilians. Yet few of them wish the punishment of minors on similar terms as those for adults or the building of more prisons.

In conclusion we can say that a city's history, the nature of its institutions and its specific culture all need to be taken into account and be added to the range of explanations for the diverse forms that inequality and violence take on in different locations. They also play a role in the responses that a city comes up with to new urban vulnerabilities.

For example, Mumbai was part of an empire, the prerogative of which was to provide all residents with safety. But when the city acquired its autonomy and over time became a global city, its institutions, including those of justice, the police and urban planning were slow to meet the expectations of its very heterogeneous residents. Ethnic divisions and widespread deprivation hamper the aim of a more equal and inclusive society.

Likewise, São Paulo had to exert violence against Portuguese domination and subsequently dictatorship, before finding its own autonomy and modernity. This specific history and culture may explain why its top issues are related to a lack of cohesion and more generally to public services. There is a lot of work still to be done to provide equal justice to all and to improve policing, all the more so in the *favelas*.

Istanbul also stood at the head of an empire, spread on two continents and made up of many layers. The current governance of this cosmopolitan city, at the hinge of Europe and Asia, shows complexity and fragmentation, with central government still exerting its domination over much of the city and thus limiting its own initiatives.

Unlike global cities in developed countries that complain they are 'broken' after each major financial crisis, the cities in the South come across as young, energetic and resilient. As said before, the scale of economic inequality that they display – which are not as high as in some developed countries – is less an expression of freedom and democracy than of their denial. Modern inequality exists because democracy is excluded from the true spheres of power.[17] There lies the urgency of the task for each of these cities. To many, cities are a promise for a better future, and they act as a conduit and as a place of events. In their unpredictability, cities offer them dizzying possibilities.

FROM UTOPIA TO YOUTOPIA

Alejandro Aravena

SECURING THE MINIMAL

There may be no instant solutions to affordable housing in squatter communities, but projects such as the Elemental initiative demonstrate that minimal infrastructure and secure tenure make an important difference.

To have more and more people living in cities is, in principle, good news. Cities are powerful vehicles for creating wealth as well as shortcuts towards equality.

Proposition One: Cities offer Critical Mass
Knowledge creation is the key factor for economic growth. Face-to-face contact is of crucial importance in the knowledge economy, so the kind of urban concentrations and the critical mass they offer make that interaction more likely to happen. In the context of a global economy, the knowledge creators can command more or less the same financial rewards anywhere. They are therefore able to choose where they live on the basis of the quality of life that they enjoy. As a result those cities that are able to offer a balance between internal and external connectivity both physical and virtual, and such amenities as better restaurants, museums, houses, a more convenient airport, a university higher up the global league table, and a sense that they are at the centre of the cultural landscape, will do better in attracting the gifted wealth creators than those which can't.

Proposition Two: Cities are a Concentration of Opportunities
This is the fundamental reason that drives people to move to cities. They are places that offer more access to better jobs, education, sanitation and health care, recreation and social mobility. This innate concentration of opportunities, combined with the right public policies, is crucial for the fight against poverty. Cities offer the best chance for equitable social conditions. If strategically planned, innovative urban projects can serve as shortcuts towards equality since they can efficiently improve the quality of life of the poor without being dependent on income redistribution.

Global South Challenge One: Subsidize the Rich?
Developing countries are not so much faced with the challenge of attracting new knowledge creators as with the threat of discouraging the flight of those that they already have. But for a city to spend money on attracting the elite, by focusing on the private sphere, corporate or individual, rather than the public realm is hard to justify, and will miss the target. The real challenge in creating urban quality takes place at the larger public scale. Thus the process of improving the quality of urban life depends on investing funds in urban elements that are as democratic and redistributive as possible.

Global South Challenge Two: Scale, Speed and Scarcity
To cope with the process of urbanization, developing countries will each week have to build a city for 1 million people that can generate an average income of US$10,000 per family. Even if governments cannot cope with these new urban dwellers, people will not stop coming to cities; they will come anyway, but as slum dwellers. Informality will be the form this urban migration will assume.

One Possibility: The Elemental Case[1]

Half of a Good House instead of a Small One
When there is sufficient money, be it from personal savings, mortgage funds or state subsidy, a middle class family usually opts for a home of around 80 square metres. Poorer families have no capacity for saving or the security to qualify for mortgages. They depend on state subsidies for their housing.

What do governments do when there isn't enough money? How does the market respond when only US$10,000 is available for every unit? It reduces and displaces. The conventional trend is to design what is in essence the same middle-class house chosen by those who can afford it, but to make it smaller, and to build it outside the city, where land is cheaper.

So, the first thing we did was to reframe the problem: instead of thinking of 40 square metres as a small house, we asked ourselves, 'what if we think of 40 square metres as half of a good house?' Once the problem is framed as designing half of a good house, the key question is: 'which half do we build?' We thought that with public money, we had to do the half that a family would never be able to achieve on its own. We identified five design conditions that define that initial more difficult half of a house.

As a consequence of this approach, it is evident that we will be then dealing with incremental housing. The magnitude of the urban challenge will not be solved if we leave the auto-construction capacity of families out of the equation.

Housing as Investment
When buying a house, we expect its value to increase over time. We thought there was no reason why social housing should not behave the same way. Unfortunately, in the current conditions, social housing is more similar to a car than a house: its value decreases every day once it's finished.

In a property-oriented policy like the Chilean one, within which we started working, families become owners of the units. Housing subsidies therefore are the biggest aid a beneficiary will ever receive from the state. So it is highly desirable that a transfer of public assets to individuals can gain value over time. If such a thing happens, we might be giving a poor family a tool in being able to use their household as capital.[2] With a unit and a property capable to increase its value, a family might be able to go to a bank and ask for a loan to start a small business or to finance a better education; or the value gain might simply express the capacity of a family to have gone beyond mere survival and actually have been able to spend part of their income to improve their home.

We identified five design conditions that are crucial for the value appreciation of a property over time, and those design conditions are exactly those that a family is not easily able to achieve on their own. Those conditions are:

1. Location, Location, Location

Location within the city is not only what a family will never be able to modify, but it is the factor that most affects the value of the house. As a city is not an accumulation of houses but a network of opportunities, a good location guarantees the inclusion of a family in that network, increasing the likelihood to overcome poverty.

It is infinitely preferable to deliver a smaller house in a good neighbourhood than a poorly situated bigger unit; instead of making the effort to deliver larger houses, which is usually done by buying cheap land on the outskirts, those efforts should be invested in delivering half of good houses on well-situated plots within the city.

To obtain a good location, or, to be able to pay for an expensive plot with a modest amount of subsidies, depends on achieving a sufficiently high density. That density has to be achieved with individual direct access of every property to the ground, avoiding common vertical or horizontal circulations, which often contribute to social conflict and urban deterioration.

The difficulty lies in the fact that we must ensure that each house can be enlarged to twice its initial size. Therefore, the design condition may be expressed as the need of obtaining density, with low-rise buildings, allowing growth, without overcrowding. Another way of putting it is that we need to develop typologies that are dense like apartments, but also expandable like houses.

2. Self-build as Customization

In progressive housing there is always the risk of deterioration of the urban environment by spontaneous building of uncertain quality; if the urban surroundings deteriorate, the value of the home decreases.

To ensure an integrated development of the complex, we need to define at least 50 per cent of the urban front with the initial dwelling. Since it's difficult to control how the expansions will be made, the aim should be to separate and frame them. The basic idea is that the design of the first half is a porous structure within which expansions can take place. It's important that the 'initial building' be strategically placed towards the plot edges to guarantee the urban front.

The criticism historically made of social housing, is that it is incapable of embracing the diversity of composition, economy, tastes or sensibilities of the residents when cost reduction techniques such as modularity and repetition are employed. In the case of progressive housing, monotony and repetition are the only ways to guarantee to avoid uncertain and unsafe scenarios when residents begin building expansions in the future. In this way, auto-construction is no longer seen as a threat of deterioration and becomes a viable alternative for personalizing urban space. On the other hand, the industrialization processes in construction no longer have a negative connotation and can be used in good conscience because of their regularity, and even their monotony, which define a neutral support, key to the appreciation of the investment.

3. Collective Space for the Extended Family

It is very expensive to be poor. The multi-family occupation of a plot, although overcrowded, is not only the expression of the impossibility of having a house of one's own. It is also a survival strategy; an intermediate level of economical association in fragile social environments is key. A key condition for the economic development of many low-income families lies in the existence of a space where the 'extended family' may develop.

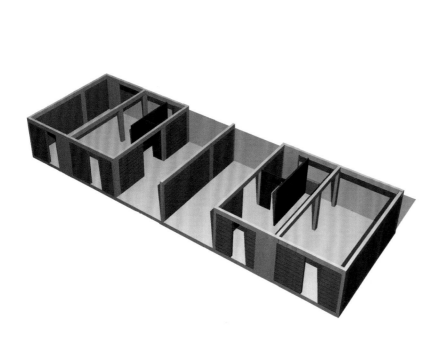

MAKING HOUSING AFFORDABLE

The Elemental housing project is based on the idea that residents take part in the building process as and when they can, using the equity that comes from having security of tenure. The first phase provides infrastructure and a minimal amount of space.

It could be said that the urban fabric tends to have a binary structure: there is either a public space or a private space, there are either streets or private plots. In social housing it is very important to introduce a collective space, a common property of restricted access where the economic and social unity of the extended family may take place. The size of the collective space will be determined by the amount of families that can reach an agreement, which, in practice, is usually around 20.

4. Structure for an Uncertain Future

The usual structure/finishes ratio in a building is around 30/70. In social housing it changes to 80/20. This means that all the savings made on structure are fundamental; but it also means that its design defines very radically the conditions of the dwelling, from the way occupation is going to happen to the urban presence of the building. The structural skeleton has to provide therefore a supporting, unconstrained framework for improvised construction, but will also perform as the skin of the final built body.

Success in progressive housing should be measured by the capacity of a family to keep on adding to the initial unit, in a quick, safe and economical way. Avoiding complex structural operations is crucial in achieving this.

5. Middle-class DNA

When working in an incremental way it is very important to bear in mind that the size of rooms and the standard of elements are measured and designed not as if they belong to a small house, but as if they are components of a middle-class dwelling. This is particularly true for all the elements that are difficult to modify afterwards, like bathrooms and kitchens, partition walls and stairs.

According to our experience with families, we have found out that size matters. But more than a bigger unit to start with, what families are interested in is the final size that they might achieve with the expansions.

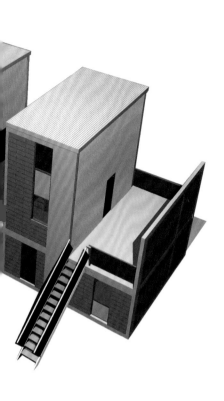

Pop Urbanism

When working with incremental housing, families must participate in the process. Participation means in the first place to communicate restrictions and constraints. To have an informed counterpart is important because the second notion of participation is to have families as responsible for establishing priorities. In progressive housing, by definition not everything can be delivered, so it is important that users understand that to prefer something will necessary mean to give up something else. Finally, participation means to arrive at an agreement of how to divide tasks. If a significant part of the house is going to be built incrementally over time, it is more efficient to have a clear understanding from the very beginning of who is going to do what. It should be open to popular discussion: what is going to be the responsibility of the public sector and what is going to be left open to private initiative?

From Utopia to Youtopia

One of the positive outcomes of an open system like the one of incremental housing, is that it is forced to reduce and concentrate resources to an extreme. And once the problem is synthesized to an irreducible core, that core tends to be universal. Basic needs tend to be the same everywhere in the world. The need to answer with what is only strictly the case, has the potential to create common solutions (in the sense of simple and shared).

And if that core is approached as an open system – as if it is only the starting point of an operation that will be completed over time – then the second halves will naturally adjust to local conditions. If the initial public, efficient and repetitive half is strategically designed, then a generic utopian beginning may well naturally be tempered by individual interventions to become a rather pragmatic, unpredictable, deeply human You-topia.

SURVIVING IN AN URBAN AGE

David Satterthwaite

CHASING INSTANT SOLUTIONS

In the face of national emergencies, apparently instant solutions in the shape of the airborne distribution of supplies may not work as well as more considered long-term engagement.

Very few of those who read this text will have had their homes bulldozed – with no compensation, with little or no warning and little chance to gather possessions and recover building materials. But among low-income urban households in low- and middle-income nations, such evictions are common – and many households have experienced such evictions more than once.[1] If any provision is made to rehouse them, it is usually in distant locations in poor quality housing (or even on undeveloped land sites), far away from employment possibilities, shops, government services and their network of contacts.

Mass evictions of low-income households are still common in urban areas in Africa and Asia and, although less so now, in Latin America. Although the largest forced evictions may be associated with non-democratic regimes – the military dictatorships in Latin America in the 1970s and 1980s,[2] the millions forcibly evicted in Seoul during the 1970s and 1980s,[3] and the evictions in Zimbabwe in 2005[4] – they remain commonplace in many democracies, including in India, the world's largest one.[5]

Very few of those who read this text will live in a house that has no piped water supply or sink, no provision for a toilet, no waste collection service – or have had to spend years negotiating with local government or local utilities suppliers to address these issues. Or to find themselves excluded from schools or health care or the voters' register because they live in an informal settlement and lack a legal address. This too happens to a large proportion of people in urban centres in democracies. It is common to live in informal settlements for between a third and two-thirds of the population in cities in most African, many Asian and some Latin American nations. There are no accurate figures for the proportion of the urban population with reliable, piped water and a decent toilet in their home because most surveys that provide data on water and sanitation are not detailed enough to provide such information. But estimates in 2000 suggested that at least 680 million urban dwellers lacked such provision for water and 850 million lacked such provision for sanitation.[6] The numbers have probably grown by several hundred million since then – as the urban population in low- and middle-income nations has grown by around 590 million since 2000 and little attention is given by most governments and aid agencies to improving the water and sanitation provision.

For hundreds of millions of urban dwellers, a regular feature of life is seeing their homes flooded or destroyed by storms or earthquakes.[7] They often show considerable

ingenuity in coping with these disasters – Mumbai for example came out of its last serious floods in much better shape than New Orleans. But every disaster has a heavy cost in loss of life and damage, and of course there is no insurance available to them to help rebuild their homes and livelihoods.[8]

One of the great privileges of living in a democracy in high-income nations is the number of our daily needs that are met on a routine basis without having to negotiate with government agencies or utility providers – or to become part of a collective organization to get the political leverage to get needs met or resort to the law to get rights realized. We do not question the fact that we get water of drinking quality delivered straight into our homes and waste water removed, and electricity and often natural gas supplied 24 hours a day. Or that we have toilets in each house or apartment where human waste is conveniently extracted by flushing and household waste collected regularly. For most of us, the costs of water, sanitation, fuel for cooking and, where needed, heating, electricity and rubbish collection represent a very small part of our income. There are also schools and health centres to which even the lowest-income households have access. There are emergency services (fire, ambulance, police) available to all, when needed. There are local politicians through whom we can make demands and voice grievances. It is easy to get on the voters' register without a lot of negotiation. Legislation and courts protect us from eviction, discrimination, exploitation and pollution. There are safety nets for those who lose their jobs or fall ill – and pensions when we retire. There are lawyers, ombudsmen, consumer groups and watchdogs we can turn to if we feel we have been mistreated. All of this is possible because of local government institutions, which are in turn overseen by democratic structures.

Little more than a century ago, infant and child mortality rates in cities in Europe were like those still common in cities or in informal settlements in low-income nations today.[9] Democratic structures were key to the setting up of this web of institutions serving our needs and remain key for ensuring their continuing presence, especially during recessions. But what does democracy mean in a city when for 20 to 70 per cent of the population few, if any of the institutions noted above serve them? What are the political levers or means available to the poor to address the issue of these lacking? And what is the role for the official aid agencies and development banks – do these really serve the needs and priorities of the urban poor? What roles and responsibilities should they have for the urban poor if national and local governments have little interest in addressing urban poverty?

It is worth reflecting on the words of Jockin Arputham, the founder and head of the National Slum Dwellers Federation in India. As South Africa moved out of the apartheid era into its first democratic, fully representative government in the early 1990s, Arputham warned South Africa's housing activists that even after 50 years of democracy in India, a very large proportion of the country's urban population lived in slums or on the pavements. Democracy does not automatically deliver for the urban poor, he highlighted. The African National Congress might be in power, but for the housing needs of the urban poor to be addressed would require the poor to be organized.[10]

India has a long, rich history of collective organization and protest by a range of civil society organizations including unions and slum dwellers.[11] Arputham himself had used the conventional range of measures to protect the settlement where he had lived since 1963 – Janata Colony – when its 70,000 residents were threatened with eviction. This included mobilizing the inhabitants for mass protests, peaceful acts of civil disobedience and use of the courts. It included contacts with key politicians to get their support and finally an audience with the Indian Prime Minister at that time, Indira Gandhi. This helped delay their eviction but it did not stop it.[12]

What the partnership of the National Slum Dwellers Federation, Mahila Milan and SPARC developed was an alternative approach. They realized that few, if any, pro-poor solutions were possible if politicians and senior civil servants always saw 'slum dwellers' and 'pavement dwellers' as problems. What they sought to do was to show those in power the knowledge and capacity of the urban poor and to offer the state a partnership in addressing their needs. When a group of women from some informal settlement wait in the office of a politician or civil servant to lobby for land for housing or for a public toilet in their community, they can easily be dismissed as a nuisance – or as complaining about needs that are not legitimate because they live in an informal settlement. When this same group of women invite the politician and civil servant to see the housing units of quality, or the public toilet they designed and built and are able to prove through accounts how much unit costs were kept down, this helps change official attitudes. These three organizations also supported all the savings groups to try out their own initiatives and to visit each other's initiatives. They developed the capacity to produce detailed maps and household censuses of informal settlements – which is essential information needed for planning and the installation of infrastructure and services.[13] Comparable federations of slum or shack dwellers with mostly women-managed savings groups as their foundation have developed in at least 25 other nations and many more are emerging.[14] These federations have formed their own international umbrella group, Shack/Slum Dwellers International, which helps them promote their members' agendas in international agencies and supports exchanges between them. They also developed their own Urban Poor Fund International to support their work.

It is only when the urban poor and their organizations can push for and help form a web of local public institutions that are accountable to them and work with them that progress is possible at a larger scale. This is also needed to ensure that the investments and interventions of national governments, international agencies and private companies recognize, respond to and are accountable to local needs. This requires local governments that are able to listen to and work with urban poor groups. It requires local institutions with the knowledge and capacity to ensure basic infrastructure and services are available to all and that are prepared to look at new ways of providing these – drawing on the experiences in nations and cities where again partnerships between local governments and low-income groups and their organizations produced much needed infrastructure and services at costs that were affordable. For instance, there are the hundreds of community-designed and -managed toilets and washing facilities and hundreds of community-police partnerships in informal settlements in India.[15] There is the example of the Community Organizations Development Institute in Thailand that has supported hundreds of savings groups in informal settlements to develop their own plans for getting legal land tenure and building good quality homes served with infrastructure.[16] There are the many nations where the federations have succeeded in negotiating for land sites on which members have built good quality homes – for instance in Malawi[17] and South Africa.[18] And also in Namibia, where the Namibian federation succeeded in getting plot sizes and infrastructure standards changed so that official legal plots for housing were more affordable.[19]

The existence of well-organized representative organizations of the urban poor that offer local government partnerships does not guarantee pro-poor urban development. In Mumbai, the residents of Dharavi, a high-density informal township with around 600,000 inhabitants, have long been under threat from a government scheme to sell the land on which it sits to developers.[20] The 'airport slums' in Mumbai that house several hundred thousand people are also at risk of eviction.[21] In both areas, there is the potential for upgrading in ways that improve housing, support local livelihoods and install infrastructure and services, yet minimize the disruption to people's homes and livelihoods. But this would need the government authorities to prioritize what worked best for the residents instead of seeing them as 'slum dwellers', occupying land that developers want.

In all the nations where slum or shack dweller federations have developed, there is the potential of another form of urban development in which the urban poor and their homes and livelihoods are recognized as critical parts of a city and national economy and society and slowly the public institutions and regulatory frameworks are changed to serve them, not criminalize them. As the Argentine urbanist Jorge Hardoy noted several decades ago, there is something wrong with laws that declare the homes and livelihoods of large sections of the urban population illegal.[22]

There is also the example of democracies in some Latin American nations that have followed more conventional routes, where organizations of the urban poor were a key part of political change that led from military dictatorships to democratic governments. Mayors often have particular importance, as they are the head of the institution that provides or should provide a range of infrastructure and services to the homes and settlements of the urban poor. In many nations, upgrading programmes for 'slums' and informal settlements became a routine part of what local government does (often with support from higher levels of government). Evictions became far less common. Slowly, the basic structures of functioning local democracies with their web of institutions serving those who live (or lived) in informal settlements were built. Much remains to be done, but a significant proportion of low-income urban dwellers is now far better served by local government than in the past.

Well-governed cities have among the world's highest life expectancies. So it is possible to see cities in low- and middle-income nations becoming centres for good standards of living for their low-income populations and with democratic structures being an important part of this. Here there is a possibly insurmountable institutional challenge for official aid agencies and development banks. These were set up to channel funding to national governments. Many have long refused to work in urban areas, sometimes even claiming that there is little poverty in urban areas[23] – as if the scale of the urban population with very high infant and child mortality rates living in very poor quality homes lacking infrastructure and services was not sufficient evidence of poverty. Some international agencies recognize the legitimacy of the urban poor organizations and federations, but they do not know how to support them – and of course national and local governments do not want international funding flowing to urban poor organizations.

Official aid agencies and development banks do not implement initiatives on the ground, they fund others to do so. So they are only as effective as the local institutions they fund. If they are funding governments (including local governments) that have no relationships with or accountability to the urban poor, they are reinforcing undemocratic structures. The very existence of these official agencies and development banks is legitimated on the basis of the needs of the (rural and urban) poor. Yet they often do not even have the capacity to talk to the organizations of the poor and they provide little or no scope for the poor to make choices and define ways of working that serve them. One much neglected aspect of poverty is never having the possibility of influencing what is provided by governments and international agencies. These international agencies are often helping to fund major projects or investments that are profoundly undemocratic, because the populations in the areas where they take place have so little power to influence them. The billion or so urban dwellers suffering from poverty have no vote in bilateral donor agencies or within the governments that supervise them. In multilateral agencies, the urban poor's government may have a vote (although in the most powerful institutions, most voting power is retained by high-income nations), but their governments rarely represent their views. If the urban poor get any infrastructure or service provided with donor support, it is very rare for them to have been consulted about what their needs and priorities are and their preferred means to address these. These agencies need to rethink how they as institutions and funders relate to urban poor organizations, including consulting them, working with them and thinking about accountability to them. Of course this presents very difficult challenges to these agencies, as their political masters believe that an efficient agency is one that minimizes staff costs. But this is inappropriate if it helps explain the lack of staff contact with the organizations of the poor.

And now there is climate change. So on top of all the risks that low-income groups face because of the incapacity or unwillingness of their governments, aid agencies and development banks to work with them, now there are the added risks and vulnerabilities from climate change, which manifest themselves through for instance more or more intense extreme weather events, sea-level rise and for many urban centres serious constraints on fresh water supplies. But again, cities present potential advantages: well-governed cities with a web of local institutions noted earlier are also much more resilient to the impacts of climate change. Well-governed cities have far lower mortality rates than poorly governed cities, when hit by storms or earthquakes of comparable magnitudes. Indeed, for well-governed cities, most extreme weather events do not constitute disasters as no one is killed or seriously injured. This is because risks were reduced or removed by the web of local institutions noted above – or by institutions that helped ensure rapid and effective responses when a disaster does hit.

So in conclusion, far more attention is needed from governments and international agencies to building and improving the local institutions that are accountable to and work with urban poor groups. These are also central to the capacity to adapt to climate change. The discussion on the balance needed globally (and within cities) between adaptation and mitigation should be informed by the level of the capacity to adapt. If there is little or no adaptive capacity for a very large part of the urban (and rural) populations in the global South, because of the failures or limitations of governments and international agencies, it makes it all the more pressing that high-income nations and high-income individuals dramatically reduce greenhouse gas emissions.

GETTING TO WORK

Fabio Casiroli

PLANNING FOR TRANSPORT

As cities grow, too often they turn their backs on older public transport systems in favour of the perceived modernity of costly urban motorways that rarely achieve their objectives. Over time these cities may return to the idea of mass transit.

If we analyze the critical issues that city dwellers, rich or poor, place at the top of their list of concerns, their primary one is almost always 'mobility', as the opinion polls conducted by the Urban Age clearly demonstrate. Transport is a central issue, and should not be seen as a peripheral one.

This is a bird's-eye view of the part that transport policies can play in making cities work better. It is based on a synthesis of the essential issues facing giant cities as they manifest themselves in a number of specific cities, rather than an in-depth study of the conditions on the ground in each. This may perhaps offer a way of coming up with a set of proposals that have wider practical relevance to an understanding of the nature of transport planning in the evolution of cities. It is underpinned by the application of effective, though simplified, working methodologies that allow us to read the forma urbis generated by different means of transport at different times of the day and to interpret the resulting 'Urban Mobility Footprints'.

São Paulo's transport system is characterized by a set of unusual features: a vast metropolitan area, a growing population (currently around 18 million) expressing a rapidly increasing demand for mobility, fairly high and constantly increasing levels of private car ownership and a public transport network that although it is expanding still can't cope.

Urban sprawl is now a dramatic reality in the São Paulo megacity but we believe that the application of a comparative methodology has allowed us to identify some potentially viable solutions. The most telling comparison was with the Milan area and Lombardy. This part of Italy presented significant similarities with the South American metropolis with respect to its economic importance, the saturation of its territory, traffic congestion and the existence of old railway networks during the post-World War II period. Especially the presence of old railway systems as a shared feature represents an opportunity to be exploited for two fundamental reasons.

Firstly, railway stations can be powerful 'seeds' for the regeneration of areas of the city, as they are able to communicate with the rest of the territory rapidly while using sustainable modes of transport. Locating important urban amenities in their vicinity rather than dispersing them elsewhere in the city makes it possible to limit people's dependence on cars and ensures that railway services are used at sufficient levels to make them economically viable. Secondly, of all modes of transport, rail networks are the most effective at controlling urban expansion, because they encourage poly-centric growth and help to prevent formless development. In the case of Milan,

THE DISCONNECT

Cutting first-world roads through third-world cities is an inadequate response to transport planning for Mumbai where toll roads are too expensive for the poor to use them.

which we have chosen as a point of comparison, had the existing railway network (built and managed profitably by skilled English and Belgian entrepreneurs between the late-nineteenth and early-twentieth century) been used to good effect more recently with the implementation of a well-considered town-planning policy, the quality of life in this wealthy region would have been better.

As well as the idea of rehabilitating the railway network, derelict interchanges and stations, we think it is worth stressing the potential impact of an extensive and well-organized Bus Rapid Transit system in São Paulo. The effects of projects that could be implemented quickly and at limited cost have been quantified through a first approximation and turned out to be extremely interesting.

Istanbul, a megacity that links two continents, suffers from progressive gigantism. Its geographical complexity and system of transport connections is unable to satisfy high levels of demand for everyday mobility. Large infrastructure projects have been planned, some of which are in progress, but the most serious issue that the city will face in the near future is the rise in *per capita* income and the consequent increase in car ownership. Today Istanbul has a very small number of cars per head of population, only 0.14, yet despite this road congestion is a serious problem. We can easily imagine what will happen as soon as car ownerships reaches higher values.

In this case, too, a comparison with other contexts allowed us to measure the extent of these problems and to suggest some proposed interventions to obtain a significant improvement in urban mobility within a reasonably short time.

Today Istanbul has 8 kilometres (4.8 miles) of reserved lanes for public transport per million inhabitants. Madrid has 92 (55.8), Rome 108 (65), Paris 152 (92), London 176 (107). In applying this strategy through the TransMilenio, Bogotá, a well-known example, has reduced public transport travel times by a third and emissions by 40 per cent; accidents along the TransMilenio route have fallen by 90 per cent.

Istanbul today has 167 park and ride spaces for every million inhabitants, Madrid has 3,700, Milan 13,000. We suggest capturing the demand near the region. In Madrid this practice has allowed for a reduction of rush-hour traffic within the city by around 20,000 cars.

In Istanbul today the capacity of the existing Bosporus bridges is approximately 12,000 vehicles per hour in either direction, which equals about 14,000 people in total. This leads to huge delays crossing the Bosporus so we suggest the use of alternating odd and even number plates and reserving a couple of lanes on each bridge for a Bus Rapid Transport (BRT). In addition, in Istanbul we can forecast that these two BRT lines would have a capacity of about 24,000 passengers per hour in each direction, exactly double the current road capacity, but using one lane instead of four. In Istanbul cycle lanes are practically non-existent. We know that the geography of the city is complicated, but we suggest building a cycle lane network (where possible) and supporting the purchase of electric bicycles. In Paris, the Vélib system has 170,000 subscribers and is used 41 million times a year by citizens and city users.

Extensive and well-integrated transport networks can drastically reduce the need for car ownership. Berlin is a truly polycentric city that has succeeded in ensuring effective connections between its various centres through extensive public transport systems and a capillary network of cycle lanes. For decades the German capital has invested massive resources in creating one of the world's most complex public transport networks and it continues to invest today, especially in the extension of rail networks. As a result about 80 out of 100 journeys are now carried out on tram, metropolitan railway and railway networks. The universal availability of public

THE FUTURE IS A BUS

As an affordable alternative to fixed rail mass transit, the dedicated bus lane has proven itself throughout Latin America as an effective form of public transport systems capable of revitalizing cities, and has been implemented in other parts of the world, too.

transport makes it possible to keep the number of private vehicles to a minimum: approximately 322 cars per 1,000 inhabitants (compared to 728 in Milan and almost 900 in Rome).

In order to function properly as polycentric entities, cities require effective public transport connections. Madrid is an important example of a city that is attempting to grow along a 'polycentric' pattern, which is evident in its peripheries. The interesting aspect of this growth lies in the simultaneous construction of public transport systems (the extension of the underground network, new Light Rail Transit, tram and Bus Rapid Transit networks) that do not in fact always have the necessary capacity. Nonetheless Madrid is an excellent example of integrated city and transport planning.

Even car-obsessed cities can adapt and design better environments for their citizens. For decades Los Angeles has represented a paradigm of the car-obsessed city, crossed by huge inner-city freeways built under the illusion that an initially overabundant capacity would allow everyone to move freely and rapidly. That this was an illusion is now clear to everyone, just as it would be a misconception to think that simply substituting cars with internal combustion engines by electric vehicles, aside from reducing pollution (a positive outcome), would also resolve the problems of congestion or the lack of parking spaces (on average each resident of Los Angeles wastes about 100 hours a year in traffic). It is no coincidence that the Californian

metropolis is also investing large sums in the creation of public rail transport infrastructure today, including a high speed rail link with San Francisco and San Diego. There is still a long way to go, but a new era seems to have begun.

Simple measures can have enormous impact. In 1986, the first time I saw Beijing I was literally stunned by the rivers of bicycles rushing through the city, barely held back at traffic lights by zealous police officers. Today China's economy is, as are the numbers of private cars, responsible for some of the world's worst environmental pollution. For the 2008 Olympic Games, under pressure from the International Olympic Committee and the athletes themselves, concerned about competing under unhealthy conditions, the authorities decided to introduce a system alternating number plate days for the duration of the sporting event. The results obtained were excellent, reducing vehicle emissions by 63 per cent. After the Games ended these restrictions were abolished with the result that traffic and pollution levels doubled overnight. For a while it seemed that the authorities, shocked by this rapid return to intolerable conditions, would reinstate the restrictions. Pressures of various types prevented this from happening, with devastating consequences: a well-known instance is the motorway north of Beijing being blocked due to maintenance work in August 2010, by 100 kilometres (60.6 miles) of standstill traffic. Those stuck in the massive traffic jam were for days on end provided with food by peasants from the villages located along the road. They were travelling at an average speed of 1 kilometre (0.6 mile) a day. On the other hand, it should be remembered that Beijing is in the process of building numerous new heavy metro lines at record speed: once these become operational, however, it would be worth considering the idea of introducing restrictions on private car use, as a good provision of public transport is insufficient in itself to guarantee extensive, rapid and egalitarian mobility.

Cities have numerous mobility 'magnets', a natural reflection of the complexity of city life. Unfortunately, situations in which the spatial location of large mobility magnets is determined exclusively by reasons of profit or, more simply, the availability of space are common. All this without any consideration for the mobility needs of those travelling to them. In the case of São Paulo, both the main university and the Morumbi Stadium, to mention but two examples, attract thousands of journeys at various times of day, but are poorly served by public transport and therefore difficult to access. Barcelona's Nou Camp stadium, the Milan Polytechnic, Canary Wharf in London, Lower Manhattan in New York, all highly accessible by public transport, represent positive examples. Locating urban mobility magnets in the vicinity of public transport nodes is essential if cities, as a whole, are to be rendered more accessible to all and therefore more democratic and equitable.

Identifying an intelligent location for urban amenities means governing the processes by which cities develop, their destiny and that of those who live in or 'use' them. In order to resist the inevitable pressure exerted by aggressive private interests it is essential for those called to govern the res publica to be courageous and farsighted. Inevitably these administrators will also have to deal with the dilemma of 'what to do' regarding the interventions on infrastructure needed to repair existing or emerging gaps in accessibility. The temptation is often to increase the capacity of the road network, under the illusion of restoring fluidity to inter- and intra-city communications (this is happening in Istanbul with the third Bosporus bridge, and in Mumbai with the Bandra-Worli Sea Link). These remedies are often purely illusory, and history has shown that building heavy road infrastructure is the first step towards inevitable disaster instead of towards a resolution of the problem. The most interesting example we were able to observe at first hand is that of Bogotá, where a courageous and farsighted mayor, Enrique Peñalosa, resisted the temptation to build dozens of kilometres of new urban motorways, choosing instead to promote the birth of the TransMilenio, an extremely efficient Bus Rapid Transit system serving the Colombian capital. The construction of hundreds of kilometres of cycle lanes and the regeneration of public spaces then sparked the city's rebirth, providing all of its citizens, even the poorest, with an opportunity to access places previously only dreamed of.

Looking at Istanbul from the top of its skyscrapers, it is immediately apparent that the quickest way to move between the districts that literally 'cling' to the hillsides and those in low-lying areas are not the tortuous existing routes, often extremely steep and so narrow that buses are unable to pass, but direct and linear connections. In the specific case of Istanbul, old but effective systems (stairs and funicular railways) may be vital for connecting parts of this geographically complex city. In this context Barcelona represents one of the world's best known examples, in particular because the escalators allow people to ascend the Montjuïc; Perugia, a little Italian gem, has equally effective escalators. Numerous cities squeezed between the sea and the mountains (Genoa, Lisbon, Hong Kong and Istanbul itself, to name but a few) also use funicular railways, an old but low energy mode of transport, able to ensure direct and linear connections. We have proposed that the Turkish city also take their carefully planned use into serious consideration.

In all the places we explored we found, to a greater or lesser extent and in more or less interesting locations, large derelict urban spaces, old obsolete factories, unused railway stations, abandoned districts. Rehabilitating these and restoring their dignity, integrating them as much as possible into the contemporary urban tissue through effective transport connections should be one of the goals of urbanists and administrators. Were such projects to be based around a variety of uses and proximity to services used on a daily basis they could have a marked positive impact on the demand for mobility, potentially leading to a drastic reduction in the need for private vehicles and even for public transport. Since most journeys would be short, low impact mobility (pedestrian and bicycle) and micro mobility (small electric rental vehicles) would become major players in balanced and pleasant urban environments.

The historic figure of the transport engineer with his solid scientific background, responsible for technologically effective solutions, can no longer be considered the 'key player' capable of resolving the complex issues posed by modern cities. Examining what actually happens in the Urban Age cities has confirmed the belief that transport planning is an essential component of city planning, not a separate technical discipline. Yet proposing just infrastructure solutions, however advanced in technological terms, does not help cities to build a better future. Often these solutions are illusory, as noted above, destined sooner or later to reveal their own weaknesses. Today we need more complex modes of thinking about the city as a whole that consider integrated transport networks as an opportunity to rebalance social imbalances of our urban fabric.

FACING THE METRO CHALLENGE

Bruce Katz

NEW JOBS FOR OLD

Even as Western cities have lost jobs and factories to Asia, some of them have created new ones by returning to manufacturing. Textile businesses can operate with migrant labour, while old-style industries cannot.

The United States stands at an economic crossroads. The Great Recession revealed an American economy dangerously out of balance, fuelled by excessive consumption and financial engineering. The nation's economic recovery remains sluggish with high unemployment and underemployment. Rising nations like China, India and Brazil (and metropolitan engines like Shanghai, Mumbai and São Paulo) are now leading the way to global economic recovery, given their rapid urbanization, industrialization and growth of the middle classes. Other disruptive changes are under way, most importantly the transition to low carbon energy sources and the growth in demand for sustainable infrastructure and products.

These and other seismic economic shifts have reinforced calls in the US for a different kind of growth model, one that is driven by exports, powered by low carbon, fuelled by innovation and rich with opportunity. This is a vision in which the US exports more and wastes less, innovates in what matters, produces and deploys more of what we invent, and ensures that working families share fully in the benefits of national prosperity.

The vision of the next economy is triggering a new appreciation for the role of cities and metropolitan areas in American economic life. The United States, traditionally anti-urban in its politics and culture, is coming to appreciate the 'power of place'. As in other parts of the world, American cities and metropolitan areas are the vanguards of national economic transformation. They are the hubs of trade, commerce and migration and the centres for talent, capital and innovation. They contain the infrastructure to move people, goods, ideas and energy efficiently and the institutions to educate and train the workforce of the future.

A new 'Metro Policy' is slowly emerging, to link the macro vision of the next economy to the metro realities of the places where that economy will largely occur. Metro Policy contends that national economic renewal is dependent on metropolitan prosperity and leveraging the competitive assets, attributes and advantages of metropolitan communities. This represents a sharp departure from traditional 'urban' policy in the United States, which has been parochial in scope (exclusively focused on cities and neighbourhoods rather than broader metropolitan areas), narrow in reach (engaged with affordable housing rather than broader economic interventions) and overly deficit- rather than asset-oriented.

Metro Policy has made an auspicious though fledgling start under the Administration of President Barack Obama. With Congressional help,

the Administration has pursued a three-part Metro Policy playbook, making signature investments in the assets that drive metropolitan and national prosperity (innovation, human capital and infrastructure), creating new institutions and mechanisms to design and deliver these investments in coordinated ways and taking important steps to reshape urban and metropolitan growth and governance in service of the next economy.

Given the growing political polarization at the federal level, the mantle of policy innovation is likely to shift to states and metropolitan areas over the next several years. There, a pragmatic caucus of governors, mayors and county leaders will work closely with a network of business, university, philanthropic and community leaders to restructure metropolitan economies.

Context

The US economy is slowly and unevenly emerging from a painful Great Recession. The dramatic downturn exacerbated longstanding structural challenges in the American economy such as excessive consumption, lagging exports and innovation, wage stagnation, and persistent racial and ethnic disparities in education, income and wealth generation.

A broad cross section of business leaders and economists have contended the US economy cannot simply 'return to normal', because the over-leveraged, debt-driven economy that preceded the recession was anything but normal. Consumer spending and residential investment stood at 75 per cent of GDP in 2007, before the beginning of the recession, up from 67 per cent in 1980. During the same period, earnings in financial services increased while American leadership on indicators of innovation – the historic catalyst and fuel for innovative growth – slipped. Financial services expanded from 10 per cent of earnings among Standard & Poor's 500 indexed companies (which include many of the largest American firms) in the 1980s to 45 per cent the last decade. But, the United States' share of new patents is declining, and its share of global R & D spending is falling.

In 2000 the US trade deficit was US$380 (€279) billion, and that doubled by 2007, to US$760 (€558) billion. The United States' economy has become dependent on imports rather than driven by exports. Exporting has become an almost unnatural act, with only 1 per cent of US firms selling their goods or services abroad. The disruption, specifically in manufacturing sectors, has been particularly harsh; half of the car manufacturing workforce has been shed since 2000.

These economic trends have had a dramatic impact on workers. Over the past 30 years, the average wage for individuals with a high school degree has stayed virtually the same as monetary rewards have mostly risen for people with college degrees and above. These trends continued in the 2000s: between 2000 and 2008, hourly earnings for high-wage workers increased 3 per cent, compared with declines of 4 per cent for middle-wage workers, and 8 per cent for low-wage workers.

The Great Recession revealed the limitations of an economy based on over-leveraged consumption and financial manipulation. So what will succeed it? According to Lawrence H. Summers, the Director of President Obama's National Economic Council, 'The rebuilt American Economy must be more export-oriented and less consumption-oriented, more environmentally-oriented and less fossil-energy-oriented, more bio- and software-engineering-oriented and less financial-engineering oriented, more middle-class-oriented and less oriented to income growth that disproportionately favours a very small share of the population.' In other words, the next economy must be export-oriented, lower carbon, innovation-fuelled and opportunity rich.

While experts debate America's ability to restructure its economy, one thing is clear: the next economy will be led by metropolitan areas. The world may be 'flat', as Thomas Friedman famously concluded, but the spatial reality of modern economies is their intense concentration in a relatively small number of particular places.

The real heart of the American economy lies in 100 metropolitan areas which, even after decades of growth, take up only 12 per cent of the nation's land mass, but harbour two thirds of its population and generate 75 per cent of its gross domestic product. Across the US, metropolitan areas concentrate those assets that matter most in today's economy.

On innovation, they produce 78 per cent of all patents, 82 per cent of National Institutes of Health and National Science Foundation research funding and 94 per cent of venture capital funding.

On human capital, they gather 74 per cent of adults with a college degree and 75 per cent of workers with a graduate degree and account for 76 per cent of all knowledge economy jobs.

On infrastructure, they concentrate 72 per cent of all seaport tonnage, 79 per cent of all US air cargo weight, and 92 per cent of all air passenger boardings. With these formidable assets, it is not surprising that metropolitan areas are where the breakthroughs in innovation, in products for export, and in lower-carbon technology and design are likely to be made, marketed and deployed. The message is clear: the next economy, in the US and abroad, will be shaped, determined and delivered by metropolitan areas.

Achievements by the Obama Administration

The Obama Administration has worked hard over the past two years to mitigate the effects of the recession in the United States and set forth an agenda for productive and sustainable economic growth. President Obama has been sweeping in his vision for the next economy. His State of the Union speech delivered in January 2010 called for an array of signature federal interventions on education, research, health care, infrastructure and energy. Unusual for an American politician, he ascribed numerical targets to key parts of the agenda: calling for a doubling of exports in five years and an increase in the number of individuals with post-secondary credentials by 5 million in 10 years.

The President has been explicit that cities and metropolitan areas are vehicles for national economic transformation. At the paradigmatic level, the Administration talks about city and metropolitan areas in a sophisticated way, a sharp departure from traditional rhetoric that exclusively discussed cities (ignoring their suburbs) and deficits like poverty and crime (ignoring their assets). The President's 'Urban Policy Statement', is illustrative: 'To maximize economic productivity and opportunity in a 21st Century economy, federal policy must reflect the new metropolitan reality – that strong cities are the building blocks of strong regions, which in turn, are essential for a strong America.'

To connect the macro economy vision to this metropolitan reality, the Administration has pursued what amounts to a three-part playbook:

Investing in the assets that drive the next economy: innovation, human capital and infrastructure;

Creating new kinds of mechanisms and institutions to leverage these assets in integrated, smart and strategic ways; and

Remaking cities and metropolitan areas to strengthen the connections between innovation, human capital and infrastructure.

The record to date is impressive, although much work remains to be done.

Investing in Assets

In February 2009, just one month after President Obama's inauguration, Congress enacted the Administration's Recovery and Reinvestment Act of 2009 (ARRA or the Recovery Act). Due to the need to affect the economy quickly, some parts of this legislation were aimed at traditional spending programmes and legacy delivery systems. But the Recovery Act also made a series of game-changing, market-shaping investments that have been long deferred. Most significantly, the Recovery Act invests in the assets that drive prosperity: innovation, human capital and infrastructure.

On innovation, ARRA invests tens of billions of dollars in federal research and development. On human capital, the Recovery Act provides tens of billions of dollars in direct funding for education, including billions of dollars for incentives to states and innovations in urban school districts. On infrastructure, the Recovery Act invests tens of billions of dollars to repair declining 'old' infrastructure as well as investing in next generation systems like high-speed rail, smart energy grids and health care information technology.

Since early 2009, the Administration has built on these initial investments by seeking to align federal policy with the spatial clustering of economic sectors. Clusters reflect the economic power of place. They are geographic concentrations of interconnected companies, specialized suppliers, service providers, firms in related industries and associated institutions that compete but also interact and cooperate. And they are why the economic map has organized itself into scores of local agglomerations: biotechnology in Boston, information technology in Silicon Valley, financial services in New York, entertainment in Hollywood, aircraft production in Wichita, and so on.

The Administration has put forth a Regional Innovation Clusters (RICs) paradigm to leverage the disparate competitive strengths of distinct metros to boost job creation and economic growth. In 2010, the RICs approach has penetrated the Economic Development Administration and Department of Energy, and is now taking hold in agencies as disparate as the Small Business Administration, National Science Foundation and Department of Agriculture.

The Administration is particularly focused on growing nascent low carbon clusters. In August 2010, the Department of Energy (DOE) announced the winner of its Energy Regional Innovation Cluster (E-RIC) competition, which will provide up to US$130 (€95.4) million from seven cooperating agencies to a Philadelphia-based consortium that will help translate advanced research on building efficiency technologies into private investment and job creation.

New Institutions

The Administration's organization of the White House and the Cabinet recognizes that complex challenges facing US metros require new institutions and integrated solutions that cross traditional policy and bureaucratic silos. The Administration has created several mechanisms – a White House Office of Urban Affairs, a White House Office of Energy and Climate Change Policy and a White House Council on Automotive Communities and Workers – to promote coordinated activity across the specialized agencies of the federal government.

The level of inter-agency collaboration envisioned and undertaken to date is truly remarkable by historic standards. The principal focus of action has been on the emerging low carbon market. Prompted by the Recovery Act, for example, the Department of Housing and Urban Development (HUD), DOE, and the Environmental Protection Agency (EPA) have forged a close partnership to catalyze a green, energy-efficient residential sector. On the broader metropolitan scale, HUD, the Department of Transportation (DOT) and EPA are collaborating on new initiatives around liveable and sustainable communities.

Beyond new coordinating mechanisms, the Administration has also sought to create new kinds of institutions – smaller, leaner, more entrepreneurial and responsive to markets – to catalyze economic recovery and transformation. Most significantly, the Administration has proposed a National Infrastructure Bank that would make market-shaping investments based on merit rather than political calculation. Federal investments through an infrastructure bank would leverage private capital for inter-modal facilities at congested ports, high-speed passenger and freight rail as in Germany and France, and modern transmission lines to carry renewable energy seamlessly across state lines.

Remaking Cities and Metropolitan Areas

The Obama Administration has recognized that the distended, sprawling landscape of most American cities and metropolitan areas is not spatially efficient and serves to weaken rather than strengthen the economic competitiveness of places. The Administration has, therefore, worked closely with Congress to invest in the making of quality, liveable places. As with the broader economic interventions, the Recovery Act invests tens of billions of dollars to retrofit homes, convert vacant and foreclosed properties to productive use, remediate brownfields and extend metropolitan transit.

These efforts have continued and intensified since the Recovery Act. In 2009, the Administration proposed and Congress approved a US$150 (€110) million Sustainable Communities Initiative, administered by the Department of Housing and Urban Development, to encourage the development of integrated regional plans that link housing, transport, jobs and land use and create more compact and transit rich communities. This programme challenges states and local agencies to reform land use and conduct state of the art research using the latest data and most sophisticated analytic, modelling and mapping tools available. The Administration has since proposed expanding this effort with additional investments through the Department of Transportation and the Environmental Protection Agency.

A Work in Progress

The Obama Administration's economic policy and its accompanying focus on metropolitan communities remains, of course, a work in progress. Despite Olympian achievements, critical proposals to restructure the national and metropolitan economies have yet to be enacted.

At the moment of writing of this essay, for example, action on comprehensive climate change legislation (which would help catalyze markets for clean energy technologies through the de facto pricing of carbon) has stalled. Congress has yet to approve funding requests to bolster investments in community colleges, high-speed rail, freight infrastructure, sustainable communities, metropolitan transit and port infrastructure. Despite Presidential engagement, the creation and capitalization of new twenty-first-century institutions like a National Infrastructure Bank appears unlikely in the short term.

It is doubtful whether any signature reforms can be achieved before the 2012 mid-term elections. Washington has become a nasty, politically polarized environment, characterized by hyper partisanship. With the mid-term elections in November 2010 the Republicans have regained control of the House and made significant gains in the Senate, arguing for a humbled, if not paralyzed federal government over the next two years. Federal activism will be dialled down, although executive decisions on some next economy related initiatives remain possible. Concerns over debt and deficit will be dialled up, particularly given the scheduled release of the National Commission on Fiscal Responsibility and Reform report in December.

Back to the States and Metros

With the likelihood of federal stalemate in the next several years, innovation on Metro Policy will pass from the federal government to state and metropolitan leaders. With 37 races for governor in 2010, it is certain that new governors will take the helm in such major states as California, Colorado, Florida, Georgia, Michigan, Minnesota, Nevada, New York, Pennsylvania, Tennessee and Wisconsin. These governors will join a pragmatic crop of mayors and their business and civic allies in metropolitan areas as diverse as Detroit and Denver, Memphis and Minneapolis, New York and Philadelphia.

The following policy areas appear ripe for state and local innovation in a select group of 'smart' states and metropolitan areas. Given the sluggish economic recovery and constrained fiscal resources, smart states and localities are likely to re-examine traditional economic development strategies. Those strategies have been heavily tilted towards consumption, following an easy to replicate 'Starbucks and stadia' recipe. Those strategies will fall out of favour and the smart communities will instead build on the burgeoning national framework and use *regional innovation clusters* to exploit the distinctive productive strengths of their metropolitan areas, including tailored interventions on land, labour and capital as well as marketing and promotion. This could include the development and implementation of metropolitan export initiatives.

With regards to investments, smart states and metros are likely to focus on bolstering their human capital assets, since funding for education is principally a state and local concern in the United States. The smart places will strengthen technology transfer and commercialization efforts at the universities and colleges, which will bolster metro clusters. In addition, they will support greater investment in and collaboration between community colleges to take advantage of their ability to retain workers, and support cluster-led economic transformation in their communities.

With regards to institution building, several states might, in the absence of federal action, create their own infrastructure banks to leverage private financing for critical investments to facilitate exports (for example through multi-modal facilities at major air, rail and water hubs) as well as accelerate the transition to a low-carbon economy (for example through green infrastructure). Traditional industrial states like Michigan might even entertain the creation of laboratories for advanced manufacturing. This would provide support for manufacturing innovation commonly found in metropolitan areas like Munich and Stuttgart: engineering research for early-stage applications that are useful in a range of manufacturing processes, export promotion assistance, credit for diversification into new products, and training investments for manufacturing's human capital.

With regards to place making, several advances are probable. In Detroit,

Cleveland and other older industrial metros, where central cities and inner suburbs have endured significant population and job losses over the last 50 years, there is considerable momentum to 'right size' communities. That means focusing revitalization and economic development efforts around anchor institutions, such as universities, medical centres, and the hubs of industry clusters and transportation. The city of Leipzig in Germany is a model worthy of replication.

Inspired by federal activism and fiscal realities, smart states and metropolitan areas more generally will work to integrate transport, housing, land use and economic development. Metropolitan areas will seek to draw closer connections between the places where low-skilled employment congregates and low-skilled workers live. In addition, the states will reinforce these initiatives by reforming their own development shaping rules and investments.

The shift to a low-carbon economy will spark large-scale application of smart technologies (such as electric vehicles, congestion pricing, utility metering) and the deployment of infrastructure to support them (advanced charging stations for instance). To spur markets and achieve sustainable goals, cities and metros will compete to be the vanguard of green development and twenty-first-century infrastructure. Global innovations in metros as diverse as Singapore, Copenhagen, Hamburg and Tel Aviv are being mined as examples for application in the American context.

State and metropolitan actions alone, of course, will not be sufficient to rebalance America's economy. In the end, federal action on trade and currency will be critical to boosting exports. A unified national strategy on carbon will be essential to catalyzing markets in clean and green technology. Federal investments and reforms will drive progress on infrastructure.

Yet American history has shown that state and metropolitan innovations today have a tendency to become federal policies tomorrow. During the 1920s, New York Governor Franklin Roosevelt experimented with interventions that ultimately became the New Deal. During the 1950s, states like California and North Carolina spurred the development of public universities, setting the foundation for the high-tech federal investments of the 1960s and 1970s. During the 1980s, a bipartisan network of governors experimented with welfare and health care reforms, paving the way for federal advances in the next decade.

The next several years could see the similar impact of bottom-up innovation. If the polarization of Washington can be mitigated and ultimately replaced with the pragmatism of state capitols, city halls and their business and non-profit allies, America may yet emerge from this recession stronger than ever.

Conclusion

The Great Recession has forced private and public sector leaders to re-examine the very structure of the American economy and begin a path towards restructuring. With the recognition that cities and metropolitan areas are the vanguard of economic transformation, the Obama Administration has experimented with a new vision of Metro Policy. A group of states and metropolitan areas are now likely to take this new framework to the next level. These innovators could drive a fundamental remaking of how national and state governments engage with and support their metropolitan engines. The pay-off will be greater economic vitality and sustainability, more and better jobs, and greater security for our nation and our people.

ON THE GROUND: THE DEUTSCHE BANK URBAN AGE AWARDS

Adam Kaasa with Marcos Rosa and Priya Shankar*

*The annual Deutsche Bank Urban Age Award (DBUAA) is worth US$100,000 and is administered by the Alfred Herrhausen Society. Full detailed descriptions of DBUAA criteria, selection process, shortlists, special mentions and winners, can be found at: http://www.alfred-herrhausen-society.org/en/38.html. See page 427 for the full list of DBUAA Jury Members and award coordinators.

The Ordinary and the Spectacular

While the majority of the people on earth live in urban areas, the majority of those urban areas are not in the dynamic, rich, and extraordinary hearts of Mumbai, São Paulo, Istanbul or Mexico City; they are in the rather more, for want of a better phrase, ordinary places. The spectacular movements of architectural auteurs remain in those well-known cities that can simultaneously attract, promote and sustain them, financially and politically. And yet we know that the vast majority of built urban landscape constructed in the world every year, continues to be built autonomously, often without government or corporate investment, often without architects, engineers or planners, and nearly always collaboratively at the community level. The sobering UN-Habitat statistic that in 2010 a third of the global urban population lives in slums (that is equivalent to over 820,000,000 people!), evidences this trend. [1] And while slums are certainly not what many would term ordinary places, as they too are often subject to spectacular and sometimes misinforming media coverage, still they, and other less centrifugal urban spaces, can be easily overlooked when we talk about urban solutions, interventions and scalar urban change.

It is generally assumed that solutions to current urban problems, like the unequal distribution of resources, or scarcity of access to services like toilets and green spaces, or oft forgotten urban populations like young children, new immigrants, vulnerable women and young unemployed men, are the result of individual vision, and that the spectacular is the best expression to define a workable and inspiring intervention. This is the idea that inspiration for change can trickle down from the grandiose and well-intentioned actions of the few, to more mundane and daily urban interactions, plans and buildings. [2] This is simply not the case. If we widen our analytic lens to those very small, and locally embedded urban projects and actors, and take seriously the implications of their work, then we might find surprising alternatives to some of the most routinely expounded urban best practice. Looking for what we might call the ordinary, leads us to engaged, insurgent citizenries that organize, plan and implement identifiably local interventions in their own urban environments. They navigate the schizophrenic nature of community consultations, of collaborative and participatory planning, and find partnerships that make sense. What better place to start the work of investigating and learning from these kinds of ordinary spaces, than on the ground?

LEVERAGING THE PUBLIC GOOD

The Triratna Prerana Mandal initiative, joint winner of the 2007 Mumbai Deutsche Bank Urban Age Award, was recognized for forging new alliances and improving the environment at the heart of one of the city's slums. These before and after shots show how a community toilet has been upgraded to provide better sanitation for men and women as well as office space, computer classes, childcare and community kitchens.

Two years after the Urban Age conferences began the challenging work of an interdisciplinary debate that facilitates shared learning across cities, continents and urban professions, the Deutsche Bank Urban Age Award (DBUAA) was created to recognize and celebrate the mirror image of this debate taking place at a very micro scale. Its sponsors saw it as a move from the macro discussion of global urban policy and best practice, to those areas where discussion is made concrete, to the lived, everyday urban condition on the ground in cities around the world. In their words, the award was designed 'to honour alliances that improve the quality of life in cities to enable inhabitants to become citizens. No one group can solve today's urban problems alone. The prize celebrates shared responsibility between residents, companies, NGOs, universities, public bodies etc. Through the award, we hope to create a network of urban initiatives at the grassroots level.' Since 2007 the award has moved annually from Mumbai to São Paulo, Istanbul and Mexico City, showcasing the proactive solutions to social and spatial problems in an increasingly urbanized and unequal world.

The award-winning projects that are described below are more collective than individual, more YouTube than Hollywood, and more embedded and committed than rootless and temporary. They are based on the assertion that urban problems are complex and contingent, and that urban solutions need to be collaborative and responsible interventions that look to ordinary places for spectacular solutions. Indeed, as Jennifer Robinson so succinctly argues, 'insisting that all cities are best understood as ordinary will ensure that cities everywhere can inform urban theory.'[3]

Mumbai: Accessing the Public Good

One of the most urgent spatial negotiations taking place in Mumbai revolves around the role that access to urban public space and services has in the promotion of a democratic and engaged civic society. Mumbaikars are privy to just 0.03 acres (1,307 square feet) of open public space/1000 people. In New York that number is 5.33 (232,175), in London 4.84 (210,830) and even in the world's most populated city, Tokyo, it is higher, at 0.68 (29,621).[4] In the densest area of Mumbai, over 100,000 people are crammed into just one square kilometre (or 259,000 per square mile).[5] Therefore it came as no surprise that some of the strongest projects submitted for the Mumbai DBUAA were concerned with doing more with less, in terms of the city's public space. One of the joint winners, the Mumbai Waterfronts Centre, focuses on reclaiming the waterfront on the western coast of the city. The other initiative, Triratna Prerana Mandal, secures and maintains public toilet facilities, leveraging them to develop community centres as part of that public shared good. The Urban Design Research Institute, which received an honourable mention, conducts heritage and conservation research to influence urban policy development.

The Mumbai Waterfronts Centre (MWC) emerged from the initiatives of determined residents of Bandra, a neighbourhood to the northwest of the centre, to reclaim their waterfront. Abused as a rubbish dump, used for raw sewage disposal, and vulnerable to the whims of private land grabs and corporate encroachment, the unique waterfronts of Mumbai were far from accessible spaces. With more length than the equally ambitious Manhattan Waterfront Greenway project, and far less access to resources, it was here that the MWC would direct political pressure.[6] While certainly overlooked, the waterfront could become either a spectacular commercial investment, or one of a more humble kind;

ACTIVATING THE WATERFRONTS

The Mumbai Waterfronts project has transformed an unloved and abandoned stretch of seafront into a promenade used by millions of Mumbaikars annually seeking respite from the dense and overcrowded city.

an ordinary space for the majority of Mumbai's residents. The key to the success of the MWC was the strong partnerships and creative alliances among a large number of community organizations, residents' associations and area committees, along with local MPs, and state departments. The MWC has already helped improve and reclaim seven kilometres (4.24 miles) of Mumbai's western waterfronts. Currently it is working on revitalizing the four kilometres (2.42 miles) of erosion-plagued Dadar-Prabhadevi beach. With funding from the public sector and local-resident-led and regulated small-scale private sponsorship for maintenance, the MWC proves the common assumption that the only way to fund these kinds of interventions at city scale is by leveraging the profits from private land sales and benevolent developers is a false one. While the physical transformation of the Bandra waterfront is a phenomenal testament to the effectiveness of the MWC, the real success has been the humility of the development and the protection of the waterfront as a truly public space.

Moving from the defining water of Mumbai's coasts to the private space of the restroom, our next project operates within the politics of public services. Globally, 2.6 billion people do not have access to improved sanitation facilities.[7] In developed regions, over 99 per cent of the population enjoys the privilege, while in India, that number is just 31 per cent.[8] The toilet is 'a tool for figuring out just how a society functions – what it values, how it separates people from one another' argues a new study by Harvey Molotch.[9] Paromita Vohra, whose film *Q2P* set in Mumbai highlights the gender and class dimensions of access to restrooms, agrees, 'When you go out and see who has to queue to pee, you figure out who has a stake in the country's development.'[10] From its inception in 1991 up until 1999, the Triratna Prerana Mandal initiative (TPM) cleaned and maintained shared neighbourhood toilets. If Molotch is guiding us in seeing the inequity of societies based on access to fundamental services like toilets, the actions of TPM during the first decade of their work points us to their fundamental commitment to respect and dignity of the human, a redistribution of resources and services to underprivileged urban areas, and an indictment against the continuing social stigma of those whose work it traditionally is to clean up after others.

TPM started out when the Silver Star Cricket Club decided to add social service and environmental conservation projects to a long list of sporting and cultural activities. From the early success and community involvement with the public toilet blocks, in 2002 it became a registered Community-Based Organisation (CBO). Between 2001 and 2003, the Municipal Corporation of Greater Mumbai (MCGM) funded TPM's reconstruction of 16 local public toilet blocks. Now TPM not only maintains the toilets, but also utilizes the buildings to set up offices and launch activities such as computer classes and a childcare centre. In recent years, TPM started a rain-harvesting programme, and collecting, sorting and recycling waste from 40 institutions and 3,500 slum dwellers locally, providing an urban service, and creating employment opportunities by working on a 'No Profit- No Loss' model. They also provide support to self-help groups of over 50 women, who then turn around and contribute more than 2,000 meals to under-nourished children every day. TPM works because its aim is to balance access to core services in underprivileged urban areas, starting with the basics, a toilet, and moving onwards to food, education and recycling programmes. By using the politics of shared public goods in urban areas, TPM leverages multi-scalar partnerships and funding for crucial and equalizing activities.

A little further south in Mumbai, the Urban Design Research Institute (UDRI) has been working to list and protect the historic Fort Area from rampant development pressures. Located in the eighteenth-century city, the area was named after the British East India Company's Fort St George, which now sits at the heart of the financial district of Mumbai and faces extreme development pressures. UDRI worked quickly to develop a proposal for the conservation of the Fort, mapping, photographing and cataloguing its entire stock of buildings and developing a management plan. Through its advocacy for the area, UDRI built strong relationships with government authorities, and local residents, raising awareness of the city's history and heritage, and enabling an agreement with local government to facilitate the restoration of spaces and buildings.

São Paulo: Securing Tenure and Employment

In 2002, a representative from UNESCO's Management of Social Transformations urban programme remarked that 'in the majority of the developing world, the proportion of "informal" urban space, that is to say without the attention of professionals, is roughly 70 per cent. Inhabitants of those areas in the city, subject to various forms of segregation, but principally economic and political, without services or dignified housing, are not the priority of urban professionals, but they should be.'[11] Part call to arms to urban practitioners in the audience at the Universidade de São Paulo to be proactive agents in equalizing urban change, the statement also sets the context against which the majority of projects that were shortlisted for the award set themselves. Many initiatives submitted for the São Paulo DBUAA worked in forgotten spaces that lacked the attention of the professional classes, and aimed at improving the living conditions of urban residents through improved security of housing and access to employment through the work of cooperatives.

The winning DBUAA project, Do Cortiço da Rua Solón ao Edificio União (From the Tenement on Solón Street to Union Building), united residents with students, architects and engineers to identify and carry out needs-based redevelopment of the building. Three other projects stood out for their ability to forge new relationships 'on the ground' and were recognized with special mentions. BioUrban carries out place making activities in the *favela* Mauro through greening, public art projects and a community centre. The Instituto ACAIA is a training facility within the Vila Leopoldina *favela* that aims to develop skills capacity among local youth. And Cooperativa de Reciclagem Nova Esperança (New Hope Recycling Cooperative) in the Pantanal neighbourhood offers key urban waste management services where none existed before and thus income to a deprived area.

In 2007 the 468 resident families of Prestes Maia, then the largest squatted building in South America, were forcefully evicted, making headlines around the world.[12] In 2002 the Movimento de Sem-Teto do Centro (Homeless Movement of Central São Paulo), occupied Prestes Maia, cleaned up spaces and organized residents in this disused office block, or *cortiço*, in the city centre. Government support in the past 20 years has focused political will and funding on *favelas* in the city and city peripheries rather than the inner-city tenements of the *cortiços*[13] which have been left vulnerable to the whims of increasing private capital and downtown land values.[14] While work in *favelas* is leading to 'legalization of tenure and upgrading', the disturbing trend with vulnerable populations in rundown *cortiços* like Prestes Maia is eviction and redevelopment.[15] Still, over 600,000

NEEDS BASED REGENERATION

Do Cortiço da Rua Solón ao Edificio União (From the Tenement on Solon Street to Union Building), in São Paulo, captured the jury's imagination for its engagement of different stakeholders – including local families and the city university – who transformed an overcrowded and unfinished tower block into well-serviced apartments in one of the city's central districts, close to jobs and other social facilities.

housing units remain unoccupied in the Metropolitan Region of São Paulo.[16] With complications about unpaid taxes, increased land values, and the implementation at the federal level of the City Statute in 2001, debates about how best to provide access to secure tenure and quality social housing remain at a standstill.[17]

The project Do Cortiço da Rua Solón ao Edifício União lies at the heart of this debate. Like many other buildings of its period, 934 Rua Solón is a raw, partially completed concrete-frame multi-storey structure located in the Bom Retiro neighbourhood close to São Paulo's central district. Constructed in the 1970s, the building remained unfinished due to the death of the developer, who left no heir, and was subsequently occupied by families in the 1980s. As with many other 'invaded buildings', the early residents established a precarious system of electrical and water supply with exposed wires and unreliable water provision, and a very basic form of waste and rubbish disposal. Overcrowding became severe with 73 families crammed into the building, using all available spaces including the incomplete lift shafts.

In 2002, staff and students from São Paulo's Faculty of Architecture (FAU) initiated a collaborative project, Cortiço Vivo, aimed at reimagining how tenement redevelopment could become more respective and responsive to current inhabitants. Recognizing the uniqueness of the project, the Department for Housing in the city, SEHAB, got involved. At the same time, a neighbouring Itaú Bank filed a lawsuit in an effort to ban the *cortiço*, arguing it was a physical danger to the community. The legal action triggered the desire to secure legal tenure for the residents, and collectively retrofit the building to safe standards. The Gaspar Garcia Centre for Human Rights used the recently invoked Article 240 of São Paulo's Strategic Master Plan that grants possession to residents over five years where no contestation on possession exists, to pursue securing tenure rights. Students and residents alike joined up to make dramatic physical changes to their building.[18]

The action resulted in three immediately visible results. First, the *mutirões* or collective initiatives between the students and the residents to clean the site and the installation of a collective powergrid enabling reliable electricity bills and reduced fire risks. Second, 42 families who had five years' residence were granted possession, with the 30 remaining families agreeing to be housed off-site, subsequently reducing the level of overcrowding. Third, they improved the facade and windows of the building with structural reinforcement, paint, security gates, and named it Edifício União. No longer was this building simply the slum on Solón Street, but now a place: the Union Building.

Inspired by their own agency in making it happen, the physical improvements to the 'look' of the building and its common areas triggered a new-found motivation that led many of the residents to make improvements inside their own apartments. Internal walls have been rendered and painted, new kitchens and bathrooms have been installed, with a determined interest in the collective improvement and maintenance of the site. Openings have been introduced into dark corridors and stairwells to improve the environment and reduce electricity consumption.

The story of Edifício União is inspirational, however, it is also exceptional. The vast majority of *cortiços* in São Paulo, and around Latin America, have contested histories of possession making any move for secured tenure a struggle. The nature of accommodations for the urban poor mean that tenement landlords often take advantage of these vulnerable populations.[19] And because of the oppressive living conditions in most of them, tenants rarely stay in one place for long.[20] Structural inequalities become embedded through tenure to the extent that where you live is both a symptom and a cause of vast differences in income, health and other quality of life measures. For example, 14 per cent of people living in *favelas* or *cortiços* make the lower quartile of incomes in São Paulo, compared with 4.6 per cent of those who don't; the numbers in the upper quartile of income are as telling – 2.9 per cent to 18 per cent.[21] Over 60 per cent of the unemployed in São Paulo are made up of the urban poor, and in some poor areas the incidence of violence is more than two and a half times the city average.[22] Therefore, the confluence of the kind of community cohesion and ownership status that exists now within Edifício União is rare, and must not lessen the urgent attention required to address the continued lack of housing security in the Metropolitan Region of São Paulo.

Still, it can teach us many things. First, these infrastructural improvements were made possible through the innovative partnership between a university institution, future practising architects, the Department of Housing, human rights organizations and the residents of the Edifício União. Second, a key ingredient to the project was the importance of place making, of building a sense of belonging and a sense of pride among the residents. Consolidating a diverse vertical community around the hope offered in collective and responsible action delivers a promise to Henri Lefebvre's right to the city. As David Harvey so concisely noted, 'The right to the city is far more than the individual liberty to access urban resources: it is a right to change ourselves by changing the city.'[23]

On the other side of the city, but with a similar impulse, BioUrban implemented a series of aesthetic measures that have transformed the spatial quality of the *favela* Mauro, a *favela* that in 2002 was subject to a military police invasion.[24] Spearheaded by a young sociologist, Jeff Anderson, the project trains local partners to activate the micro spaces of communities, injecting thought and intention into forgotten or overlooked sites. These include the cleaning up of small spaces and areas in front of people's homes, planting gardens in place of concrete kerbs, introducing colours and materials to humanize the facades of buildings and exposed infrastructures, creating public artworks by local children and the staging of collective activities such as painting sessions within these 'found' urban places. Very much in the place-making spirit of Austrian artist and architect Friedensreich Hundertwasser, whose 1958 *Mouldiness Manifesto against Rationalism* advocated 'the right to the window',[25] BioUrban works hard to create a sense of place and shared ownership through collective, committed and consistent action in space.

While place making can help to improve confidence, develop a sense of self-worth and create the spatial commitment from which community cohesion can grow, material inequality still persists and is spatially concentrated. Located near Vila Leopoldina, the Instituto ACAIA is an arts and crafts workshop providing extensive training facilities in the middle of a rapidly changing industrial area. The neighbourhood hosts the city's wholesale food market, a large source of employment, and is struggling to accommodate the nearly 1,000 families that have moved into informal housing to work at the market since 2006. The Instituto ACAIA was able to team up with various residents' associations to develop strategic plans for spatial improvements to help with a burgeoning and transient population. In addition to the construction of a new sewage system and paved streets throughout the dense and compact *favela,* the initiative has created a new public space with play equipment and an 'art cabin' used extensively by local children. Operating at the intersection of the social and spatial complexities of *favela* life in São Paulo, Insituto ACAIA illustrates a commitment to thinking in multifaceted terms about the relationship between larger trends of inequalities and the micro-scale interventions that work for particular communities at particular points in time.

The Cooperativa de Reciclagem Nova Esperança (New Hope Recycling Cooperative) is an innovative partnership between the State of São Paulo's housing agency (CDHU) and local residents developed under the Integrated Program of Urbanization of the Pantanal neighbourhood. Over 30,000 people live in a former floodplain of the River Tietê at the eastern periphery of São Paulo – the site of numerous landfills during the past 30 years. The project has pioneered a new system of waste and rubbish collection that both generates income for the cooperative and reduces the volume of waste previously deposited in the local streets, public spaces and water supplies. In addition, the project aims to create an open space for the community by recovering a stretch of the River Tietê. Many members of the cooperative also create artworks from recovered materials and in 2007 they were commissioned to create Christmas decorations for the Natal do Conjunto Nacional in São Paulo, one of the most anticipated seasonal events of the year.[26] Because of the continued success of the programme, the cooperative's scale and their backing by the CDHU, they were able to negotiate a deal in August 2009 with Owens-Illinois Inc., a Fortune 500 company and producer of half of the world's glass containers. Owens-Illinois provides agreed-upon food baskets in return for set amounts of recycled glassware. Translated into dollar equivalents, the deal more than quintupled their earnings from an average of between R\$0.15–R\$0.22/kg (US\$0.09–US\$0.13/kg) up to R\$1.17/kg (US\$0.69/kg).[27] This is great news for the cooperative, but also breaks conventional thinking about waste services in urban areas, and acts as a challenge to create meaningful and recognized work for vulnerable populations.

Istanbul: Enabling the Forgotten

Cities are consistently contradictory places. Saskia Sassen reminds us that 'on the one hand they concentrate a disproportionate share of corporate power and are one of the key sites for the overvalorization of the corporate economy; on the other, they concentrate a disproportionate share of the disadvantaged and are one of the key sites for their devalorization.'[28] A politics of the disadvantaged, then, requires work on two fronts. The first is an urgency to redistribute the social, political and economic resources of power more equally among all participants in the urban realm. The second is the call to recognize and value those members of society who have been excluded, or as Sassen puts it, to 'valorize the evicted components of the economy in a system that values the centre.'[29] Istanbul is one of the largest cities in the world and is a city largely made up of migrants. As discussed elsewhere in this volume, many of these migrants come from other parts of Turkey, from Anatolia or the Black Sea coast, but still, in such a multicultural country they all bring their own differences to the Bosporus, differences that both serve to include and exclude them from the multiplicity of Istanbul.

Many of the projects shortlisted for the Istanbul DBUAA addressed some of the critical problems faced by the city's most fragile communities – new immigrants, isolated women, disadvantaged children, and disabled and homeless young men.

Kadın Emeğini Değerlendirme Vakfı (Foundation for Support of Women's Work) and Umut Çocukları Derneği, Bakırköy Gençlik Evi (Children of Hope Foundation, Bakırköy Youth House) – projects which received special mention – both serve vulnerable populations and demonstrate the relationship between gender and space. The winner of the award, Barış İçin Müzik (Music for Peace) works specifically with economically disenfranchised children through music programmes. All shortlisted projects seek to bring a sense of value back to populations 'evicted' from the social and economic life of the city through work and doing, by making space for them at the heart of their communities.

In Nurtepe, a neighbourhood in Istanbul that lies along the Kağıthane stream, Kadın Emeğini Değerlendirme Vakfı (the Foundation for Support of Women's Work) provides childcare and education facilities designed to empower local women. A mixed and socially fragmented area, Nurtepe continues to act as an entry point for new migrants, many of whom are not able to access the resources and services of the city. Run on a volunteer basis by the First Step Women's Environment, Culture and Enterprise Cooperative, the centre offers classes on leadership, entrepreneurship and domestic violence, as well as networking opportunities for women from all backgrounds to help them overcome marginalization, and build the confidence to engage fully in the city. At the same time, they offer access to cooperative childcare support, enabling mothers to bring their children to the centre while they engage in these activities. Women immigrants to the city experience a difficult transition, losing the support of traditional networks. They are often unable, or denied the opportunity, to find employment in an urban economy. This project has tried to overcome the problem by using the power of making things together to engender an enabling sense of possibility and pride, at the same time as producing small craft-like items that help finance other initiatives in the centre. Discussions that ensue while making things create an opening to discuss more difficult debates around domestic violence, racism and unemployment. The women in the cooperative set the learning agenda for the year, go out and learn things for themselves, and then teach them to their communities.

On the motorway out to the airport, seemingly a site of transience, another centre provides support for young men who have fallen, or were pushed, through the cracks. After the age of 18, young women and men are no longer eligible for state support if they become marginalized and homeless; there is a policy gap that makes young, disenfranchised people economically vulnerable. Umut Çocukları Derneği – Bakırköy Gençlik Evi, the Children of Hope Foundation is a city-wide initiative which provides a safe haven for the primarily young men who have been involved in family violence, crime and drug addiction and have nowhere else to go. Similar to the Foundation for Women's Work, the central element of this project is the spatial one. The Children of Hope Foundation provides clean and safe, short-term accommodation for the underprivileged, and it is here that they receive health and social advice, and vocational training which helps them reintegrate themselves into society. Many social engagement projects operate training, learning and vocational work, but don't address the struggle and material and psychological stresses of spatial inequalities. At Children of Hope, the intersection of spatial security and access to crucial services like health and education is reinforced.

The winning Istanbul DBUAA project, located in the heart Edirnekapı, one of the city's most disadvantaged neighbourhoods, relies on music as a catalyst for

COMMUNITY ANCHORS

Barış İçin Müzik (Music for Peace) is located
in one of Istanbul's poorer inner-city districts
and provides music training facilities, meals
and after-school care for children of local
disadvantaged families. The recently completed
new building provides improved training and
performance activities for teenagers who wish
to stay in the neighborhood and continue their
education.

social and spatial change. On the face of it, Barış İçin Müzik (Music for Peace) offers free musical education to local schoolchildren from the ages of seven to 14. However, underneath the surface the project is a complex social infrastructure that acts as a vocational training school and a community centre, which provides meals for children and afterschool childcare. It is further developing into a self-sustaining space that provides employment for teaching assistants and members of the newly formed Music for Peace Foundation for students who decide to continue with their musical education. The project has far-reaching impacts socially and spatially, particularly with the completion of its new building that will house the Foundation, which will run the project, and a new, small concert hall to act as an anchor institution in the community.

Music for Peace began its work in the basement of several schools in the neighbourhood, and quickly won the interest and trust of its participants. Students learn to play a multitude of instruments, from the accordion to the flute to drums, violin, cello and piano. While the project is seemingly the brainchild of one man, the architect Mehmet Selim Baki, who up until now has been the sponsor of the entire project, he is the first to recognize the impossibility of success without the strong collaboration with partners. His list includes the schools, students and families involved in the project, but also the Children of Hope Foundation who introduced them to the Ulubatlı Hasan Primary School, where the project first started. This is a project that began with a simple idea, has wide-reaching social effects, and activates and leverages the true urban capacity of Istanbul to the benefit of poor young children. With over 250 students enrolled, Music for Peace has the long-term sustainability of the project at heart, and aims to turn it into an employer of its own alumni as it grows. The youth choir at Music for Peace has inspired like-minded parents and members of the community to begin an adult choir as well. Music here acts like the medium through which access and connection to the plentiful social- and capacity-building resources of the city are transmitted through to this vulnerable and oft forgotten segment of the population.

Mexico City: Living In Complexity

Like many other fast urbanizing urban regions in the world, Mexico City illustrates the layers of complexity involved in accounting for urban inequalities. Néstor García Canclini rightly calls Mexico City a 'city-continent', referring to the fact that its population is roughly equivalent to that of Central America, and its social, political and economic diversity is as complex.[30] Indeed Canclini goes so far as to argue that there are multiple cities operating in the city at any one time. 'What predominates today,' he argues, 'is a conflictive intersection between the different cities of Mexico City.'[31]

The three shortlisted projects for the Mexico City DBUAA respond to the natural complexities of any megacity, but at the level of the specific local space which best holds the opportunities for change. The winning initiative, Asamblea Comunitaria de Miravalle (Miravalle Community Council), is an umbrella organization in a marginal community on the peri-urban outskirts of Mexico City that makes connections between various community organizations and citizens in need. One of the two special mentions, Casa de Cultura Consejo Agrarista – CODECO (Cultural Centre Consejo Agrarista), emerged out of the dramatic shift in consciousness among 30 competing gangs to form a community centre for recovery and retraining. The other, Recuperando Espacios para la Vida (Recovering

Spaces for Life), works to improve the spatial conditions of Santa Fe where impoverished historic neighbourhoods rub elbows with the most dramatic elite urban restructuring process in Mexico. The diversity of these three projects asserts the multiplicity of urban issues at play at any given time, the cities within cities.

The colonia Miravalle in the southeast periphery of Mexico City is a low-income neighbourhood hosting many new migrants from the states of Oaxaca, Puebla and the State of Mexico. Many new migrants enter the city through peripheral neighbourhood communities, this one on the precarious slopes of Sierra de Santa Catarina. With just over 10,000 people, Colonia Miravalle is also very young, with the majority of the population between the ages of 12 and 25, and with only 2.3 per cent of people moving on to any kind of higher education or vocational training.[32] Asamblea Comunitaria de Miravalle (Miravalle Community Council) works to consolidate the multiple community-based projects in the neighbourhood and connect them to people in need.

As such it runs a comprehensive set of cultural, health, environmental, educational and employment programmes. They run a broad-based project that includes the collection and recycling of two tonnes of PET plastic per week, generating employment for 30 young people. In a community vegetable garden they grow some of the food on offer at their low-budget canteen, which provides a balanced diet for 300 members of the community. They also offer a wide variety of sporting and cultural activities, such as art workshops, dance and music classes, a skateboarding court, and an educational programme aimed at bridging the technological gap. They have a library with 25 computers that is open seven days a week, and after-school workshops to help children with homework. In the pipeline are plans for a rainwater harvesting system and the expansion of the community farm, the construction of 100 rubbish containers to expand the network of plastic waste collection in the neighbourhood, a digital laboratory that trains young people on the use of the Internet, digital photography, video and radio, and the purchase of musical instruments to develop the musical talents of local bands. Among their first achievements was the transformation of a former waste dump into a new public space with green spaces and a community amphitheatre.

Because the Miravalle Community Council works in such a diverse range of areas, and represents a large segment of community organizations in the neighbourhood, they are able to leverage partnerships with municipal and state government bodies for funding and capacity support, as well as local architecture schools and human rights organizations. Rather than reinventing the wheel, the Miravalle Community Council works more like a network hub, which means more consolidation of activities, more collaboration among organizations, and more sharing of resources in the delivery of increased services, training and support for the citizens of Miravalle.

In the same borough as the Miravalle Community Council, Iztapalapa, Casa de Cultura Consejo Agrarista – CODECO (Cultural Centre Consejo Agrarista) works within the context of drugs wars and neighbourhood gangs. In December 2010, the president of Mexico Felipe Calderón announced that over 30,000 people have been killed in relation to drug crime since the government deployed national troops to crisis areas in 2007.[33] In the same period there were just over 42,000 documented civilian deaths in occupied Iraq.[34] The continual rise of violence and the impunity exercised by both drug gangs and military police forces in Mexico has far-reaching consequences. Within this context, CODECO is a cultural centre founded by 30

CONSOLIDATING COMPLEXITY

The award jury was impressed by the multiple activities of the multiple activities of the Asamblea Comunitaria de Miravalle (Miravalle Community Council) which operates in one of the city's most deprived informal settlements. Apart from creating a covered public space at the heart of the neighbourhood, a rare commodity in Mexico City, the initiative involves a community kitchen, library and computer classes as well as a recycling centre that generates income for the community.

gangs after they agreed on a truce. The organization works to provide graphic arts training including drawing, graffiti, airbrushing and silk-screening as an alternative to involvement with gangs. They are also very aware of the importance that participation and shared ownership have in the spatial development of a neighbourhood. As its organizers are local residents, CODECO works to provide needs-based urbanism. Both the truce and the community cultural centre have made a major contribution towards the recovery of an entire neighbourhood.

On the other side of the city, disempowered neighbourhoods lie cheek by jowl with the new central business district of Santa Fe. Since the early 1970s plans for a business district in the area have existed, and in 1982, the Universidad Iberoamericana was located on site. With the financial crisis of 1994, it took until 2004 for plans to resurface, and the past six years of building frenzy means that Santa Fe now accounts for 14 per cent of the office space in the entire city. As a result of increased land values, of cross-cutting motorway systems and development pressures, many small and impoverished communities near the development have seen little improvement. Recuperando Espacios para la Vida (Recovering Spaces for Life) is a project supported by the Universidad Iberoamericana and focuses on poverty reduction through unique and lasting partnerships between large institutions and the public. They leverage financial contributions from many of the large multinational corporations in Santa Fe to help recover public spaces long abandoned by local residents. With the help of the university's Housing Department, residents work collaboratively to design improvements to their houses while using the partnership with the university to get financial credit from the National Housing Institute (INVI). Internship positions and training opportunities at the university in subjects like landscape design and maintenance, and urban planning, are under way with the support of the General Office of Employment and Training. Architecture students from the university also take part in community activities working on colour design and then help to implement it with a community painting session. Through participatory research, training and implementation of work in urban spaces, Recovering Spaces for Life creates meaningful and locally relevant public spaces. These in turn create a sense of belonging, encourage the creation of productive projects and promote the leadership of local community members.

Insurgent Groundings

Over recent+ years, the Deutsche Bank Urban Age Award has travelled from Mumbai to São Paulo, and from Istanbul to Mexico City with the aim to activate discussion about projects and programmes in those cities that work at the intersection of the social and spatial struggles of our urban condition. While the projects explored in this essay represent the winners and special mentions of those award processes, there are hundreds, if not thousands, of similar initiatives taking place around the world. All together, 486 projects have so far applied for the award, representing just a tiny portion of all the activities, organizations, and ordinary intentional insurgent citizenship transforming cities across the globe. They were all imbued with local histories, struggles and communities, and operated mainly as cooperatives with multiple partners, volunteers and stakeholders. Above all, they remind us that sometimes the most spectacular agents of change operate in the most ordinary of spaces.

Confronting the future of the Endless City: Istanbul's expanding suburbs.

NOTES

LIVING IN THE URBAN AGE / Ricky Burdett and Philipp Rode

1 The OECD has estimated that global infrastructure investments needed up to 2030 represent an annual investment requirement for telecommunications, road, rail, electricity and water of around 2.5 per cent of world GDP, of which a major part will be invested in cities. OECD, Infrastructure to 2030: Telecom, Land Transport, Water and Electricity (Paris, 2006).
2 L. Kamal-Chaoui and A. Robert, 'Competitive cities and climate change', OECD Regional Development Working Papers 2009/2, (OECD, Public Governance and Territorial Development Directorate, 2009); UN Population Division, World urbanisation prospects: The 2009 revision (New York, 2010).
3 M. Ravallion, S. Chen and P. Sangraula, 'New evidence on the urbanization of global poverty', Population and Development Review, Vol. 33, No. 4, 2007, pp. 667-701.
4 E. Glaeser, Cities, agglomeration and spatial equilibrium, (Oxford, 2008) and P. Krugman, 'Increasing returns and economic geography', Journal of Political Economy, Vol. 99, No. 3, 1991, pp. 483–99.
5 UN-Habitat State of the World's Cities Report 2008/09: Harmonious Cities (London, 2008); D. Satterthwaite, The Transition to a Predominantly Urban World and its Underpinnings, IIED Working Paper (London, 2007, available online at http://www.iied.org/pubs/pdfs/10550IIED.pdf); World Bank, World Development Report 2009: Reshaping Economic Geography (Washington, DC, 2009).
6 A. Schlomo, S. Sheppard and D. L. Civco, The Dynamics of Global Urban Expansion, Transport and Urban Development Department, (Washington, DC, 2005), available online at http://www.williams.edu/Economics/UrbanGrowth/WorkingPapers_files/WorldBankReportSept2005.doc)
7 P. Newman and J. R. Kenworthy, Cities and automobile dependence: a sourcebook (Aldershot, 1989); R. Burgess, 'The compact city debate: A global perspective', in M. Jenks and R. Burgess, eds, Compact cities: Sustainable urban forms for developing countries (London, 2000); A. Bertaud, The spatial organization of cities: Deliberate outcome or unforeseen consequence?, Working Paper 2004-01. (Berkeley, CA, 2004); M. Jenks, E. Burton and K. Williams, eds, The compact city: a sustainable urban form? (London and New York, 1996).
8 R. Burdett and D. Sudjic, eds, The Endless City (London, 2007 [hardback], 2010 [paperback]).
9 See S. Mehta, 'The Bird of Gold', p. 106.
10 The notion of 'Maximum City' is borrowed from S. Mehta's book Maximum City: Bombay Lost and Found (London, 2004).
11 A. Berube, A. Friedhoff, C. Nadeau, P. Rode, A. Paccoud, J. Kandt, T. Just and R. Schemm-Gregory, Global Metro Monitor: The path to economic recovery (Washington, D.C. and London, 2010).
12 Istanbul: City of Intersections, Urban Age conference newspaper (London, 2007).
13 See http://www.urban-age.net/ and quarterly e-bulletins http://www.urban-age.net/publications/ebulletins/subscription.
14 D. Sudjic, 'The City too Big to Fail', p. 206

THE ECONOMIES OF CITIES / Saskia Sassen

1 For data and bibliography on the issues discussed in this brief article, please see S. Sassen, Cities in a World Economy, fourth edition (Thousand Oaks, CA, 2011), and S. Sassen, Cities and the New Wars (London, 2011).
2 For one of the most exhaustive examinations of all the knowledge sectors in today's economies see J. Bryson and P. Daniels, eds, The Handbook of Service Industries in the Global Economy (Boston, 2007).
3 See J. Fitzgerald, 'Cities on the Front Line', The American Prospect, 13 April 2007, available online at http://www.prospect.org/cs/articles?article=cities_on_the_front_lines.
4 This use of the term 'slum' needs to be distinguished from the exclusively negative conventional understandings, whether in literature or in the UN-Habitat practice. The recovery of the term slum comes from leaderships inside some of the major slums in the world. Slum here is a knowing choice of word. It is not the category of the observer, but of the actor from inside the slum. Most slums are probably too overwhelmed by poverty and ill health to take on this knowing political stance, though they may be structurally a condition that is political. I develop some of this in Cities and the New Wars (London, 2011).
5 See in this regard also Gratz's chapter on manufacturing in New York City linked to top-level design sectors, e.g. making classic style furniture replicas to be sold through the Museum of Modern Art, in R. B. Gratz, The Battle for Gotham: New York in the shadow of Robert Moses and Jane Jacobs (New York, 2010). Another example is that of American Apparel, a fashion store that made a point of manufacturing in inner Los Angeles, and became hugely successful, though eventually it suffered setbacks.
6 D. Swinney, 'Chicago Green Manufacturing Network. Illinois Future: The global leader in manufacturing the products of the future', (Chicago, 2009), available on www.clcr.org; see also www.chicagomanufacturing.org

A MATTER OF PEOPLE / Darryl D'Monte

Source of the image in the text is R. Prasad et al, A Study on Migration, Health & Employment in Mumbai Urban Agglomeration (Mumbai, 2006), p. 11.

THE STATIC AND THE KINETIC / Rahul Mehrotra

This article is based on an essay entitled 'Negotiating the Static and Kinetic Cities' published in A. Huyssen, ed., Urban Imaginaries (Durham, NC, 2007).
1 See A. King, Colonial Urban Development: Culture, Social Power and Environment (London 1976).
2 This unprecedented shift in demography has not only transformed the social make-up of Indian cities, but has perpetuated an incomprehensible landscape charged with intense dualities, which are cultural, social and economic. This new demography consists mainly of rural migrants, who form the urban poor and bring with them new skills, social values and cultural attitudes that not only determine their ability to survive in an urban environment, but are in the process also of altering the very structure of the city. The presence of the urban poor makes another crucial divide explicit – between those that have access to the formal city and the infrastructure that goes with it, and those that don't and therefore lack the basic amenities.
3 See also P. Shetty, Stories of Entrepreneurship (New Delhi, 2005).
4 See P. Chatterjee, 'Are Indians becoming bourgeois at last?', in Body. City. Siting contemporary culture in India (Berlin, 2003).
5 The idea that distinct manufacturing zones and spatial segregation have now shifted to services and manufacturing occurring in fragmented areas in the city networked through the efficient transportation system the city offers.
6 See R. Sundaram, 'Recycling Modernity: Pirate electronic cultures in India', in Sarai Reader: The Cities of Everyday Life (New Delhi, 2001).
7 Chatterjee, op. cit.
8 Weddings are an example of how the rich too are engaged in the making of the Kinetic City. The lack of formal spaces for weddings as the cultural outlet for ostentation have resulted in public open space being colonized temporarily as spaces for the spectacle of elaborate weddings. Often very complex wedding sets are constructed and removed within 12 hours. Again the margins of the urban system are momentarily expanded.
9 The Ganeshotsava (as it is referred to locally) in its present form was reinvented in the late-nineteenth century by Lokmanya Tilak, as a symbol of resistance to the British colonial regime. Tilak took a domestic and private idiom of worship and translated it into a collective and public rite of self-assertion.
10 See R. Hoskote, 'Scenes from a festival', in The Hindu Folio, The Hindu (Chennai, 14 January 2001).
11 See also R. Mehrotra, 'Bazaar City: A Metaphor for South Asian Urbanism', in A. Fitz, ed., Kapital & Karma (Vienna, 2002).
12 Conservation Legislation was introduced in Mumbai in 1995 – the first of its kind in India. Over the last 10 years the debate about Historic Preservation or Conservation (as it is more commonly referred to in Mumbai) has become a well-articulated one. A number of NGOs are involved in activism and advocacy to lobby for the protection of listed buildings. Unfortunately most debates about the practice of conservation are biased towards British practices, because most Indian architects trained in conservation at universities in the UK. They tend to bring a Britain-centric view to the protection of colonial buildings, often totally out of sync with contemporary Indian urban realities. Their benchmarks are British and European standards – which often contribute to the drawing of conservation practice into the realm of the elite (banks, government agencies etc.), which results in it being perceived as an exclusionary activity.
13 The notion of cultural significance first emerged in what is referred to as the Burra Charter – one of the many resolutions made by the International Charter for the Conservation and Restoration of Monuments and Sites (ICOMOS) to define and guide conservation practice. The Burra Charter (adopted in Burra, South Australia in 1979) defined cultural significance as the 'aesthetic, historic, scientific or social value for past, present and future generations'.
14 These ideas were first presented at a seminar in Adelaide in July 2000 titled 'Cultural Significance: Construct or Criterion?' at the Center for Architecture and Middle Eastern Studies, University of Adelaide, Australia. I am grateful to Professor Peter Scriver for his input in developing these ideas.
15 For examples of works / projects that have attempted to translate these ideas, see R. Mehrotra, 'Planning for Conservation – Looking at Bombay's Historic Fort Area, Future Anterior', Journal of Historic Preservation, History, Theory and Criticism, Vol.1, No. 2, 2004.
16 See V. Venkataraman and S. Mirto, 'Network/Design', in Domus, No. 887 (Milan, 2005).
17 See R. Khosla, The Loneliness of a Long Distant Future – Dilemmas of Contemporary Architecture (New Delhi, 2002).
18 As organized manufacturing disappeared from Mumbai, skilled labourers were left with no other choice but to fend for themselves. Small manufacturing centres with agents working to network them have become the emergent paradigm. This system allows for an incredible web of distribution with the informal areas serving as centres of production.
19 Before Shanghai, Singapore was the metaphor for a successful city until the late 1990s – and the question politicians asked was 'why can't Mumbai become like Singapore?' The levels of hygiene, the cleanliness, the efficient functioning all set in an tropical landscape was something Mumbai and its citizens could easily imagine happening there.
20 This is a political question because India and China have extremely different political systems: one is an autocracy and the other a democracy. Big infrastructure projects or generally big moves in a city are difficult and slow in a democracy. And therefore the use of Singapore or Shanghai as a metaphor for the physical expression of Mumbai's aspiration is naive, as it does not factor in the political system behind the expression.
21 See A. Appadurai, 'Deep democracy: urban governmentality and the horizon of politics', in Environment and Urbanization, Vol. 13, No. 2, 2001.
22 Charles Correa, the eminent Indian architect has described Mumbai as 'a Great city, terrible place'. In this expression, utopia is the cultural and economic landscape of the city and dystopia the physical landscape.

BEYOND THE MAXIMUM / Geetam Tiwari

1 Registrar General of India, 'Census of India 2001', published by Government of India. 'National Urban Transport Policy' (New Delhi, 2006).
2 'Traffic and Transport Policies and Strategies in Urban Areas in India', final report prepared for the Ministry of Urban Affairs and Employment (New Delhi, 1998).
3 Ministry of Transport and Power, Government of National Capital Territory of Delhi, (Delhi, 2006).
4 G. Tiwari and M. Advani, 'Demand for Metro Systems in Indian Cities', TRIPP working paper (Delhi, 2006).
5 E. Sreedharan, 'Mobility in major cities', Good Governance of India, Vol. 1, No. 4.
6 Ministry of Urban Development, 'National Urban Transport Policy' (New Delhi, 2006).

FILLING THE POLITICAL VACUUM / Jeroen Klink

1 See E. Maricato, Metrópole na periferia do capitalismo: ilegalidade, desigualdade e violência (São Paulo, 1996).
2 L. C. Q. Ribeiro, ed., Metrópoles: entre a coesão e a fragmentação, a cooperação e o conflito (São Paulo, 2004).

3 E. Rojas, J. R. Cuadrado-Roura and J. M. F. Güell, *Governing the Metropolis: principles and cases* (Washington DC, 2008).
4 G. Thuillier, 'Gated communities in the metropolitan area of Buenos Aires, Argentina: A challenge for town planning', *Housing Studies*, Vol. 20, No. 2, 2005, pp. 255–71.
5 T. Araújo, *Ensaios sobre o desenvolvimento brasileiro. Heranças e urgências* (Rio de Janeiro, 2000).
6 As illustrated by J. L. Fiori, 'O federalismo diante do desafio da globalização', in R. de B. A. Afonso and P. L. B. Silva, eds, *A Federação em perspectiva. Ensaios selecionados* (São Paulo, 1995).
7 L. Guimarães Neto, *Questão regional no Brasil: reflexões sobre os processos recentes, Cadernos de estudos sociais*, No. 6, 1990, pp. 131–61.
8 See C. C. Diniz, 'Desenvolvimento poligonal no Brasil: Nem desconcentração nem contínua polarização', *Revista Nova Economia*, No. 3, 1993, pp. 35–61.
9 See J. Rabinovitch and J. Leitman, 'Urban planning in Curitiba', *Scientific American*, No. 274, 1996, pp. 46–54; and also T. Campbell, *Learning Cities: Knowledge, capacity and competitiveness*, Habitat International, No. 33, 2009, pp. 195–201
10 That is, car ownership has grown from 448 (cars per thousand people) in 2000 to 800 in 2009. See http://ippucnet.ippuc.org.br/Bancodedados/Curitibaemdados/Curitiba_em_dados_Pesquisa.asp.

THE CULTURES OF THE METROPOLIS / Gareth A. Jones
1 G. Simmel, 'The Metropolis and Mental Life' (1905), in K. Wolff, ed., *The Sociology of Georg Simmel* (Glencoe, IL, 1950).
2 C. Monsiváis, *Mexican Postcards* (London, 1997).

WORLDS SET APART / Teresa Caldeira
1 For 1920, see N. G. Bonduki, 'Habitação popular: contribuição para estudo da evolução urbana de São Paulo', in L. do Prado Valladares, ed., *Habitação em Questão* (Rio de Janeiro, 1983) pp. 135-68. For 1960–2000, see IBGE Censuses.
2 See T. P. R. Caldeira, *City of Walls: Crime, Segregation, and Citizenship in São Paulo* (Berkeley, CA, 2000), Chapter 6. J. Holston, *Insurgent Citizenship – Disjunctions of Democracy and Modernity in Brazil* (Princeton, NJ, 2008), Chapter 6.
3 C. Saraiva and E. Marques. 'A dinâmica social das favelas da região metropolitana de São Paulo', in E. Marques and H. Torres, eds, *São Paulo: Segregação, Pobreza e Desigualdades Sociais* (São Paulo, 2004), pp. 143–68.
4 Data from Pro-Aim / SMS-SP, IBGE, and Fundação Seade. Rates by district tabulated by the Núcleo de Estudos da Violência of the University of São Paulo. See http://nevusp.org/downloads/bancodedados/homicidios/distritossp/taxa-homicidios-distritos-2000-2007.htm.
5 See Caldeira, op. cit. The following argument about fear of crime and the production of separations is developed at length in this book.

LIVING ON THE EDGE / Fernando de Mello Franco
I would like to thank Sophia da Silva Telles for her careful reading of the text.
1 The city of São Paulo had a population of 130,755 inhabitants in 1893. By the year 2000, the population of the city proper had leapt to 10,406,166 while that of the Greater Metropolitan Region was 17,821,326. See N. Reis, *São Paulo: Vila, Cidade, Metrópole* (São Paulo, 2004) p. 253.
2 Published by Emplasa. Available at http://www.emplasa.sp.gov.br/portalemplasa/infometropolitana/rmsp/imagens_gif/tabela_pib.gif [24 October 2010].
3 Published by Emplasa. Available at http://www.emplasa.sp.gov.br/portalemplasa/infometropolitana/metropoles/tabelas_metropoles/tabela11.htm [24 October 2010].
4 A treaty signed between the Portuguese and Spanish in 1494, with the aim of dividing the 'territories discovered and to be discovered' by way of an arbitrary line, drawn from north to south, which was clearly favourable to the Spanish crown.
5 S. R. Perillo, 'Novos Caminhos da Migração no Estado de São Paulo', in *São Paulo em Perspectiva*, Vol. 10, No. 2, 1996, p. 74. Available at: http://www.seade.gov.br/produtos/spp/v10n02/v10n02_10.pdf. [24 October 2010].
6 Fundação Seade. Available at: http://www.seade.gov.br/produtos/imp/index.php?page=tabela [24 October 2010].
7 Ibid.
8 The Bolsa Família is a recently deployed government programme that provides a monthly stipend to families on the condition that their children attend school and are vaccinated.
9 From a speech by José Isaac Peres, a Brazilian billionaire who made his fortune in the development of shopping centres in Brazil. Excerpt from the article 'Multiplan vai investir R$1,3 bilhão em novos shoppings e estuda aquisições' [Multiplan to invest R$1.3 billion in new shopping malls and study acquisitions], in *OESP*, 7 July 2010, p. 10.
10 Class C is defined as those households with an income between R$1,115 and R$4,807 (US$655 / €480 to US$2,824 / €2,073).
11 Currently, 81.23 per cent of the national population is urban. In São Paulo, this index corresponds to 90.52 per cent of the metropolis. Between 1995 and 2000 the influx of migrants to the city of São Paulo corresponded with 5.1 per cent of the population, only part of this contingent hailing from the countryside. See IBGE, 2000 Census and S. R. Perillo, 'Novos Caminhos da Migração no Estado de São Paulo', in *São Paulo em Perspectiva*, Vol.10, No. 2, 1996, p. 74. Available at: http://www.seade.gov.br/produtos/spp/v10n02/v10n02_10.pdf [24 October 2010].
12 See A. Souza and B. Lamounier, *A Classe média brasileira: ambições, valores e projetos de sociedade* (Rio de Janeiro, 2010).
13 See C. Nobre et al., Vulnerabilidade das Megacidades Brasileiras às Mudanças Climáticas: Região Metropolitanta de São Paulo', Executive summary, 2010. Available at www.inpe.br/noticias/arquivos/pdf/megacidades.pdf.

BRIDGING HISTORIES / İlhan Tekeli
1 İ. Tekeli, 'An Exploratory Approach to Urban Historiography Through a New Paradigm: The Case of Turkey', in H. Sarkıs and N. Turan, eds, *A Turkish Triangle: Ankara, Istanbul and Izmir at The Gates of Europe* (Cambridge, MA, 2009).
2 K. H. Karpat, *Osmanlı Nüfusu (1830–1914)* (Istanbul, 2003).
3 On this subject, see *From the Imperial Capital to the Republican Modern City: Henri Prost's Planning of İstanbul (1936–1951)* (Istanbul, 2010).
4 For a more detailed analysis on this topic, see *Turkey National Report and Plan of Action* (Istanbul, 1996).
5 See also M. Güvenç and E. Yücesoy, 'Urban Spaces in and Around Istanbul', in *Istanbul City of Intersections* (London, 2009).
6 See also J. Friedmann, 'The World City Hypothesis', in *Development and Change*, Vol.17, 1986, pp. 69–84. And J. Friedmann, 'Where We Stand: A Decade of World City Research', in P. Knox and P. Taylor, eds, *World Cities in a World System* (Cambridge, MA, 1995).
7 See Toplu Konut İdaresi, IULA-EMME, *Geleceğin İstanbul'u* (Istanbul, 1993).
8 TÜBA Yerleşme Bilimleri Öngörü Çalışma Grubu, *Yerleşme Bilimleri/ Çalışmaları İçin Öngörüler* (Ankara, 2006).

THE HINGE CITY / Richard Sennett
1 Detailed accounts of the first six Urban Age conferences in New York, Shanghai, London, Mexico City, Johannesburg and Berlin can be found in R. Burdett and D. Sudjic, eds, *The Endless City* (London, 2007).

IT'S ISTANBUL (NOT GLOBALIZATION) / Hashim Sarkis
1 The soap opera was titled *Gümüş* (Turkish for 'silver') and it actually did not fare that well with the Turkish audiences.
2 See 'The Turkish Soap Opera "Noor" More Real than Life', by A. Hackensberger in *Qantara.de*, available at: http://www.qantara.de/webcom/show_article.php/_c-478/_nr-801/i.html.
3 See for example 'Noor-mania shows no signs of abating' in *The Kuwaiti Times*, 26 August 2008, available at: http://www.kuwaittimes.net/read_news.php?newsid=MTE0MTI3NTUwMg==.
4 This was observed by the anonymous author(s) of the Wikipedia article on the song. See http://en.wikipedia.org/wiki/Istanbul_(Not_Constantinople).
5 For an analysis of the relationship between geography and cosmopolitanism, see D. Harvey, *Cosmopolitanism and the Geographies of Freedom* (New York, 2009).
6 N. Brenner and R. Keil illustrate this issue in their introduction to *The Global Cities Reader* (London and New York, 2006), pp. 12–13.
7 For an assessment of the impact of this cosmopolitan vision of Istanbul on its urban politics and policies, see S. T. Rosenthal, *The Politics of Dependency: Urban Reform in Istanbul* (Westport, CT, 1980). And also A. Mango, 'Istanbul Lives', in *The Turks Today* (Woodstock and New York, 2004), pp. 189–206.
8 See for example D. Abulafia, *The Mediterranean in History* (Los Angeles, CA, 2003).
9 The analysis of the sixteenth- and seventeenth-century governance comes from R. M. Unger, *Plasticity into Power: Comparative-Historical Studies on the Institutional Conditions of Economic and Military Success* (Cambridge and New York, 1987).
10 See for example D. R. Khoury, *State And Provincial Society In The Ottoman Empire: Mosul, 1540–1834* (Cambridge, 1997), and H. Watenpaugh, *The Image of an Ottoman City, Imperial Architecture and Urban Experience in Aleppo in the 16th and 17th Centuries*, (Leiden and Boston, 2004).
11 For a critical assessment of the nineteenth-century model, see J. Hanssen, T. Philipp and S. Weber, eds, *The Empire in the City, Arab Provincial Capitals in the Late Ottoman Empire* (Beirut, 2002), pp. 1–25.
12 Ibid. See also T. Philipp, *Acre: The Rise and Fall of an Palestinian City, 1730-1831* (New York, 2002). On the clock towers in the late-nineteenth century and early-twentieth century Ottoman modernization efforts see J. Hansen, *Fin de Siécle Beirut: The Making of an Ottoman Provincial Capital* (Oxford, 2005). See also S. Tamari, 'Riffraff', in P. Misselwitz and T. Rieniets, eds, *City of Collision, Jerusalem and the Principles of Conflict Urbanism* (Basel/Boston/Berlin, 2006), pp. 305–12.
13 For a good account of this period see D. Fromkin, *A Peace to End All Peace: The Fall of the Ottoman Empire and the Creation of the Modern Middle East*, (New York, 1989).
14 G. E. Fuller, *The New Turkish Republic, Turkey as a Pivotal State in the Muslim World*, (Washington DC, 2008), pp. 19–23. See also R. Khalidi et al., eds, *The Origins of Arab Nationalism* (New York, 1991).
15 This initiative was actively undertaken between the Syrian and Turkish prime ministers during the Turkish Arab Economic Forum of 2009.
16 See H. Kaptan and Z. Merey Enlil, 'Istanbul: Global Aspirations and Socio-Spatial Restructuring in an Era of New Internationalism' in *A Turkish Triangle: Ankara, Istanbul and Izmir at the Gates of Europe* (Cambridge, MA, 2009), p. 27.
17 M. E. Yapp, *The Near East Since the First World War, A History to 1995* (London and New York, 1996), p. 147. A UN population survey.
18 M. S. Abdu et al., 'Jeddah Urban Growth and Development Process: The Underlying Factors', *Scientific Journal of King Faisal University*, Vol. 3, No. 1, March 2002, pp. 111–36.
19 H. Kaptan and Z. Merey Enlil, op. cit.
20 http://whc.unesco.org/en/list.
21 T. Mitchell, *Rule of Experts, Egypt, Techno-Politics, Modernity* (Berkeley/Los Angeles/London, 2002), p. 287.
22 Fuller, op. cit., p. 84.
23 The 3rd Turkish Arab Economic Forum, 12–13 June 2008, conference brochure, p. 4.
24 For an insightful essay on the formation of this model see N. Turan, 'The Dubai Effect Archipelago', in A. Kanna, ed., *The Superlative City: Dubai and the Urban Condition in the Early Twenty-First Century* (Cambridge, MA, 2009).
25 Mitchell, op. cit., pp. 272–5.
26 Fuller, op. cit., p. 125.
27 See F. Braudel, *The Mediterranean and the Mediterranean World in the Age of Philip II* (New York, 1973).
28 I have greatly benefited from the feedback of several colleagues, namely Sibel Bozdoğan, Shirine Hamadeh, Gülru Necipoglu, Nasser Rabbat, and Neyran Turan. The responses of the participants in the Urban Age Istanbul Conference, particularly Ayşe Öncü, have been very helpful in reworking the essay for publication. This essay is dedicated to the memory of Wissam Ezzeddine, who opened my eyes to Istanbul.

THE VIOLENCE OF CHANGE / Asu Aksoy
1 Ç. Keyder, 'Globalization and Social Exclusion in Istanbul', *International Journal of Urban and Regional Research*, Vol. 29, No. 1, 2005, p. 130.
2 A. Alp and O. Şentürk, 'İstanbul'da 1 Milyon ev yıkılacak', *Ekonomist*, 11 November 2007.
3 E. Boztepe, 'Topbaş: İstanbul'un trafik sorununu çözmek için 15 milyar dolar lazım', *Radikal*, 2 January 2007.
4 A. Aksoy, and K. Robins, 'Istanbul between Civilization and Discontent', *New Perspectives on Turkey*, No. 10, Spring 1994.
5 S. Menkes, 'A futuristic mall is new Turkish playground', *International Herald Tribune*, 4 December 2006.
6 IMP, 'İstanbul Çevre Düzeni Planı: Özet Raporu', Istanbul, July 2006.
7 E. Boztepe, op. cit.
8 F. Özkan, 'Vatandaş Omuz Vermezse Kentsel Dönüşüme 500Yıl da Yetmez' [If Citizens do not lend support, even 500 years will not be enough for urban regeneration], *Radikal*, 10 January 2008.
9 G. Uras, '"İstanbul" un Marka Değerini Düşürüyoruz' [We are reducing Istanbul's brand value], *Milliyet*, 26 December 2007.
10 O. Esen, 'The tightrope walk of the middle class in a fractured Istanbul', in *Writings from the 9th International Istanbul Biennial* (Istanbul, 2005).
11 D. Behar and T. İslam, eds, *Istanbul'da 'Soylulaştırma'* ('Gentrification' in Istanbul) (İstanbul, 2006). See also O. Işık, and M. Pınarcıoğlu, *Nöbetleşe Yoksulluk* (Poverty in Turn) (Istanbul, 2001); H. Kurtuluş, ed., *Istanbul'da Kentsel Ayrışma* (Urban Polarization in Istanbul) (Istanbul, 2005); *Art, City and Politics in an Expanding World: Writings from the 9th International Istanbul Biennale* (Istanbul, 2005).
12 'The Worrying Tayyip Erdoğan', *The Economist*, 27 November 2008.
13 N. Smith, 'Which new urbanism? The revanchist '90s', *Perspecta*, Vol. 30, 1999, pp. 98–105.

THE CONTOURS OF CONCRETE / Ömer Kanıpak
1 See http://www.worldvaluessurvey.org/ [6 August 2010] and http://www.bilgicagi.com/Yazilar/2027-hosgorusuzluk_ve_guvensizlik_toplumsal_karakterimizde_var.aspx [6 August 2010].

NO FRILLS AND BARE LIFE / Alejandro Zaero-Polo
This text was first published in issue No. 18 of *Log* Journal.
1 The relationship between merchandise and political culture has been widely analyzed in other economic contexts, in particular the American post-war period. See W. Leach, *Land of Desire: Merchants, Power, and the Rise of a New American Culture* (New York, 1994).
2 L. Cohen, *A Consumers' Republic: The Politics of Mass Consumption in Postwar America* (New York, 2003).
3 R. Booth, 'Tory controlled borough of Barnet adopts budget airline model', *The Guardian*, 27 August 2009.
4 G. Agamben, *Homo Sacer: Sovereign Power and Bare Life*, trans. Daniel Heller-Roazen (Palo Alto, CA, 1998), p. 44.
5 In his book *The State of Exception*, Agamben questions Carl Schmitt's crypto-totalitarian legitimization of the suspension of individual rights by the state, an excess of power implicit in sovereignty. See G. Agamben, *State of Exception*, trans. Kevin Attell (Chicago, 2005).
6 Peter Sloterdijk uses the term explicitation as an alternative process to revolution and emancipation. The history of explicitation is made increasingly intelligible in the spheres and objects to which we are attached. The categories of the French Revolution and left and right, each with their particular techniques of classification and of positioning, no longer correspond to the order of things, itself no longer hierarchical but heterarchical. Whether we talk about carbon footprints, deregulation, genetically modified foods, congestion pricing, or public transport, these issues give rise to a variety of political configurations that exceed the left-right distinction. The left-right divide still exists, but has been diluted by a multitude of alternative attitudes. See P. Sloterdijk, *ESFERAS III. Espumas. Esferologia plural* (Madrid, 2006). 'Explicitation' is derived from Sloterdijk's term *explikation*, and as a neologism is best rendered in English as such, versus 'explication', which is merely to explain.
7 Considered a boon to the Los Angeles economy, American Apparel recently was required to fire a significant portion of its workforce, as it was inordinately stacked with 'undocumented workers'. While not in any way diminishing their reputation, or perhaps instead perversely enhancing it, the reliance on, in this case, well-paid but copious urban labour is part of the new model called 'vertical integration'.
8 *This is Not a Time for Dreaming* (2004) was commissioned by Harvard University to mark the 40th anniversary of the Carpenter Center. In Huyghe's version, a bird flies by and drops a single seed and the Carpenter Center is engulfed in vines and all but disappears.

CITY SOLUTIONS TO GLOBAL PROBLEMS / Nicholas Stern, Dimitri Zhengelis and Philipp Rode
1 World Bank, *Cities and Climate Change: An Urgent Agenda* (Washington DC, 2010).
2 D. Hoornweg, L. Sugar, & C. L. Trejos Gómez, 'Cities and Greenhouse Gas Emissions: Moving Forward', *Environment & Urbanization* (forthcoming at date of print).
3 T. Litman, 'Understanding Smart Growth Savings. What We Know About Public Infrastructure and Service Cost Savings, And How They are Misrepresented by Critics', (Victoria, BC, 2009), available from http://www.vtpi.org/documents/smart.php.
4 Sedegly and Elmslie present evidence to show that agglomeration economies far outweigh congestion effects in dense cities. See N. Sedegly and B. Elmslie, 'The Geographic Concentration of Knowledge: Scale, Agglomeration, and Congestion in Innovation across U.S. States', *International Regional Science Review*, Vol. 27, No. 2, pp. 111–37.

5 L. Kamal-Chaoui and A. Robert, eds, 'Competitive Cities and Climate Change', *OECD Regional Development Working Papers*, No. 2 (Paris, 2009), pp.16. See also D. Strumsky, J. Lobo and L. Fleming, *Metropolitan Patenting, Inventor Agglomeration and Social Networks: A Tale of Two Effects*, (Los Alamos, NM, 2004).
6 Two separate studies conducted for the OECD outline the numerous co-benefits of climate action at the urban level. See also S. Hallegatte, F. Henriet and J. Corfee-Morlot, *The Economics of Climate Change Impacts and Policy Benefits at City Scale: A Conceptual Framework* (Paris, 2008). And also J. Bollen, B. Guay, S. Jamet and J. Corfee-Morlot, *Co-benefits of Climate Change Mitigation Policies: Literature Review and New Results* (Paris, 2009),
7 R. Montezuma, 'The Transformation of Bogotá, Colombia, 1995-2000: Investing in Citizenship and Urban Mobility', *Global Urban Development magazine*, Vol. 1, No. 1, 2005, p. 6.
8 See C. Dora, 'Health Effects', *Seminar*, No. 579, 2007, pp. 26–30. And C. Dora, 'Health burden of urban transport: The technical challenge', *Sādhanā*, Vol. 32, No. 4, 2007, pp. 285–92.
9 See 'The Eddington Transport Study: The case for action: Sir Rod Eddington's advice to Government' (December 2006), Executive Summary, p. 5, UK Department for Transport, www.dft.gov.uk/162259/187604/206711/executivesummary.
10 World Bank, *Cities on the Move: A World Bank Urban Transport Strategy Review* (Washington DC, 2002). Also available on http://siteresources.worldbank.org/INTURBANTRANSPORT/Resources/cities_on_the_move.pdf.
11 Transport for London, *Congestion Charging Central London – Impacts Monitoring: Second Annual Report* (London, April 2004), available on-line athttp://www.tfl.gov.uk/assets/downloads/Impacts-monitoring-report-2.pdf.
12 S. Beevers and D. Carslaw, 'The impact of congestion charging on vehicle emissions in London', *Atmospheric Environment*, No. 39, 2005, pp. 1–5. Also available on http://www.thepep.org/ClearingHouse/docfiles/congestion%20charge%20london.pdf.
13 A. Mahendra, 'Vehicle Restrictions in Four Latin American Cities: Is Congestion Pricing Possible?', *Transport Reviews*, Vol. 28, No. 1, 2008, pp. 105–33.
14 World Resource Institute, 'World Greenhouse Gas Emissions for 2005' (Washington DC, 2009).
15 *San Francisco Solar Power System (2004–2010)*, C40 Cities Climate Leadership Group, 2010. Available online: http://www.c40cities.org/bestpractices/buildings/sanfrancisco_eco.jsp).
16 Other energy related green strategies for cities include lake water air conditioning as implemented in Toronto and Amsterdam and seawater heating. Increasingly, smart grids and smart meters will play a key role in urban energy markets and can significantly reduce energy demand by providing more information to end-consumers.
17 C40 Cities Climate Leadership Group, 'Best Practices Copenhagen', 2010. Available online at http://www.c40cities.org/bestpractices/waste/.
18 World Resource Institute, 'World Greenhouse Gas Emissions for 2005'. Available online at http://pdf.wri.org/world_greenhouse_gas_emissions_2005_chart.pdf.
19 C40 Cities Climate Leadership Group, 'Best Practices Buildings', http://www.c40cities.org/bestpractices/buildings/.
20 See D. Hoornweg et al, 'City Indicators: Now to Nanjing' (Washington DC, 2007).
21 Connected Urban Development, 2010, available on http://www.connectedurbandevelopment.org/blog/?cat=12.
22 See N. Stern, *A Blueprint for a Safer Planet* (London, 2009).
23 See http://www.nextgenpe.com/news/global-green-investments [4 January 2011].

DEMOCRACY AND GOVERNANCE / Gerald E. Frug
1 J. Friedmann, 'The World City Hypothesis', in P. Knox and P. Taylor, *World Cities in a World System* (Cambridge, 1995), p. 317.
2 See for example A. Appadurai, 'Deep Democracy: Urban Governmentality and the Horizon of Politics', *Public Culture*, Vol. 14, No. 21, 2002, p. 24.
3 F. Erkip, 'Global Transformations Versus Local Dynamics in Istanbul: Planning in a Fragmented Metropolis', *Cities*, Vol. 17, No. 5, 2000, p. 317.
4 S. Erder, 'Local Governance in Istanbul', in *Istanbul: City of Intersections* (London, 2009), p. 46.
5 See Friedmann, op. cit. and S. Sassen, *The Global City*, second edition (New York, 2001).

UNEVEN LANDSCAPES / Sophie Body-Gendrot
1 See S. Body-Gendrot, 'A plea for urban disorder', *British Journal of Sociology*, Vol. 60, No. 1, 2009, p. 72.
2 See P. Wilkinson and K. Pickett, *The Spirit Level* (London, 2010), p. 250.
3 See the table on page 301 for the GINI data.
4 See A. Bertho, *Le temps des émeutes* (Paris, 2009), pp. 58–9.
5 See E. Weede, 'Some new evidence on correlates of political violence: income inequality regime repressiveness, and economic development', *European Sociological Review*, Vol. 3, No. 2, September 1987, pp. 97–108.
6 See S. Sassen, 'When the City Itself Becomes a Technology of War', in *Theory, Culture & Society*, Vol. 27, No. 5, 2010, pp. 1–18.
7 See A. Appadurai, *Fear of Small Numbers* (Durham, 2007), p. 124.
8 See Sassen, op. cit.
9 See L. Weinstein, 'Mumbai's Development Mafias: Globalization, Organized Crime and Land Development', in *International Journal of Urban and Regional Research*, Vol. 32, No. 1, March 2008, pp. 22–39.
10 See Weinstein, op. cit., p. 29.
11 See Sassen, op.cit.
12 See T. Caldeira, this volume, pp. 168–175
13 R.J. Sampson, 'Disparity and Diversity in the contemporary city: social disorder (re) visited', *British Journal of Sociology*, Vol. 60, No. 1, 2009, pp.1–31.
14 See T. Caldeira, this volume, pp. 168–175
15 See Sassen, op. cit.
16 See M. Poyraz, 'La jeunesse des varos d'Istanbul et des quartiers dits sensibles en banlieue parisienne', Sociétés et jeunesses en difficulté (available online) http//:sejed.revues.org/index 6651.htlm [8 November 2010].
17 See Wilkinson and Pickett, op. cit., p. 264.

FROM UTOPIA TO YOUTOPIA / Alejandro Aravena
1 We will focus here on the housing projects that Elemental has developed. For more information about other urban projects in areas like infrastructure, public space or transportation, visit www.elementalchile.cl.
2 As Hernando de Soto has said in *The Mystery of Capital* (New York, 2000).

SURVIVING IN AN URBAN AGE / David Satterthwaite
1 See the website of the Centre on Housing Rights and Evictions http://www.cohre.org/GFEP for many reports on this; see also G. Bhan, 'This is no longer the city I once knew; Evictions, the urban poor and the right to the city in Millennial Delhi', in *Environment and Urbanization*, Vol. 21, No. 1, 2009, pp. 127–42.
2 A. Portes, 'Housing policy, urban poverty and the state: the favelas of Rio de Janeiro', *Latin American Research Review*, No. 14, Summer 1979, pp. 3–24; J. E. Hardoy and D. Satterthwaite *Squatter Citizen: Life in the Urban Third World* (London, 1989).
3 ACHR/Asian Coalition for Housing Rights, 'Evictions in Seoul, South Korea', *Environment and Urbanization*, Vol. 1, No. 1, 1989, pp. 89–94.
4 A. K. Tibaijuka, *Report of the Fact-Finding Mission to Zimbabwe to Assess the Scope and Impact of Operation Murambatsvina* (New York, 2009).
5 Bhan, op. cit.
6 UN-Habitat, *Water and Sanitation in the World's Cities; Local Action for Global Goals*, (London, 2003).
7 I. Douglas et al., 'Unjust waters: climate change, flooding and the urban poor in Africa', *Environment and Urbanization*, Vol. 20, No. 1, 2008, pp. 187–206; H. Jabeen, A. Allen and C. Johnson, 'Built-in resilience: learning from grassroots coping strategies to climate variability', *Environment and Urbanization*, Vol. 22, No. 2, 2010.
8 See references in note 7; also C. Stephens, R. Patnaik and S. Lewin, *This is My Beautiful Home: Risk Perceptions towards Flooding and Environment in Low Income Urban Communities: A Case Study in Indore, India* (London, 1996).
9 P. Bairoch, *Cities and Economic Development: From the Dawn of History to the Present* (London, 1988).
10 T. Baumann, J. Bolnick and D. Mitlin, 'The age of cities and organizations of the urban poor: the work of the South African Homeless People's Federation', in D. Mitlin and D. Satterthwaite, eds, *Empowering Squatter Citizen; Local Government, Civil Society and Urban Poverty Reduction* (London, 2004), pp. 193–215.
11 E. Mageli, 'Housing mobilization in Calcutta: empowerment for the masses or awareness for the few?', *Environment and Urbanization* Vol. 16, No. 1, 2004, pp. 129–38; A. Pal, 'Scope for bottom-up planning in Kolkata: rhetoric vs reality', *Environment and Urbanization*, Vol. 18, No. 2, 2006, pp. 501–22.
12 Arputham, op cit.
13 S. Patel, C. d'Cruz and S. Burra, 'Beyond evictions in a global city; people-managed resettlement in Mumbai', *Environment and Urbanization*, Vol. 14, No. 1, 2002, pp. 159–72.
14 D. Mitlin, 'With and beyond the state; co-production as a route to political influence, power and transformation for grassroots organizations', *Environment and Urbanization* Vol. 20, No. 2, 2008, pp. 339–60; see also the website of Shack/Slum Dwellers International - http://www.sdinet.org/.
15 S. Burra, S. Patel and T. Kerr, 'Community-designed, built and managed toilet blocks in Indian cities', *Environment and Urbanization*, Vol. 15, No. 2, 2003, pp. 11–32; A. Roy, J. Arputhan, A. Javed, 'Community police stations in Mumbai's slums', *Environment and Urbanization*, Vol. 16, No. 2, 2004, pp. 135–38.
16 S. Boonyabancha, 'Baan Mankong; going to scale with "slum" and squatter upgrading in Thailand', *Environment and Urbanization*, Vol. 17, No. 1, 2005, pp. 21–46.
17 Mtafu A. Zeleza Manta, 'Mchenga – urban poor housing fund in Malawi', *Environment and Urbanization*, Vol. 19, No. 2, 2007, pp. 337–59.
18 B. Bradlow, J. Bolnick and C. Shearing, 'Housing, institutions, money: The failures and promise of human settlements policy and practice in South Africa', *Environment and Urbanization*, Vol. 23, No. 1, 2011.
19 D. Mitlin and A. Muller, 'Windhoek, Namibia: towards progressive urban land policies in Southern Africa', *International Development Planning Review*, Vol. 26, No. 2, 2004, pp. 167–86.
20 S. Patel and J. Arputham, 'An offer of partnership or a promise of conflict in Dharavi, Mumbai?', *Environment and Urbanization*, Vol. 19, No. 2, 2007, pp. 501–8.
21 S. Patel and J. Arputham, 'Recent developments in plans for Dharavi and for the airport slums in Mumbai', *Environment and Urbanization*, Vol. 22, No. 2, 2010.
22 Hardoy and Satterthwaite, op. cit.
23 In many low- and middle-income nations, urban poverty is greatly underestimated because poverty lines are set with little or no account taken of the costs low-income groups have to pay for housing, water, sanitation, health care, schools, transport and other non-food needs. If poverty lines are set too low, there can appear to be very little urban poverty when a large proportion of the urban population live in very poor quality accommodation, lacking infrastructure and services and with high levels of under-nutrition.

ON THE GROUND: THE DEUTSCHE BANK URBAN AGE AWARDS / Adam Kaasa with Marcos Rosa and Priya Shankar
1 UN-Habitat, State of the World's Cities 2010/2011: Bridging the Urban Divide (city, 2010), p. 32.
2 James Holston's work on insurgent citizenship is a useful framework for thinking through the ways in which minding the overlooked can help us reflect on our own assumptions about the guiding principles of our urban practices. Here, *insurgent* insists not in the moralizing right or wrong, but 'describes a process that is an acting counter, a counterpolitics, that destabilizes the present and renders it fragile, defamiliarizing the coherence with which it usually presents itself. ...In this view, the present is like a bog: leaky, full of holes, gaps, contradictions, and misunderstandings. These exist just beneath all the taken-for-granted assumptions that give the present its apparent consistency.' See James Holston, 2008, *Insurgent Citizenship: Disjunctions of Democracy and Modernity in Brazil*, (Princeton: Princeton UP), p. 34.
3 Jennifer Robinson, *Ordinary Cities: Between modernity and development*, (Routledge: Milton Park, 2006), p.64
4 Presentation by P.K. Das, Waterfront Expo International Conference and Exhibition, 2005, Riga, p. 3 accessed: www.pkdas.com/pdfs/Riga-WaterfrontExpo.pdf
5 See Data section of this book for full density data details, pp. 252–321.
6 For information on the Manhattan Waterfront Greenway project, please see http://www.nyc.gov/html/dcp/html/transportation/td_projectbicycle.shtml
7 World Health Organization and UNICEF, 2010, *Progress on Sanitation and Drinking-Water: 2010 Update*, WHO/UNICEF Joint Monitoring Programme for Water Supply and Sanitation, p. 6.
8 Ibid. p. 43.
9 H. Molotch and L. Noren, *Toilet: Public Restrooms and the Politics of Sharing* (New York, 2010), p. 8.
10 S. Gupta, 'Flush hour: The pot comes out of the closet', *Indian Express*, 18 August 2009, p.7. Available on-line at www.parodevi.com/pdfs/reviews_for_q2p.pdf [15 December 2010].
11 Author's translation. Original text: 'En la mayoría de las regiones en desarrollo del mundo, la proporción del espacio urbano "informal", es decir, sin atención profesional, alcanza ya casi el 70%. Estos habitantes de la ciudad, objetos de diferentes formas de segregación, principalmente la económica y política, sin servicios y ni viviendas dignas, no son los clientes de los profesionales de la ciudad, pero podrían llegar a serlo. Los diseños arquitectónicos y la gestión urbana, tal como se practican actualmente, están lejos de ofrecer soluciones viables a los problemas básicos de nuestras ciudades.' G Solinis, Keynote at UNESCO, Professionals in the City conference, São Paulo, Brazil, 26–9 June 2002. Available on-line at http://www.unesco.org/most/cityprofs2002_informe.htm [[16 December 2010].
12 See http://www.amnesty.org.uk/actions_details.asp?ActionID=251; http://www.guardian.co.uk/world/2006/jan/23/brazil.uknews1; http://www.independent.co.uk/news/world/americas/the-two-faces-of-sao-paulo-439849.html; http://news.bbc.co.uk/1/hi/world/americas/6563359.stm.
13 The *cortiço* has a long history dating back to the final decades of the nineteenth century when rapid immigration diversified the Brazilian population and labour force. In 1890, foreshadowing later works depicting urban conditions in twentieth-century Boston, Chicago and New York, Aluísio Azevedo wrote *O Cortiço* (*The Slum*). The book weaves a tale of nineteenth-century new migrants in a Rio de Janeiro slum, their living conditions, differences, and accentuations of class and race. The hidden character of the story is the *cortiço*.
14 See United Nations Human Settlements Programme, 2003, *The Challenge of Slums: Global Report on Human Settlements 2003*, pp. 226–7.
15 Ibid.
16 See UN-Habitat and Fundacao Sistema Estadual de Analise de Dados (SEADE), 'São Paulo: A Tale of Two Cities' in *Cities & Citizens Series: Bridging the Urban Divide*, 2010, pp. 112–7.
17 Ibid.
18 For a full overview of the project, see the review by project leader Professor Maria Ruth Amaral de Sampaio of FAU-USP here: http://www.usp.br/prc/revista/pp1.html
19 See UN-Habitat and Fundacao Sistema Estadual de Analise de Dados (SEADE), op. cit., p. 76.
20 Ibid. pp. 112–7.
21 Ibid. p. 36.
22 Ibid. pp. 52 and 70.
23 D. Harvey, 'The Right to the City', *New Left Review*, Vol. 53, September–October 2008, p. 1.
24 'PM apreende armas e drogas em favela da zona sul de SP', *Folha de São Paulo*, 2 August 2002, http://www1.folha.uol.com.br/folha/cotidiano/ult95u56138.shtml.
25 Friedensreich Hundertwasser's (1928–2000) right to the window centred on the firm belief that anyone renting housing should be able to lean out of the window and paint the surface of the building within arm's reach in an effort to appear as a creative and present agent within larger structures of space. His 'tree duty' from 1972 called upon urban residents to plant trees as an obligation. See *Catalogue Raisonné Friedensreich Hundertwasser* (Cologne, 2003).
26 See http://www.itu.com.br/conteudo/detalhe.asp?cod_conteudo=11500.
27 See press release http://www.revistasustentabilidade.com.br/noticias/copy2_of_cdhu-owens-illinois-e-cooperativa-de-catadores-lancam-projeto-de-coleta-de-vidro.
28 S. Sassen, 'Analytic Borderlands: Race, Gender and Representation in the New City', in A. D. King, ed., *Re-Presenting the City: Ethnicity, Capital and Culture in the 21st-Century Metropolis* (New York, 1996), p. 196.
29 Ibid., p. 184.
30 N. G. Canclini, 'Makeshift Globalization', in R. Burdett and D. Sudjic, *The Endless City* (London, 2008), p. 188.
31 Ibid., 191.
32 See http://comunidadmiravalle.blogspot.com/p/quienes-somos.html.
33 See http://www.bbc.co.uk/news/world-latin-america-12012425.
34 See http://www.iraqbodycount.org/.

CREDITS

264–265: The changing nature of urban work – Mumbai: Population and Employment Profile of Mumbai Metropolitan Region, Mumbai Metropolitan Region Development Agency, 2003, http://www.mmrdamumbai.org/docs/Population%20and%20Employment%20profile%20of%20MMR.pdf; São Paulo: Pesquisas, Cadastral Centro De Empresas, Tabela 1735, Sistema IGBE de Recuperação Automática (SIDRA), http://www.sidra.ibge.gov.br/bda/tabela/listabl.asp?z=p&o=1&i=P&c=1734; Istanbul: Eurostat, http://epp.eurostat.ec.europa.eu/portal/page/portal/statistics/search_database; New York City: Quarterly Census of Employment and Wages (QCEW), http://www.labor.ny.gov/stats/ins.asp; Shanghai: China Statistical Yearbook, 2009, http://www.stats.gov.cn/tjsj/ndsj/2009/html/E0410e.xls; London: Eurostat, http://epp.eurostat.ec.europa.eu/portal/page/portal/statistics/search_database; Mexico City: INEGI, 2004, http://www.inegi.gob.mx/est/contenidos/espanol/proyectos/censos/ce2004/pdfs/CT_DF.pdf; Johannesburg: Statssa Interactive, Labour Force Survey 2007, Average Values of March and September 2007, http://interactive.statssa.gov.za:8282/webview/; Berlin: Eurostat, http://epp.eurostat.ec.europa.eu/portal/page/portal/statistics/search_database. Please note the percentages in the inner circle of each chart have been rounded up to the nearest whole number.

266–285: Capturing Urban Density and Density Peak points – all density graphics have been prepared by Urban Age with the data retrieved from local census statistics.

286–287: Infrastructure of Mobility – all maps are drawn with data gathered from local data sources regarding transport networks. Most of the transport network lines are originated from GIS-based drawings supplied by official sources. Where this is not the case, they have been drawn to represent the real network lines in the most accurate way possible. All maps are drawn to the same scale.

288–289: Travelling to Work – Mumbai: Data received by Urban Age from the Jurisdiction of Municipal Corporation of Greater Mumbai, 2007; São Paulo: Companhia do Metropolitano de São Paulo, http://www.metro.sp.gov.br/empresa/pesquisas/od_2007/teod.asp?act=dw&cnpj=LSE&arq=viagens_atracao_modo.xls; Istanbul: Information has been provided by Mr. Muzaffer Hacimustafaoglu, Head of the Transport Department of Istanbul Metropolitan Municipality, at an interview held on 15 October 2008; New York City: U.S. Census Bureau, 2008 American Community Survey, American Factfinder, http://factfinder.census.gov/servlet/DTGeoSearchByListServlet?ds_name=ACS_2007_1YR_G00_&_lang=en&_ts=260173996650; Shanghai: Information retrieved from a presentation by Professor Xiaohong Chen at the School of Transportation Engineering, Tongji University, 2006; London: Transport For London: Travel in London, Report 2, http://www.tfl.gov.uk/assets/downloads/corporate/Travel_in_London_Report_2.pdf; Mexico City: Secretaria de Communicaciones y Transportes, http://www.setravi.df.gob.mx/wb/stv/programa_integral_de_transportes_y_vialidad; City of Johannesburg, Intergrated Transport Plan 2003/2008, http://www.joburg-archive.co.za/2007/pdfs/transport/vol1/statusquo5.pdf; Berlin, Urban Audit, http://www.urbanaudit.org/index.aspx.

290–291: Connecting Density to Public Transport – data on all of the maps are a combination of the data used for Capturing Urban Density and Density Peak points (pp. 266–285) and Infrastructure of Mobility (pp. 286–287).

293: Current population in the city - figures correspond to population figures that fall within the areas covered for the respective cities' maps displayed in Urban Footprint: Mapping People and Power (pp. 254–255).

293: Current population in the metropolitan region – Mumbai: MCGM – Greater Mumbai City Development Plan (2005 to 2025), chapter 2, Table 5, http://www.mcgm.gov.in/irj/portalapps/com.mcgm.ahome_keyprojects/docs/2-1%20Demography.pdf; São Paulo: IBGE 2007 Population Count, http://www.ibge.gov.br/home/estatistica/populacao/contagem2007/defaulttab.shtm; Istanbul: State Institute of Statistics, Turkey; New York City: U.S. Census Bureau, 2007 American Community Survey, American Factfinder, http://factfinder.census.gov/servlet/DTGeoSearchByListServlet?ds_name=ACS_2007_1YR_G00_&_lang=en&_ts=260173996650, Shanghai: http://www.stats.gov.cn/tjsj/ndsj/2007/indexeh.htm; London: http://www.london.gov.uk/gla/publications/factsandfigures/DMAG-Update-14.pdf; Mexico City: Gobierno de Mexico, CONAPO, http://www.conapo.gob.mx/index.php?option=com_content&view=article&id=133&Itemid=212, Johannesburg: Statistics South Africa, Community Survey, 2007, http://www.statsonline.gov.za/publications/statsdownload.asp?ppn=P0301.1&SCH=4117; Berlin: http://www.stadtentwicklung.berlin.de/archiv/metropolis2005/de/berlin/.

293: Central area density (people per km^2) – All figures are derived from calculations done with the data used for the density information (pp. 266–285) and census data (p. 293) for all cities.

293: Projected growth 2010–2025 (people per hour) – 2009 Revision of World Urbanization Prospects, United Nations, 2009, http://esa.un.org/unpd/wup/.

296: City as a percentage of national population – all figures are derived from calculations done with the data on population census statistics of all cities and their respective countries.

296: GDP per capita (US$) – Mumbai: http://mu.ac.in/arts/social_science/economics/pdf/vibhuti/wp18.pdf; São Paulo: http://www.ibge.gov.br/home/estatistica/economia/pibmunicipios/2006/tab01.pdf; Istanbul: http://tuikapp.tuik.gov.tr/ulusalgostergeler/menuAction.do; New York City: http://www.comptroller.nyc.gov/cnote/economic-indicators/122208/12-22-08_gcp.pdf; Shanghai: http://www.stats-sh.gov.cn/2003shtj/tjnj/nje06.htm?d1=2006tjnje/E0401.htm; London: http://www.statistics.gov.uk/statbase/tsdtables1.asp?vlnk=ragv; Mexico City: http://dgcnesyp.inegi.gob.mx/cgi-win/bdieintsi.exe/NIVM150002000700100005#ARBOL; Johannesburg: http://www.joburg-archive.co.za/2007/pdfs/joburg_overview2.pdf; Berlin: https://www-genesis.destatis.de/genesis/online/logon?language=en.

296: City as a percentage of national GDP: the figures are derived from calculations done with the data on GDP of the cities and their respective countries where the data were collected from sources that are the same for the city and the country in some instances but different in others. Therefore the full account of the information on the data sources for the countries' GDPs for their respective cities are as follows: Mumbai: http://mospi.nic.in/6_gsdp_cur_9394ser.htm; São Paulo: http://www.ibge.gov.br/home/estatistica/economia/pibmunicipios/2006/tab01.pdf; Istanbul: http://www.tuik.gov.tr/PrelstatistikTablo.do?istab_id=533; New York City: http://www.bea.gov/national/xls/gdplev.xls; Shanghai: http://chinadataonline.org/member/macroy/macroytshow.asp?code=A0101; London: http://www.statistics.gov.uk/statbase/tsdtables1.asp?vlnk=ragv; Mexico City: http://dgcnesyp.inegi.gob.mx/cgi-win/bdieintsi.exe/NIVM150002000700100005#ARBOL; Johannesburg: http://www.joburg-archive.co.za/2007/pdfs/joburg_overview2.pdf; Berlin: https://www-genesis.destatis.de/genesis/online/logon?language=en.

296: Average annual growth in GVA 1993 – 2010: the figures have been generated by the research made by the LSE Cities as indicated for Where Urban Economies Are Going map (pp. 38–39).

301: Percentage of the population under 20 – please see Signs of Ageing (pp. 260–261).

301: Income inequality (measured by the GINI Index) – Mumbai: http://www.wider.unu.edu/publications/working-papers/research-papers/2004/en_GB/rp2004-053/; São Paulo: http://www.earthscan.co.uk/Portals/0/Files/SotWC%20Data%20Tables/3.%20Gini%20in%20capital%202.pdf, OECD Territorial review Istanbul, Turkey, p. 99; New York City: U.S. Census Bureau, 2007 American Community Survey, American Factfinder, http://factfinder.census.gov/servlet/DTGeoSearchByListServlet?ds_name=ACS_2007_1YR_G00_&_lang=en&_ts=260173996650; Shanghai: http://www.uic.edu/depts/soci/xmchen/Chen-NewShanghai.pdf; London: http://www3.interscience.wiley.com/cgi-bin/fulltext/118502820/PDFSTART; Mexico City: http://www.earthscan.co.uk/Portals/0/Files/SotWC%20Data%20Tables/3.%20Gini%20in%20capital%202.pdf; Johannesburg: http://www.earthscan.co.uk/Portals/0/Files/SotWC%20Data%20Tables/3.%20Gini%20in%20capital%202.pdf.

301: Human Development Index – please see The Human Potential of Cities (pp. 40–41).

301: Murder rate (homicides per 100,000 inhabitants) – Mumbai: http://www.mumbaipolice.org/statistics.htm; São Paulo: http://www9.prefeitura.sp.gov.br/sempla/md/index.php?pageNum_sql=1&totalRows_sql=63&texto=table; Istanbul: State Institute of Statistics, Turkey, http://tuikapp.tuik.gov.tr/Bolgesel/menuAction.do; New York City: http://nyc.gov/html/nypd/downloads/pdf/crime_statistics/cscity.pdf; Shanghai: http://www.stats-sh.gov.cn/2003shtj/tjnj/nje06.htm?d1=2006tjnje/E2405.htm; London: http://maps.met.police.uk/datatables/2006-07.xls; Mexico City: http://www.inegi.org.mx/est/contenidos/espanol/rutinas/ept.asp?t=mvio31&s=est&c=7040&e=09; Johannesburg: http://www.saps.gov.za/statistics/reports/crimestats/2007/_pdf/province/gauteng/johannesburg/johannesburg_area_total.pdf; Berlin: http://www.statistik-berlin-brandenburg.de/produkte/jahrbuch/jb2008/BE_Jahrbuch_2008.pdf.

304: Percentage of daily trips on foot or by cycle – please see Travelling to Work (pp. 288–289).

304: Rail network system length (km) – please see Infrastructure of Mobility (pp. 286–287).

304: Metro ticket price in 2010 (US$) – Mumbai: http://www.mumbaimetro1.com/HTML/faqs.html#q5; São Paulo: http://www.metro.sp.gov.br/informacao/tarifas/exclusivo/teexclusivo.shtml; Istanbul: http://www.istanbul-ulasim.com.tr/default.asp?page=yolcuhizmetleri&category=ucrettarifeleri; New York City: http://www.mta.info/metrocard/mcgtreng.htm; Shanghai: http://www.urbanrail.net/as/shan/shanghai.htm; London: http://www.tfl.gov.uk/tickets/14416.aspx; Mexico City: http://www.metro.df.gob.mx/red/index.html#c; Berlin: http://www.bvg.de/index.php/de/3786/name/Tarifuebersicht.html

304: Car ownership rate (per 1,000 inhabitants) – Mumbai: http://unpan1.un.org/intradoc/groups/public/documents/apcity/unpan030171.pdf; São Paulo: http://www.denatran.gov.br/download/frota/Frota2007.zip; Istanbul: http://tuikrapor.tuik.gov.tr/reports/rwservlet?ulastirmadb2=&report=tablo22.RDF&p_yil1=2009&p_ar1=1&p_ay1=12&p_tur=2&p_duz1=TR1&desformat=pdf&ENVID=ulastirmadb2Env; New York City: http://nydmv.state.ny.us/Statistics/regin08.htm; Shanghai: http://www.stats-sh.gov.cn/2003shtj/tjnj/nje07.htm?d1=2007tjnje/e1409.htm; London: http://www.dft.gov.uk/excel/173025/221412/221552/228038/458107/datatables2008.xls; Mexico City: http://www.inegi.org.mx/est/contenidos/espanol/proyectos/continuas/economicas/bd/transporte/vehiculos.asp?s=est&c=13158#; Johannesburg: http://www.transport.gov.za/library/docs/stats/2001/table2.3a.pdf; Berlin: http://www.statistik-berlin-brandenburg.de/produkte/jahrbuch/jb2008/BE_Jahrbuch_2008.pdf

307: Annual waste production (kg per capita) – Mumbai: S. Rathi, optimization model for integrated municipal solid waste management in Mumbai India, in *Environment and Development Economics*, 2007, Volume 12, Issue 01, pp. 105–121; São Paulo: http://sempla.prefeitura.sp.gov.br/infocidade/tabelas/11_coleta_de_lixo_segundo_origem_1980_557.xls; Istanbul: TUIK 2006; New York City: http://www.nyc.gov/html/planyc2030/downloads/pdf/emissions_inventory.pdf; Shanghai: http://www.iges.or.jp/en/ue/activity/mega-city/article/pdf/far46.pdf; London: http://www.citylimitslondon.com/downloads/Complete%20report.pdf; Mexico City: http://www.clintonfoundation.org/what-we-do/clinton-climate-initiative/i/mexico-city-waste-management; Johannesburg: http://www.joburg-archive.co.za/2007/pdfs/sector_plans/environment.pdf; Berlin: http://www.wu-wien.ac.at/itnp/downloads/kongress2007/05berlin-en.pdf

307: Daily water consumption (litres per capita) - Mumbai: http://www.thehindubusinessline.com/2005/04/02/stories/2005040201460900.htm; São Paulo: http://www.sabesp.com/br/CalandraWeb/CalandraRedirect/?temp=4&proj=sabesp&pub=T&db=&docid=1E088E6DDF9CEF7F8325734E00545EE2; Istanbul: Data received from ISKI over an email exchange, 2009; New York City: http://www.nyc.gov/html/dep/html/drinking_water/droughthist.shtml; Shanghai: http://www.stats-sh.gov.cn/2003shtj/tjnj/nje06.htm?d1=2006tjnje/E1109.htm; London: http://www.city-data.com/world-cities/Mexico-City-Environment.html; Mexico City: http://www.city-data.com/world-cities/Mexico-City-Environment.html; Berlin: http://www.bvsde.paho.org/bvsacd/cd63/measures.pdf

307: Annual electricity use (kWh per capita) - Mumbai: http://unpan1.un.org/intradoc/groups/public/documents/apcity/unpan030171.pdf; São Paulo: http://www.seade.gov.br/index.php; Istanbul: TUIK 2007; New York City: http://www.nyc.gov/html/planyc2030/downloads/pdf/progress_2008_energy.pdf; Shanghai: http://www.stats-sh.gov.cn/2003shtj/tjnj/nje06.htm?d1=2006tjnje/E1109.htm; London: http://www.citylimitslondon.com/downloads/Complete%20report.pdf; Johannesburg: http://www.joburg-archive.co.za/2009/pdfs/report_evironment/enviro_climatology.pdf; Berlin: http://www.statistik-berlin-brandenburg.de/Publikationen/Stat_Berichte/2008/SB_E4-4_j05_BE.pdf

307: Annual CO_2 emissions (kg per capita) – Mumbai: http://papers.ssrn.com/sol3/papers.cfm?abstract_id=999353; São Paulo: http://ww2.prefeitura.sp.gov.br/arquivos/secretarias/meio_ambiente/Sintesedoinventario.pdf; Istanbul: Data received from ISKI over an email exchange, 2009; New York City: http://www.nyc.gov/html/planyc2030/downloads/pdf/inventory_nyc_ghg_emissions_2008_-_feb09update_web.pdf; Shanghai: http://www.gcp-urcm.org/files/A20080204/Workshop/Li.pdf; London: http://www.citylimitslondon.com/downloads/Complete%20report.pdf; Mexico City: http://www.hewlett.org/AboutUs/News/Foundation+Newsletter/A+Breath+of+Fresh+Air+Mexico+City.htm; Johannesburg: http://www.joburg-archive.co.za/2009/pdfs/report_evironment/enviro_climatology.pdf; Berlin: http://www.statistik-berlin-brandenburg.de/Publikationen/Stat_Berichte/2008/SB_E4-4_j05_BE.pdf

310–320: All graphs are products of the Urban Age City Surveys research project. Data on Mumbai, São Paulo and Istanbul are part of the research done by Urban Age and Ipsos KMG. Data on London are part of the 2007 Greater London Authority Survey.

344: Relating Pollution To Affluence – Urban Age.

CONTRIBUTORS

Asu Aksoy is in charge of international project development at SantralIstanbul, a new international arts and culture initiative at Istanbul Bilgi University, and a visiting fellow at Goldsmiths College, London. Dr Aksoy's work focuses on urban and cultural transformation in the context of migration, globalization and technological change.

Alejandro Aravena is Director of ELEMENTAL S.A. a for-profit company with social interest working in projects of infrastructure, transportation, public space and housing. He founded Alejandro Aravena Architects in 1994, was a visiting professor at Harvard GSD between 2000 and 2005, and has been named an International Fellow of the Royal Institute of British Architects (RIBA).

Sophie Body-Gendrot is Director of the Center for Urban Studies at Université-Sorbonne-Paris IV and a CNRS researcher. Specializing in cross-national comparisons on urban violence and security, her research focuses also on the role of the state and public policies, social efficiency, the built environment, citizen participation and inclusive cities.

Ricky Burdett is Professor of Urban Studies at the London School of Economics and Political Science (LSE), Director of LSE Cities and the Urban Age programme. He has worked as Chief Adviser on Architecture and Urbanism for the London 2012 Olympics, as architectural adviser to the Mayor of London and advises the Olympic Park Legacy Company. He was Director of the 2006 Architecture Biennale in Venice, curator of 'Global Cities' at Tate Modern and is a member of the Milan Expo 2015 masterplan team.

Teresa Caldeira is a Professor of City and Regional Planning at the University of California, Berkeley. Caldeira's research addresses questions of social discrimination, spatial segregation, and urban change.

Fabio Casiroli is a Visiting Professor at DPA Milan Polytechnic. He is a founding partner of Systematica, an urban and transport planning consultancy, and the author of *Khrónopolis, Accessible City, Feasible City* (Viareggio, 2008).

Charles Correa is Principal and founder of Charles Correa Associates of Mumbai. His work covers a wide range, from the Mahatma Gandhi Memorial at the Sabarmati Ashram, to the State Assembly for Madhya Pradesh – as well as housing projects and townships in Delhi, Mumbai, Ahmedabad and Bangalore. He was Chief Architect for Navi Mumbai, the new city of 2 million people, and in 1985 Prime Minister Rajiv Gandhi appointed him Chairman of the National Commission on Urbanisation.

Darryl D'Monte, former Resident Editor of *The Times of India*, is the Chairman of the Forum of Environmental Journalists of India (FEJI) and writes a column on the environment and development.

Fernando de Mello Franco is Professor at São Judas Tadeu University in São Paulo. He co-founded MMBB Architects in 1990. He is a Design Critic in Landscape Architecture at the Harvard Graduate School of Design. He co-curated the exhibition 'São Paulo: networks and places' at the Venice Architecture Biennale in 2006 and also the travelling exhibition 'Coletivo: Contemporary Architecture from São Paulo'.

Gerald Frug is the Louis D. Brandeis Professor of Law at Harvard Law School. He worked as a Special Assistant to the Chairman of the Equal Employment Opportunity Commission, in Washington, DC, and as Health Services Administrator of the City of New York. He previously taught at the University of Pennsylvania Law School.

Gareth Jones is a Senior Lecturer at the LSE, and co-editor of the Cambridge University Press's *Journal of Latin American Studies*.

Adam Kaasa is a PhD candidate in the Cities Programme at the LSE with a focus on the circulations of ideas about architecture and urbanism. He is the Communications Manager at LSE Cities, and coordinates the NYLON seminars, a transatlantic intellectual working group between universities in and around London and New York.

Ömer Kanıpak founded Arkitera Architecture Center after taking his Master's degree from MIT School of Architecture. He has been responsible for the international relations and educational projects of the centre.

Bruce Katz is a Vice President at the Brookings Institution and founding Director of the Brookings Metropolitan Policy Program. He received the Heinz Award in Public Policy for his contributions to urban and metropolitan America. Katz served as Chief of Staff to Henry G. Cisneros, former Secretary of the US Department of Housing and Urban Development.

Çağlar Keyder is a native of Istanbul and works on historical, urban and developmental studies. He has published *Istanbul: between the Global and the Local* (Lanham, MD, 1999) and teaches at Boğaziçi University, Istanbul and the State University of New York at Binghamton.

Jeroen Klink is the Director of Institute of Science, Technology and Society of the Federal University of the ABC Region in São Paulo. Klink was formerly the Secretary for Local Economic Development in Santo André.

Raul Juste Lores is the business and economics editor for *Folha de São Paulo*. He has served as editor and Buenos Aires correspondent for *Veja* magazine and as an anchor and editor for Cultura TV.

José de Souza Martins is a sociologist and an Emeritus Professor at the University of São Paulo. He has published books on agrarian issues, migration, social movements and life in the Paulista suburbs and periphery.

Justin McGuirk writes for the Guardian newspaper on design culture. He was formerly the editor of *Icon*, the international architecture and design magazine and is a regular commentator on design issues for national newspapers and the broadcast media.

Rahul Mehrotra is an architect and is Professor and Chair of the Department of Urban Planning and Design, Graduate School of Design, Harvard University. Professor Mehrotra is founder of Rahul Mehrotra Associates, a Mumbai-based architectural practice, and has written extensively on Mumbai.

Suketu Mehta is an Associate Professor in the Department of Journalism at New York University and the author of *Maximum City: Bombay Lost and Found* (New York, 2004), which was a finalist for the 2005 Pulitzer Prize.

Wolfgang Nowak is Managing Director of the Alfred Herrhausen Society, the International Forum of Deutsche Bank. He has held various senior positions in Germany's state and federal governments, France's Centre Nationale de la Recherche Scientifique in Paris and UNESCO. A former State Secretary, Nowak was Director-General for Political Analysis and Planning at the German Federal Chancellery from 1999 to 2002.

Philipp Rode is Executive Director of LSE Cities and the Urban Age Programme at the LSE. Rode is the Ove Arup Fellow with the LSE Cities Programme and co-convenes the 'City Making: The Politics of Urban Form' course. As researcher and consultant he manages interdisciplinary projects comprising urban governance, transport, city planning and urban design.

Marcos Rosa is a Brazilian architect and urban planner currently teaching and conducting research at the Institute for Architecture and Urbanism at ETH Zürich. He is the editor of *Microplanning. Urban Creative Practices*, 2011, and was the coordinator of the Deutsche Bank Urban Age Award São Paulo.

Hashim Sarkis is the Aga Khan Professor at Harvard University Graduate School of Design, and an architect. Sarkis is author of several publications including *Circa 1958: Lebanon in the Pictures and Plans of Constantinos Doxiadis* (Beirut, 2003) and co-editor, with Eric Mumford, of *Josep Lluís Sert: The Architect of Urban Design* (New Haven, CT, 2008).

Saskia Sassen is the Lynd Professor of Sociology and Co-Chair of The Committee on Global Thought at Columbia University, and an Urban Age Advisor. Her recent publications include *Territory, Authority, Rights: From Medieval to Global Assemblages* (Princeton, NJ, 2008).

David Satterthwaite is a Senior Fellow at the International Institute for Environment and Development and editor of the international journal *Environment and Urbanization*.

Richard Sennett writes about cities, labour and culture. He is a professor of humanities at New York University, Emeritus Professor of sociology at LSE and is co-chair of the Urban Age Advisory Board. He is a fellow of the American Academy of Arts and Sciences, the Royal Society of Literature, the Royal Society of the Arts, and the Academia Europea.

Priya Shankar is a Senior Project Manager and Researcher at Policy Network. She co-ordinates the Foresight project and previously worked with the Alfred Herrhausen Society and the LSE on the Deutsche Bank Urban Age Award. Having worked with NGOs and publications in India, her research interests include international affairs, governance, and development issues.

K. C. Sivaramakrishnan is an Honorary Visiting Professor at the Centre for Policy Research in New Delhi, India. Professor Sivaramakrishnan has written extensively on urbanization and governance in India.

Nicholas Stern is the Chair of the Board at the Grantham Research Institute on Climate Change and the Environment at the LSE and is IG Patel Chair and Director at the LSE Asia Research Centre. Professor Stern is best known for his insights on the economics of climate change.

Deyan Sudjic is the Director of the Design Museum in London, co-chair of the Urban Age Advisory Board and co-editor of *The Endless City* (London, 2008). Sudjic curated 'Design Cities', which opened at Istanbul Modern in 2008. Sudjic was formerly the design and architecture critic at *The Observer* and has published several books on the subjects of design, architecture and cities.

İlhan Tekeli is a professor of city and regional planning at the Middle East Technical University, Ankara and member of the Turkish Academy of Sciences. The founding chairman of the History Foundation of Turkey and Chairman of the National Committee of Turkey for the HABITAT II United Nations Conference on Human Settlements in Istanbul, he writes on city and regional planning, planning theory, macro geography, migration, local administrations in Turkey and the economic history of Turkey.

Geetam Tiwari has been Chair and Associate Professor for Transport Planning as part of the Transportation Research and Injury Prevention Programme (TRIPP) at the Indian Institute of Technology in New Delhi since 1990. She has published over 60 research papers on transportation planning and safety and has edited four books.

Tony Travers is Director of LSE London, a research centre at the London School of Economics. He has been Expenditure Advisor to the House of Commons Select Committee on Education and Skills, a Senior Associate at the King's Fund and a member of the Arts Council of England's Touring Panel. He was, between 1992 and 1997, a member of the Audit Commission and has worked for a number of other Parliamentary select committees.

Anthony Williams is Chief Executive Officer of Primum Public Realty Trust. Williams served two terms as the fourth mayor of the District of Columbia from January 1999 to December 2006. While in office, Mayor Williams was elected president of the Washington DC-based National League of Cities in December 2004. In 1997, *Governing* magazine named him Public Official of the Year. He was also on the award jury for the 2007 Opus Prize.

Alejandro Zaera-Polo founded Foreign Office Architects in 1992 together with Farshid Moussavi. FOA is an international practice of architecture and urban design, dedicated to the exploration of contemporary urban conditions, lifestyles and construction technologies. Zaera-Polo is currently on the research board of the Berlage Institute and lectures at several architectural schools around the world.

Dimitri Zenghelis is a visiting senior fellow at the Grantham Research Institute on Climate Change at the London School of Economics and Political Science. He is a Chief Economist at Cisco Climate Change Practice, and an Associate Fellow of the Energy for the Environment and Development Programme at Chatham House.

URBAN AGE CONFERENCE
PARTICIPANTS 2007-2009

Alex Abiko, Professor, Construction Engineering, Universidade de São Paulo
Milene Abla Scala, Architect Coordinator, Tecnico, Aflalo & Gasperini Arquitetos, São Paulo
Marina Acayaba, Architect, FAU, Universidade de São Paulo
Josef Ackermann, Chairman of the Group Executive Committee, Deutsche Bank and Chairman of the Board of Trustees, Alfred Herrhausen Society
Arvind Adarkar, Joint Director of Architecture, Academy of Architecture Rachana Sansad, Mumbai
Neera Adarkar, Architect and Urban Researcher, Adarkar Associates, Mumbai
Dalberto Adulis, Executive Director, ABDL, Associação Brasileira para o Desenvolvimento de Lideranças, São Paulo
Uma Adusumilli, Chief of the Planning Division, Mumbai Metropolitan Regional Development Authority, Mumbai
Girish Vice Agarwaal, Managing Director, DNA, Diligent Media Corporation, Mumbai
Roberto Agosta, Director, Facultad de Ingenieria, Departamento de Transporte, Universidad de Buenos Aires
Sabrina Agostini Harris, Research Student, FAU, Universidade de São Paulo
Ali Ağaoğlu, Columnist, Vatan, Istanbul
Duygu Ağar, Member of Executive Board, TMMOB Şehir Plancıları Odası, Istanbul Şubesi
Meltem Ahıska, Professor, Sosyoloji Bölümü, Fen-Edebiyat Fakültesi, Boğaziçi Üniversitesi, Istanbul
Bahriye Ak, Urban Planner, Istanbul Metropoliten Planlama ve Kentsel Tasarım Merkezi
Behiç Ak, Architect and Cartoonist, Cumhuriyet Gazetesi, Istanbul
Öznur Akalın, Member of Executive Board, TMMOB Şehir Plancıları Odası, Istanbul Şubesi
Şule Akalp, Urban Planner, Kentsel Strateji, Istanbul
Asaf Savaş Akat, Columnist, Vatan, Istanbul
Şengül Akçar, Director and Founder, Foundation for the Support of Women's Work, Istanbul
Müge Akgün, Culture Editor, Referans Gazetesi, Istanbul
Ulaş Akın, Urban Planner, Researcher, Istanbul Metropoliten Planlama ve Kentsel Tasarım Merkezi
İpek Akpınar, Assistant Professor of Architectural Design, Mimarlık Fakültesi, Istanbul Teknik Üniversitesi
Asu Aksoy, Associate Professor, Cultural Management MA Programme, Santral Istanbul, Istanbul Bilgi Üniversitesi
Suay Aksoy, Director, Cultural Heritage and Museums, Istanbul 2010 European Capital of Culture Agency
Ersin Akyüz, Chief Country Officer, CEO, Deutsche Bank Turkey, Istanbul
Tamar Al Hajjeh, Minister of Local Administration, Damascus
Felipe Aldunate-Montes, Editorial Director, America Economia, Santiago de Chile
Leon Alexander, President, Toronto Com.
Materiais e Administraçao, São Paulo
Giorgos Alexandrou, Giorgos Alexandrou, Architect, University of Patras
Thiago Allis, Professor, Campus Sorocaba, Universidade Federal de São Carlos
Nüket Algan, Coordinator, Deutsche Bank Turkey, Istanbul

Rashid Ali, Lecturer, Institute of Architecture, University of Nottingham
Orlando Almeida Filho, Secretary of Housing and Urban Development, Prefeitura de São Paulo
Zeren Alpagut, Urban Planner, Istanbul Metropoliten Planlama ve Kentsel Tasarım Merkezi
Burak Altınışık, Instructor of Architecture, Mimarlık ve Tasarım Fakültesi, Bahçeşehir Üniversitesi, Istanbul
Andy Altman, Chief Executive, Olympic Park Legacy Company, London
Evrim Altuğ, Editor, Sabah Gazetesi, Istanbul
Ana Alvarez, Citámbulos, Mexico City
Bernardo G. Alvim, Researcher, CEPESP, FGV, São Paulo
Tata Amaral, Filmmaker and Co-founder, Coraçao da Selva, São Paulo
Shriya Anand, Centre for Development Finance, Institute for Financial Management and Research, Chennai
Jeff Anderson, BioUrban, São Paulo
Maira Andre, Student, FAU, Universidade de São Paulo
Tomas Antonio Moreira, Professor, Gestão Urbana, Pontificia Universidade Católica do Parana
Denise Antonucci, Professor, FAU, Instituto Presbiterano Mackenzie
Helena Aparecida A. Silva, Professor, Departamento de Projeto, FAU, Universidade de São Paulo
Maria Apostolidi, Researcher, Accounting and Finance, London School of Economics and Political Science
Metin Ar, President & Chief Executive, Garanti Yatırım, Istanbul
Ricardo Araujo, General Coordinator, Secretaria de Saneamento e Energia, Governo do Estado de São Paulo
Luiz Ricardo Araujo Florence, Espaco de Cultura Cohab Raposo Tavares, São Paulo
Alejandro Aravena, Executive Director, Elemental S.A., Santiago de Chile
Erbay Arıkboğa, Professor of Political Science, Sosyal Bilimler Meslek Yüksekokulu, Marmara Üniversitesi, Istanbul
Sophie Arie, Foreign Editor, Monocle, London
José Armenio De Brito Cruz, Partner Director, Piratininga Arquitetos Associados Ltda, São Paulo
Vivianne Armitage, Executive Director, Fundacion Sidoc, Acopi Yumbo
Salvador Arriola, Consul, Consulado Geral do Mexico, São Paulo
Osman Arolat, Columnist, Dünya Gazetesi, Istanbul
Jockin Arputham, Director, National Slum Dwellers Federation, Mumbai
Cemil Arslan, Head of Financial Services Department, Istanbul Büyükşehir Belediyesi
Pınar Arslan, Assistant Editor, DEPO Yayıncılık, Istanbul
Sinan Arslaner, CEO, cfs Danışmanlık, Istanbul
Kerem Arslanlı, Researcher, Çevre ve Şehircilik Uygulama Araştırma Merkezi, Istanbul Teknik Üniversitesi
Kate Ascher, Development Director, Vornado Realty Trust, New York
Bruno Assami, Director, Assuntos Institucionais, Instituto Tomie Ohtake
Valdir Assef Jr., Advisor, Secretaria de Seguranca Publica, Prefeitura Municipal de São Paulo

Ahmet Atil Aşıcı, Professor of Industrial Engineering and Economy, Istanbul Teknik Üniversitesi
İdris Atabay, Director of Urban Transformation, Istanbul Büyükşehir Belediyesi
Serpil Atalay, Economist Specialist, Türkiye Cumhuriyeti Merkez Bankası, Ankara
Ulus Atayurt, Journalist, Istanbul Dergisi
Celso Athayde, Founder, Central Única de Favelas, Rio de Janeiro
Maria Teresa Augusti, President, Instituto Florestan Fernandes, São Paulo
Jose Auriemo Neto, President, JHSF Investor Relations, São Paulo
Adam Austerfield, Director of Projects, ELSE, London School of Economics and Political Science
Gökhan Avcıoğlu, Founding Partner, GAD Mimarlık, Istanbul / New York
George Avelino, Coordinator, CEPESP, FGV, São Paulo
Sergio Avelleda, President Director, CPTM Governo de São Paulo
Maira Avila, Researcher, University of British Columbia, Vancouver
Ceren Aydın, Head of Relations with Professional Organisations and Regional Development Unit, TÜSİAD, Istanbul
Semra Aydınlı, Professor of Architecture, Mimarlık Fakültesi, Istanbul Teknik Üniversitesi
Pushan Ayub, Professor, Tata Institute of Fundamental Research (TIFR), Mumbai
Vanessa Azavedo, Research Officer, Youth for Unity and Voluntary Action (YUVA) Research Project, Mumbai
Shabana Azmi, Actress and Member, National Integration Council and National AIDS Commission, Mumbai
Gruia Badescu, Researcher, Cities Programme, London School of Economics
Lee Baca, Sheriff, Los Angeles County
Mehmet Selim Baki, Founder, Barış için Müzik, Istanbul
Burçin Bakkaloğlu, Project Manager, Ipsos KMG, Istanbul
Ashok Bal, Deputy Chairman, Ministry of Shipping, Mumbai Port Trust, Mumbai
Mauna Baldini Soares, Researcher, CEPESP, FGV, São Paulo
Bruno Silva Balthazar, Architect and Urban Planner, FAU, Universidade de São Paulo
Nelson Baltrusis, Social Development and Territorial Planning, Universidade Catolica de Salvador
Alapan Bandyopadhyay, Municipal Commissioner, Kolkata Municipal Corporation, Kolkata
Ian Banerjee, Assistant Professor, Vienna Technical University
Bia Bansen, Founder, Comunicacao Bansen and Associados, São Paulo
Fernanda Barbara, Partner Architect, UNA Arquitetos, São Paulo
İlke Barka, Co-Founder, GB Mimarlik Muhendislik, Istanbul
Monica Barroso Keel, 2009 Kleinhans Fellow, Rainforest Alliance, New York
Jessica Barthel, Project Manager, Alfred Herrhausen Society
Kaustabh Basu, Principal Consultant, PricewaterhouseCoopers Pvt. Ltd., Kolkata
Ezgi Başaran, Columnist, Hürriyet, Istanbul
Cüheyda Başık, Marketing and Sales Coordinator,

Arkitera Mimarlık Merkezi, Istanbul
Adem Baştürk, General Secretary, Istanbul Büyükşehir Belediyesi
Leandro Batista de Oliveira, President, Capital Social, São Paulo
Ratan Batliboi, Architect, Ratan J. Batliboi Architects, Mumbai
Emin Batmazoğlu, Assistant to Mayor, Esenyurt Belediyesi, Istanbul
Bilgehan Baykal, Researcher, Marmara Üniversitesi, Istanbul
Ayşegül Baykan, Senior Visiting Fellow, Cities Programme, London School of Economics and Political Science
Mete Başar Baypınar, Research Assistant on Architecture, Mimarlık Fakültesi, Istanbul Teknik Üniversitesi
Sevince Bayrak, Partner, SO Mimarlık, Istanbul
Erdoğan Bayraktar, Executive Director, Toplu Konut İdaresi Başkanlığı, Ankara
İbrahim Baz, Coordinator, Istanbul Metropoliten Planlama ve Kentsel Tasarım Merkezi
Nefise Bazoğlu, Former Chief in Kenya for Monitoring and Evaluation, UN-Habitat, Istanbul
Jo Beall, Professor of Development Studies, Development Studies Institute (DESTIN), London School of Economics and Political Science
Rengin Beceren Öztürk, Lecturer in Architecture, Mimarlık Fakültesi, Uludağ Üniversitesi, Bursa
Daniel Becker, Director, Programa Brasil, Instituto Synergos, Rio de Janeiro
Regina Beda, Independent consultant, São Paulo
Murat Belge, Professor of Comparative Literature, Bilgi Üniversitesi, Istanbul
Gustavo Belic Cherubine, Educator, Energia Solar, ONG Sociedade do Sol, São Paulo
Huser Benedikt, Urban Planner, Zurich
Gila Benmayor, Columnist, Hürriyet, Istanbul
Bruna Benvenga, Architect, Development, McDonald's Brazil, São Paulo
Özlem Berber, Professor of Social Science, Sosyal Bilimler Enstitüsü, Istanbul Teknik Üniversitesi
Christian Berkes, Editor, Arch+, Berlin
Claudio Bernardes, Vice-President, SECOVI-SP, São Paulo
Wolfram Bernhardt, Zeppelin University, Friedrichshafen
Enrique Betancourt, Deputy General Director, Urban Development, Secretaria de Desarrollo Social, Gobierno Federal de Mexico
Carlos Andres Betancur C., Project Director, Oficinas de Proyectos Urbanos (OPUS), Medellin, Colombia
Rodrigo Bethlem, Secretary-Elect of Public Order, Rio de Janeiro
Joost Beunderman, Architect, 00:/, London
Gustavo Beuttenmuller, Expert on Urban Development, Secretaria Municipal do Verde e do Meio Ambiente, Prefeitura de São Paulo
Francisco Bezerra Baião, Deutsche Bank Urban Age Award Winner 2008, São Paulo
Luis Renato Bezerra Pequeno, Professor, FAU, Universidade Federal do Ceara
Ram B. Bhagat, Professor, International Institute for Population Sciences, Mumbai
Shirin Bharucha, Managing Trustee, Urban Design Research Institute (UDRI), Mumbai
Bikash Ranjan Bhattacharya, Mayor, Kolkata Municipal Corporation, Kolkata
Amita Bhide, Associate Professor, Department of Urban and Rural Development, Tata Institute of Social Sciences (TISS), Mumbai
Manas Ranjan Bhunia, Leader, West Bengal

Congress Legislature Party, Kolkata
Özcan Biçer, Planner, İlke Planlama, Istanbul
José Bicudo, President, Presidencia, Cia. City de Desenvolvimento
Ciro Biderman, Professor, Centro de Estudos em Política e Economia do Setor Público, FGV
İhsan Bilgin, Director, MimariTasarım Programı and Dean, Fen-Edebiyat Fakültesi, Bilgi Üniversitesi, Istanbul
Özgür Bingöl, Co-Founder, GB Mimarlik Muhendislik, Istanbul
Rodin Bingöl, Founder and Director, engelleri kaldir renovatio, Istanbul
Anna Birkefeld, Designer, Editorial Staff, Arch+ Berlin
Mario Biselli, Principal, Biselli & Katchborian Arquitetos Associados, São Paulo
Peter Bishop, London Development Agency Group Director of Design, Development and Environment and Deputy Chief Executive
Renato Boareto, Director, Departamento de Mobilidade Humana, Governo Federal do Brasil
Klaus Bode, Founding Partner, BDSP Partnership, London
Sophie Body-Gendrot, Director, Centre for Urban Studies, Université-Sorbonne-Paris IV, Paris
Rajaram Bojji, Director, Atri Knowledge Embedded Infrastructure Lab Pvt. Ltd., Hyderabad
Fabiano Bolcato Rangel, Partner Consultant,Txai Cidadania e Desenvolvimento Social, São Paulo
Elvis Bonassa, Director, Kairos Desenvolvimento Social, São Paulo
Cintia Bonder, Project Officer, UNESCO, Porto Alegre
Agatha Bonizzoni, Espaço Eventos, São Paulo
Ana Bonomi, Student, Fundacao Getulio Vargas, São Paulo
Ana Maria Bonomi Barufi, Student, Faculdade de Economia, Administracao e Contabilidade, Universidade de São Paulo
Katherine Boo, Staff Writer, The New Yorker, Washington D.C.
Jose Borelli Neto, Assistant Professor, FAU, Universidade de São Paulo
Ranjan K. Bose, Senior Fellow, The Energy and Resources Institute, New Delhi
Recep Bozlağan, Secretary General, Union of Municipalities of the Marmara Region, Istanbul
Fadime Boztaş, Specialist, Urban Projects Coordination, Istanbul 2010 European Capital of Culture Agency
Elisa Bracher, Founder, Instituto Acaia, São Paulo
Milton Braga, Architect, MMBB Arquitetos, São Paulo
Rodrigo Brancatelli, Journalist, Caderno Metrópole, O Estado de S. Paulo, São Paulo
Juarez Rubens Brandão Lopes, Sociologist and Advisor, Empresa Paulista de Planejamento Metropolitano SA (EMPLASA), São Paulo
Julia Bravo Caldeira, Architect, Todescan Siciliano Arquitetura
Lindsay Bremner, Professor, Department of Architecture, Tyler School of Art, Temple University, Philadelphia, Pennsylvania
Luís Eduardo Brettas, Urban Projects Manager, Diretoria de Projetos Meio Ambiente e Paisagem Urbana, Empresa Municipal de Urbanização, São Paulo
Alfredo Brillembourg, Principal, Urban Think Tank, Caracas
Richard Brown, Urban Policy Consultant, London
George Brugmans, Director, Internationale Architectuur Biennale Rotterdam
Miguel Bucalem, Head of Advisory, Secretaria de Planejamento, Prefeitura de São Paulo
Funda Budak, Advisor, United Cities and Local Governments, Middle East and West Asia Section, Istanbul
Maria Lidia Bueno Fernandes, Professor, Escola Cidade Jardim, São Paulo
Sibel Bulay, Director, EMBARQ, Istanbul
Lucy Bullivant, Architectural Curator, Critic and Author, London
Özlem Bulut, Director, Exco Member, Marketing Quantitative, Ipsos KMG, Istanbul
Amanda Burden, Director, Department of City Planning, New York City
Mika Burdett, Designer, London
Ricky Burdett, Director, Urban Age & LSE Cities, London School of Economics and Political Science
Zara Burdett, Graduate, New York University
Sundar Burra, Advisor, Society for the Promotion of Area Resource Centres (SPARC), Mumbai
Gürcan Büyüksalih, Assistant Professor of Urban Planning, Istanbul Metropoliten Planlama ve KentselTasarım Merkezi
Bruno Caetano Raimundo, Secretary, Secretaria de Comunicacao, Governo do Estado de São Paulo
Alexandre Cafcalas, Architect, Cafcalas Arquitetos
Andrea Calabi, Professor, Faculdade de Economia e Administracao, Universidade de São Paulo
Luis Otavio Calagian, Consultant, CEPESP, FGV, São Paulo
Jorge Caldeira, Director, Editora Mameluco, São Paulo
Marina Caldeira, Diretora, Editora Mameluco, São Paulo
Teresa Caldeira, Professor of City and Regional Planning, College of Environmental Design, University of California, Berkeley
Anna G. H. Callejas, Student, FAU, Universidade de São Paulo
Ana Cristina C. Camargo, Psychological Coordinator, Instituto Acaia, São Paulo
Sergio Raul Cammarano Gonzalez, Technical Director, Companhia de Desenvolvimento Habitacional e Urbano do Estado de São Paulo
Beatriz Campos, Associate Director, Space Syntax, London
Orion Campos, Student, FAU, Universidade Estadual Paulista, Bauru
Mauricio Camps, Government of Mexico City
Aynur Can, Assistant Professor of Urban Aesthetics, KamuYönetimi Ana Bilim DalıYerel Yönetimler Programı, Marmara Üniversitesi, Istanbul
Ayfer Bartu Candan, Professor of Sociology, Sosyoloji Bölümü, Fen-Edebiyat Fakültesi, Boğaziçi Üniversitesi, Istanbul
Canan Candan, Researcher, Sanat ve Sosyal Bilimler Fakültesi, Sabancı Üniversitesi, Istanbul
Aline Cannataro Figueiredo, Student, FAU, Universidade de São Paulo
Ege Cansen, Columnist, Hürriyet, Istanbul
Ariadna Cantis, Architecture Urbanism Curator, Madrid
Ana Maria Cardachevski, Assistant to Director, SESC, São Paulo
Luiz Carlos Salem Bouabci, Integracao de Redes, Ashoka - Empreendedores Sociais, São Paulo
Rosely Carmona, International Relations Manager, Fundação Memorial da América Latina, São Paulo
Adriano Carneiro De Mendonça, Architect And Professor, FAU, Pontifícia Universidade Católica de Rio de Janeiro
Fabio Casiroli, Chairman, Systematica; Professor of Transport Planning, Faculty of Civil Architecture, Polytechnic of Milan, Milan
Luis Castaneda Lossio, Metropolitan Mayor of Lima
Eduardo Castanho, Intern, SupervisãoTécnica de Planejamento da Subprefeitura do Butantã, Prefeitura de São Paulo
José Castillo, Principal, Arquitectura 911sc, Mexico City
Lorenzo Castro, Architect, Lorenzo Castro Arquitectos, Bogota
Cristina Catunda, Director of Projects, Consultoria Ambiental, COPAM, São Paulo
Rodrigo Cavalcante, Post Graduation Student, Departamento deTecnologia, FAU, Universidade de São Paulo
Jose Cazarin, Principal, AXPE Negocios Imobiliarios, S
Hüseyin Cengiz, Head of City and Regional Planning, YıldızTeknik Üniversitesi, Istanbul
Frederico Celentano, Director, Microdv, São Paulo
Gunit Chadha, Managing Director and Chief Executive Officer, Deutsche Bank India, Mumbai
Neeta Chalke, Advisor, Special Projects and Public Relations, Slum Rehabilitation Society, Mumbai
Christopher Champalle, Bangalore
Min-Cheng Chang, Student, Southern California Institute of Architecture (SCI-Arc), Los Angeles
Margarita Charriere, President, Comision de Urbanismo y Medio Ambiente, Universidad de Buenos Aires
Tathagata Chatterji, Director, Centre for Information and Research on Urban Settlements, New Delhi
Xiangming Chen, Dean and Director, Center for Urban and Global Studies, Trinity College, Hartford, Connecticut
Susan Chivaratanond, Southern California Institute of Architecture (SCI-Arc), Los Angeles
Kees Christiaanse, Chair of Architecture and Urban Design, Institute of Urban Design, The Swiss Federal Institute of Technology, ETH Zurich
Shiuan-Wen Chu, Researcher, International Architecture Biennale Rotterdam, Rotterdam
Fernando Chucre, Federal Deputy, Camara dos Deputados Governo Federal do Brasil
Ana Maria Ciccacio, Editor, Publicacoes, Viva o Centro, São Paulo
Juliana Cipolletta, Researcher, Departamento de História de Estética do Projeto, Universidade de São Paulo
Joan Clos i Matheu, Executive Director, United Nations Human Settlements Programme (UN-HABITAT), Nairobi
Henry Cobb, Founding Partner, Pei Cobb Freed & Partners Architects LLP, New York
Gustavo Coelho, Professor, Geografia, Pontificia Universidade Catolica de São Paulo
Michael Cohen, Director of the International Affairs Program, New School University
Wagner Colombini Martins, President, Diretoria, Logit Engenharia Consultiva Ltda, São Paulo
Joanna Conceicao, Student, LABAUT, FAU, Universidade de São Paulo
Frederick Cooper, Dean, Facultad de Arquitectura y Urbanismo, Pontificia Universidad Católica del Perú
Hafeez Contractor, Architect, Hafeez Contractor Architects, Mumbai
Charles Correa, Founding Partner, Charles Correa Associates, Mumbai
Renato Correa Baena, Secretary, Secretaria Municipal da Pessoa com Deficiencia e Mobilidade Reduzida, Prefeitura de São Paulo
Norberto Correa da Silva Moura, Professor, FAU, Universidade de São Paulo
Luiz Antonio Cortez Ferreira, Coordinator of International Relations, Secretaria de Estado dos Transportes Metropolitanos, Governo de São Paulo
Fernanda Costa, Director Advisor, Cobansa Cia Hipotecaria, São Paulo
Roberto Costa de Oliveira, President, ViSão Mundial ONG, Recife
Diogo R. Coutinho, Professor, Faculdade de Direito, Universidade de São Paulo
Pierre Alain Croset, Professor, Facolta' di Architettura, Politecnico di Torino, Turin
James Crowe, Parish Priest, Sociedade Santos Mártires, São Paulo
Maria Augusta Cunha, Student, FAU, Universidade de São Paulo
Camila Curi, Student, FAU, Universidade Federal Fluminense
Otavio Cury, Producer, Outros Filmes, São Paulo
Eliana Maria Custodio, Coordinator, Politicas Publicas, GELEDES Instituto da Mulher Negra, São Paulo
Renato Cymbalista, Architect and Urban Planner, Instituto Polis, São Paulo
Hüseyin Çağlayan, Fashion Designer, London
Arzu Çahantimur, Professor of Architecture, Mimarlık Fakültesi, Uludağ Üniversitesi, Bursa
Hasan Çalışlar, Partner, Erginoğlu & Çalışlar Mimarlık, Istanbul
Vural Çakır, CEO, Ipsos KMG, Istanbul
Mehmet Emin Çakırkaya, Partner, Tekeli-Sisa Mimarlık, Istanbul
Perihan Çakıroğlu, Columnist, Bugün Gazetesi, Istanbul
Ayşe Çavdar, Journalist, Post Express Dergisi, Istanbul
Ali Çavuşoğlu, Chairman of ÇBS Holding, Istanbul
Ömer Çavuşoğlu, Researcher, Urban Age and LSE Cities, London School of Economics and Political Science
Sonat Çavuşoğlu, Industrial Engineer, Istanbul
Buğra Çelik, Project Partner, Engelleri kaldir renovatio, Istanbul
Devrim Çimen, Co-Founder, 8Artı Mimarlık, Istanbul
Candan Çınar, Professor of Architecture, Yıldız Teknik Üniversitesi, Istanbul
Alişan Çırakoğlu, Partner, Çırakoğlu Mimarlık, Istanbul
Nuri Çolakoğlu, Member of the Executive Board, DoğanYayın Holding, Istanbul
Francisco Da Costa, Director, Departamento de Planejamento e Avaliação da Política, Transportes do Ministério, São Paulo
Gerson Da Cunha, Columnist, Activist and Trustee, Action for Good Governance and Networking in India, Mumbai
Eugenio Da Motta Singer, Executive Director, Instituto Pharos, Santana do Parnaiba, SP
Maria Da Piedade Morais, Instituto de Pesquisa Economica Aplicada, State of São Paulo
Wagner Luciano da Silva, Project Advisor, Programacao Acao Familia, FundacaoTide Setubal
Ariadne Daher Dos Santos, Architect, Jaime Lerner Arquitetos Associados and Professor of Urban Planning and Landscape Design, UniversidadeTuiuti do Paraná, Curitiba
Caroline Dahl, Southern California Institute of Architecture (SCI-Arc), Los Angeles
Juliana Dalbello, Student, FAU, Universidade Presbiteriana Mackenzie, São Paulo
Özlem Dalga, Columnist, Habertürk, Istanbul
Ali İhsan Dalgıç, Senior Advisor, United Cities and Local Governments, Middle East and West Asia Section, Istanbul
Didem Danış, Lecturer, Sociology, University of Galatasaray
Joao Paulo Daolio, Engineer, Obra Arquitetos, São Paulo
Murat Daoudov, Director, EU & International Relations Centre, Union of Municipalities of the Marmara Region, Istanbul
Bratati Bal Das, Journalist and Voice Artist, Pragati Association, Mumbai
P. K. Das, Architect, PK Das and Associates, Mumbai
Howard Davies, Director, London School of Economics and Political Science
Aparecida De Abreu N. Simoes, Bio Urban
Maria Cecilia de Almeida Barbosa das Eiras, Coordinator, Policidadania, São Paulo
Jose De Filippi Junior, Mayor of Diadema
Dirce Bertan De Freitas, Specialist in Transportation Planning, Companhia do Metropolitano de São Paulo
Walter De Mattos Filho, President, Lance and Candidacy for Olympics 2016, Rio de Janeiro
Cynthia de Lima Krahenbuhl, Assitant, Secretaria de Assuntos Juridicos, Prefeitura do Municipio deTaboão da Serra, São Paulo
Fernanda de Macedo Haddad, Professor, Departamento de Urbanismo, Universidade Paulista (UNIP)
Luciana M. V. De Mattos, Student, CEPESP, FGV, São Paulo
Paulo De Mello Bastos, President, Arquiteto Paulo Bastos e Associados Ltda, São Paulo
Fernando De Mello Franco, Partner, MMBB Arquitetos, São Paulo
Raimundo de Oliveira Bitencourt, Buildings Technical, Projetos, Risco Zero Assessoria em Arquitetura Ltda, São Paulo
Gesner de Oliveira Filho, Diretor, Companhia de Saneamento Básico do Estado de São Paulo
Juan Diego De OliveiraTeixeira, Student, FAU, Universidade Federal do Rio de Janeiro
Gilberto de Palma, Institutional Director, Defesa do Eleitor e da Democracia, Instituto Agora, São Paulo
Ana Luiza L. C. De Paula, Programme Assistant, Logistics and Communication, Urban Age, São Paulo
Evelyn De Rothschild, Chairman, N.M. Rothschild & Sons Limited, London
Maria Ruth Amaral de Sampaio, Professor, Faculdade de Arquitetura e Urbanismo, Universidade de São Paulo
Pedro De Sales, Architect, Secretaria Municipal de Planejamento, Prefeitura de São Paulo
Filipe Lage de Souza , Economist, Banco Nacional do Desenvolvimento Economico e Social, São Paulo
Jose Eduardo N. De Souza Alves, Architect, Frentes Arquitetura, São Paulo
Pedro Ivo De Souza Batista, Advisory Council, Nucleo de Brasília, Associação Alternativa Terrazul
Pedro Luis De Souza Lopes, Criminal Analyst, Comando de Policiamento da Capital, Policia Militar do Estado de São Paulo
José De Souza Martins, Emeritus Professor, Letras Ciencias Humanas, Universidade de São Paulo
Jacobine De Zwaan, Policy Advisor, Fire Department, Municipality of Amsterdam
Eduardo Della Manna, Director of Urban Legislation, SECOVI, São Paulo
Ahmet Misbah Demircan, Mayor, Beyoğlu Belediyesi, Istanbul
Erhan Demirdizen, Head, TMMOB Şehir Plancıları Odası, Istanbul Şubesi
Jayant Deo, Member, World Energy Council, Pune
Milind Deora, Member of Parliament, India National Parliament, Mumbai
Kemal Derviş, Vice-President and Director of Global Economy and Development Program, The Brookings Institution, Washington DC and Senior Advisor, Sabancı University, Istanbul
Pelin Derviş, Curator, Garanti Galeri, Istanbul
Vilasrao Deshmukh, Chief Minister, Government of Maharashtra, Mumbai
Del DeSouza, Deputy Director, Slum Rehabilitation Society, Mumbai
Alejandra Maria Devecchi, Architect and Coordenador, Coordenadoria de Planejamento Ambiental, Prefeitura de São Paulo
Eloisa Dezen Kempter, Architect, Departamento de Coordenacao de Projeto, Universidade Estadual De Campinas
Sergio Dias, Secretary-Elect of Urbanism, Rio de Janeiro
Oscar Edmundo Diaz, Senior Program Director, Institute for Transportation and Development Policy in Colombia, Bogota
Rodrigo Diaz, Director of America Economia Intelligence
Anna Dietzsch, Architect, Architecture and Urban Design, DBB Brasil, São Paulo
Sheila Dikshit, Chief Minister, Government of National Capital Territory of Delhi, New Delhi
Gilberto Dimenstein, Member of the Editorial Council, Jornal Folha de São Paulo
Kadir Dikbaş, Columnist, Zaman, Istanbul
Sandra Dini Kliukas, Espaço Eventos, São Paulo
Flavia Diniz, International Affairs Assistant, Assuntos Internacionais, Prefeitura Municipal de Diadema

Ajit Kumar Jain, Principal Secretary, Water Supply and Sanitation Department, Government of Maharashtra, Mumbai
Trupti Jain, Executive Director, City Managers' Association Gujarat, India
Suraj P. Jakhanwal, Director General, School of Urban Management, Amity University, New Delhi
K. R. S. Jamwal, Vice President, Strategy, Tata Sons Ltd., Mumbai
Flavio Janches, Architect and Urban Designer, Faculty of Architecture and Urbanism, Universidad de Buenos Aires
Paulo Jannuzzi, Professor, Instituto Brasileiro de Geografia e Estatistica, São Paulo
Marcio Jeha Chede, Director, Chéde Construções e Empreendimentos Ltda, São Paulo
Xu Jiexia, Student, Southern California Institute of Architecture (SCI-Arc), Los Angeles
Gregory John, Rede Cultural Beija-flor, São Paulo
Joseph Edmund Johnson, Bureau Chief of India, Financial Times, New Delhi
Gareth Jones, Senior Lecturer, Geography and Environment Department, London School of Economics and Political Science
Eduardo Jorge, Secretary of Environment, Municipality of São Paulo
George Jose, Executive Member, Collective Research Initiatives Trust (CRIT), Mumbai
Johny Joseph, Chief Secretary, Government of Maharashtra, Mumbai
Pankaj Joshi, Executive Director, Urban Design Research Institute, Mumbai
Marlova Jovchelovitch Noleto, General Programme and Social and Human Sciences Coordinator, UNESCO, Brasilia
Tessa Jowell, Minister for the Olympics and London, Department for Culture, Media and Sport, Government of the United Kingdom, London
Carla Juca Amrein, Masters Student, FEA, Universidade de São Paulo
David Judson, Columnist, Referans and Hürriyet Daily News, Istanbul
Adam Kaasa, Communications and Outreach Manager, Urban Age and LSE Cities, London School of Economics and Political Science
Rod Kaasa, Doctor, Edmonton
Terry Kaasa, Chaplain, Royal Alexandra Hospital, Edmonton
Betül Kabahasanoğlu, Columnist, Posta, Istanbul
Şelale Kadak, Columnist, Sabah, Istanbul
Hasan Bülent Kahraman, Associate Professor of Social Science, Sanat ve Sosyal Bilimler Fakültesi, Sabancı Üniversitesi; and Columnist, Sabah Gazetesi, Istanbul
Tayfun Kahraman, Secretary, TMMOB Şehir Plancıları Odası, Istanbul Şubesi
Hüseyin Kahvecioğlu, Professor of Architecture, Mimarlık Fakültesi, Istanbul Teknik Üniversitesi
Vijay G. Kalantri, Chairman and Managing Director, Dighi Port Ltd., Mumbai
Jamsheed Kanga, Kala Ghoda Association, Mumbai
Ömer Kanıpak, Founding Partner, Arkitera Mimarlık Merkezi, Istanbul
Ayşegül Kapısız, Architect, Kreatif Mimarlık, Istanbul
Gabriela Kappeler, Student, FAU, Pontificia Universidade Catolica do Parana
Hüseyin Kaptan, Partner, Atelye 70 Planlama ve Tasarım Grubu and Former 1st Director, Istanbul Metropoliten Planlama ve Kentsel Tasarım Merkezi
Mariana Kara Jose, Urbanist, Alianca de Cidades, São Paulo
Özkan Karababa, Architect, ArchBox, Istanbul
Haydar Karabey, Partner, Limited Mimarlık, Istanbul
Ahmet Karacahisarlı, Executive Director of Finance, Çelik Halat ve Tel Sanayi A.Ş., Istanbul
Enise Burcu Karaçizmeli, Assistant Editor, XXI Mimarlık, Tasarım, Mekan Dergisi, Istanbul
Nuray Karakurt, Architect and Guest Editor, Arch+ Berlin
Aykut Karaman, Head of Urban and Regional Planning Department, Mimarlık Fakültesi, Mimar
Necmi Karaman, Southern California Institute of Architecture (SCI-Arc), Los Angeles
Sinan Güzel Sanatlar Üniversitesi, Istanbul
Necmi Karaman, Architect, Istanbul Ulaşım A.Ş.
Nuri Karamollaoğlu, Assistant Researcher, Visual Arts Programme, Sanat ve Sosyal Bilimler Fakültesi, Sabancı Üniversitesi, Istanbul
Funda Karatay Evren, Urban Planner, Istanbul Metropoliten Planlama ve Kentsel Tasarım Merkezi
Işıl Karter, Member for Istanbul Provincial Council, Esenyurt Belediyesi, Istanbul
Uğur Kasımoğlu, Urban Planner on Renewal and Regeneration, Istanbul Yenileme Alanları Kültür ve Tabiat Varlıklarını Koruma Bölge Kurulu
Bruce Katz, Vice President & Director, Metropolitan Policy Program, Brookings Institution, Washington DC
Ruth Kattumuri, Head, LSE-India, London School of Economics and Political Science
Stephen Kausch, Architect, DFZ-Architekten, Hamburg
Kemal Kaya, Private Secretary to Mayor, Pendik Belediyesi, Istanbul
Christian Keim, Researcher, EIFER, Karlsruhe
Çağlar Keyder, Professor, Atatürk Institute for Modern Turkish History, Sosyoloji Departmanı, Boğaziçi Üniversitesi, Istanbul; Department of Sociology, Binghamton Unviversity, State University of New York, Binghamton
Fuat Keyman, Professor of International Relations, İktisadi ve İdari Bilimler Fakültesi, Koç Üniversitesi, Istanbul
Babu Khan, Director, Confederation of Indian Industry (CII), New Delhi
Ajay Khanna, Deputy Director General, Confederation of Indian Industry (CII), Mumbai
Uttam Khobragade, General Manager and Chief Executive Officer, Brihan Mumbai Electric Supply and Transport Undertakings (BEST), Mumbai
Heng Chye Kiang, Dean, School of Design and Environment, National University of Singapore, Singapore
Caroline Kihato, Researcher, Graduate School of Humanities, University of South Africa, Johannesburg
Ceren Kılıç, Architect, Potansiyel Araştırmalar Birimi, Istanbul
He Nem Kim Seo, Student, FAU, Universidade de São Paulo
Elif Kısar Koramaz, Urban Planner, Istanbul Metropoliten Planlama ve Kentsel Tasarım Merkezi
Kay Kitazawa, Research Officer, Urban Age, London School of Economics and Political Science
Cengiz Kirli, Professor, Sociology Department, Boğaziçi Üniversitesi, Istanbul
Rosa Grena Kliass, Landscaping Architect, Rosa Kliass - Arquitetura e Paisagismo, São Paulo
Carolin Kleist, Editor, Arch+, Berlin
Mariane Klettenhofer, Researcher, Departamento de Tecnologia, FAU, Universidade de São Paulo
Jeroen Klink, Director, Centro de Engenharia, Modelagem e Ciências Sociais Aplicadas, Universidade Federal do ABC
Danielle Klintowitz, Architect and Urban Planner, Politica Urbana, Instituto Via Pública, São Paulo
Hubert Klumpner, Principal, Urban Think Tank, Caracas
Mahmut Kocameşe, Head of Real-Estate Development, Istanbul Büyükşehir Belediyesi
Anne Kockelkorn, Editor, Arch+, Berlin
Levent Koç, Programme Manager, İyiYönetişim Programı, TESEV, Istanbul
Dirce Koga, Reasercher, Universidade Cruzeiro do Sul, São Paulo
David Kohn, Founder, David Kohn Architects, London
Şulan Kolatan, Principal, KOL/MAC LLC Architecture + Design, New York
Biray Kolluoğlu, Assistant Professor of Sociology, Boğaziçi Üniversitesi, Istanbul
Jorge Andre Königsberger, Co-Director, Königsberger Vannucchi Arquitetos Associados Ltda., São Paulo
Güzin Konuk, Professor of Architecture, Mimarlık Fakültesi, Mimar Sinan Güzel Sanatlar Üniversitesi, Istanbul
Tansel Korkmaz, Assistant Professor, İletişim Fakültesi, Bilgi Üniversitesi, Istanbul
Vasıf Kortun, Director, Platform Garanti Güncel Sanat Merkezi, Istanbul
Nilüfer Kozikoğlu, Principal, TUSPA Architectural Design Studio, Istanbul
Sait Ali Köknar, Researcher on Architecture, Mimarlık Fakültesi, Istanbul Teknik Üniversitesi
Tavit Köletavitoğlu, Vice-Chair, Urban Land Institute, Istanbul
Somanahalli Mallaiah Krishna, Governor, State of Maharashtra
Lakshminarasimhan Krishnan, Chief Executive Officer, Infrastructure Leasing and Financial Services Ltd., Chennai
S. S. Kshatriya, Principal Secretary, Housing Department, Government of Maharashtra, Mumbai
Zeynep Kuban, Assistant Professor of Architecture, Mimarlık Fakültesi, Istanbul Teknik Üniversitesi
Nikolaus Kuhnert, Editor, Arch+, Berlin
Manish Kumar, Managing Director, Dreams Consultant Pvt.
Rakesh Kumar, Deputy Director, National Environmental Engineering Research Institute Zonal Laboratories (NEERI), Mumbai
Venkatesh Kumar, Associate Professor, Department of Civics and Politics, University of Mumbai, Mumbai
Ercan Kumcu, Columnist, Habertürk, Istanbul
Matiko Kume Vidal, President Director, Instituto de Reciclagem do Adolescente - Reciclar
Amitabh, Kundu, Professor of Economics, Centre for the Study of Regional Development, Jawaharlal Nehru University, New Delhi
Ali Kural, Partner, Kural Mimarlık, Istanbul
Nerkis Kural, Partner, Kural Mimarlık, Istanbul
Hatice Kurtuluş, Professor of Urban Sociology, Fen ve Edebiyat Fakültesi, Muğla Üniversitesi
Pieter Kuster, Architect
Monica Yukie Kuwahara, Professor, Economia do Centro de Ciencias Sociais e Aplicadas, Universidade Presbiteriana Mackenzie
Tuna Kuyucu, Researcher, Department of Sociology, University of Washington, Washington, D.C.
Lisette Lagnado, Professor of Visual Arts, Universidade de São Paulo
Rajan Lakule, Principal, J. J. School of Architecture, Mumbai
Abha Narain Lambah, Principal, Abha Narain Lambah Associates, Mumbai
Thais Lapp, Architect, Construtora Ferreira de Souza, São Paulo
Dieter Läpple, Professor, Hamburg University of Technology, Hamburg
Simone Laubach, Manager, BDA Bayern Architects, Munich
Andrew Lauck, MSc Student, Urbanisation and Development and Programme Assistant, Urban Age, London School of Economics and Political Science
Reynaldo Ledgard, Architect, FAU, Pontificia Universidad Católica del Perú
Franklin Lee, Visiting Instructor, Architectural Association, London
Kyung Mi Lee, Architect, Superintendência de Planejamento Habitacional, Cia Desenvolvimento Habitacional e Urbano do Estado de São Paulo
Goetz Lehmann, Producer, Timespot, Germany
Andre Leirner, Researcher, CAPG, FGV, São Paulo
Carlos Leite, Professor of Architecture, Mackenzie Presbyterian University, São Paulo
Suzana Leite Nogueira Karagiannidis, Director, Planejamento Urbano, Lenog Arquitetura
Christina Lenart, Editor, Arch+, Berlin
Arno Loebbecke, Architect, Arch+ Berlin
Ana Leonardo Nassar de Oliveira, Coordinator of Social Networks, Museu da Pessoa
Jaime Lerner, President, Instituto Jaime Lerner
Marina Lessa, Student, FAU, Universidade de São Paulo
Adriana Lessa de Oliveira, Researcher and Consultant, LABAUT, FAU, Universidade de São Paulo
Joaquim Levy, Secretary of Finance, State of Rio de Janeiro
Ramiro Levy, Student, FAU, Universidade de São Paulo
Mariana Levy Piza Fontes, General Coordinator of Studies and Research, Ministry of Justice, Federal Government of Brazil
Igor Vinicius Lima Valentim, Researcher, Ciencias Sociais, Universidade Tecnica de Lisboa
Maria C. L. D' Ottaviano, Professor, Centro de Estudos Urbanos, Universidade São Francisco, Itatiba
Eduardo Lopes, Architect, BAU arquitetura, São Paulo
Eduardo Lopes, Cooperativa de Reciclagem Nova Esperanca, São Paulo
Marcos Lopes, Assistant Reseacher, CEPESP, Fundacao Getulio Vargas, São Paulo
Melina Lopez Calvo, Technical Assistant, Ministerio de Desarrollo Urbano Gobierno, Buenos Aires
Xin Lu, Architect, Ibo-Concepts, Shanghai
Martin Luce, Fellow, Faculty of Architecture, Technische Universität Munich
Pedro Luis, Divisao Operacional, Centro de Policiamento da Capital
Yun Luo, Department of Graduate Studies, China Foreign Affairs University, Beijing
Bruna Luz, Tecnologia da Arquitetura, FAU, Universidade de São Paulo
Ana Claudia Maeda, Espaço Eventos, São Paulo
Jose Guilherme Magnani, Coordinator, Nucleo de Antropologia Urbana (NAU), São Paulo
Adalberto Maluf, São Paulo City Coordinator, Climate Change Initiative, Clinton Foundation
Mariana Malufe, Architect, Architectural Association School of Architecture
Fred Manson, Former Director of Regeneration & Environment, London Borough of Southwark and Associate Director of Heatherwick Studio
Alessandra Marchand, Research Associate, Urban Age, London School of Economics and Political Science
Monica Marcondes, Researcher, Departamento de Tecnologia da Arquitetura LABAUT, FAU, Universidade de São Paulo
Stefan Mahrdt, Chief Country Officer, Sri Lanka, Deutsche Bank AG, Colombo
Rohit Manchanda, Chief Representative in Mumbai, London Development Agency (LDA) and Mayor's Office, Mumbai
Erminia Maricato, Professor, Laboratório de Habitação e Assentamentos Humanos (LABHAB), FAU, Universidade de São Paulo
Eduardo Marques, Director, Centro de Estudos da Metrópole, São Paulo
Patricia Marra Sepe, Specialist in Urban Development, Secretaria Municipal Do Verde e Meio Ambiente, Prefeitura de São Paulo
Luca Martinazzoli, Freelance Journalist, Milan
Deise Josiane Martins, International Advisor, São Paulo State Government, São Paulo
Paulo Adolfo Martins, Student, FAU, Universidade de São Paulo
Eliana Martins de Mello, Planning and Development Analyst, Gerencia de Desenvolvimento, Empresa Metropolitana de Transportes Urbanos
Marta Martinz Magalhães, Advisor, Instituto Pereira Passos, Prefeitura do Rio de Janeiro, Rio de Janeiro
Ronaldo Marzagao, State Secretary, Public Security, State of São Paulo
Douglas Mattos Siqueira, Director, Instituto Navega São Paulo
Thomas Matussek, Ambassador of Germany to India, Ständige Vertretung der Bundesrepublik Deutschland bei den Vereinten Nationen
Maria Carolina Mauro, Associate, Triptyque, São Paulo
Semra Cerit Mazlum, Assistant Professor of International Relations, Siyaset Bilimi ve Uluslararası İlişkiler Bölümü, Marmara Üniversitesi, Istanbul
Shelagh McCartney, Doctoral Candidate, Urban Planning and Design, Harvard University
Justin McGuirk, Editor of ICON Magazine, London
Rocky McKnight, Head of Corporate Relations, London School of Economics and Political Science
Rahul Mehrotra, Principal, Rahul Mehrotra Associates, Mumbai
Mukesh Mehta, Chairman, MM Project Consultants Pvt. Ltd., Mumbai
Suketu Mehta, Author, Maximum City and Associate Professor, School of Journalism, New York University
José Renato Melhem, Arquiteto, Secretaria Municipal de Coordenação das Subprefeituras, Prefeitura de São Paulo
Danielly Melo Ordanini, Research Colaborator, Programa para Uso Eficiente de Energia na USP, Universidade de São Paulo
Güngör Mengi, Columnist, Vatan, Istanbul
Muhsin Mengütürk, Member of Board of Directors, Doğuş Holding, Istanbul
Javier Mendiondo, Researcher Professor, Facultad de Arquitectura, Universidad Catolica de Santa Fe
Cristina Mendonca, Director, Clinton Climate Initiative, Fundacao Clinto, Rio de Janeiro
Rualdo Menegat, Professor, Institute of Geosciences, Federal University of Rio Grande do Sul
Emine Merdim Yilmaz, Publications Coordinator, Arkitera Mimarlık Merkezi, Istanbul
Angela Merkel, Chancellor, Government of Germany, Berlin
Markus Merkel, Security
Regina Meyer, Coordinator of LUME, FAU, Universidade de São Paulo
Tanja Meyle, Meylenstein, Berlin
Anna Miana, PhD Student, Tecnologia da Arquitetura, FAU, Universidade de São Paulo
Cristiano Miglioranza Mercado, Sociologist, Mogi Mirim
Raphael Milion, Student, FAU, Universidade de São Paulo
Luis Minoru Shibata, Managing Director, Assuntos Publicos, Ipsos, São Paulo
Paula Miraglia, Executive Director, United Nations Latin American Institute for the Prevention of Crime and the Treatment of Offenders, São Paulo
Ashish Mishra, Manager, Emerging Markets, London Development Agency, London
Philipp Misselwitz, Sub-Curator, Internationale Architectuur Biennale Rotterdam
Nisha Mistry, Researcher, Cities Programme, London School of Economics and Political Science
Yasuyuki Miwa, Senior Researcher, The Mori Memorial Foundation, Tokyo
Denis Mizne, Executive Director, Instituto Sou da Paz, São Paulo
Pankaj Modi, Senior Vice President, Urban Planning, NMSEZ Ltd., Mumbai
Renu Modi, Centre for African Studies, Mumbai
Tarique Mohammad, Program Officer, Koshish Field Action Project on Homelessness and Destitution, Tata Institute of Social Sciences (TISS), Mumbai
Dinesh Mohan, Professor and Coordinator, Transportation Research and Injury Prevention Programme, Indian Institute of Technology (IIT) Delhi, New Delhi

Rakesh Mohan, Deputy Governor, Reserve Bank of India, Mumbai
Sudha Mohan, Associate Professor, Department of Civics and Politics, University of Mumbai, Mumbai
P. K. Mohanty, Joint Secretary, Ministry of Housing and Urban Poverty Alleviation, New Delhi
Helena Monteiro, Campus Party
Antonio M. V. Monteiro, Coordinator, Instituto Nacional de Pesquisas Espaciais, São Jose dos Campos
Leonardo Monteiro, Researcher, Departamento deTecnologia, FAU, Universidade de São Paulo
Talita Montiel D´Oliveira Castro, Analyst of Projects, FundacaoTelefonica, São Paulo
Marcos Moraes, Coordinator, Artes Plasticas, FAAP - Fundacao Armando Alvares Penteado
Marta Moreira, Architect, MMBB Arquitetos, São Paulo
Polise Moreira De Marchi, Professor, Design, Senac São Paulo
Monica Moreno, Architect and Urban Planner, Departamento deTecnologia, FAU, Universidade de São Paulo
Marcelo Morgado, Environmental Advisor, SABESP, Governo do Estado de São Paulo
Tan Morgül, Editor-in-Chief, Istanbul Dergisi
Rosemeire Mori, Deutsche Bank Urban Age Award Winner 2008, São Paulo
Elizaveta Mosina, Urbanist, Editorial Staff, Arch+, Berlin
Arthur Motta Parkinson, Founder, Parkinson Desenvolvimento Imobiliario
Renata Moura Santoniero, Student, FAU, Universidade Presbiteriana Mackenzie, São Paulo
Fernanda Mourão Lopes, Student, FAU, Universidade Presbiteriana Mackenzie, São Paulo
Dipti Mukherji, Reader, Department of Geography, University of Mumbai, Mumbai
Roberta C. K. Mülfarth, Professor, FAU, Universidade de São Paulo
Mauro Munhoz, Director, Mauro Munhoz Arquitetos, São Paulo
Cristiane Muniz, Partner Architect, UNA Arquitetos, São Paulo
Nasser Munjee, Chairman, Development Credit Bank, India
Talat Munshi, Associate Fellow, The Energy and Resources Institute, New Delhi
Yu Muraoka, Researcher, International Project Research Center, Mitsubishi Research Institute, Tokyo
Burcu Mutman, Environmental Engineer, Bureau Veritas, Istanbul
Demet Mutman, UA 2009 Istanbul Award Co-ordinator, Deutsche Bank, Alfred Herrhausen Society
Alessandro Muzi, Architect, Companhia de Projeto, São Paulo
Cynthia Myntti, Anthropologist and Scholar, Paris, Cairo
Vanessa Nadalin, PhD Student, FEA, Universidade de São Paulo
Kazuo Nakano, Senior architect, Nucleo de urbanismo, Instituto Polis
Paul Nakazawa, Lecturer, Department of Architecture, Harvard University, Boston
Marly Namur, Professor, Departamento de Projeto, FAU, Universidade de São Paulo
Priscila Napoli, Manager, Desenvolvimento Institucional, Save Brasil
Gabriel Nascimento Pinto, Student, Direito Internacional, Universidade de São Paulo
Regina Nascimento, Rio Grande do Norte Comunicacao Dirigida
Thiago Natal Duarte, Engineer, Obra Arquitetos, São Paulo
Mario Navarro, CEO, Paz Brasil, Barueri, São Paulo
Nayanika Nayak, Architect, The Design Platform, Mumbai
Narinder Nayar, Chairman and Director, Governing Board, Bombay First, Mumbai
Virginia Nehmi, Researcher, Departamento de Tecnologia, FAU, Universidade de São Paulo
Anja Nelle, Architect, Projetos Sociais, Fundacao de Desenvolvimento Habitacional de Fortaleza
Marcelo Nery, Project Adviser, Instituto São Paulo Contra a Violencia
Helio Neves, Cabinet Chief, Secretaria do Verde e do Meio Ambiente, Prefeitura de São Paulo
Marketa Newcova, Architect, Istanbul Ulaşım A.Ş.
Anh-linh Ngo, Editor, Arch+ Berlin
Manju Nichani, Principal, Kishinchand Chellaram College, Mumbai
Ignacio Niño Perez, General Coordinator of Strategy and International Action, Madrid Global
Ligia Nobre, Independent Researcher, São Paulo
Regina Nogueira, Assistant, Coordenadoria de Relações Institucionais, Secretaria dos Transportes Metropolitanos, Governo do Estado de São Paulo
Bruno Nogueira de França Santos, Student, FAU, Universidade de São Paulo
Enrique Norten, Architect, TEN Arquitectos, Mexico City and New York City
Wolfgang Nowak, Managing Director, Alfred Herrhausen Society, Berlin
Felipe Nunes, Architect, Rio de Janeiro
Kerem Okumuş, Regional Vice-director for Turkey and the Black Sea, The Regional Environmental Center for Central and Eastern Europe, Istanbul
Meliha Okur, Columnist, Sabah, Istanbul
Luci Oliveira, Manager, Assuntos Publicos, Ipsos, São Paulo
Roberto Oliveira, Coordinator of Communication and Projects
Sinan Omacan, Partner, Atölye Mimarlık, Istanbul
Yusuf Omar, Consul, Consulado Geral da Africa do Sul, São Paulo
Mehmet Onaner, Former Public Officer on International Commerce and Treasury, Istanbul
Barış Onay, Deputy Director, Yapı Endüstri Merkezi, Istanbul
Nicole Opel, Architect, Editorial Staff, Arch+ Berlin
Suna Birsen Otay, Partner, Trafo Mimarlik, Istanbul
Henk Ovink, Director, National Spatial Planning, Strategy and Design, Ministerie van VROM, The Hague
Pınar Öğünç, Columnist, Radikal, Istanbul
Ayse Öncü, Professor of Sociology, Sanat ve Sosyal Bilimler Fakültesi, Sabancı Üniversitesi, Istanbul
Meriç Öner, Editor, Garanti Galeri, Istanbul
Jose Orenstein de Almeida, Intern, Secretaria de Relacoes Internacionais, Prefeitura de São Paulo
Edsom Ortega, Coordinator of Public Security, Secretary of Governance, Municipality of São Paulo
Catherine Otondo, Architect and Urbanist, Instituto Acaia, São Paulo
Seçil Özalp, Urban Planner, Istanbul Metropoliten Planlama ve Kentsel Tasarım Merkezi
Nazan Özbaydar, Member of Executive Board, TMMOB Şehir Plancıları Odası, Istanbul Şubesi
Ahmet Özgüner, Partner, Paralel 41 Mimarlık, Istanbul
Ali Ercan Özgür, Programme Manager, İyi Yönetişim Programı, TESEV, Istanbul
Funda Özkan, Columnist, Radikal, Istanbul
Miray Özkan, Urban Planner, Kentsel Strateji, Istanbul
Begüm Özkaynak, Professor of Environmental and Ecological Economics, İktisadi ve İdari Bilimler Fakültesi, Boğaziçi Üniversitesi, Istanbul
Umut Özkırımlı, Professor of International Relations, Bilgi Üniversitesi, Istanbul
Orhan Öztürk, Civil Engineer, Istanbul
Ayşe Özyetgin, Researcher, Mimarlik Fakultesi, Istanbul Teknik Universitesi
Mariana Paál Fernandes, Project Assistant, Associação Brasileira para o Desenvolvimento de Liderancas, São Paulo
Antoine Paccoud, Researcher, Urban Age and LSE Cities, London School of Economics and Political Science
Vanessa Padia, Technical Coordinator, Projeto Heliópolis, Superintendência de Habitação Popular, Prefeitura do Municipio de São Paulo
Vaijayanti Padiyar, Regional Head, Infrastructure Leasing and Financial Services, Urban Infrastructure Managers Ltd., Mumbai
Eduardo Paes, Mayor-Elect of Rio de Janeiro
Ben Page, Chief Executive, Ipsos MORI UK and Ireland, London
Ricardo Pagliuso Regatieri, Analyst for Social and Urban Development, Companhia de Desenvolvimento Habitacional e Urbano, Estado de São Paulo
Balçiçek Pamir, Columnist, Habertürk, Istanbul
Şevket Pamuk, Chair, Contemporary Turkish Studies, London School of Economics and Political Science
Sneha Palnitkar, Director and Professor, All India Institute of Local Self-Government, Mumbai
Sudhir Panse, Adjunct Professor, University Institute of Chemical Technology, Mumbai
S. Parasuraman, Director, Tata Institute of Social Sciences (TISS), Mumbai
Anuradha Parikh, Founder, Matrix Architecture, Mumbai
P. S. Pasricha, Director General of Police, Maharashtra State Police, Mumbai
Kevin Parker, Global Head of Asset Management, Deutsche Bank, Berlin
Meltem Parlak, Urban Planner, Kentsel Strateji, Istanbul
Bernardo Parnes, Chief Country Officer, Deutsche Bank, São Paulo
Barbara Pasik, City Planning Adjunct Secretary, Ministerio de Desarrollo Urbano Gobierno, Buenos Aires
Claudia Pasquero, Partner, ecoLogicStudio, London
P. S. Pasricha, Director-General, Maharashtra State Police, Mumbai
Clara Passaro, Student, Departamento de Tecnologia, Faculdade de Arquitetura e Urbanismo, Universidade de São Paulo
Suzana Pasternak, Professor, FAU, Universidade de São Paulo
Anand Patel, Architect, HCP Design and Project Management Pvt. Ltd., Ahmedabad
Bimal Patel, Director, HCP Design and Project Management Pvt. Ltd., Ahmedabad
Jabbar Patel, Shastriya Nagar Housing Society, Mumbai
Sheela Patel, Founder, Society for the Promotion of Area Resource Centres (SPARC), Mumbai
Shirish Patel, Chairman Emeritus, SPA Consultants Pvt. Ltd., Mumbai
Anita Patil Deshmukh, Executive Director, Partners for Urban Knowledge Action and Research, Mumbai
Jayant Patil, Minister of Finance, Maharashtra State, Mumbai
Anirudh Paul, Director, Kamala Raheja Vidyanidhi Institute for Architecture, Mumbai
Aline Pek Di Salvo, Universidade Presbiteriana Mackenzie, São Paulo
Enrique Peñalosa, Mayor of Bogotá (1998 – 2000)
Jose Marcos Pereira de Araujo, Technical advisor, Secretaria Municipal de Planejamento, Prefeitura de São Paulo
Glauco Peres, Pesquisador, CEPESP, FGV, São Paulo
Jenny Perez, Architect and Urbanist, Arquitetura e Urbanismo e Gestão Ambiental, FiamFaam e FMU, São Paulo
Reinaldo Paul Pérez Machado, Professor, Faculdade de Filosofia, Letras, Ciencias Sociais e Historia, Universidade de São Paulo
Jorge Pessoa De Carvalho, Architect and Urbanist, Instituto Acaia, São Paulo
Abhay Pethe, Vibhooti Chair in Urban Economics, Department of Economics, University of Mumbai, Mumbai
Stefan Pfefferle, Southern California Institute of Architecture (SCI-Arc), Los Angeles
Jairaj M. Phatak, Municipal Commissioner, Brihan Mumbai Municipal Corporation, Mumbai
Vidyadhar K. Phatak, Consultant, Urban Planning and Management, V. K. Phatak, Mumbai
Juliana Pimentel Nogueira, Student, FAU, Universidade Presbiteriana Mackenzie
Eduardo Pimentel Pizarro, Student, Departamento deTecnolgia da Arquitetura, FAU, Universidade de São Paulo
Minar Pimple, Deputy Director, Asia, United Nations Millennium Campaign, Bangkok
Juliana Pinheiro Gonçalves, Student, FAU, Universidade de São Paulo
Andre Luiz Pinto, Manager, Unidade de Gerenciamento de Projetos, SMC Consultoria, Rio de Janeiro
Ciro Pirondi, Director, Escola da Cidade, São Paulo
Caio Piza, Professor, Centro de Ciencias Sociais e Aplicadas, Universidade Presbiteriana Mackenzie
Daniela Platsch, Key Account Manager, Austrian Trade Commission, London
Gunter W. Pollack, Gerente Relações Internacionais, Fundação de Rotarianos de São Paulo
Jose Luis Portella, Secretary of Transport, State of São Paulo
Ricardo Porto de Almeida, Editor, Telejornalismo, Fundacao Casper Libero, São Paulo
Chandrashekhar Prabhu, Editor, Indian Institute of Architects and Economic Digest, Mumbai
Tiyok Prasetyoadi, Managing Director, Associate Architect and Urban Designer, Planning & Development Workshop, Indonesia
Arun Prasad Raja, PhD Student, University of Leipzig, Leipzig
Pamela Puchalski, Projects Coordinator 2007-2009, Urban Age, London School of Economics and Political Science
Neera Punj, Convenor, CitiSpace: Citizens Forum for the Protection of Public Spaces, Mumbai
Silvia Pupareli, Project Adviser, Administración de Infraestructuras Ferroviarias, Ministerio de Planificación e Infraestructura, Buenos Aires
Ana Silvia Puppim, Project Coordinator, Centro de Direitos Humanos e Educacao Popular Defesa da Vida, São Paulo
Shoba Purushothaman, Founder and Chief Executive Officer, The NewsMarket, New York
Isabelle Putseys, Southern California Institute of Architecture (SCI-Arc), Los Angeles
Joaquim Racy, Professor, Economia, Pontificia Universidade Catolica de São Paulo
Parimal Rai, Chairman, New Delhi Municipal Council, New Delhi
Champaka Rajagopal, Urban Designer, Bangalore
B. Rajaram, Director, Atri Knowledge Embedded Infrastructure Lab Pvt. Ltd., Hyderabad
R. A. Rajeev, Additional Municipal Commissioner, Municipal Corporation of Greater Mumbai, Mumbai
R. V. Rama Rao, Chief Project Coordinator and Member, National Technical Advisory Group, Jawaharlal Nehru National Urban Renewal Mission, Ministry of Housing and Urban Poverty Alleviation, Government of India, Visakhapatnam
Ramesh Ramanathan, Co-Founder, Janaagraha Centre for Citizenship and Democracy, Bangalore
Radhika Ramasubban, Member, National Technical Advisory Group, and Director, Centre for Social and Technological Change, Mumbai
Bruce Ramer, Chairperson, Gang, Tyre, Ramer & Brown Inc., Beverly Hills
Frederico Roman Ramos, Research Associate, Urban Age, London School of Economics and Political Science
Jose Ovidio Ramos, Professor, Departamento deTecnologia - LABAUT, FAU, Universidade de São Paulo
Sueli Terezinha Ramos Schiffer, Professor, FAU, Universidade de São Paulo
Sean Randolph, President and Chief Executive Officer, Bay Area Economic Forum, San Francisco
Manjula Rao, Head of Programmes, British Council Division, British Deputy High Commission, Mumbai
Anand Rao, Professor, Centre for Technology Alternatives for Rural Areas (CTARA), Indian Institute of Technology (IIT) Bombay, Mumbai
Anupam Rastogi, Principal, Infrastructure Development Financial Corporation, Mumbai
Cordula Rau, Journalist, Walverwandtschaften, Munich
Shubha Raul, Mayor, Brihan Mumbai Municipal Corporation, Mumbai
Martin Raven, Consul, Consulado Geral da Gra-Bretanha, São Paulo
K.T. Ravindran, Head, Department of Urban Design, School of Planning and Architecture, New Delhi
Barun Kumar Ray, Secretary, Kolkata Metropolitan Development Authority, Kolkata
Tomás Rebollo, Architect, FAU, Universidade de São Paulo
Elias Redstone, Senior Curator, The Architecture Foundation, London
Thais Reis Cardoso, Student, Escritório Público De Arquitetura, Universidade Federal do Rio de Janeiro
Camila Renault, Supervisor, Incorporacao, Camargo Correa Desenvolvimento Imobiliario, São Paulo
Joao Rett Lemos, Student Researcher, Laboratorio da Paisagem Projeto QUAPA, FAU, Universidade de São Paulo
Amelia Reynaldo, Universidade Catolica de Pernambuco
Hennie Reynders, Head of Department of Interior Architecture and Designed Objects, School of the Art Institute of Chicago
E. F. N. Ribeiro, Principal, Ribeiro Associates, New Delhi
Manoel Ribeiro, Urban Planner and UNESCO consultant, Rio de Janeiro
Bernd Rieger, CEO, Rieger Reurbanização, São Paulo
Tim Rieniets, Researcher and Chair for Architecture and Urban Design, The Swiss Federal Institute of Technology, ETH Zurich
Gabriela Rimoldi Cunha, Student, FAU, Universidade de São Paulo
Daniela Risafi de Pontes, Student, Ludwig-Maximilians-Universität München
Melina Risso, Director, Desenvolvimento Institucional, Instituto Sou da Paz, São Paulo
Luiz Guilherme Rivera De Castro, Coordinating Professor of Urbanism, FAU, Universidade Presbiteriana Mackenzie
Guido Robazza, Researcher, Urban Age, London School of Economics and Political Science
Christoph Rode, Account Manager, T-Systems Enterprise Services GmbH, Stuttgart
Philipp Rode, Executive Director, Urban Age & LSE Cities, London School of Economics and Political Science
Pravin Rodrigues, Associate Professor, Communication Arts, Ashland University, Ashland, Ohio
Guida Rodrigues, Espaço Eventos, São Paulo
Thais Rodrigues Corral, President, Associação Brasileira para o Desenvolvimento de Liderancas ABDL, Rio de Janeiro
Daniela Rodrigues Damaceno, Coordinator, Movimento dos Trabalhadores Sem Teto, São Paulo
Alessandra Rodrigues Prata Shimomura, Researcher, Tecnologia, LABAUT, FAU, Universidade de São Paulo
Klemens Roel, Vice President, Deutsche Bank AG, São Paulo
Richard Rogers, Chairman, Rogers Stirk Harbour + Partners, London
Eduardo Rojas, Principal Urban Development Specialist, Inter-American Development Bank BID
Valentina Rojas Loa Salazar, Author, Citambulos Mexico City

Raquel Rolnik, Architect and Professor, Pontifícia Universidade Católica de Campinas
MariaTereza Romero Leal, Co-founder, Coordenacao Artistica e Executiva, COOPA-ROCA, Rio de Janeiro
Patricia Romero Lankao, Deputy Director, Institute for the Study of Society and Environment, National Centre for Atmospheric Research, Boulder
Alex M. Rosa, Architect, Cia. Publica Municipal Pró-Habitação, Embu
Carlos Rosa, Coordinator, Coletivo Dulcineia Catadora, São Paulo
Elisabet Rosa, ProfesoraTitular, Geografia Humana, Universitat de Barcelona
Lucia G. L. Rosa, Coordinator, Coletivo Dulcineia Catadora
Marcos Rosa, Project Manager, Deutsche Bank Urban Age Award São Paulo, Alfred Herrhausen Society, Berlin
Eli Rosenbaum, Harvard Law School, Harvard University, Cambridge, Massachusetts
Tomas Rosenfeld, Student, Relacoes Internacionais,Faculdade de Economia e Administracao (FEA), Universidade de São Paulo
Renato Roseno De Oliveira, Advisor, Associação Nacional dos Centros de Defesa da Criança e do Adolescente, Fortaleza
Dunu Roy, Director, Hazard Centre, New Delhi
Katia Beatris Rovaron Moreira, PhD Student, Tecnologia da Construcao, FAU, Universidade de São Paulo
Nancy Rubens, Artist, NewYork
Rick Rubens, Professor of Psychology, Department of Counseling & Clinical Psychology, Columbia University, NewYork
Mariana Rudge, Manager, Cia. Desenvolvimento Habitacional e Urbano, Superintendencia de Planejamento, Estado de São Paulo
Beatriz Rufino, Student, Faculdade de Arquitetura e Urbanismo, Universidade de São Paulo
Lizzie Rusbridger, Administrator, Urban Age, London School of Economics and Political Science
Filomena Russo, Partner, Foster + Partners, London
Suzan Sabancı Dinçer, Member of the Board and Managing Director, Akbank, Istanbul
Janette Sadik-Khan, Commissioner, Department ofTransportation, NewYork City
Prabhat Sahai, Chief Mechanical Engineer, Mumbai RailwayVikas Corporation Ltd., Mumbai
Bittu Sahgal, Editor, Sanctuary, Mumbai
Sare Sahil, Head of Architecture Department, Mimarlık Fakültesi, Uludağ Üniversitesi, Bursa
Carina Saito, Architect, Desenvolvimento de Mercado, Associação Brasileira de Cimento Portland
Güven Sak, Director,Türkiye Ekonomi Politikaları Araştırma Merkezi, Ankara
Patricia Sakata, Research Assistant, Architecture School, Harvard University, Cambridge
Dilgün Saklar, Partner,Tekeli-Sisa Mimarlık, Istanbul
Rachel Salamander, Publicist andWriter, Munich
Violeta Saldanha Kubrusly,Technical Ccoordinator, Superintendência de Habitação Popular, Prefeitura Municipal de São Paulo
Yıldız Salman, Assistant Professor in Architecture, Mimarlık Fakültesi, IstanbulTeknik Üniversitesi
Rubens Salles, President, Instituto Artesocial, São Paulo
Alexis Sanal, Partner, Sanal Mimarlık, Istanbul
Murat Sanal, Partner, Sanal Mimarlık, Istanbul
Manuel Sanches, Associate Professor, Ciência Politica, Universidade Federal do Rio de Janeiro
Patricia Mara Sanches, Architect and Urban Planner, Desenho Urbano Sustentavel Luz, FAU, Universidade de São Paulo
Renata Sandoli, Researcher, Departamento de Tecnolodia - LABAUT, FAU, Universidade de São Paulo
Elton Santa Fe, Secretary, Secretaria de Habitacao, Prefeitura Municiapal de São Paulo
Vladimir Santana, PhD Student, Escola Brasileira de Administração Pública e de Empresas, FGV, São Paulo
Paulo Santiago, Director and Founder, Novo Olhar
Paula Santoro, Urban Planner, Programa Mananciais, Instituto Socioambiental
Danilo Santos De Miranda, Director,The Social Service of Commerce, São Paulo
Sanjeev Sanyal, Chief Economist and Senior Investment Advisor, Deutsche Bank Singapore
Arup Sarbadhikari,Trustee, Bandra Bandstand Residence Association, Mumbai
Nandini Sardesai, Professor, Department of Sociology, St. Xavier's College, Mumbai
Hashim Sarkis, Aga Khan Professor of Landscape Architecture and Urbanism, Graduate School of Design, Harvard University, Cambridge, Massachusetts
Saskia Sassen, Helen and Robert Lynd Professor of Sociology, Columbia University, NewYork City
Stephan Sattler, Journalist, Focus Magazine, Munich
Anne Save de Beaurecueil, Adjunct Assistant Professor, Architectural Association, London
Ana Paula Sayao, Espaço Eventos, São Paulo
Haluk Sayar, CEO, Ecofys, Istanbul
Muriel Schenkel, MA Student, Public Management and Governance, Zeppelin University, Wiesbaden
Tatiane Schilaro, Coordinator Architect, Apoio Tecnico, Associação Viva o Centro, São Paulo
Inge Schmidt-Barthel, Heilpraktiker, Warstein
Rolf Schmidt-Holz, Sony BMG Music Entertainment
Folke Schuppert, Professor for Governance, Wissenschaftszentrum Berlin für Sozialforschung
Giorgio Romano Schutte, Coordinator, Alianca de Cidades, São Paulo
Luciana Schwandner Ferreira, Researcher, FAU, Universidade de São Paulo
Martin Schwegmann, Architect, Urban Passion, Berlin
Renata Semin, Director, Piratininga Arquitetos Associados, São Paulo
Richard Sennett, University Professor of the Humanities, NewYork University, NewYork City; Emeritus Professor of Sociology, London School of Economics
Josef-Fidelis Senn, Vice President of Human Resources, Volkswagen do Brasil, São Paulo
Arıl Seren, Chairman, Istanbul Menkul Kıymetler Borsası
Utku Serkan Zengin, Urban Planner, Istanbul Metropoliten Planlama ve KentselTasarım Merkezi
Alejandra Serna, Student, Escola da Cidade, São Paulo
Eva Serra, Architect and Senior Planner, Barcelona Regional
José Serra, Governor of the State of São Paulo (2007 – 2010)
Sibel Sezer Eralp, Regional Director forTurkey and the Black Sea,The Regional Environmental Center for Central and Eastern Europe, Ankara
Eunice Helena Sguizzardi Abascal, Professor, FAU, Universidade Presbiteriana Mackenzie, São Paulo
Rupa Shah, Vice Chancellor, SNDTWomen's University, Mumbai
Bashar Shakra, Assistant Project Manager, Syrian-GermanTechnical Cooperation GTZ, Damascus
Priya Shankar, Policy Researcher, Policy Network, London
Deepak Kumar Sharma
Suresh Sharma, Director, Centre for the Study of Developing Societies, New Delhi
Utpal Sharma, Dean, School of Planning, Centre for Environmental Planning andTechnology (CEPT) University, Ahmedabad
Vikas Sharma, General Manager,Traffic and Transportation Planning, LEA Associates, Mumbai
Prasad Shetty, Executive Member, Collective Research InitiativesTrust (CRIT), Mumbai
Simone Shoji, Researcher, FAU, Universidade de São Paulo
Kapil Sibal, Minister of State, Science and Technology and Minister of Earth Sciences, Indian National Congress, New Delhi
Rosimeire Silva, Researcher, Centro de Estudos Sociais, Universidade de Coimbra
Rafael Silva Brandao, Researcher, Departamento deTecnologia, FAU, Universidade de São Paulo
Denise Helena Silva Duarte, Professor, Departamento deTecnologia, FAU, Universidade de São Paulo
Maria Laura Silveira, Researcher and Lecturer, LABOPLAN - FFCL, Universidade de São Paulo
Gabriela Simoes Garcia, Student, FAU, Universidade de São Paulo
Hillary Simon, SLUMLAB, Columbia University, NewYork
Regina Simpson, ODAR, London School of Economics and Political Science
Richard Simpson, MRes student, Human Geography, Department of Geography and Environment, and Researcher, Urban Age, London School of Economics and Political Science
Subir Hari Singh, Metropolitan Commissioner, Urban Development, Bangalore Metropolitan Region Development Authority, Bangalore
Manfred Sinz, Head of Spatial Planning Group, Federal Ministry ofTransport, Berlin
Charles Siqueira, Project Coordinator, Rede de Desenvolvimento Humano, Instituto Polen, Rio de Janeiro
Renata Siqueira, Student, FAU, Universidade de São Paulo
Maria Sisternas, Researcher, Cities Programme, London School of Economics and Political Science
K. C. Sivaramakrishnan, HonoraryVisiting Professor, Centre for Policy Research, New Delhi
Danielle Snellen, Researcher, Planbureau voor de Leefomgeving,The Hague
Medha Somaiya, Coordinator, Centre for Slum Studies, Ramnarayan Ruia College, Mumbai
Vinay Somani, Karmayog, Mumbai
Brinda Somaya, Principal Architect, Somaya & Kalappa Consultants Pvt. Ltd., Mumbai
Nadia Somekh, Director, FAU, Universidade Presbiteriana Mackenzie
Semra Somersan, Associate Professor, İletişim Fakültesi, Bilgi Üniversitesi, Istanbul
Clair Souki, Southern California Institute of Architecture (SCI-Arc), Los Angeles
Lucia Sousa e Silva, Reseacher, LUME, FAU, Universidade de São Paulo
Firuz Soyuer, Managing Partner and Co-founder, DTZ Pamir & Soyuer, Istanbul
Mustafa Sönmez, Economist, Istanbul
Özdemir Sönmez, Urban Design and Competition Group Coordinator, Istanbul Metropoliten Planlama ve KentselTasarım Merkezi
Aldaiza Sposati, Coordinator, Centro de Estudos de Desigualdades Socio-Territoriais, Pontifícia Universidade Católica de São Paulo
Albert Speer, Managing Partner, Albert Speer + Partner, Frankfurt
Saidee Springall, Founding Partner, Arquitectura 911 SC, Mexico City
S. Sriraman, Walachand Hirachand Professor of Transport Economics, Department of Economics, University of Mumbai, Mumbai
Manu Kumar Srivastava, Additional Municipal Commissioner, Brihan Mumbai Municipal Corporation, Mumbai
Rahul Srivastava, Research Advisor, Partners for Urban Knowledge, Action and Research, Mumbai
Surendra Srivastava, Lok Satta, Mumbai
Lord Nicholas Stern, Chair, Grantham Research Institute on Climate Change and the Environment; IG Patel Chair and Director, Asia Research Centre and India Observatory, Department of Economics, London School of Economics and Political Science
Jaime Stiglich, Consul, Consulado Geral do Peru, São Paulo
Kristine Stiphany, Architect, Brasil Arquitetura
Thomas Stini, Founder, Onorthodox, Vienna
Heloisa Strobel, Architect, Instituto Jaime Lerner, Curitiba
Fabiana Stuchi, Coordinator Architect, Piratininga Arquitetos Associados, São Paulo
Yedla Sudhakar, Associate Professor, Urban Environmental Management, Indira Gandhi Institute of Development Research, Mumbai
Deyan Sudjic, Director, Design Museum, London
Dattaraya M. Sukthankar, Vice Chairman, Action for Good Governance and Networking in India, Mumbai
Haluk Sur, Chair, Urban Land Institute, Istanbul
K.T. Suresh, Executive Director,Youth of Unity and Voluntary Action (YUVA), Mumbai
Evrim Sümer, Manager of Corporate Communications, Hürriyet Gazetesi, Istanbul
Birgitte Svarre, Research Coordinator, Gehl Architects, Urban Quality Consultants, Copenhagen
Ilona Szabo de Carvalho, Senior Manager, Instituto Synergos, Rio de Janeiro
Salih Kenan Şahin, Mayor, Pendik Belediyesi, Istanbul
Aytug Şaşmaz, Project Assitant, Eğitim Reform Girişimi, Istanbul Politikalar Merkezi, Sabancı Üniversitesi, Istanbul
Remzi Şeker, Deputy Mayor, Pendik Belediyesi, Istanbul
Kubra Şen, Member of Executive Board,TMMOB Şehir Plancıları Odası, Istanbul Şubesi
Uğur Şenarslan, Urban Planner, Istanbul Metropoliten Planlama ve KentselTasarım Merkezi
Serap Şengül, Director ofTransport Planning, Istanbul Metropoliten Planlama ve Kentsel Tasarım Merkezi
RenatoTagnin, Architect and Professor, Servico Nacional de Aprendizagem Comercial, São Paulo
MeralTamer, Columnist, Milliyet Gazetesi, Istanbul
PelinTan, Sociologist, Art Historian, Sosyal Bilimler Enstitüsü, IstanbulTeknik Üniversitesi
LuiTanaka, Advisor, Gerencia de Comunicacao e Marketing, Companhia do Metropolitano de São Paulo
KöksalTandıroğlu, Head of Strategy Development Department, Istanbul Büyükşehir Belediyesi
GörgünTaner, General Director, Istanbul Foundation for Culture and Arts
AliTaptık, Freelance Photographer, Istanbul
AngelicaTanus Benatti Alvim, Research Coordinator, FAU, Universidade Presbiteriana Mackenzie
NelsonTapias, Director of Programs, SESC, Pompei
BülentTaşar, Managing Director, Siemens Finansal Kiralama, Istanbul
GuilhermeTeixeira, Director, Acao Cultural e Educativa, Centro Cultural São Paulo
PauloTeixeira, Federal Deputy, Camara dos Deputados, Brasilia
DoğanTekeli, Founding Partner,Tekeli-Sisa Mimarlık, Istanbul
İlhanTekeli, Professor of City and Regional Planning, Orta DoğuTeknik Üniversitesi, Ankara
Antonio AugustoTelles Machado, Nacional Director, Projeto IncluSão Social Urbana - 'Nos do Centro', São Paulo
Anne ter Steege, Advisor, Strategy and Finance, Slum Rehabilitation Society, Mumbai
ElaineTerrin, Student, FAU, Universidade de São Paulo
FatihTerzi, Researcher on Architecture, Mimarlık Fakültesi, IstanbulTeknik Üniversitesi
NatznetTesfay, Project Associate, Urban Age, London School of Economics and Political Science
GregersTangThomsen, Founding Partner, Superpool, Istanbul
PhichaiThaengthong, Student, Southern California Institute of Architecture (SCI-Arc), Los Angeles
BhaktiThakoor, Project Head, Urban Design, Ratan J. Batliboi Architects, Mumbai
CenkTıkız, Co-ordinator, United Cities and Local Governments, Middle East andWest Asia Section, Istanbul
AnandTiwari, Director, Public Relations, New Delhi Municipal Council, New Delhi
GeetamTiwari, Chair and Associate Professor, TRIPP, Indian Institute ofTechnology, New Delhi
FikretToksöz, Programme Director, İyiYönetişim Programı,TESEV, Istanbul
RicardoToledo, Deputy Secretary, Water Sanitation and Environment, State of São Paulo
GermanTorres, Advisor to Metropolitan Mayor of Lima
EduardoTrani, Secretario Adjunto, Secretaria de Estado da Habitacao, State of São Paulo
LucianaTravassos, Researcher, LUME, FAU, Universidade de São Paulo
TonyTravers, Director, LSE London, London School of Economics and Political Science
UpendraTripathy, Managing Director, Bangalore MetropolitanTransport Corporation, Bangalore
Paulo JoséTripoloni, Architect, Criação, Grupo Artless
Patricia D.Truzzi, Student, FAU, Universidade de São Paulo
AlpTümertekin, Partner, Managing Director, Mimarlar Design, Istanbul
SebastianTurner, Partner of Scholz & Friends Group GmbH and Member of the Board of Trustees of the Herrhausen-Gesellschaft
HakanTüzün Şengün, Lecturer in Architecture, Mimarlık Fakültesi, IstanbulTeknik Üniversitesi
Sanjay Ubale, Secretary, Special Projects, General Administration Department, Government of Maharashtra, Mumbai
Natalia Ubilla, Espaço Eventos, São Paulo
Aydın Uğur, Professor of Communications, Bilgi Üniversitesi, Istanbul
Osman Ulagay, Columnist, Milliyet, Istanbul
Öykü Uluçay, İyiYönetişim Programı,TESEV, Istanbul
Bülent Uluengin, Professor of Architecture, Mimarlık Fakültesi, Bahçeşehir Üniversitesi, Istanbul
Belkıs Uluoğlu, Assistant Professor of Architecture, Mimarlık Fakültesi, IstanbulTeknik Üniversitesi
Erica Mitie Umakoshi, Researcher, Departamento deTecnologia da Arquitetura LABAUT, FAU, Universidade de São Paulo
Andre Urani, Executive Director, Instituto de Estudos deTrabalho e Sociedade, Rio de Janeiro
İdil Üçer Karababa,Teaching Assistant, Foundations Development, Sabancı Üniversitesi, Istanbul
Sinan Ülgen, Chairman, EDAM
Alper Ünlü, Professor of Architecture, Mimarlık Fakültesi, IstanbulTeknik Üniversitesi
Deniz Ünsal, Assistant Professor, İletişim Fakültesi, Bilgi Üniveresitesi, Istanbul
Fatma Ünsal, Professor of Urban and Regional Planning, Mimarlık Fakültesi, Mimar Sinan Güzel Sanatlar Üniversitesi, Istanbul
Özlem Ünsal, Researcher, Department of Sociology, City University, London
MirianVaccari, Architect, Oxford Brookes University
DavidVan Der Leer, Assistant Curator for Architecture and Design, Solomon R. Guggenheim Museum, NewYork
AntonVan Hoorn, Researcher, Planbureau voor de Leefomgeving,The Hague
TiagoValente, Architect,Valente Arquitetos, São Paulo
AlfonsoValenzuela-Aguilera, Professor, Institute of Urban and Regional Development, University of California, Berkeley
GianfrancoVannucchi, Co-Director, Königsberger

Vannucchi Arquitetos Associados Ltda, São Paulo
Eduardo Vasconcellos, Consultant, Associação Nacional de Transportes Publicos
Daniel Vasquez, Researcher, Centro de Estudos da Metropole, Centro Brasileiro de Análise e Planejamento, São Paulo
Gündüz Vassaf, Author, Psychologist, Istanbul
João Alberto Vaz Massler, Engineer, Consultoria de Transportes, Urbanismo Transporte Modelagem Ltda.
Achyut Vaze, Director, Institute of Mass Media, Mumbai Educational Trust (MET), Mumbai
Murat Vefkioğlu, Urban Design and Competition Group Director, Istanbul Metropoliten Planlama ve Kentsel Tasarım Merkezi
America Vera-Zavala, Writer, Playwright, Stockholm and Member of the Alfred Herrhausen Society Board of Trustees, Deutsche Bank
Savvas Verdis, Tutorial Fellow, Cities Programme, London School of Economics and Political Science
Javier Vergara Petrescu, Editor, Plataforma Urbana, Santiago de Chile
Francisco Vidal Luna, Secretary of State, Secretaria de Economia e Planejamento, Governo do Estado de São Paulo
Fernando Felippe Viegas, Architect, UNA Arquitetos, São Paulo
Pablo Viejo, Project Manager, EIFER, Karlsruhe
Joao Vieira, Director, Departamento de Aguas e Energia Eletrica, Secretaria de Saneamento e Energia, Governo do Estado de São Paulo
Tuca Vieira, Photographer
Maria Rita Villela, Senior Researcher, Programa Meio Ambiente de Desenvolvimento, Instituto de Estudos da Religiao
Marcos Virgilio, Advisor on Social-Environmental studies, Grupo de Projetos Integrados, Diasonal Urbana Consultoria
Aydan Volkan, Partner, Kreatif Mimarlık, Istanbul
Hilmar Von Lojewski, Program Manager, Syrian-German Technical Cooperation GTZ, Damascus
Christian Vonwissel, Author, Citambulos Mexico City
Subodh Wagle, Professor, Tata Institute of Social Sciences (TISS), Mumbai
Darren Walker, Vice-President, The Rockefeller Foundation
Chuck Ware, Southern California Institute of Architecture (SCI-Arc), Los Angeles
Alexandros Washburn, Chief Urban Designer, City of New York
Shridar Washikar, Manager, Urban Planning, NMSEZ Pvt. Ltd., Mumbai
Julio Watanabe Jr, Technical Director, Departamento de Planejamento Urbano, Prefeitura de Barueri, SP
Ben Watt-Meyer, Designer, Chernoff Thompson Architects, Vancouver
Mark Watts, Former Environmental Advisor to Ken Livingstone, Mayor of London 2004-2008
Ute Weiland, Deputy Director, Alfred Herrhausen Society, Berlin
Barry Weisberg, PhD Candidate, Research Associate, Criminoloqy, Law and Justice Department, University of Illinois
Matthieu Wellner, Researcher, Technische Universität Munich
Christian Werthmann, Associate Professor in Landscape Architecture, Graduate School of Design, Harvard University
Joseph West, Southern California Institute of Architecture (SCI-Arc), Los Angeles
Francine Wey, Head of Communications, Deutsche Bank, São Paulo
Jorge Wilheim, Principal, Jorge Wilheim Consultores e Associados, São Paulo
Anthony Williams, Mayor of Washington DC (1999–2006)
Darien Williams, Southern California Institute of Architecture (SCI-Arc), Los Angeles
Alison Wolanski, Researcher, Management of Technology, Federal Polytechnic School of Lausanne
Kari Wolanski, Senior Policy Analyst, Income Security, Government of Canada
Richard Woolhouse, Senior Economist, Centre for Cities, London
Sarah Worthington, Pro-Director, London School of Economics and Political Science
Arthur Xavier, Former Deputy Mayor, Subprefeitura de Tiradentes, Municipality of São Paulo
Murat Yalçıntan, Professor of City and Regional Planning, Mimarlık Fakültesi, Mimar Sinan Güzel Sanatlar Üniversitesi, Istanbul
Yeliz Yalın, Volunteer, Barış için Müzik, Istanbul
Vitor Yamamoto, Student, FAU, Universidade Presbiteriana Mackenzie
Birgül Yavuz, Director of Information Center, Yapı Endüstri Merkezi, Istanbul
Hakan Yener, Coordinator, Urban Land Institute, Istanbul
Musa Yetim, General Director, Istanbul Konut A.Ş.

Burçin Yıldırım, Co-Founder, Potansiyel Araştırmalar Birimi, Istanbul
Eyyüp Yıldırım, Foreign Relations Specialist, Dış İlişkiler Müdürlüğü, Istanbul Büyükşehir Belediyesi
Kerimcan Yıldırım, Projects Officer, United Cities and Local Governments, Middle East and West Asia Section, Istanbul
Selahattin Yıldırım, Secretary General, United Cities and Local Governments, Middle East and West Asia Section, Istanbul
Demet Yıldız, Researcher, Foundations Development, Sabancı Üniversitesi, Istanbul
Erdoğan Yıldız, Representative, Istanbul Mahalle Dernekleri Platformu
Sevin Yıldız, Researcher on Architecture, New Jersey Institute of Technology
Ömer Yılmaz, Partner, Arkitera Mimarlık Merkezi, Istanbul
Serpil Yılmaz, Columnist, Milliyet, Istanbul
Hakki Yırtıcı, Assistant Professor of Architecture, Mimarlık Fakültesi, Istanbul Kültür Universitesi
Emine Yilmazgil, Architect, Istanbul
Anupam Yog, Chief Executive Officer, Mirabilis Advisory, Delhi
Cristiane Yoshimura, Architect, Comercial, Sinalmig Sinais e Sistemas Ltda, São Paulo
Eda Yücesoy, Assistant Professor, Mimari Tasarım Programı, Bilgi Üniversitesi, Istanbul
Özlem Yüzak, Columnist, Cumhuriyet Gazetesi, Istanbul
Alejandro Zaera-Polo, Joint Director, Foreign Office Architects, London
Ramesh Zalki, Managing Director, Karnataka Road Development Corporation Ltd., Bangalore
Leticia Zamolo Duque, Student, Departamento de Tecnologia, FAU, Universidade de São Paulo
Julia Zanghieri, Corporate Relations Manager, CRU, London School of Economics and Political Science
Adrian Zeller, Architect, Massimo Lopreno Architects and Independent Architect, Switzerland
Dimitri Zenghelis, Visiting Senior Fellow, Grantham Research Institute on Climate Change and the Environment, London School of Economics and Political Science; Chief Climate Economist, Cisco
Ignacio Zervino, Economist, Fundación AVINA, Buenos Aires
Silvana Zioni, Architect and Professor, FAU, Universidade Presbiteriana Mackenzie, São Paulo
Maria Helena Zonzini, Espaço Eventos, São Paulo
Maria Zulmira de Souza, Journalist, TV Cultura, São Paulo
Harald Peter Zwetkoff, Director, Companhia de Concessões Rodoviárias, São Paulo

INDEX

Page numbers in *italics* refer to illustrative material or information in the caption. **Bold** pages indicate the main discussion of a city.

Abdul Hamid II 231
Abu Dhabi 227
Ackermann, Dr Josef 7
Africa 61, 94; and multiculturalism in São Paulo 165-6
age structure of cities 260-1, 301, 302-3
air travel: global connections *30-1*; low-cost airlines *332, 333*, 334, 335, 340
Aix-en-Provence 326
Aleppo 22, 227, 228, 230-1
Alexandria 222, 227
Algeria 206, 222
American Apparel *60*, 339
Amman 227, 228
Amsterdam 24-5, 121, 346, 348
Anatolian migrants in Istanbul 208, *218*, *219*, 295
Ankara 206, 210, 212, 213, 227, *228*, 246
Appudarai, Arjun 115, 362
Arab cities 22, 224-31
Arab League 230
Arab nationalism 227
Aravena, Alejandro *46*, 52-3
architecture 18, 44-55; Istanbul 44, *47*, 51-2, 246, *247*; Mumbai 44, *45*, *48*, 53-5, 88; 'no-frills' 334, *336*, 336-7, *337*, 338, 340; plate glass walls 328-9; preservation campaigns 4; São Paulo 44, *49*, *136-7*, 149, 178, 181, 182
Argentina 155, 159, *see also* Buenos Aires
Aputham, Jockin 376
Arte Povera 337-8
Ataturk, Kemal 206, 208, *228*
Atlanta 344

Baghdad 209, 227
Baghdad Pact 227
the Balkans: and Istanbul 226, 227
Balyan, Sarkis 231
Bananare, Juó (Alexandre Marcondes Machado): *La Divina Increnca* 162-5
Bangladesh 94
Bangladore 15, 86, 88, 94, 122
Barcelona 24-5, *47*, 51, 181, 222, 344
Bardi, Lino Bo 149
bare-life politics 240, 335-7
Bastide, Roger 166
Beijing 327, 385-6
Beirut 22, 222, 227, *228*, 228, 230, 231
Bengal 86, 88
Berlage, Hendrik Petrus 25
Berlin 14; age pyramid 261, 303; carbon emissions 303, 304, 305, 307; cycling 298; GDP statistics 296; government structures 256, 257; Neukölln *285*; population density 266, 267, *284-5*, 293; social disadvantage 263; social equity 305, 306; transport 286, 287, 288, 289, 290, 291, 383-4; urban economy 301; urban footprint 254, 255; workforce 265
Bhagat, Dr R.B. 96
bicycles and cycling 122, 125, 298, 384, 385, 386
Bihar 104
Boeing 60-1
Bogotá 14, 18, 19, 25, 116, 146-8, 152-3, 158, 160, 180, 327; bus system 345; carbon emissions reductions 346
Bolivian immigrants in São Paulo 165

boundaries and borders 24, 324-31; edges 324-6, 330-1; views 329-30; walls 326-9
Brasilia 146, 149
Braudel, Fernand 222, 231
Brazil 11, 153-5, 388; ABC City Region 154-5; carbon emissions 303; crime and the police 148; Curitiba 146, 153-4, 358; economy 148, 153; government structures 259; middle class 186; polygon region 153, *see also* Rio de Janeiro; São Paulo
BRIC nations 19, 148, 208
BRT (Bus Rapid Transit) in India 126-7
Budapest 218, 221
Buenos Aires 15-18, 19, 148, 152, 159, 160, 161, 180, 329, 345
building trades: and urban manufacturing 62, 63
Burdett, Ricky 47
Burgess's concentric city model 262
Burnham, Daniel 25, 329
Burra, Sunder 98
buses *342, 343*, 345, *384*; Mumbai 122, 125, 126-7; São Paulo 383

Cairo 22, 208, 227, 228, 229, 230, 231
Calcutta *see* Kolkata (Calcutta)
Cameron, David 335, 341
Campana brothers 149
Caracas *328*
carbon emissions 11, 14, 17, 303-5, 307, *346*; reduction policies 342-9
cars and car ownership 297-8, 302; Curitiba 154; Istanbul *202-3*, 297-8; London 298; Mexico City 298; Mumbai 119, 122, *123*, 124, 127, 298; São Paulo *138-9*, 176, 298; Shanghai 298; transport planning 384-6, *385*
Casablanca 222, 229
Catholics in Mumbai 97
Celant, Germano 337-8
Central Asia and Istanbul 226, 227
Cerda, Idelfonso 24-5, 181, 222
Chandigarh 116
Charles, Prince of Wales 49, 50, *52*
Charney, Dov *60*
Chennai 94, 116, 122
Chicago 24-5; knowledge econoy 61; lakefront 329; 'pork bellies' 58; and urban manufacturing 62-3
Chicago Manufacturing Renaissance Council: Wind Turbine Supply Chain Project 63
Chile: Elemental projects *46*, 52-3; Santiago 150-2
China 10, 49, 388; environmental impact of cities 11; and India 86, 88; one-child policy 303; transport planning 385-6, *see also* Shanghai
citizenship 170, 340, 341
City of God (film) 174, 245
climate change effects 24, 303-5, 342-9; and poverty 379; São Paulo 187
clothing stores 335, 339
Cohn-Bendit, Daniel 334
'compact city' model 14
Constantinople 222, *see also* Istanbul
Copenhagen 14, 240, 346
Correa, Charles 88, 94, 96, 104
cost of living: public opinion on 310, 311, 312
creative classes: and the economies of cities 58, 64
crime and safety: Bogotá 146-8; and gated communities 107; inequalities and urban violence 362-7; Mumbai 107, 314-16;

public opinion on 23, 310-11, 312, 313-16; São Paulo 148, 170, 171, 174-5, 179, 186, 313-14, 315, 316
cultural industries: and urban manufacturing 59, 62
culture in Istanbul 216, 235-7
Curitiba 146, 153-4, 358

Damascus 228
Davis, Mike 174, 295, 297
deep democracy 115
deep economic histories of cities 56, 59-61, 65
Delhi 8, 15, 86, 88, 94, 116; transport 122, 124, 126-7
democracy: and daily life in high-income nations 376; and governance of cities 350-5; Mumbai 90-3, 115
design industries 58, 59; and urban manufacturing 58, 59, 62, 63
Dhaka 8, 344
Dharavi (Mumbai) 10, 44, 59, 89, 98-9, *101*, 294, 295
Dink, Hrant 232
disorder in cities 360-7
Doha 230
Dubai 176, 208, 231, 330

eastern Europe and Istanbul 215
ecological footprint 46
economics of cities 18, 56-65, 300-3; Brazil 148, 153; Istanbul 56, 59, 65, 213, 216; urban economies *38-9*; urban manufacturing 58-9, 62-5; US Metro Policy 388-95
Ecuador 160
Eczacibasi, Bülent 51
edge cities 49
edges 324-6; centre and edge 330-1
Edinburgh 52
Egli, Ernst 229
Egypt 222, 227; Alexandria 222, 227; Cairo 22, 208, 227, 228, 229, 230, 231
Eisenman, Peter 55
electricity consumption 11, 307
Elemental project 24, *46*, 52-3, *368, 369*, 370-3
employment: opportunities in cities 310, 311, 312; urban workforce 264-5, 300-2; urban workforce, Mumbai 86, 87, 96, 98, 99, *113*, 113, 264
The Endless City 7, 14
energy consumption 11, 307
energy efficiency 346-7
environmental impacts 316-18; green cities 24, 61, 343-9, 395; human footprints 11, 14, *28-9*, 254-5, 298-300, *see also* carbon emissions; climate change effects
equality: politics 334; securing in cities 368-73
Erder, Sema 354
Erdogan, Tayyip 248, 354
Erikson, Erik 330-1
European Union: and hinge cities 218, 220-1, 222; and Istanbul 208, 215, 232
extended families, housing for 371-2

Fenty, Adrian 358
Fez 229
financial futures 58
flexible production systems: and Istanbul 216
flooding 11, 374-6, *375*; Mumbai *82-3*, 103, 305, 374-6; São Paulo 187, 305
football clubs in Latin America 161
Ford, Tom 339

Foster, Norman 328-9
Frankfurt 22, 218, 220, 223
Friedan, Betty 334

Gandhi, Rajiv 90
Ganesh festival in Mumbai *109*, 110-11
gangs in Latin American cities 158-9
gated communities 6, 10, 107, 152, 222, 231, 327
Gates, Bill 334
GDP (gross domestic product) 8, 296, 300, 302, 305; and carbon emissions 303; São Paulo 147, 148, 182, 296, 300
Gehry, Frank 237
Genoa 387
GINI index 305-6, 362
Glasgow 313
glass production: and advanced economic sectors 59
global cities: deep histories of 56; slums in 58, 59; visual orders and topographies of 58
global urbanization 10-14
global-local distinction 356-8
globalization: democracy and governance 354-5; inequalities and urban disorders 260-5; and Istanbul 22-3, 210, 224-6, 232-9, 246-51; and 'no-frills' economic models 332-41
Goa 121
governance of cities 6, 24, 318-19, 320; and democracy 350-5; government structures 256-60; and urban footprints 298-300
green cities 24, 61, 343-9, 395
Greenspan, Alan 334, 335
Guevara, Che 334
Gujarat 120
Gulf States 49, 227, 231

Hadid, Zaha 44, 49, 51-2, 209, 230, 235
The Hague 121
Haifa 227
Hamburg 218
Hardoy, Jorge 378
Harvey, David 226
Haussmann, Baron 25, *47*, 51, 52
Havel, Václav 47
HDI (Human Development Index) 11, *40-1*, 305-6
health care: public opinion on 23, 319-21
Herzog, Jacques 44, *49*
Hindus in Mumbai 97
hinge cities 22, 218-23; centre/periphery distinction 220-1; and public space 222-3
Hong Kong *53*, 97, 344, 387
housing 10; Elemental project 24, *46*, 52-3, *368, 369*, 370-3; Istanbul 10, *194-5*, 208-9, 213-14, 216, 217, *232, 233*, 234-5, 236-9, 249-50; Mumbai 10, *80-1*, 87, 96, 97, 105-6, *112*, 114; São Paulo *142-3*, 168-71, *172-3*, 180; Turkish state housing programme (TOKI) 208-9, 216, 234-5, 249-50, *see also* slums
Houston 344
human footprints 11, 14, *28-9*, 254-5, 298-300
Hungary 218, 220
Huyghe, Pierre 340-1
Hyderabad 94

ideal city concept 306
identity: and living-edge urbanism 330-1
image of cities 312-13
income inequality 305-6

incremental housing 370-3
India: Bangladore 15, 86, 88, 94, 122; Bengal 86, 88; Bihar 104; Calcutta (Kolkata) 15, 86, 88, 94, 116, 120, 122; carbon emissions 303; cars and car ownership 119, 127; Chandigarh 116; Chennai 94, 116, 122; colonial roots 86, 120; Delhi 8, 15, 86, 88, 94, 116, 122, 124, 126-7; democracy and the 74th Amendment 90-3, 352-3; economic growth 388; employment 86; environmental impact of cities 11; Goa 121; government structures 258; Gujarat 120; house building 88-9; Hyderabad 94; Independence Day 111; infrastructure 88; Kerala 92, 121; Kinetic City 108-10; Madras 120; Maharashtra state government 94, 104, 121, 258, 350-2; National Slum Dwellers Federation 115, 376-7; National Urban Transport Policy (NUTP) 126; pollution *347*; post-colonial partition 86; Pune 122; railways 119; rural hinterland 86; Silicon Valley 88-9; Special Economic Zones 88; state governments 92, 93; urban growth 94; urban planning 92; urban shift 86-9; urban transport infrastructure 124-7; Uttar Pradesh 104, *see also* Mumbai
Industrial Revolution 8
inequalities in cities 305-6; Istanbul 208-9, 239, 305-6; Mumbai 305, 306; São Paulo 19-22, *132-3*, *168*, 168-75, *169*, *172*, *173*, 305; and urban disorders 360-3
infant mortality 376
informal economy 56
infrastructure 14, 299; green cities 347-8; Istanbul 227; São Paulo 154-5, 170, 176, 184, 185, 186, *see also* transport
integrated technologies 347-8
International Institute for Environment & Development: "The Transition to a Predominantly Urban World" 94
International Institute of Political Sciences (IIPS) 96
Israel 230
Istanbul 14, 22-3, *190-205*, **206-45**, *228*, *241*; age pyramid 261, 303; and Arab cities 22, 224-31; architecture 44, *47*, 51-2, 246, *247*; bridges *190-1*, 209; built environment patterns 244; business districts *47*, 52, 214-15, 216-17; carbon emissions 304, 307; cars and car ownership *202-3*, 297-8; city centre *194-5*, *220*; crime and safety in 313, 314, 315, 316, 327, 365-6, 367; culture 216, 235-7; deep economic history of 18, 56, 59, 65; deepening capitalism in 251; earthquake 209; edges 327; environmental issues 316-18; and the European Union 208, 215; gated communities 107; GDP statistics 296; *gecekondu* neighbourhoods 213, 214, 215, 217, 238, 240, 249; gentrification 217, 237-9; geography and topography 226, 240-3, *242*; and globalization 22-3, 210, 224-6, 232-9, 246-51; governance 257, 258, 259, 318-19, 320, 353-4; Güngören 273, 295; hinge city status 218-23, *223*; hinterland *215*; history of urban development 206, *210*, 210-17, *211*, *214*; housing 10, *194-5*, 208-9, 213-14, 216, 217, *232*, *233*, 234-5, 236-9, 249-50; image of 313; industries 215, 216; inequalities 208-9, 239, 305, 305-6, 307, 362; Kanyon shopping centre 51, *200-1*, 236; Kartal 51, 209; Levent 51, 208; linear sub centres 209; mayors 229-30, 231; migration/migrants 22-3, 206, 208, *218*, *219*, 235; and 'Noormania' 224, 230, 231; older neighbourhoods *202-5*; and the Ottoman Empire 52, 226-7, 230-1, 248, 250-1; Pera district 236; population density 266, 267, *272-3*, 293, 295, 297; population distribution 212; population growth 47, 207, 208, 212, 213, 216, 248-9; population stability 308-9; position and heritage *224*, *225*; public opinion on 23, 309-12, 321; public spaces 235-6, 244-5; quality of life in 240; social disadvantage 263; social psychology and the physical environment 243-4; Sultanahmet 217; Sulukule 23, 217, 235, 238, 297; Taksim-Harbiye axis 243; traffic congestion *198-9*, 210, 214; transport 209, 287, 289, 290, 297, 318, 319, 383, 386-7; Tüyap area 237; Urban Age Award 7, 405-8, *407*; urban development *192-3*; urban economy 213, 215, 228, 301, 302, 303; urban footprint 254, 255, 299; views 330; walls 327; waterways *229*, 329; workforce 265; as a World Heritage site 228; world-city status regained 215-17, *see also* Turkey
Italian immigrants in São Paulo 162, 164
Izmir 222, 227

Jacobs, Jane 94
Japanese culture in São Paulo 167
Jeddah 228, 229, 230
Jews 120, 165
JNURM (Jawaharlal Nehru Urban Renewal Mission) 125-6
Jobs, Steve 334
Johannesburg 14, 218; age pyramid 261, 303; Berea *283*; carbon emissions 304, 307; GDP statistics 296; government structures 256, 257; inequalities 306, 362; population density 266-7, *282-3*, 293, 295; social disadvantage 262, 263; Soweto 295; transport 286, 287, 289, 291; urban economy 301, 302, 303; urban footprint 255; workforce 264, 265
Johnson, Ralph 53

Katz, Bruce 358
Kerala 92, 121
Keyder, Caglar 234
Kinetic City: Mumbai 108-15
Klein, Naomi 340
knowledge economy 56, 59, 60-1, 65; and urban manufacturing 58-9, 62-3
Kolkata (Calcutta) 15, 86, 88, 94, 116; transport 122, 124
Koolhaas, Rem 48-9, 51, 55, 338
Korean culture in São Paulo 167
Krier, Leon 48-51, *52*
Kubitchek, Juscelino 146
Kurdish migrants in Istanbul 208, 235, 239
Kuwait 227

Lagerfield, Karl 339
Lagos 8, 49
Latin American cities 15-18, 94, **146-61**, *151*; alternative financial schemes 160; edges *328*; *favelas* 146, 158, 170-1; formation of new settlements 159-60; gangs and city governance 158-9; graffiti *157*, 158; impact of economic crisis 159; importance of affiliations 160-1; informal housing 374; multi-scalar vacuum 155; religion and social life 156-8; streetlife *156*, *157*; structural adjustment programmes 150; transport *384*; urbanization patterns 150-3, *see also* Bogotá; Brasil; São Paulo
Le Corbusier 49, 340
leapfrogging technology **61**
Lebanon 222, 226
Lerner, Jamie 96
life expectancy 302, 305, 378
Lille 338
Lima 18, 19, 148, 159-60
Lisbon 18, 107, 387
living-edge urbanism 330-1
Ljubljana 50
London 14, 46, 218, 220, 240; age pyramid 261, 303; carbon emissions 303, 304, 305, 307, 344; cars and car ownership 298; congestion charge 346; crime and safety in 313, 314; cycling 298; docks 329; edges 327; environmental issues 316-18; GDP statistics 296; governance 256, 257, 350; image of 313; and Mumbai 306; new City Hall 328-9; Notting Hill *279*, 295; population density 266, 267, *278-9*, 293, 294, 295; population stability 308-9, public opinion on 23; social disadvantage 262, 263; social equity 305, 306; social housing 44; transport 116-18, 287, 289, 291, 297, 318, 319; urban economy 301, 302; urban footprint 254, 255, 300; views 329, 330; waterways 329; workforce 265
Los Angeles 14, 327, 339, 384-5
LSE Cities 7
Lula, Brazilian President 7

MacNeil, William 222
Madras 120
Madrid 344, 384
Maharashtra 94, 104, 121, 258, 350-2
Mahila Milan 115
Malcolm X 334
Manchester: post-war restoration 218
manufacturing cities 18, 58-9, 62-5, 302; urban manufacturing networks 63-4; and US Metro Policy *388*, *389*
Mao Zedong 344
material economies 58, 60-1
mayors 6, 318, 320, 321, 356-9; Istanbul 229-30, 231, 320; United States *356*, *357*
Mecca 231
Mediterranean hinge cities 22, 222
megacities 10
Mehta, Mukesh 98
Mehta, Sukhetu: *Maximum City* 89
Merkel, Angela 106-7
Metro Policy (United States) 388-95
metro systems: in Indian cities 124-5; Istanbul 209
Meuron, Pierre de 44, *49*
Mexico 208, 221
Mexico City 14, 19, 146, 148, 176, 180; age pyramid 260; carbon emissions 303, 304, 307; cars and car ownership 298; GDP statistics 296; government structures 256; inequalities 362; population density 266, 267, *280-1*, 293, 297; population growth 8; religion in social life 156-8; social disadvantage 262; social equity 305, 306; traffic congestion 345, 346; transport 14, 286, 288, 290; Urban Age Award 7, 408-11, *410*; urban economy 301, 302; urban footprint 254, 299; workforce 264
Miami 146
Microsoft Corporation 334, 337
middle class: Brazil 186
migration/migrants 8, 308-9; and equality in cities 368-70; and hinge cities 221; Istanbul 22-3, 206, 208, *218*, *219*, 235; Mumbai 88, 89, 94-6, *95*, 97, 102-4, 107, 120; and population density 295, 297; São Paulo 59, 148, 162-7, *167*, *see also* population growth
Milan 218; railway network 380-3
Milan, Mahila 377
Mitchell, Timothy 230
mobile phone technology 61
modernism 51
Monbiot, George 48
Monsiváis, Carlos 156
moral panics 46
Morocco 206, 222
Morris, William 86; *News from Nowhere* 46
Moses, Robert 206
motorways 326-7
multiculturalism in São Paulo 22, 162-7
Mumbai 14, 15, 18-19, *70-85*, **86-127**, *91*, 221, 388; age pyramid 260, 303; architecture 44, *45*, *48*, 53-5, 88; assistance networks 102, 104; bicycles 122, 125; buses 122, 125; carbon emissions 304, 305, 307; cars and car ownership 119, 122, *123*, 124, 127, 298; Chhatrapati terminal 88; crime and safety in 107, 314-16; deep economic history of 56, 59; democracy and the 74th Amendment 90-3; Dharavi 10, 44, 59, 89, 98-9, *101*, 294, 295; environmental issues 316-18; financial institutions 120; floods *82-3*, 103, 305, 374-6; Fort area 96, 97, 111-12; future of urban growth 120-1; Ganesh festival *109*, 110-11; GDP statistics 296; Girgaum 97; governance 99-100, 114, 120, 318, 319, 320, 350-3; government structures 256, 258; Greater Mumbai 94; Historic District bazaars 111-13; history 88; housing 10, *80-1*, 87, 96, 97, 105-6, *112*, 114; image of 313; inequalities 305, 306, 362; infrastructure 89, 104; Kamathipura 269, 294-5; Kinetic City 108-15; and London 306; and Maharashtra state 94, 104, 121, 350-2; Metropolitan Region 94, 96; migration/migrants 88, 89, 94-6, *95*, 97, 102-4, 107, 120; Municipal Corporation 89; Navi Mumbai (New Mumbai) 19, 120-1, 300; population density 96-7, 266, 267, *268-9*, 292-5, 297; population growth 8, 47, 94-6, 97, 102, 120, 121; population stability 308-9; poverty *75*; public opinion on 23, 309-12, 321; railways *74*, 88, 89, *103*, **113**, 114, 116, *117*, 119, 297; redevelopment 104-7, religious diversity *70-1*, *72-3*, 97, *109*, 110-11; rickshaws 122, 125; roads *78-9*, *126*, 126; and São Paulo 101; schools *84-5*; slums 88, 89, 96, 97-9, *99*, 100, 105, *324*, *325*; social disadvantage 262; squatters 101; SRA (Slum Rehabilitation Authority) 105; state government 104; Static City 108-15; street vendors 89; terrorist attacks (2007) 97, 363-4; transport 14, 100-1, 116-19, *117*, *118*, 121, 122-7, 124-7, *125*, *126*, 286, 288, 290, 297, 318, 319, *382*; Urban Age Award 7, 396, 398-401; Urban Age conference 15-18; Urban Age project 86; urban economy 301, 302, 303; urban footprint 254, 300; vaccination stations 88; water supplies 89; Waterfronts Centre (MWC) 398-400, *399*; waterways 329; wealth *76-7*; workforce 86, 87, 96, 98, 99, *113*, 113, 264; as a world city 121
music 174
Muslims in Mumbai 97

nagarpalikas (India) 90-2
Namibia 377
Napoleon, French emperor 231
Navi Mumbai (New Mumbai) 19, 120-1, 300
Nepal 94
New Orleans 102, 376
New Urbanism 50, *52*
New York City 51, 52, 344; age pyramid 260, 303; carbon emissions 303, 304, 305, 307; GDP statistics 296; government structures 256; image of 313; inequalities 362; and Istanbul 206; Lower East Side 105; Manhattan 44, 116, 331; population density 266, 267, *274-5*, 292, 293, 294, 295; population stability 309; social disadvantage 262; social equity 305, 306, 307; Spanish Harlem community 331; traffic congestion reductions 346; transport 286, 288, 290, 318; urban economy 301, 302; urban footprint 254, 299; and urban manufacturing 62; views 329, 330; waterways 329; workforce 264
Niemeyer, Oscar 146, 181
'no-frills' economic models 332-41
Noor (Turkish soap opera) 224, 230, 231
North American transport systems 119

Obama, Barack: and Metro Policy 388-90, 395
office buildings 64
O'Neill, Tip 90
Ottoman Empire 52, 226-7, 230-1, 248, 250-1
Oxford 49

Pakistan 94, 97
Paris 24-5, *47*, 51, 52, 220, 318, 344; suburbs *356*, *357*
Patel, Sheela 98
pedestrianization 327
Phoenix 14
photovoltaic (PV) systems 346
Planet of Slums 174, 297
plate glass walls 328-9
Poland 218, 220
population control 48
population density 9, 266-85; Berlin 266, 267, *284-5*, 293; global population distribution *26-7*; Istanbul 266, 267, *272-3*, 293, 295, 297; Johannesburg 266-7, *282-3*, 293, 295; London 266, 267, *278-9*, 293, 294, 295; Mexico City 266, 267, *280-1*, 293, 297; Mumbai 96-7, 266, 267, *268-9*, 292-5, 297; New York City 266, 267, *274-5*, 292, 293, 294, 295; and quality of life 294-5; São Paulo 266, 267, *270-1*, 293, 297; Shanghai 266, 267, *276-7*, 293, 295, 297
population growth 8, 10, 11-14, 47-8; Istanbul 47, 207, 208, 212, 213, 216, 248-9; Mumbai 8, 47, 94-6, 97, 102, 120, 121; patterns of *36-7*; São Paulo 47, 147, 185, *see also* migration/migrants
population stability and 'churn' 308-9
'pork bellies' 58
Portland 240, 344, 347
postmodern cities 340
Poundbury 50, *52*
poverty 11, *20*, 21, 58; aid agencies and development banks 378-9; Mumbai *75*, 97-8; and population density 294; São Paulo 168, 170, 174
Prague 47, 50
Primark 340
Prost, Henri 212, 214, 229
Protestantism in Latin America 158, 165
public opinion on cities 23, 308-321; environmental impacts 316-18; good and bad things 309-12; image 312-13; population stability and 'churn' 308-9; transport 318, 319
public spaces: and hinge cities 222-3; Istanbul 235-6, 244-5
public transport *see* transport
Pune 122

quality of life: and population density 294-5
Queiroz, Renato da Silva 166

railways: funicular 387; Istanbul 209; Mumbai *74*, 88, 89, 116, *117*, 119, 297; networks 380-3; São Paulo 185
Randstad (Holland) 121
Rao, Narasimha 90
recycling 347
religion and religious festivals: Istanbul 206; Mexico City 156-8; Mumbai *70-1*, *72-3*, 97, *109*, 110-11; São Paulo 158, 165, 166
religious affiliations: and urban violence 363-4, *364*
resilience of cities 359
Rio de Janeiro 18, 19, 146, 149, 158, 159, 161, 184; *favelas* 170-1
risk hotspots *42-3*
Riyadh 230, 231
Roma population in Istanbul 23, 217, 235, 238, 297
Rome 220, 326, 344
Roosevelt, Franklin 395
Rubinato, João (Adoniran Barbosa) 164-5
Ruskin, John 86
Russia and Istanbul 215

safety *see* crime and safety
St Louis 44
St Petersburg 208
San Diego 385
San Francisco 22, 385; Bay Area 121
Santiago 150-2
São Paulo 14, 15, 19-22, 101, 106, *130-45*, 388; ABC City Region 154-5; age pyramid 260, 261, 303; architecture 44, *49*, *136-7*, 149, 178, 181, 182; Avenida Paulista 178-9; beautification strategy *54*, *55*; and Buenos Aires 148; buses 383; carbon

emissions 303, 304, 305, 307, 344; cars and car ownership *138-9*, 176, 298; city centre *140-1*, 180-1; Clean City project 181; climate change 187; Conjunto Nacional 178-9; cosmopolitan identity *163, 164*; crime and safety in 148, 170, 171, 174-5, 179, 186, 313-14, 315, 316, 327, 364-5; deep economic history of 56, 59; developmental change 184-5; edges 327; environmental issues 316-18; *favelas* 185; flooding 187, 305; formation of new settlements 159; GDP statistics 147, 148, 182, 296; governance 257, 258, 259, 318, 319, 320, 353; governmental aid programmes 185; graffiti 175; helicopter commuters *134-5*; housing *142-3*, 168-71, *172-3*, 180; image of 313; inequalities 19-22, *132-3, 168*, 168-75, *169, 172, 173*, 305, 362; infrastructure 154-5, 170, 176, 184, 185, 186; market segmentation 186; Metropolitan Region 146, 155; migration/migrants 59, 148, 162-7, *167*; multiculturalism 22, 162-7; *Nordestino* neighbourhoods 165; Paraisópolis 101, 168; *pixações* 175; population 147, 185; population density 266, 267, *270-1*, 297; population growth 47, 147, 185; population stability 308-9; post-war development 218; public opinion on 23, 309-12, 321; railways 185; religion 158, 165, 166; Roosevelt Square 180-1; security *144-5*, 171-4, 176, 186; shopping malls 179, 185-6; slums 59, 178; social disadvantage 262, 263; street children 148; *televovela* 149; theatres 179-80; Tietê River *183*, 184; transport 176, 178, 286, 287, 288, 289, 290, 291, 318, 319, 380, 383, 386; Urban Age Award 7, 401-5, *402*; urban development 10, *130-2*, 176-87, *177*, 221; urban economy 301, 302, 303; urban footprint 254, 255, 299, 300; urban social movements 170; views 330; workforce 264, 265
Sassoon, Victor 120
Saudi Arabia 224, 230
schools: Mumbai *84-5*; public opinion on 310, 311, 312
sea connections *32-3*
Seattle 14, 240
security in São Paulo *144-5*, 171-4, 176, 186
Seoul 345, 374
service industries: and urban manufacturing 58, 62, 63-4
Shanghai 104, 114, 146, 176, 181, 221, 388; age pyramid 260, 261, 303; carbon emissions 303, 304, 305, 307; cars and car ownership 298; GDP statistics 296; government structures 256, 257; housing 10; population density 266, 267, *276-7*, 293, 295, 297; population stability 309; social disadvantage 262, 263; transport 287, 288, 289, 290, 291, 297, 298; urban economy 301, 302; urban footprint 254, 255, 299; waterways 329; workforce 265
Silva, Vital Fernandes da 165
Simmel, Georg 19, 156, 161
Singapore 14, 97
Singh, Professor D.P. 94
Singh, Simreet 98
Singh, V.P. 90
slavery: and multiculturalism in São Paulo 165-6
Slumdog Millionaire 245, 295
slums 10, 13, 374-9; Dharavi (Mumbai) 10, 44, 59, 89, 98-9, *101*, 294, 295, 378; ghettoes *324, 325*; in global cities 58, 59; mass evictions 374; Mumbai 88, 89, 96, 97-9, *99, 100, 122, 324, 325*; National Slum Dwellers Federation (India) 115, 376-7; Slum/Shack Dwellers International 377; squatter communities *368, 369*; and transport 122, 124; and urban manufacturing 59
small businesses 56
'smart city' design 327-8, 331
Smithson, Alison and Peter 44
soap operas, Turkish 224, 230, 231
social disadvantage in cities 262-3
social equity *see* inequalities in cities
social reform in cities 8
Society for the Promotion of Area Resources (SPAARC) 115
solar power 346
South Africa 376
South America *see* Latin American cities
Soviet Union collapse: and Turkey 208
Sri Lanka 94
Stevens, F.W. 88
Stuttgart 327
suburbanization 8
Sullivan, Louis 329
symbolic knowledge workers 58

Tel Aviv 221
terrorism 362, 363-4
Thailand: Community Organizations Development Institute 377

Thessaloniki 227
Tokyo 8, 97, 101, 149, 176, 179, 300, 344
Toledo 59
tolerance culture *360, 361*
Topbas, Kadir 235, 237
Topshop 339
Toronto 309
tourism 62, 64
trade unions in Argentina 159
traffic congestion 345-6; costs of 345; public opinion on 311-12
transport 286-91, 297-8, 299; air connections *30-1*; Berlin 286, 287, 288, 289, 290, 291, 383-4; Bogotá 146; and carbon emissions *342, 343*, 344, 345-6, 349; Curitiba 153, 154; Istanbul 209, 287, 289, 290, 297, 318, 319, 383, 386-7; Johannesburg 286, 287, 289, 291; Lima 148; London 116-18, 287, 289, 291, 297, 318, 319; Mexico City 14, 286, 288, 290; Mumbai 14, 100-1, 116-19, *117, 118*, 121, 122-7, 124-7, *125, 126*, 286, 288, 290, 297, 318, 319, *382*; New York City 286, 288, 290; planning and policies *380*, 380-7, *381, 382*; politicians *350, 351*; public opinion on 318, 319; São Paulo 176, 178, 286, 287, 288, 289, 290, 291, 318, 319, 380, 383, 386; sea connections *32-3*; Shanghai 287, 288, 289, 290, 291, 297; smart 348, *see also* railways
Turkey 232; AKP government 232, 237-8, 246-7, 354; Ankara 206, 210, 212, 213, 227, *228*, 246; carbon emissions 303; government structures 259; nation-state development 210-12; TOKI state housing programme 208-9, 216, 234-5, 249-50; urbanization 206, *see also* Istanbul
Turkish Arab Economic Forum 230
Turkish nationalism 227

United Arab Emirates 230
United States: Great Recession 390-1, 395; mayors *356, 357*; Metro Policy 388-95; post-war American cities 218; St Louis 44
Urban Age Awards 7, 24, 350, 396-411, *397, 412-13*
Urban Age conferences 7, 15-18, 218
Urban Age Project 8, 14-18, 24, 46
urban footprints 11, 14, *28-9*, 254-5, 298-300
urbanization 10-14, *11, 12, 34-5*, 332
Utrecht 121
Uttar Pradesh 104

Vancouver 240, 344
Venice 22, 221-2, 223; ghetto *324, 325*
Vienna 344
views 329-30

Wal-Mart 362
walls 326-9
Warsaw 218, 221
water consumption 11, 307
waterways 329
wealth: Mumbai *76-7*; São Paulo 168, 170
Whyte, William H. 218
women: and democracy in India 90-2
World War II: post-war Istanbul 228; restoration of cities following 218

Yamasaki, Minou 44
young people 6, 366

Zara 334, 337, 339

EDITORS' ACKNOWLEDGMENTS

LIVING IN THE ENDLESS CITY
URBAN AGE PRODUCTION TEAM

Editors
Ricky Burdett
Deyan Sudjic

Assistant Editor
Ömer Çavuşoğlu

Mapping, Research and Information Graphics
Guido Robazza
Jens Kandt
Antoine Paccoud
Kay Kitazawa
Atakan Guven
Bruno Moser

Copy-editor
Gerrie van Noord

URBAN AGE TEAM

Urban Age Board
Andy Altman, *Chief Executive, Olympic Park Legacy Company, London*
Ricky Burdett, *Director, Urban Age & LSE Cities, LSE*
Bruce Katz, *Vice President & Director, Metropolitan Policy Program, Brookings Institution, Washington DC*
Wolfgang Nowak, *Managing Director, Alfred Herrhausen Society, Berlin*
Philipp Rode, *Executive Director, Urban Age & LSE Cities, LSE*
Ute Weiland, *Deputy Director, Alfred Herrhausen Society, Berlin*

Advisory Board
Richard Sennett (Co-chair), *University Professor of the Humanities, New York University, New York City; Emeritus Professor of Sociology, LSE*
Deyan Sudjic (Co-chair), *Director, Design Museum, London*
Klaus Bode, *Founding Partner, BDSP Partnership, London*
Sophie Body-Gendrot, *Director, Centre for Urban Studies, Universite Paris-Sorbonne, Paris*
Lindsay Bremner, *Professor, Department of Architecture, Tyler School of Art, Temple University, Philadelphia, Pennsylvania*
Richard Brown, *Urban Policy Consultant, London*
Amanda Burden, *Director, Department of City Planning, New York City*
Fabio Casiroli, *Professor of Transport Planning, Faculty of Civil Architecture, Polytechnic of Milan, Milan*
José Castillo, *Principal, Arquitectura 911 SC, Mexico City*
Job Cohen, *Mayor of Amsterdam (2001 – 2010)*
Xiangming Chen, *Dean and Director, Center for Urban and Global Studies, Trinity College, Hartford, Connecticut*
Joan Clos i Matheu, *Executive Director, United Nations Human Settlements Programme (UN-HABITAT), Nairobi*
Charles Correa, *Founding Partner, Charles Correa Associates, Mumbai*
Frank Duffy, *Founder, DEGW, London*
Gerald Frug, *Louis D. Brandeis Professor of Law, Harvard University, Cambridge, Massachusetts*
Hermann Knoflacher, *Professor of Transport Planning, Vienna University of Technology, Vienna*
Rem Koolhaas, *Principal, Office for Metropolitan Architecture, Rotterdam*

Dieter Läpple, *Professor, Hamburg University of Technology, Hamburg*
Guy Nordenson, *Engineer, Guy Nordenson and Associates, New York City*
Enrique Norten, *Architect, TEN Arquitectos, Mexico City and New York City*
Enrique Peñalosa, *Mayor of Bogotá (1998 – 2001)*
Anne Power, *Professor of Social Policy, LSE*
Saskia Sassen, *Helen and Robert Lynd Professor of Sociology, Columbia University, New York City*
Ed Soja, *Distinguished Professor of Urban Planning, UCLA, Los Angeles, California*
Geetam Tiwari, *Chair and Associate Professor, TRIPP, Indian Institute of Technology, New Delhi*
Tony Travers, *Director, LSE London, LSE*
Lawrence Vale, *Ford Professor of Urban Design and Planning, MIT, Cambridge, Massachusetts*
Anthony Williams, *Mayor of Washington DC (1999–2006)*
Alejandro Zaera-Polo, *Joint Director, Foreign Office Architects, London*

Executive Group
Ricky Burdett, *Director, Urban Age & LSE Cities, LSE*
Philipp Rode, *Executive Director, Urban Age & LSE Cities, LSE*
Ute Weiland, *Deputy Director, Alfred Herrhausen Society, Berlin*

Staff, Urban Age, The London School of Economics and Political Science
Cristina Alaimo, *Researcher*
Ömer Çavuşoğlu, *Researcher*
Andrea Colantonio, *Research Officer*
Emily Cruz, *Publications Manager*
Sarah Davis, *Management Accounts Coordinator*
Atakan Guven, *Research Officer*
Miranda Iossifidis, *Graphic Designer*
Mariane Jang, *Project Manager*
Ayako Iba, *Events Co-ordinator*
Sarah Ichioka, *Research Associate*
Adam Kaasa, *Communications and Outreach Manager*
Jens Kandt, *Researcher*
Gesine Kippenberg, *Researcher*
Kay Kitazawa, *Research Officer*
Christos Konstantinou, *Researcher*
Mira Krusteff, *Programme Assistant*
Bruno Moser, *Research Associate*
Miguel Kanai, *Project Researcher*
Iliana Ortega-Alcazar, *Researcher*
Antoine Paccoud, *Researcher*
Pamela Puchalski, *Project Coordinator*

Emma Rees, *Executive and Admin Assistant*
Guido Robazza, *Researcher*
Andrea Rota, *Web Editor*
Elizabeth Rusbridger, *Administrator*
James Schofield, *Researcher*
Peter Schwinger, *Researcher*
Richard Simpson, *Researcher*
Nell Stevens, *Outreach and Communications Coordinator*
Daniela Tanner, *Administrator*
Myfanwy Taylor, *Researcher*
Natznet Tesfay, *Researcher*
Katherine Wallis, *Centre Administrator*

Staff, Alfred Herrhausen Society, The International Forum of Deutsche Bank
Jessica Barthel, *Project Manager*
Anja Fritzsch, *Project Manager*
Christiane Timmerhaus, *Project Manager*
Freya Tebbenhoff, *Assistant to the Management Board*

Staff, Deutsche Bank Urban Age Award
Demet Mutman, *Istanbul Award Co-rdinator*
Marcos Rosa, *São Paulo Award Coordinator*
Priya Shankar, *Mumbai Award Coordinator*
Ana Álvarez Velasco, *Mexico City Award Coordinator*

Phaidon Press Ltd
Regent's Wharf
All Saints Street
London N1 9PA

Phaidon Press Inc.
180 Varick Street
New York, NY 10014

www.phaidon.com

First published 2011
© 2011 Phaidon Press Limited

ISBN 978 0 7148 6118 0

A CIP catalogue record for this book is available
from the British Library.

Designed by
Quentin Newark and Paola Faoro, Atelierworks

Printed in China